THE

MEMOIR AND WRITINGS

OF

JAMES HANDASYD PERKINS.

VOL. II.

THE

MEMOIR AND WRITINGS

OF

JAMES HANDASYD PERKINS.

EDITED BY

WILLIAM HENRY CHANNING.

IN TWO VOLUMES.

VOL. II.

BOSTON:
WM. CROSBY AND H. P. NICHOLS,

CINCINNATI:
TRUEMAN & SPOFFORD.

1851.

CAMBRIDGE:
METCALF AND COMPANY,
PRINTERS TO THE UNIVERSITY.

CONTENTS.

HISTORICAL SKETCHES.

HISTORICAL SKETCHES.

I.

MOHAMMED.*

SISMONDI and Carlyle have done something, of late years, to make us believe that the old orthodox notion of Mahomet's, or Mohammed's, power and success is not as well founded as might be. They have tried to convince the world that naked, selfish, mean imposition never could have done what the spirit of the founder of Islam did. God, according to their doctrine, has not endowed shallow craft and unlimited lying with such mighty control over human souls as that which the great Arabian possessed. But the mass of those who write on the prophet still write in the tone of the Crusaders; they buckle on their armour to do battle with the false leader of the infidel host, in place of opening their eyes and purging their minds, to see and understand aright one of the great phenomena of history, that is to say, one of the great facts in God's government of the world. And is it not truly a great fact, that a wild, illiterate, unregenerate Arab was able to breathe a spirit of advancement, of daring, of enterprise, of civilization even, into those desert children, which has lasted for so many centuries, and swept clean so many countries? Count over

* *The Koran, commonly called the Alcoran, of Mohammed; translated into English, with Explanatory Notes, and a Preliminary Discourse.* By GEORGE SALE. London. 1838. 8vo.

From the North American Review, for October, 1846.

your great men, your Alexanders, Solons, Platos, Homers, — how many of them have influenced human destinies, moulded human laws, ruled in palaces, judged in courts, led in battles, taken the child in the cradle and guided it even to the tomb, as this rude Ishmaelite has done? Let us not, even if we can, shut our eyes to the fact, that in the success of Mohammed God has placed before us a riddle worthy our reading; and let us not forget, that, when he places before us a lesson to be learned, we are little better than blasphemers, if we fail at least to study it. It is in the hope that we may do something for some minds toward reading this riddle, that we write the few following pages.

And, in the first place, it should be clearly understood that we know very little with certainty respecting the prophet. Neither Saracens nor Christians are to be believed. He that reads must read *as Niebuhr* did. He must question every statement, weigh every intimation, compare friend and enemy on every point of praise and dispraise. The Koran alone may be trusted, and to the study of that more than all else the inquirer should turn, and strive to find the needle which shall guide him in that vast stack of mingled weeds, flowers, and food.

In the next place, the different periods of Mohammed's life must be distinguished, and each one made to throw light upon the others. And this must be done with a constant prayer that God will enable us to set aside prejudice, and judge of this man as we should judge of another. With these two thoughts to aid us, let us enter upon the inquiry, What was Mohammed, and how came he to play so great a part in the world's history? His life consisted of three periods; the first extending from his birth to the commencement of his mission, at about the age of forty; the second including his years of trial and suffering, and closing with his flight to Medina, in the fifty-third year of his age; the third, his period of triumph, ending with his death, ten years after his flight. What was this man in these three periods?

In a narrow valley, hemmed in by barren mountains, a valley without pastures, or grain-fields, or even springs of sweet water, stood the holy city of Mecca. Many tribes of the keen, nervous Arab race lived there, but none of them was so noble as the Koreish, and of that tribe no house was so powerful as the house of Hashem, who kept the key of the Caaba, the holy temple, where the sevenfold stone bound with silver, which the archangel Gabriel brought from heaven when God made the world, stood for the reverential kiss of the sons of Ishmael. Gabriel brought it milk-white from above, but the sins of man had in early ages changed its color to black. Of the house of Hashem, in the year of our Lord 569, there were living Abdol Motalleb, his thirteen sons, and six daughters. Among these sons was Abdallah, the light of the East, whose smile no maiden could withstand. Flashing eyes followed his stately person, wherever he moved; warm Arab hearts beat quicker, whenever his noble countenance was seen; and when the rumor spread through the Holy City, and sped out on swift coursers even to the daughters of the desert, that Amina was the chosen bride of the beautiful grandson of Hashem, many a bosom felt that void which nothing can fill. Amina, like her husband, was of the tribe of the Koreish, and of a noble house of that tribe. We may be sure it was a princely wedding. Grand old men with flowing beards, and stately women, and free-moving youths in their light Eastern costume, and wondering children with their open eyes, we may feel certain graced the ceremony; the youngest of them died twelve hundred years ago, and yet is that wedding memorable, for from the union sprang Mohammed.

The little boy, who inherited his father's beauty, and whose mind and temper were from the cradle noticeable, was just beginning to climb that father's knee, and to listen and answer as they sat upon the house-top in the twilight, when the angel of death took Abdallah from the earth; the son of Hashem saw the fairest of his nineteen children fall the first. Can we bring before us the widowed Amina, with her little prophet by her side? Can we imagine how he, with his quick, wild soul and keen sense of justice, was educated into a horror and hatred of the customs of his country by the injustice of his uncles, who, according to usage, seized his father's wealth, and left him and his mother stripped? Will not the two years, sad and lonely years, which he passed with the mourning and suffering bride of Abdallah, show us something of the creation of the Arabian Reformer? Two lonely years, and then the weary heart of Amina herself stood still. Silence reigned in the house; silently friends moved round the bed of death; and he stood there, a little child of four years old, with the heart and the imagination of a child, — looked on the pallid face, the speechless lips, and knew that it was the cruel treatment allowed by the pagan faith he lived under, which had robbed the eye Abdallah had loved of its beauty, and brought the young bride to her grave. He knew it all, but did not know he knew it; it was in his imagination and soul, not in his understanding. Many words had that weeping mother spoken to him, which had sunk into his heart to lie for years, and prepare the way for Islam.

Amina was laid in her tomb, and Mohammed looked up into the sorrowing face of his grandfather, who took the orphan-boy kindly by the hand and led him home. He was a kind old man, Abdol Motalleb, and he loved and cared tenderly for Abdallah's child. For two more years Mohammed grew in strength, beauty, and intelligence under the patriarch's eye; then the son of Hashem called the stripling to him, and having sent for Abdallah's eldest brother, Abu

Taleb, he gave the orphan to his uncle, saying, — "I am dying. Take this child, whose father and mother have been called away from this world, and rear him as if he were your own." The uncle promised him protection, and in a little while the boy followed to the grave his third, his last parent. So early was his spirit purified and made strong by sorrow.

Let us pass by twenty years, and look at Abdallah's son a grown man, faintly visible as he is in the pages of biography. He is a merchant or factor, not trading on his own account, but heretofore agent for his uncle, and lately advanced into the service of a rich lady of Mecca, Cadijah, already twice a widow. He had travelled; he had been in Syria; had seen Christians and Jews; had listened to the history and the poetry of the old Hebrews. Calm, acute, quick, imaginative, and devout by nature, and devout also through suffering, Mohammed saw and heard realities; and in silence, half consciously, weighed the faith and the practice of his own pagan Arabia against the simple deism and the sublime morality of Moses. Among his companions, kind, considerate, and remarkable for his purity; in business exact and thorough; with a person of uncommon beauty, an address of remarkable grace, a fine intellect, and a spotless character, — none of the descendants of Hashem promised better than the son of Abdallah. And now he is leaving again, in the service of Cadijah, to spend some years in Syria. Will he not carry still farther his inquiries into Judaism and Christianity? Will he not think yet more earnestly of a change among his own wild brethren, that shall do away with those savage customs which made his childhood one of dependence, and brought Amina to the grave? Can we not from all the fables about the Nestorian monk Sergius take simply this kernel, that Mohammed, in his various journeys to Syria, became well acquainted with the faith of Moses and with that of Jesus, and leave all the husks of time, place, and circumstance to those who please to quarrel about them? Are we not authorized to feel sure, that, when the factor of the rich Meccan widow, at the age of twenty-eight, became her husband, and rose through her wealth to the place which he might claim as his own by birth, he was already earnestly, silently meditating that great reform in the faith and practice of his countrymen which twelve years later he commenced?

Slowly do the great births of time, material or spiritual, take place. Napoleon may rise in an instant to his zenith of influence, but so he falls, too; Mohammed through twenty years quietly meditates his mission, and leaves an impress on the world for twenty centuries; Christianity yet more slowly grows towards power; the Arab lived to triumph, Jesus died upon the tree; and now the crescent is passing away before the cross. No meteor hangs long in the firmament. Through twenty years Mohammed listened, thought, and prayed, — through eight years of active life, through twelve of quiet retirement. Imagine the effect of retirement, of earnest, solitary meditation, on a mind of vast, uneducated powers; a soul of mighty passion, chastened and curbed by a will of iron. He saw the evils of Arabian society, of Arabian law, of Arabian religion, — that is, of paganism; he saw, too, that, wherever great progress had been made, it had proceeded from revelation; Moses and Jesus were prophets of the one God. Was God dead? Had he ceased to take an interest in mankind? Did he care less for the offspring of Hagar than for those of Sarah? Was no other prophet to arise, no further revelation to be made? Nay, did not even Judaism and Christianity require another revelation to purify them? Had not Jesus promised another to complete his work, the Comforter?

Twenty years of such questioning, and deep meditation thereon, might produce an impostor or an enthusiast, a liar or a self-deceiver. Which was Mohammed? Before seeking an answer in his after life, look at him as he is, and which is the most probable character for him to live in? He is noble, his ambition is thereby gratified; he is rich, he can hope no more from wealth; he is looked on as a man of leading mind, love of power and fame on that score is satisfied; his character is so pure, so faultless, that men point him out as a model to their sons. Will he, profoundly false, plan to deceive his countrymen into a system better than their own, and gain nothing himself? That surely would not be human nature. And what could he gain for himself? What did Jesus gain? What did Moses gain, or any true servant of God? Would these fierce idolaters — these worshippers of the sun, and moon, and stars, these kissers of the Black Stone — make him their king and prophet because he *pretended* to have a mission from God? The Israelites, with their old traditions, so much stronger and fresher than those of the Ishmaelites, could scarce yield to Moses with all his miracles; would he, without any miracle, succeed, where the rod of the Hebrew lawgiver and the thunders of Sinai were so weak? He was a shrewd man, this Mohammed; in worldly matters he had sped well; he was an astute, cautious, judicious merchant of forty. In England or the United States, he would, in our day, have been president of a bank, chief director in a railroad or canal company. Now, to him coolly calculating, what sort of a speculation was this of prophecy? On the one hand, certain rank, certain wealth, certain respect and estimation; on the other, every thing uncertain, but persecution probable, and little to be hoped at last save the production of a faith in one God, for whom — on this imposture theory — he cared not a straw. Would any judicious Yankee have gone into this business of humbug with such odds? It was not a case of quack medicines, or perpetual-motion machines. Mohammed was trying his patent invention against the intensest prejudices of one of the intensest races this earth has been occupied by. Imagine a Dutch merchant of old times, say 1650, going to preach the gospel of peace and forgiveness among the Mohawks *on speculation;* or a wise Boston dealer of our day starting, — not for Texas or Oregon, — but for the Blackfeet or Crows on a like mission; — imagine this, and then you have a conception of Mohammed playing the part of impostor. Out on the idea! Paley's argument for the honesty of the Apostles is worth nothing, if Mohammed was an impostor, — leaving out of sight, what we have presently to present, his after life. O, no! whether rogue or not afterwards, let us so far respect our own hearts and heads, — human nature, fallen as it is, — as to believe that this unlettered, imaginative, world-oppressed, heaven-seeking Arab was no mere cheat, but one to whose imagination heaven was opened, and to whom Gabriel came, *subjectively at least*, in truth. Twenty years of earnest thought on the questions, "Will God never send another prophet? never heal our woes?" twenty years of earnest longing that he would, of solitary, heartfelt prayer that he might, were enough to draw Gabriel to that cave of Hara, in Mohammed's thought, if not in reality. In how many hours had Amina met her child in that quiet cave! How often had the misty form of Abdallah, even, floated near him! Was it strange, that, on the night of Al Kadr (the divine decree), the Koran drew near to the earth, — God's expressed will near to man, — and that the archangel, dark with excessive bright, told the dreamer of his mission?

The light of morning was breaking over Mecca on the 24th of the month of Ramadan, and Cadijah yet waited the coming of her husband. Many a night he had been absent in his solitude, and she had slept in peace; but for some days his mind had been so absent, so excited, so elevated, that she could not rest. Morning dawned; her husband came; never had she seen such a fire in his eye, such light in every trait of his noble countenance. Was it insanity or inspiration? To her his words, burning with the calm fervor of the sun, proved it the latter, and the new prophet had one disciple.

Now begins the second period of the prophet's life, extending through about thirteen years. Supposing him honest at the commencement of it, did he continue so? And what light does his conduct during this part of his career throw upon the previous portion of his history? Does it add to or take from the proofs of his honesty at the beginning of his mission?

His wife was his first convert; his servant his next; Ali, the son of Abu Taleb his protector, and the leading man of Mecca, was his third; Abubekir, a rich and influential citizen of the Holy City, his fourth. In four years he had gained but nine followers. Then he called together all of the house of Hashem to hear his message, for hitherto he had labored in secret, — labored rather to perfect his own conceptions, probably, than to convey them to others. His relatives, or forty of them, came at his call, curious to hear what their quiet, easy, comfortable cousin Mohammed had to say. Cousin Mohammed was a changed man since they last saw him; then he was a thriving merchant and bridegroom, who seemed likely to enjoy his wealth, bring up his children respectably, and command the regard of his fellow-citizens for his intelligence and virtue, but who would never set the world on fire. Now, at this annunciation feast, his eye, manner, voice, and words had a vehemence, fervor, and extravagance in them, heretofore unknown in him. Some wondered, some laughed, some scoffed; to a few it was inspiration, to most sheer madness, to one or two (the rogues of the family) deep hypocrisy and imposture. The family of Hashem, the kin of Abdallah, rejected him. Then he turned from his own house to the Holy City, and in public, to all men, at the doors of the Caaba, to the idolatrous pilgrims flocking thither, proclaimed the truth given through

Abraham, through Moses, through Jesus, and now again through him: — "God is one God; the eternal God; he begetteth not, neither is he begotten; and there is not any one like unto him." * "Those whose balance shall be weighty with good works shall go into paradise; but they whose balance shall be light of good works shall go into hell." † The people listened in wonder to the eloquence of their townsman; the pilgrims heard, half angry, half alarmed, his denunciations of their idol-worship. The tribe of the Koreish — from among whom the keepers of the temple were taken, and who now saw with alarm and horror one rising to overthrow that temple, from the very family to which its care had been confided — found a solace for their troubles in the suggestion, that, should the family of Hashem uphold Mohammed, the time was come to turn that house from its primacy and exalt some other to its place. Abu Taleb, calm and firm, who had promised his father to protect Abdallah's child, would not desert him in his hour of need. He knew his virtues, his integrity, his purity, his intelligence, — and while he thought him an enthusiast, perhaps a madman, he still held over him his powerful arm, and the bold prophet was unhurt. Months passed, and years passed; day after day Mohammed took his station in the open street, and proclaimed the unity of God, the terrors of hell that lay before all idolaters and evil-doers, and the certainty of his own mission. A man, as we have said, of noble appearance, of persuasive manners, of natural eloquence and grace, and of excited imagination, — all could not hear him unmoved; but the greater part cried out upon him, that he had a devil, that he was a sorcerer, that he was a man distracted, a liar and a knave. Now and then some man came to him privately, and owned himself a convert; now and then some woman fell at his knees and hailed him

* Koran, ch. 112.

† Koran, ch. 101.

as the prophet of the Most High ; but in the seventh year of his mission, all his adherents in Mecca could not much have exceeded a hundred.*

Months passed, and years passed, and still, day by day, amid the gathering storm, when his followers had to fly to other lands, when even his daughter had to seek a foreign home, and after the other families of the Koreish had bound themselves by a solemn league against the family of Hashem, — even then, Mohammed, in the streets of Mecca, poured forth his denunciations of divine wrath against the idolater and evil-doer. No threats, no dangers, daunted him ; and though death at the hands of his opponents seemed sooner or later inevitable, he never swerved from his purpose of declaring the message confided to him. Fortunately, the Meccans were not the only hearers of his message ; all the pilgrims who crowded to kiss the Black Stone came within the reach of his voice. Among them were wayfarers from Yatreb, or Medina, the city of "the people of the book," the literary emporium (as we should say in America) of Arabia. Many Jews, many half Christians, dwelt there ; to the pagans of Medina, therefore, the unity of God was not, as to other pagans, a novelty and rock of offence ; and they listened to the voice of Mohammed, and believed, and became his disciples. Returning home to Yatreb, these few disciples became apostles, and while on all sides darkness seemed closing in upon the Reformer, while Mecca was becoming a more and more perilous home for him each year, silently at the sister city his doctrines were spreading ; and behold, in the twelfth year of the mission, when at the Holy City itself civil war and the death of the prophet seemed inevitable, twelve men went up from Medina to pledge themselves to Mohammed. At night, upon the hill Al Akaba,

* One hundred and one fled to Ethiopia in that year, to escape persecution ; and these could not have been the weakest only, as Mohammed's own daughter and her husband were among them.

north of Mecca, these twelve swore to renounce all idolatry; neither to steal, commit fornication, nor kill their infant children, — the common crimes of the pagan Arabs; not to forge calumnies; and to obey the new prophet of the one true God in every thing reasonable. Such was the oath of fealty on which rested the empire of the Caliphs. They returned, with one of the better instructed of the Meccan believers, who was to be a missionary in Yatreb. Even at that juncture, when death stood on one hand, and life and power on the other, Mohammed remained fronting death. Nay, when, the next year, a larger deputation from the city of the faithful came and offered to the endangered Meccan a home, and almost a throne, he still waited in his native town until all hope of success there should have vanished.

The thirteenth year of his mission came. The brave, wise, faithful friend of Abdallah's son, Abu Taleb, had descended to the tomb, and the arm of power which shielded the prophet was withdrawn. Nor was the death of his defender his only loss; Cadijah, — for twenty-five years his wife, to whom through that quarter of a century he had been faithful as few of that land ever were, for many wives were allowed, — Cadijah, his benefactress and his first disciple, had also been recalled from the earth. It was the "year of mourning" for the Reformer, that one which thus took from him his two best friends. His heart was no longer in Mecca.

And now an enemy, a deadly enemy, filled the place of Abu Taleb, and the hour of vengeance drew near. Silently, beneath the shades of night, the leaders of the Koreish met in conclave; with hushed voices, they plotted the destruction of Mohammed; from each family one was to be chosen, and all these were to strike their daggers into the breast of the offending member of the house of Hashem, and thus would that powerful connection be forced to seek revenge upon all the other houses of the tribe. They plotted, but "God is the best layer of plots";* by unknown means those whispers reached the ear of the doomed one. Should he fly? Had not God bidden him do so, by raising up an asylum at Yatreb? But already his chamber was watched, and at midnight the daggers would be in his heart. "Give me thy mantle," cried the young, fearless, generous Ali, "and do you, O Prophet, and Abubekir escape in the twilight." Ali put on the green mantle of Mohammed, and laid himself, fearing nothing, upon the apostle's bed. Eyes of vengeance watched him there, while the daggers were whetted, and while, with noiseless steps, the founder of Islam commenced the Hegira. He fled, with Abubekir, to a cave three miles from Mecca, and there rested till pursuit was passed. As he rested, sleeping calmly, his friend touched his arm; he awoke to hear at the mouth of the cavern voices debating the probability of the fugitive being concealed there. Trembling with fear, Abubekir whispered, — "We are lost! what can we do against so many, we two?" "There is a third," was the calm reply. "Who?" asked the astonished follower, — and as his hand fell by chance in the dark on the apostle's wrist, he felt the pulsations regular as those of a child; — "Who?" he asked. "God." As they spoke, the voices receded, and they were safe. A pigeon had built her nest at the mouth of the cavern, and a spider had woven her web across the entrance. Truly, by a spider's thread at that moment hung the fate of the world! After three days' delay, the fugitives pursued their way, and reached Medina in safety. Five hundred men met the prophet, and he entered the city of his adoption in triumph.

How does this portion of his life, these thirteen years of persecution and contempt endured, and death dared hourly, correspond with the theory of imposture on speculation?

* Koran, ch. 8.

How does his answer in the cave agree with the probable feelings of one who was thinking, talking, living a lie? If the lie theory can be made to explain the second period of Mohammed's life, then, we aver, a similar theory may be made to apply to almost every great promulgator of the gospel. If thirteen years so spent are not *primâ facie* proof of honesty, nothing can be; and it is a proof so strong, that a vast, vast amount of counter evidence must be brought forward to overturn it. One who is content to reason as Professor Bush does, in his Life of Mohammed, may see no force in what is so mighty as evidence to us; but to such champions of the cross we do not speak. He, for example, disbelieves the express statement of his hero, that he was not taught to write, — because, first, his cousin Ali was; secondly, because writing was not rare among the Arabs; thirdly, because Mohammed was to be a merchant; and fourthly, because it is asserted in the Koran, the last place where truth is to be looked for; * and he actually supposes this prince of liars to have dictated to Ali this useless lie, which Ali, and Cadijah, and every body else knew to be a lie, at the time when he wished to inspire confidence, and all for no other purpose, apparently, than to have the pleasure of lying. To such reasoners we have not a word to say; but to the rest of our readers we address the question, — Does the second period of the prophet's life add to or take from the probability, created by the purity and honesty of his character during the first period, that he was honest? And we cannot doubt the answer.

Let us now pass to the third, — the shortest, last, and most mysterious portion of this man's life. And let us begin by remembering that we are looking at a man fifty-three years old, one void of ambition hitherto, and remarkably free from impurity and immorality; who has been led to feel keenly

* Bush's *Life of Mohammed* (Harpers' edition), pp. 38, 39.

the need of a great radical change in the habits of his countrymen, who believes such a change must be effected by a revelation from God through an inspired prophet, and who has, after long meditation, come apparently to the conclusion that he is so inspired. And as we proceed in this man's history, and meet, as we shall, with circumstances which would stamp a sane man as a rogue, let our inquiry be, whether they are inconsistent with what has been observed of other monomaniacs, and honest religious enthusiasts. This is the basis on which, as we conceive, all such inquiries must proceed, and on which, in common daily affairs, all men would proceed. Had we known a man sensible and upright to the age of forty, and for the next thirteen years showing undoubted signs of insanity on some one subject, should we ever after that judge of his actions as of a perfectly sane man's in matters relating to that and kindred subjects? Should we not reckon as delusion in him many things, which, in one of sound mind, we should deem clear knavery? Up to the time of the Hegira, we claim that Mohammed's life gives proof of nothing but honest self-deception, or monomania; and we also claim, that, in trying to understand the ten years of his career that remain, we are still to regard him as under the same influence, unless something which is opposed to such an idea can be shown.

Mohammed had ever proclaimed the impolicy and iniquity of religious persecution; he had advocated the propagation of his doctrines, by addressing the reason, feelings, and consciences of men. For thirteen years he had persevered in thus addressing them, and almost in vain; they had spurned his instructions, rejected his truths, and sought his life. On a sudden, without agency of his, unsought, unasked by him, lo! God had put into his hands an army of devoted followers; for what? The old Hebrew collection answered very plainly, that God chastised by physical suffering those that persisted in rebellion and unbelief; it taught him that by the sword, when all else failed, Jehovah had prepared a way for himself. Is this denied? Is it denied that an Arabian of the sixth century might, in his best senses, most naturally thus read the Holy Book? Is it denied that in modern Europe, in England, more than a thousand years after Mohammed, the idea of promulgating by force the truth, even the truth as it is in Jesus, was a common idea? Can we look at the conquest of America by the Spaniards, and hold an Arab, into whose possession Heaven had as by miracle given arms, an evident knave, and no enthusiast, for believing that God designed him to use the arms thus given for the purpose of spreading that truth which men would not otherwise receive? Nothing, perhaps, tells more against Mohammed in the popular mind, than the idea that he wished to spread his faith by the sword; and yet how strange would it have been, had he persevered in peaceful addresses to men's reason, after laboring so long in vain, and being at last empowered to use other means, — the same means that were used against him! Truly, had he refused the armies of Yatreb, he would have deserved from all of us the name of prophet, and would have proved himself one of the truest successors to the spirit of the gentle Jesus. But so great virtue was not in him; the offer of the sword was to his mind not to be refused, for God offered it. The means of conversion which the greatest monarch of Christendom tried some three centuries later, this untutored Arab appealed to. Was Charlemagne dishonest in his bloody baptisms? If not, why Mohammed? It will be said, because he once taught a better doctrine; but shall there be no end to God's forbearance? Had not a clear proof reached the fugitive from Mecca, that the day of retribution was at hand?

But Mohammed, when in power, was cruel, vindictive, and showed that he used the sword for selfish, not noble, purposes; so many appear to think. In two lives of the prophet lying before us, the fact, that, after the battle of Beder, the bodies of the Meccans were thrown by Mohammed's followers into a well, is mentioned as a striking instance of their barbarity. Did the writers of those works remember how Christians, in this nineteenth century, treat the corpses of their foes? Did it occur to them, that, in the situation of the victorious army at Beder, no other mode of burial was possible than the one adopted? and that the act which is denounced as barbarous may have been an act of unusual respect? Surely, to leave the body of an enemy to the kites and dogs is as barbarous as to bury it, even though the grave be a well. And to aid them in estimating the barbarity of the victor in that wonderful battle, they had the fact, — more important, one would think, than the disposition of the dead, — that, of seventy prisoners taken, but two suffered death. But the charge of cruelty is utterly false. Mohammed forgave the very men of Mecca who had driven him forth and hunted him like a wild beast; he probably forgave the Jewess who administered the poison which produced his death; nor does a spirit of cruelty show itself in any part of his career.

He entered Medina, as we have said, in triumph. He found himself Prophet, Priest, Lawgiver, Judge, General, and King. Never was monarch so revered by his people, as the son of Abdallah by his followers. He built a temple or mosque of the most primitive simplicity, and reared for himself a palm-tree for a pulpit. His private life was one of marked abstinence and plainness. He lit his fire, and swept his chamber; mended his own garments, and spread his own table; dates and barley-bread, milk and honey, were his food.

One charge, and only one, relative to his private conduct, is, or can be, made; he is accused of licentiousness. Into a full discussion of this subject we cannot enter; but we ask the inquirer to consider these suggestions. From his youth to the age of fifty-three, Mohammed had been a model of chastity, and this at a time when no external circumstances operated upon his mind to make him so. Is it, then, to be at once believed that he, who had been so free from licentiousness through youth and manhood, would become a profligate in his old age, when every inducement from without called upon him to control himself? He was trying to reform his countrymen in regard to the very vice of which he is accused; and should we look, in the course of nature, for utter abandonment on the part of the Reformer, heretofore so continent, just when he was preaching continence? Ought we not, before we admit so improbable a charge, to weigh well the evidence on which it rests? And what is this evidence? It is, first, the tradition of his followers; secondly, certain portions of the Koran. In regard to the first, we hold it as worthless, for it is clear that what we look on as criminal his followers viewed in a wholly different light;* and this, leading, as we know it did, to immense exaggerations and fables, vitiates the tradition entirely. And what is the evidence of the Koran? We take it to be this, and nothing more; Mohammed took a greater number of wives than he allowed to his followers, under an assumed permission from God to do so. Why? From a licentious spirit? We cannot believe it. What then? it may be asked. We answer, that the conduct of the prophet may, very probably, have been induced by the same feeling which led Napoleon to repudiate Josephine; the only sons he had appear to have died in infancy, and he had no one to succeed him in that priesthood to which God had raised him. In short, that charge of unbounded licentiousness, which Christian and infidel writers have brought against the husband of Cadijah, we believe may be regarded as a misinterpretation of the fact, that, in his desire for an heir, he

* See Gibbon, chap. 50, notes 162, &c.

supposed himself allowed by Heaven to increase the number of his wives beyond the bounds prescribed to his followers. No other explanation than this seems to us to accord with his previous purity, and this explanation coincides entirely with the idea upon which we are proceeding, that Mohammed was a monomaniac, a self-deceived enthusiast, up to the time of his flight from Mecca.

And how do the other circumstances of his life at that time accord with our theory? Take, for instance, the first noted event after his accession to power, that battle of Beder, to which we have already referred. A caravan of the Koreish was on its way to Mecca. Anticipating an attack from the followers of Mohammed, a reinforcement from Mecca, consisting of nine hundred and fifty men, went out to meet and defend their fellow-citizens. To this force the prophet could oppose only three hundred and thirteen soldiers; but he did not hesitate about engaging the superior body, assuring his followers of divine aid. At first, he stood aloof from the battle, calling on God to assist his true worshippers; but when he saw his men wavering before the overwhelming numbers of the enemy, throwing himself upon a horse, and casting a handful of sand into the air, with a loud cry he led his yielding followers back to the charge, and by his enthusiasm so inspirited his supporters, and daunted his opponents, that he gained the day.

In relation to this battle, we have another specimen of the way in which prejudice can lead a man to write. Professor Bush, after giving an account of the contest, says this triumph is often alluded to in the Koran "in a style of *self-satisfied vaunting*," and immediately quotes this passage: — "And ye slew not those who were slain at Beder yourselves, but God slew them. Neither didst thou, O Mohammed, cast the gravel into their eyes when thou didst seem to cast it, but God cast it"; together with one or two others of similar import, all ascribing the victory to God.

But perhaps no period will more fully prove a man's honesty than the hour of death. How was it then with the Arabian impostor? He knew, for many months before his death, that his end was approaching, as he died from the lingering disease produced by poison. As long as his strength permitted, he pursued his usual course, promulgating his faith by force, where the Koran was not enough. Though he knew Azrael to be so near, he changed neither in language nor action, but continued to claim to be God's messenger, and to fulfil the duties of his mission. At length his strength failed him, but not his courage, his enthusiasm, or his faith. For the last time he caused himself to be borne to the mosque, and spoke to his people. He told them that his last hour was near, and called upon any to whom he had been unjust, or whose name he had injured, to accuse him openly; and if he owed any, he prayed them to make their claims then, rather than at the day of judgment. From the crowd there came a voice making a demand; it was acknowledged and paid, with many thanks to the creditor. He then set free his slaves; arranged every thing for his funeral; appointed Abubekir to succeed him as priest, but made no mention of any successor in command; and, with his head resting on Ayesha's knee, prepared to die. When the delirium of fever was upon him, he wished to dictate new messages from God; when the delirium passed by, he bade his weeping friends be comforted. Around him were gathered his chief followers; the worthlessness of power, the poverty of the rewards of ambition, could not fail to be seen by the dying man. Did he point out their vanity to Ali and Abubekir? Were his last moments given to self-reproach, or even silent despair? Could this impostor, this liar, this greatest of quacks and deceivers, pass away, and not utter one word showing that his soul was stricken with agony, when he looked back upon the villany of his mature years? His lips moved; they leant over him to catch the feeble sounds. "O God! pardon my sins," he cried; "yes, I come among my fellow-laborers on high!" He dipped his faint hand in the water, sprinkled his face, and died. Was that a liar's death-bed?

But there is one fact in the history of Mohammed which is usually regarded as conclusive; the fact, that he had revelations to suit his own plans, wishes, and position; in any difficulty or danger, he was informed from heaven what course to pursue. This is considered as certain proof of his imposture. But we think the history of monomania would show it to be one of the most common results of that disease. An enthusiast whose mind is unsound will, in most cases, have his visions or voices, when circumstances make them desirable; his revelations will be guided by his wishes. We cannot, therefore, think this strongest of all the evidences of the Arabian's dishonesty of any weight.

We have now given the leading points which need to be considered, in estimating Mohammed's honesty. For ourselves, we look upon him as honest to the last hour of his life; and we suppose his success and his influence to have been the result of his truthfulness and his real greatness of soul. It is disheartening to think, for a moment, that a mere deceiver and cheat could rule men's minds as this man did; but it is full of comfort and food for faith, the conviction that earnest, heartfelt, fearless devotion to the cause of God, as he believed, enabled the Arab Reformer to change the fortunes of so many millions. We regard the lesson to be learned, from the study of the prophet's life, as in favor of uprightness; not, as by the imposture theory, in favor of deception and knavery.

But not only do we look on Mohammed as honest, we regard him as one of the great souls of the world. We have no room to discuss his whole character, but we would call the attention of the reader to his forgiveness of the

Meccans who had sought his life; to his ability as a soldier, though educated to arts of peace; to the fact, that he originated the laws and literature of a great people, though but partially taught himself; and to that peculiar power which he gained over all about him. Had he been less great, his honesty would not have enabled him to perform the wonders he did; and had he been otherwise than honest, we cannot believe his name would have been now known to the reader of history.

II.

GREGORY THE SEVENTH AND HIS AGE.*

Surely it is a good sign for our age, that we have such historians as Hallam, Ranke, Hurter, and Voigt, — men who can see truth and excellence out of their own peculiar range of association, their own school of truth and excellence. And surely it is a good sign for Protestantism, which has ever tended so much to worship that intolerance which is the Antichrist of her faith, that such historians are rising among her sons; men who can see good as well as evil in the Western Christendom of the Middle Ages, and who dare show to their contemporaries, that the spirit of wisdom and reformation was not reserved for our perfect days alone; — and yet who are not Puseyites or Patristics of any school, but earnest, free-spoken Lutherans. And among these writers, there is no one who has given himself to an age more worthy of thorough and careful examination than the one selected by Voigt. It was the age of Hildebrand, of William the Norman, of the white-haired, firm-hearted, well-taught Lanfranc, of Abelard, and Bernard of Clairvaux, and the wise Mussulmans of Spain; the age of rising cities,

---

* *Histoire du Pape Grégoire VII., et de son Siècle, d'après les Monuments Originaux.* Par J. Voigt, Professeur à l'Université de Halle. Traduite de l'Allemand, par M. L'Abbé Jager. Paris: A. Vaton, Libraire-Éditeur. 1838. 2 tomes. 8vo.

From the North American Review, for July, 1845.

of consolidating feudalism, of literature beginning to breathe, of democracy struggling to be born.

Since Christianity came to man, but one great element has been introduced into European life; this was the intermingling of the Northern barbarians with the civilized, Christianized, degraded Romans of the South; the marriage of the fair-haired Teuton with his half-enslaved brunette bride. And a fierce wedding it was, — a dance of torches and of swords. For five hundred years, Frank crowded on Burgundian and Visigoth; farther Frank on nearer; Saxon on the farthest Frank; Slave and Hun on him; all was bloodshed, license, licentiousness, turmoil, robbery, and woe. A prayer for aid, a cry as of millions in mortal agony, rose unceasingly toward heaven. The ploughman stood idle, with hopeless, downcast eye; the hammer of the blacksmith hung in mid-air, as he thought how fruitless was his labor; the merchant stole along the hedges, shrinking from the eye of the passer, and stepped into rivers cautiously, seeking a ford, lest the man at the bridge should rob him. Over all the West of Europe, the wassail-song of the baron, the mocking laugh of the bandit, the shriek of the virgin, the nasal twang of priestly insult to God, were the only sounds which rose above the chaos of inarticulate moaning and heartfelt prayer, that came from the half-cultured country and half-deserted town. For a time, the reign of Charlemagne acted like oil upon the waters; but the day which God gave him passed by, and all was storm again; he came as a sunbeam in a dark day, as a meteor in the tempest, dazzling and wonderful, but shedding no permanent, abiding light. Into the darkness of that tempest let us cast a glance, and try to see a clear outline or two in its great depths.

It is a law of God, that a new organization shall always be preceded by the entire dissolution of what has gone before. The mineral will crystallize anew, only after it has been completely dissolved; the vegetable and the animal must be decomposed, before their elements can recombine into other forms of life. So, too, a new society can arise, only when the old one has been wholly dissolved, its atoms freed from each other, and its old arrangements broken up, so that every particle is at liberty to become part of the new living frame, according to some other law than that which governed the formation of the old social unit. The Roman world had to be ground down and dissolved by barbarian and Christian influences, before the formation of modern society became possible. Whose eyes can watch these processes, through the dust and fumes which rise from them? From Clovis to Hugh Capet, the grinding and fermenting cease not; and it is only within the eleventh century, when every baron, in his stone nest upon the hill-top, rejoices in utter independence of law and government, that we see the freed molecules of society ready to combine anew; while within the same age, in the completed feudalism of France, the rising power of the Church, the birth of the Communes, and the song of the Troubadour, are discernible the first floating filaments of the world in which we live. When the decomposing process was completed, society may be said to have ceased, while each family and individual, passing also through a modified chaos, acquired new ideas and tended to new organizations. To use the language of electrology, each atom acquired a new polarization. Chivalry, female influence, loyalty, romantic devotion, were then born within each separate household. Virtues, which had been unknown to Roman, German, or Christian, sprang into being from the commingling of all these elements.

Would we see a man of those times, of the first half of the eleventh century, — barbarian-Christian, chaotic and contradictory? Let us take the following portrait, sketched by William of Malmesbury. Old Foulques Nerra, Count of

Anjou, having for many long years governed his county with glory, and, one act excepted, with honor, at length gave the active administration into the hands of his son, Geoffrey Martel, a haughty, quarrelsome young fellow, who, not content with the substance, would have the insignia of power, and took up arms against his father to gain them. The old man, who, in leaving the battle-field and council-court, had proposed to attend mainly to the welfare of his soul, no sooner heard of his son's disloyalty than he grew young again with anger. "Once more to horse!" cried the graybeard; "up, every true man of you! The world will go to ruin at this rate! The saints shudder in their tombs at such impiety! Let every father and true son aid me!" They came at his call, and, led to battle by the fiery old warrior, overthrew the usurper and made him prisoner. What shall be done with such an enemy to society? The wrinkled brow of the father lost not its frown, and the proud boy was sentenced to the most humiliating punishment. On his hands and knees, a saddle upon his back, he was forced to crawl for miles to the feet of his father, who sat, trembling with excitement, waiting his arrival. He came in sight, he reached his parent's feet; did that paternal heart melt? Springing up, while the young man was still prostrate, again and again he kicked him, as he cried, "Are you conquered? are you conquered, boy?" The proud youth answered, "Yes, by you, my father; none else can conquer me." The flush of anger in the withered cheek died away; the bloodshot eye filled; those words, full of his own soul, reached his heart; lifting his son from the ground, he threw his arms about him, bade him forget the insult he had received, restored him his command, and forgot the past.

Is this not enough? Look, then, at this same old Foulques Nerra, journeying with two sworn servants to Jerusalem. See him, half stripped, kneeling before the Holy Sepulchre;

a wooden yoke is on his neck, and, as the servants scourge him under the eyes of wondering Mussulmans, hear his piercing prayer, — " Receive, dear Lord, this perjured, but repentant soul! Deign, O holy Jesus, to take me to thyself!" His prayer was not granted; three times he visited the Holy Land, and died at last in Europe, engaged in war with the son he had forgiven, because he disapproved of his marriage.

Let us look at that son's employments, as recorded by another Foulques, Fulk, or Fulco, his nephew.

> "By and by Geoffrey had a war with William of Normandy, who afterwards took England, and was a great king. Then he had one with the French, and the people of Berry; one with William, Count of Poictiers; one with Emery, Viscount of Thouars; one with Hoel, Count of Nantes, and the other Breton counts who held the city of Rennes; and then one with Hugh, Count of Maine, who had failed in his fidelity to him. It was because of these wars, and the magnanimity he showed in them, that he was called the 'Hammer' (*Martel*), as being one who hammered well his enemies."

The nephew, who leaves us the memoirs from which this extract is taken, spent the eight years next after his uncle's death, he tells us, in warfare with his brother, " with now and then a truce," trying to settle the division of the domains left them. This record of constant warfare will explain the necessity which existed for the adoption of the " Truce of God," the work of the Church; the history of which we may with propriety sketch, as it was one of the most characteristic features of the times we treat of.

In the year 994, a fearful pestilence raged in the Southwest of France. The people, horror-stricken, crowded for safety to the churches, where lay the wonder-working relics of the saints; and above all, to the church of St. Martial at Limoges. Thither they flocked, though all around was disease, and death, and pollution. The flesh of the infected fell from their bones; the air reeked with the vapors of decay; day and night, groans and cries of anguish mingled with the unceasing prayers of all the bishops of Aquitaine, who officiated before the altar. The hand of God was seen in the affliction; conscience spoke to the hardened sinners who witnessed these scenes of terror, and princes and barons bound themselves, trembling, to cease their wars and robberies, and to practise peace and justice. But soon impunity made them forget their oath; and again, on every hand, violence and evil reigned unchecked. At length, in **1033**, the angel of death once more descended, and in a form more terrible than pestilence. A famine fell upon the land, which carried agony to every hearth; all animals, all roots and grass, were exhausted, and then, as in shipwrecked vessels and besieged towns, man turned on man. The last apple that was left was used to decoy some child to death, that the decoyer might feast upon it. Men became wolves; and the wolves, starving too, broke from the mountains to aid in the warfare upon human kind. Again God's hand was recognized, and when the Church raised her voice and said that men suffered thus because of the evil that was done, all, gentle and simple, for the moment bowed, and established "God's Peace."

But it was again for the time only; human nature could not yet bear total abstinence from human blood, and within a few years, "God's *Truce*" was substituted in place of "God's *Peace*." By this truce, which was nominally established throughout nearly all Europe, warfare, plunder, and bloodshed were forbidden from sunset on Wednesday to sunrise on Monday; also during the great festivals; and during the Christmas holidays and Lent, no new defences were to be erected, nor old ones repaired. But this was not all. The provisions made for the protection of the laborer, and for the produce of labor, were far more characteristic of the dawning of a new era, — the era of church power, and of the arts of peace. Peasants in hostile territories were not to be injured or confined; the tools of agriculture, the hay and grain stacks, the cattle, were all taken under the protection of the Church; if seized, it must be for use, not destruction. He that violated this truce was placed under censure of the ecclesiastical power.

This was about the year 1041, in the pontificate of the wretched Benedict the Ninth, when pilgrims dared not enter Rome for fear of robbery, and just before the great quarrel, when the rivalry of three claimants to St. Peter's chair obliged Henry of Germany to interfere. It was not then the Roman Church, which strove to civilize Europe through the "Truce of God," but the bishops of Spain and France. The Church, indeed, as yet was not a hierarchy, but rather an aristocracy. But let us look more narrowly at the position and past efforts of the Church; for, in truth, its history is the history of Europe from the fourth to the fifteenth century.

In the last days of the Empire, the only active, energetic officers were those of the great Catholic body. When the barbarians came, the bishops met and tamed them. They became in part barbarous, in order to make the Franks and Lombards in part Christian. Thus were impurity and worldliness carried into the Church. When the Roman ideas died with Charlemagne, and individualism destroyed all political unity, the unity of the Church, in part at least, was lost too. Then the worldly tendency increased, and men, devoid of all learning and spiritual graces, sought to profit by the Church revenues, either directly or indirectly,—by becoming bishops and abbots, or by selling those places to others, equally worthless. As the feudal relation spread in reference to all else, it seized upon the Church, and subordinated it to the power and pleasure of the suzerain. Still, though seemingly enslaved, the Church was in reality the life of Europe, the one feeble bond which upheld society.

She was the refuge of the distressed, the friend of the slave, the helper of the injured, the only hope of learning. To her chivalry owed its noble aspirations; to her art and agriculture looked for every improvement. The ruler from her learned some rude justice; the ruled learned faith and obedience. Let us not cling to the superstition which teaches that the Church has always upheld the cause of tyrants. Through the Middle Ages she was the only friend and advocate of the people, and of the rights of man. To her influence was it owing, that, through all that strange era, the slaves of Europe were better protected by law than are now the free blacks of our United States by the national statutes.

The Church history of the tenth and eleventh centuries especially is an epitome of the history of Europe. While it was all that we have described, it was, at the same time, filled with the records of rapine, lust, ambition, and evil. Cautiously, but widely, the effort was commencing on the part of ecclesiastics to govern the nobles by means of mingled argument and artifice. Of this effort we have some curious evidences in the earlier history of that same old Foulques who saddled his rebel son. It was then, also, that the wonderful stories of the fate of those who took Church property had their rise; for example, that of the knight who, having made free with the property of St. Clement, was attacked by rats. All day he fought against them, sword in hand; but it was useless to slay them, for new crowds constantly came. At length, when evening drew near, the poor, wearied knight was forced to have himself hung up in a cage, suspended from the wall, thinking he was there safe from his enemies. But he mistook. When his attendants in the morning opened the cage to congratulate him on the disappearance of his foes, they found only his well-picked bones.

But while more of policy begins to appear in the Church

during the first half of the eleventh century, there were yet crowds of churchmen who bore the broad stamp of barbarism. We may refer, as an illustration, to the case of the Abbot of Fulda and the Bishop of Hildesheim, as late as 1063. They contended for precedence; and the bishop, upon a certain occasion, anticipating trouble, concealed a body of soldiers in the church where the quarrel was likely to break out. These men, when it did break out, fell upon the unarmed followers of the abbot, and began a slaughter. The friends of the Fulda cause rushed in then, sword in hand, and the church was a battle-field. Standing on high, the bishop cheered on his men, bidding them forget the place and its character, and by his energy he carried the day. And this was done by churchmen, not only in the house of God, but also in the presence of their young monarch, Henry the Fourth of Germany. The abbot was heavily fined. To raise the money, he used the property of his convent unjustly, and starved his monks. The monks rebelled, the abbot was forced to fly. The monks pursued him to the king's feet; but Henry took his part, and the rebels were brought to reason by a detachment of soldiers.

A better idea, however, of the chaotic character of the age may be formed by observing the conduct of two of the chief prelates of the Empire, the Archbishops of Cologne and Bremen. The young king was under the care of his mother Agnes, whose chief counsellor was the Bishop of Augsburg. The two archbishops, together with him of Mayence, were determined to get the boy into their hands by any means. The Archbishop of Cologne, accordingly, in 1062, contrived to meet Henry on an island in the Rhine, where the young monarch was feasting. One day the prelate told the prince, as he walked with him, that there was a most beautiful bark at the shore, which he had caused to be built. This was the fact; he had prepared it for the occasion, adorned it with tapestry, gilding, carved work, and painting. So eloquent was the account he gave of it, that Henry was readily persuaded to go on board. Instantly, on a signal, hidden rowers swept the vessel from the shore. The despairing Henry cast himself into the Rhine, but was saved and brought on board again; and, followed by the curses and threats of the party of the queen-mother, the reverend robber bore away his prey to Cologne.

But Anno of Cologne was far inferior to his associate, Adalbert of Bremen. Nobly born, well educated, with a fine person, a strong mind, an unbending will, and boundless ambition, Adalbert came into the world a predestined ruler. Determined to obtain control of the young Henry, and to extend his own wealth and power, until he should be the Pope of the North, — he gave the reign to the prince's passions, and stopped not either for truth, justice, or mercy. Engaged in wars and spoliations which loosened all moral control throughout Germany, he still ruled monarch and people until 1067, when the nobles of the Empire plainly told Henry, that he must leave Adalbert, or abandon all claim to the throne. Then for a season he left the court, but soon returning, remained in power till his death in 1072.

Into such a world of fierce barons and scarcely less fierce churchmen — a world which to those of its own day seemed so bad that they thought it must soon end — was born the boy Hildebrand, at Soano, in Tuscany. The year of his birth is not known. His father, an honest carpenter, saw the lad's parts, and gave him the best education that could be had; his master was John Gratian, afterwards Gregory the Sixth, one of the three popes deposed by Henry the Third in 1046. At some unknown period, Hildebrand crossed the Alps, and became an inmate of the monastery of Cluny, near Macon, in France. In this celebrated house, surrounded by highly cultivated gardens, the young man's mind and soul were watched over by the fathers of the institution, who understood his capacity, and expected great things of his future career. No less was thought of him at the court of Germany, whither he went at a later period. The reigning emperor, Henry the Third, said that he preached God's word with more power than any one he had ever heard. But a court was not the place for Hildebrand, and he soon reached his true position as Prior of Cluny. In this part of his life, the dates are so uncertain and tangled, that we will not undertake to say any thing about them; the first sure point, chronologically, that we meet with in his life, being his entrance into Italy in 1048–49, with Bruno, who had been appointed pope.

Before that time, however, the vast plans to which Hildebrand devoted his after life were formed. In those gardens of Cluny he sat in thoughtful solitude, meditating on the chaotic world about him, and praying for God's spirit to move upon the face of the waters. Can we enter into his thoughts? Can we see the evil and the remedy as he saw them? If we can, we find the key to his life, and to the history of Christendom.

From the shades of his mountain-cinctured retreat, Hildebrand looked out upon a world filled with ignorance, violence, and evil; upon a world, wherein God's image was effaced from man's soul. The old divisions between Roman and German had melted away, and the people and their language were new and shapeless. Order or supremacy there was none, or but the faintest signs of them. In every land he saw the same scene; everywhere the material of society, but no hand busy in the manufacture. And what hand ought to reform and create anew the moral world, but that which formed the earth and the sun? And would he not do it? Could it be God's will, that men should groan in the agony of that day for ever? Surely, he would change the whole structure of society, and make justice and peace once more known among men. And how? How, unless through his Church? But had not the Church always labored against these evils and iniquities? Why was she so weak? — In silent, solitary meditation, Hildebrand weighed all these points; and as he thought, saying nothing, listening to every thing, the problems one by one were solved by the mysterious power which works in earnest meditation. He saw that the Church, to do God's will, must become far more efficiently one; must lose its independent, feudal, aristocratic character, and assume the form, substance, and strength of a despotism, — whose head should be Rome, whose agent should be the successor of St. Peter. But that, though much, would be as nothing, unless the Church were independent of the nobles, of the emperor, and of all the world. Not only the Church must be independent, but, above all, the pope must be so. Even if all were as he wished in respect to the independence of the Church, would the wild, proud, fearless, feudal nobles obey the advice of God's representative on earth? Must not that representative be prepared to order and enforce obedience, as well as to advise? And how could this be done with power and effect, — how could God's aid be looked for, unless the Church were pure, as well as independent and united? Thus there rose up in the mind of the solitary thinker in those Cluny arbours four great guiding ideas; that God's Church should be one, and Rome its efficient head; that it should be free; that it should be pure; that it should assume the tone due to it as God's inspired organ, and command the princes and powers of the earth.

Calmly impatient, Hildebrand sat revolving his great plans, and biding his time. He opened his plans to the abbot in part, and with care. The good abbot saw the evil, and trusted that God would terminate it; he knew the Church ought to be free, and prayed that it might become so; but in the great work what could they do? Pray; trust in God; live pure, and hope for the best. And truly, such a world-making as the Prior of Cluny dreamed of was no slight task. To free the bishop from the baron, and the pope from the emperor; to stop all simony, and all priest-marriages; to unite the ecclesiastics of Europe under one despotic head, and make monarchs and warriors bow to that sacred power: — would not most abbots and men have said, "Pray and hope for the best, for what can we do?" Not so thought Hildebrand; to him it was clear that the work might and must be done. It would take scores of years, perhaps centuries; his dust would return to the earth long before the Herculean task could be accomplished. But what then? It did not follow that he must die before it was *begun*.

And now, in 1048, for the third time, messengers from Rome sought the emperor to ask from him a holy pontiff. At a full synod at Worms, the excellent Bruno was unanimously agreed on, as the most worthy and fit for the chair of the Apostle. Pious, learned, pure, and mild, Henry and his counsellors thought he could reform the Church, and yet not take airs upon himself; could be made to work as they pleased, to reform up to their point. The choice was made known to him, the place accepted, and, as Leo the Ninth, he left Worms, and by easy journeys through the Vosges, reached Toul, of which he had been, and still remained, bishop; and then, in full pontificals, admired by all men, passed on his southward way toward Rome. It was Christmas day when he drew near to the far-famed monastery of Cluny; whose abbot and prior hastened out to meet the great Christian father, and to invite him to spend with them the great festival of the Church.

In prayer and sober rejoicing they commemorated the coming of their Saviour. In friendly conversation they brought before them the world, the Church, the infinite evils of Christendom. Did Jesus then come in vain? Did Peter found his Holy See in vain? Had God deserted that Church with which he promised to be while the world stood? God had not deserted it; it needed an effort on man's part; it needed faith in Christ and Christian principle; it needed self-sacrifice and courage on the part of God's representative among the nations. The excellent Bruno felt and acknowledged his duties and his difficulties; he had been chosen by the emperor, who wished truly to aid in reforming the Church, and he was bound by gratitude and honor to consult that emperor's wishes. And these wishes might clash with the true interests of Christ's people; how melancholy that the head of Christendom could not be truly and in power its head! "There was a time," said Hildebrand, "when these things were not so; when the Bishop of Rome was chosen by the people and clergy of Rome, and stood as free of the emperor as of the Caliph of Bagdad." "There was," answered the mild father of the Church; "but alas! it can never be again!" "Can it not be?" asked the Prior, earnestly; "is your Holiness sure it can never be? May not God be waiting even now for you to take the first step in a revolution which shall not merely reform, but recreate, his Church? O most venerated Father, has not Christ called you that you may serve him, and not an earthly potentate? He, by his appointed means, will make you head of his Church, but no emperor can do so. These robes, pardon me for my boldness, are not truly the insignia of Peter's successor; for never did Peter, or his Master, give to earthly monarch the power to choose the Shepherd of the world." Bruno listened; his soul kindled at the words of the bold prior; he saw history by a new light, saw duty by a new light, and was shaken as from a sleep of years.

The Christmas revels were over. The report went forth, that the pope would resume his journey toward Rome. The villagers flocked forth to see the show; the house-tops, even in that cold season, were covered with anxious spectators; the Rhone, far eastward, swarmed with barges; nobles in mail-coats, bishops in rich robes sweeping the earth, ladies in jewelry and gold, — all came to see the newly chosen head of Christendom. The monastery gates unclosed; all eyes strained to catch a glimpse; Leo came forth, — but no longer in the robes of a pontiff, with the pomp of a prince; in pilgrim weeds, and with a pilgrim's staff to support his steps, Bruno, Bishop of Toul, was on his way to ask of the Roman people and clergy confirmation of the otherwise empty imperial nomination. How noble looked at priest, and priest at peasant, and women's tongues were silent from wonder, and all the world seemed astonished for a moment, is nowhere recorded, but is easily imagined. And who walked by Bruno's side? The Prior of Cluny, henceforth manager of popes, and recreator of Europe. The Herculean task was visibly begun, and a demonstration given that something might be done by man beside praying and hoping for the best.

The strange procession reached the Eternal City; barefooted, Bruno walked the streets, and asked confirmation of the emperor's choice. It was given with full hearts and eyes. On the 2d of February, 1049, he was consecrated. Thus had Hildebrand entered his wedge; he had made his protest against the imperial appointment to St. Peter's chair; he was next to open his church batteries against the other great evils of the day. In the same year, therefore, in which he was consecrated, Bruno held at Rheims a council, wherein simony, the dependence of priests on laymen, the unlawful marriages of priests, their more unlawful custom of concubinage, their yet viler crimes, — their habits of violence, of warfare, of robbery, of injustice, — were all condemned. The Church must civilize Europe, and it must first purify itself. In twelve canons we have Hildebrand's protest against the iniquities of churchmen.

But a mere verbal protest, though very needful, was not all; an example was wanted. When Leo had made known to the king of France, that he proposed to hold a council at Rheims to look into the matter of simony, efforts were made to prevent the visit; but they were made in vain. Even if Bruno would have listened to requests, evidently made by fearful and guilty men, his sub-deacon Hildebrand would hear no such prayers. And good cause had the guilty to fear; one by one, archbishop, bishop, and abbot, — all the prelates, — were called up to state under oath whether they had ever, directly or indirectly, been guilty of simony. Two archbishops, six bishops, and one abbot could not swear that they were innocent; six of the nine were deposed.

And now, notice having been given to the emperor and the world, that the imperial nomination of the head of Christendom was nothing, unless confirmed according to old usage by the Romans; and the priesthood having been roused to the danger of buying and selling church dignities; Hildebrand, as soon as temporal matters would allow, turned Leo's mind to the final adjustment of the old quarrel with the patriarch of Constantinople. Rome, by distinct acts, must avow herself sole head of the Church. Accordingly, toward the close of 1053, legates from Rome presented themselves before the proud ruler of the Eastern Church, Michael Cerularius, and demanded the recognition of Rome's claim to be the only orthodox and supreme spiritual power on earth. Michael refused the recognition. Turmoil and threatened violence ensued. Rome would abate no jot of her claim, and her pride was met by equal pride. Her messengers then raised their voice, and in the church of St. Sophia excommunicated the patriarch and all who adhered to him; they placed a copy of their anathemas upon the high altar of the church, shook the dust from their feet, and returned to render an account of their doings. But he to whom they should have accounted, the good Bruno, had fallen asleep in the month of May, 1054, and Hildebrand was even then seeking for his successor.

In this search he had a delicate part to play; his problem was to prevent the emperor from nominating the pope, and yet not to offend the emperor. Historians differ as to the mode which he adopted, but there seems to be no doubt as to his success. He chose his man, Gebhard; compelled the emperor to nominate him, and then had the election made, as in Leo's case, at Rome. Thus, again, he openly protested against the imperial appointment as conclusive, while, at the same time, he managed not to break with the wise monarch of Germany. Gebhard, as Victor the Second, went back with Hildebrand to the Holy City. Victor lived but two years, but during those years the great plans of the subdeacon went steadily forward. In two matters especially did he gain strength and success. The one was in the result of his mission to France to repress simony; he induced seventy-two bishops and dignitaries of the Church to confess their guilt and abdicate their places! It is said that he brought about this result by miraculous means, for that, when the first one accused presented himself boldly and defied inquiry, having previously bribed the witnesses, — Hildebrand asked him to say, "Glory to the Father, Son, and Holy Ghost"; and the false prelate finding himself unable to pronounce the words "Holy Ghost," fell on his knees and confessed his bribery and his falsehood.

But without stopping to discuss this story, let us look at the other case of success, in which our world-changer laid the foundation for the supremacy of the Roman Church over kings and emperors. Thus far he had striven to free the pope from imperial power; to free the Church from baronial vendors; to purify the priesthood, and assert Rome's supremacy. The year 1055 witnessed the first step taken in the most difficult labor he had yet to perform, — the subordination of temporal to spiritual power. The circumstances were these. Ferdinand of Castile had refused to pay due homage to the emperor, and had hinted an intention of assuming that title for himself. This matter was laid before one of the synods held by Hildebrand, who agreed that the conduct of the Spanish prince was a wrong done to the imperial dignity, and through it to all Europe; but at the same time he contended, that it was easier and better to settle all such matters peaceably, and offered the intervention of the power of the pope. Henry, seeing little of the future, agreed to employ the Church to bring the rebel to his senses. Accordingly, legates set out for Spain, bearing the recognition by the ecclesiastical power of the wrong done to the emperor, and calling upon the usurper to return to his duty, and renounce all claim to the imperial title, under pain of excommunication. Ferdinand called together and consulted his own great prelates, and finding their voice to be in favor of submission to Rome, he announced to the messengers his willingness to obey the papal command. By this action, the Spanish bishops definitely admitted the idea of unity in the Church, and of Roman supremacy; while Henry and Ferdinand united to teach the princes of Europe, that the imperial dignity, the highest known in the West, was in some sense dependent upon the successor of St. Peter. Thus had Hildebrand, within seven years, promulgated widely the four great leading ideas which had risen before his mind in those Cluny arbors.

Victor died; to him succeeded Stephen the Ninth, who reigned only seven months. His view of the monk of Cluny may be gathered from his last words: "Make no choice of my successor," said he, "till Hildebrand returns." The sub-deacon was then absent in Germany, whose emperor was dead, and whose young prince was in the hands of his mother, Agnes. Before his return, however, by means of bribery, the Bishop of Velletri, under the title of Benedict the Tenth, ascended the papal throne. What course, then, was the reformer to pursue, since corruption had thus again dared to lay hands on the Holy See itself? His partisans were driven from Rome, where Benedict, supported by the nobles, ruled supreme. If he turned to the empress, he lost all he had gained toward insuring the pope's independence of the imperial power. The clergy of the North of Italy were opposed to him, because he had caused Stephen to war against their continued habit of marriage. Whither should he turn? Leaving Germany, with the consent of the empress, he called a council in Tuscany, having already fixed in his own mind on Gerard, Bishop of Florence, as Stephen's successor. At this council, he first caused Benedict to be excommunicated, and next caused the nomination of Gerard to be made. At the same time, before the council had named any one to the vacant pontificate, he had sent messengers to the young German prince, expressing the wish of the Romans, that he and his advisers should name whom they thought most fit, but recommending, in a way which Agnes understood, the Bishop of Florence, who thus, by virtue both of the imperial nomination, backed by imperial lances, and of the choice of a proper council, could lay claim to the tiara. Early in 1059, under the title of Nicholas the Second, Gerard entered Rome, while Benedict was forced to retire, crestfallen and powerless, a deposed usurper, to Velletri.

The crisis which had just passed, we may be assured, had been foreseen by Hildebrand. He knew the history of the previous century too well not to perceive from the outset, that it was as needful to set the pope free from the Roman nobles as from the German monarch. It was with pleasure, therefore, in all probability, that he regarded the futile attempt of the factious aristocracy of the Eternal City to oppose the spiritual power; for it would, of course, afford an excellent opportunity to place the election of pope beyond their control, in part at least, if not entirely. No sooner, therefore, was Nicholas fairly seated, than a council of one hundred and thirteen bishops met at the Lateran, chiefly to consider the momentous subject of papal elections. By them it was determined, that wisdom would not teach an entire and immediate abrogation of the share either of the nobles or the emperor in the choice of the Roman bishop; but that the difficult matter should be arranged thus. On the death of a pope, the cardinal bishops — that is, the seven bishops within the Roman territory — were to meet, and consider who should succeed him. They should then call in the cardinal clerks, — or twenty-eight presbyters of the chief Roman churches, — and by these thirty-five, forming the College of Cardinals, the election was to be made, subject, however, to the agreement of the rest of the Roman clergy and the people of Rome, and impliedly to the consent of the emperor; the emperor's voice in the matter being a personal right, which the Church might withhold from any one it pleased. Thus was arranged a system, which, almost of necessity, would result in the complete supremacy of the College of Cardinals, and which, in fact, did so in the year 1179. It secured perfectly Hildebrand's first object, the independence of the papal power.

This independence was not to be left without substantial support. We have not time to enter into the details of the Norman invasion of Italy; it will be enough for our purpose to remind our readers, that, when those wild, gallant pirates conquered the whole south of the beautiful peninsula, and defeated and took prisoner the good old Bruno in 1053, they bowed before him and asked his pardon, and bound themselves to be his vassals. The relation then established between Rome and the Normans of Italy was made yet stronger in 1059, when, by the influence of our pope-guiding subdeacon, Robert Guiscard became the soldier of the Church, and bound himself to fight her battles; thus insuring the independence of the Roman bishop by the aid of the best lances of the South. Nor was it by the wild Normans alone, that the Holy See was defended. Beatrice, wife of

Godfrey of Lorraine, and mother of the celebrated Countess Matilda, was also ready to throw her power, as Marchioness of Tuscany, in favor of the Roman pontiffs, and with men and arms to aid them. And well was it for Hildebrand that he had secured these stout defenders, for now the time drew near that was to make or mar his plans for ever.

In 1061, Nicholas the Second died, and the canons respecting the mode of choosing his successor were to be enforced, in opposition, probably, to the nobles of Rome, and to the empress of Germany. The cardinals met, and nominated Anselm of Lucca, who was chosen under the name of Alexander the Second. It was supposed that his great merits, his piety, goodness, and learning, would cause all parties joyfully to agree in the election, if agreement in any case was possible. But such was not the case; a faction arose, opposed to the action of the cardinals; messengers were sent to the empress; the Lombard bishops, always hostile to the wife-banishing Hildebrand, crowded to Basle; the canons of Nicholas the Second relative to the choice of pope were condemned and disavowed; and soon the Bishop of Parma, as Honorius the Second, was declared the true successor of St. Peter. It was the crisis of the plans of our monk of Cluny. Should the licentious and mercenary priests of Lombardy succeed, simony and concubinage would again be the order of things, and the power of the Church be lost, perhaps for ever. The pope's chancellor, for such had Hildebrand become, girded up his loins for the struggle; Heaven would not desert him. The profane anti-pope, Honorius, commenced his march on Rome; many hands there beckoned him forward; behind was the power of the Empire. Still Hildebrand said, "Heaven will not desert us"; and through the South of Europe, earthquakes, lightning in midwinter, fearful tempests, and fatal diseases announced to all that Heaven was not unmindful of the doings upon earth. On the 14th of April, 1062, the watchers upon the walls of

Rome saw in the distance the lances of the unholy armament. Gold, for two months tried upon the friends of Alexander and his chancellor, had failed ; the fate of Christendom must be decided by iron. In the field of Nero the two armies of the followers of Jesus met ; with stubborn will the usurper and his troops pressed onward, and it seemed certain that they would win the fight, when Godfrey, husband of Beatrice, appeared with fresh troops upon the field. The forces of Honorius, wearied and surprised, gave way, and Hildebrand triumphed by the arms of Tuscany. But Honorius, though defeated, was not dismayed ; and it was not till Anno of Cologne, as we have related, stole young Henry from his mother, and in a large council of German and Italian prelates espoused the cause of Alexander, that the anti-pope was wholly disabled, by being deprived of the support of the Empire. This occurred in the autumn of 1062. Even then he did not cease his efforts, and in the following year, by the aid of friends in Rome, he was even enabled to enter the city, and seize upon the Vatican itself ; from which he was driven, however, the next day, by a rising of the people. His partisans, even after that, continued active ; and it was not till the Council of Mantua, in 1066, decided the question, that it could be regarded as at rest.

But we must hasten on to the close of the reign of Alexander the Second. In 1067, the leading men of Germany counselled the king's marriage, hoping thereby to diminish the mischievous consequences of the early training Henry had received from Adalbert the Evil ; for a wilder, wickeder boy-monarch has not often afflicted Europe.* But the marriage did no good ; the royal couple soon entertained an honest hatred for one another, and in the very next year, Henry proposed a divorce. In the midst of civil commotions, therefore, a meeting was held at Frankfort to consider

* In 1067, Henry was seventeen years old.

the proposed measure. Henry came to the meeting unwillingly, for he had heard that a Roman legate was there to forbid the divorce. And truly there was one there, — of all men in Europe, the one best fitted for such an occasion: Peter Damien, — Peter the Hard, — the boldest, most inflexible of mortals, who reprimanded bishops as if they were schoolboys, and knocked Hildebrand himself over the knuckles without ceremony. Peter, the hater of all the voluptuous and licentious, was a special hater of an immoral king, guided by an unprincipled churchman. When, therefore, the meeting was convened, he delivered the message, with which he was charged from Rome, in the spirit of pride in which it was conceived: — "The measure contemplated by the king," said he, "is full of evil, unworthy not only of a monarch, but of any Christian. If this prince will not be bound by laws and canons, let him at least spare his reputation, and save himself from the scandal which so vile an act must cause. Let him not do that for which he would punish another. But if he will not renounce his evil purpose, the Holy Church must speak with her God-given authority, and never will the sovereign pontiff crown him emperor who dares thus to outrage the Christian faith." The bold messenger of Rome was sustained by the discontented nobles of the Empire, and the angry prince could do nothing but submit, and bear as he best could the matrimonial burden they had loaded him with.

Four more years passed by; the evil Adalbert returned to power; sin and corruption, discord and tyranny, ruled the court and the country of Germany. Alexander was drawing near to his tomb; but before he passed away, he determined to hold the language of a master to the young monarch who would not listen to the tones of a father. The Empire was in a ferment; the Saxons and Thuringians were in rebellion; the royal treasury was stripped to build strongholds to overawe the wild, fierce people; the nobles openly murmured; all good counsels were lost upon the reckless Henry. In want of money, he despatched Anno of Cologne and Herman of Bamberg to Italy, to obtain his dues from that land. They went, and came again, with his dues indeed, but not such as he sent for; they came with letters from the Holy See calling on Henry to appear before St. Peter's tribunal, there to give an account of his past life, and justify himself from the charge of simony, and other equally grave crimes. Thus had the day at length come, when Hildebrand's conception of the tone which the Church should assume was realized, and the spiritual openly claimed supremacy over the temporal head of Christendom. It had wisely been withheld till then; and then it was wisely used. The German people, who would have rushed *en masse* against Rome, had she asserted such a power against a favorite ruler, rejoiced to hear the voice of the pontiff threatening the madcap tyrant then upon the throne; and so little sympathy was expressed for Henry by his people, that, rash and foolish as he was, he could not but tremble, and promise to reform. His promises and his fears were soon forgotten, however; for on the twenty-second of March, 1073, Alexander breathed his last, and no prophet stood by Henry to tell him, that the man who, as a guiding spirit, had for twenty-four years ruled the court of Rome, was about to ascend the throne himself, and to wield the thunderbolts he had been forging.

The pope was dead; the good, almost great, Alexander had gone to render his account. From mouth to mouth, on that March morning, the news spread through Rome; and every street-group buzzed with praises of the lost pontiff. The artisan had lost a patron, the poor widow a supporter, the scholar a generous friend, the churchman a model of piety; when would Rome see his like again? "And who shall succeed our most excellent Alexander? Hildebrand knows; Hildebrand will choose; we may trust the chancellor; he will arrange it for us; has he not done so since the time of meek old Bruno?" All eyes turn to Hildebrand. The wise, cold, calm archdeacon — cold and calm like Hecla in repose — ordered a fast of three days. Meantime, the last honors should be paid to the body wherein once dwelt Anselm of Lucca, Alexander the Second. Cardinals and bishops, abbots and deacons, priests and monks, in long-drawn, solemn files, enter St. Peter's church; the heavy, wavering crowd sways this way and that, striving to open and admit the sacred throng. Slowly the throng passes in, Hildebrand in the midst of them. Murmurs run through the crowd, — "Let us name our bishop"; "Choose Hildebrand for our shepherd?" "Yes, name him, — the archdeacon, — St. Peter wishes to have him for a successor." In ever louder murmurs, the inarticulate bass of a thousand voices swells toward clear, individual utterance, when Hildebrand springs to the pulpit. The murmurs die away; he bids them to be calm as he is, and to abandon all thought of him as the successor of their sainted father, whose burial they were to celebrate. But the ground-swell of popular feeling is not to be calmed, and the deep ocean tones begin again. A cardinal rises: — "Brethren, this is the man; from the time of sainted Leo, he has guided and defended us; no one can be found so fit to rule; and in unison with your wish clearly expressed, we, cardinals and bishops, with one voice, choose Hildebrand the archdeacon for our lord and pope." The multitude reply, "Amen." And now bring forth the robes and the sacred crown, clothe him, and, as Gregory the Seventh, salute him head of Christendom.

For long years had Hildebrand looked forward to that day, and yet he shrank and trembled when it came. Was he a coward, then, — willing to fight from behind popes' backs, but fearful of being in the front? Surely his own pontificate disproves that suspicion. Was he truly modest, and afraid of his own power and goodness? Few recorded lives show more of self-reliance and dauntless pride. Did he doubt whether the hour had come for the blow to be struck which he had so long meditated? Or did he tremble with excitement? Or was his conduct all hypocrisy? Whatever the motive may have been, he shrank, as we have said, when the power was pressed upon him. Trembling, he ascended the steps of the pontifical throne; mildly and peaceably he asked the approval of the German prince, as was proper by the canons of 1059; with real or assumed humility, he declared his wish to be free from the cares and burden of the papacy. But when once seated firmly, and beyond cavil made the spiritual ruler of Christ's Church, all trembling ceased, and the most fearful outbreaks of popular or regal displeasure could not move his fixed purpose. He had planted himself on eternal truth, and the wind and the rain might beat upon, but they could never stir him. He ascended the throne; European unity began again, and the sundered nations were reunited by a new idea.

Let us look with Gregory, from that throne of his, over Europe, and see, as he saw, what had been done, and what remained to be accomplished. For twenty-four years had he been laboring, since that holiday evening when Bruno yielded to his eloquence. Which of his ideas had been realized? Neither of them. The pope was not free from the emperor; the Church was not free from the laity; Rome was not absolute; the priesthood was not pure. And yet something had been done. Did the far-seeing dreamer in those Cluny gardens expect to see all realized within one quarter of a century? Was he disappointed, when he looked at the world as it yet lay about him? Confidently we may answer, No. He knew the work he had undertaken, and knew that his dust would mingle with the earth again before one half that meditated work was done. The spirits which bring despondency may have haunted the throne of Hildebrand, but his pride and his faith strove with and vanquished them. His ideas were not yet realized; an unregenerate Europe yet heaved beneath him; so much the more need of firmness, boldness, and trust in the Most High.

In the far Northwest, William the Norman, with mailed hand, was crushing the last free hearts that struggled for English independence. And yet from that far land had the old Lanfranc come to Rome to ask of the pope his *pallium*, his robe of office; Rome was becoming wholly supreme in the island of the Atlantic.

In France and Germany, Philip and Henry, ignorant and scatter-brained boys, set an example of simony and immorality that could not fail to corrupt all who dared to be corrupted. In those lands, Hildebrand saw clearly, the battle was to be fought; the pope, single-handed, against the two strongest monarchs of Christendom. And he saw, too, that the time for half-measures and winning words was gone by; with distinctness, and as Heaven's vicegerent, he must speak and act, and leave the consequences to the God of battles. Spain, rent and chaotic, was not yet the field for the Church to act in; one day it would be preëminently the arena; for the present, he would only claim it as subject to Rome. In the North, the reverence for Rome was growing, slowly and with difficulty; Scandinavia was not yet to mingle in the religious wars of Europe.

Russia, Poland, Hungary, and the East — half pagan and half heretic — were to be regarded only as a region in which to employ and educate missionaries, and as a pathway to that Holy Land where the Moslem stood triumphant. "Would it be possible," thought Hildebrand, as he looked into the future, "to unite the whole of Christendom in an effort to drive the heathen from that blessed soil? That were indeed a bond of union, and an effort in which the Church must lead." In his busy, restless mind, he dreamed of the Crusades, and fashioned the way for them.

But France and Germany, Philip and Henry, were nearer than Palestine and the Moslem; they were first to be looked to. In March, 1073, Hildebrand became Gregory the Seventh; in December of the same year he wrote thus to the Bishop of Chalons: —

> "Among all those princes of our day, who, urged by a shameless love of lucre, sell the Church of God, and thus enslave and soil the Mother to whom they owe all honor, we learn that Philip, king of the French, ranks first. . . . . . He, therefore, must know that we will no longer tolerate this ruin of the Church, but with the authority derived from the blessed Apostles Peter and Paul, we will repress his impudent disobedience. The king must renounce this shameful, simoniacal trade; or the French, trembling beneath the edge of a universal excommunication, must decide whether they will refuse obedience to him, or abandon their Christian faith."

The Frenchman trembled and obeyed, and another rivet was fixed in the yoke with which the monk of Cluny was binding the monarchs of Europe.

Toward Henry, Gregory, in the month of April, immediately after he had ascended the throne, had assumed a tone of mingled kindness and firmness, which, united with the internal troubles of the Empire, induced that fiery young monarch to write to him in a most respectful and friendly manner; so that, at the close of the first year of Gregory's power, 1073, the appearances were of submission on the part of the two princes from whom most opposition was anticipated. But Hildebrand knew men too well to think that his end was obtained on account of this apparent submission. He understood the state of Germany, and heard of all its secret dissatisfaction; to his mind there was but one object worth living for, and he perfectly appreciated how much might be done toward attaining that object by taking advantage of the strong feelings of disgust generated by the folly of Henry. He had heard in due season of the insult offered by that prince to the counts, dukes, and bishops of Saxony, whom he invited to his palace at Goslar, and left to wait for him all day, saying that he was engaged in a game, — and who went away at last without seeing him at all. He knew also of the midnight meeting in the Goslar chapel, where the fierce descendants of those who had baffled Charlemagne prepared the means for baffling his unjust and insulting successor. The winds from beyond the Alps had borne the murmur of the great multitude, who, called together by their lords, were informed of the perfidious purposes of their king.

"Brave Saxons," cried Otto, the Bavarian, mounting a hillock, "you see there castles crowning every hill, gorged with soldiers; for what are they? To defend your country, they tell us. Defend your country here in its very centre! Defend it where there is no foe! Believe not one word of it; they are to overawe and enslave you; to them you will see your wealth carried, your daughters dragged, by the agents of this faithless king. King! no, brave men, he is no king; he has ceased to be such, for he has violated every duty of a monarch. He is the enemy of our liberty, the enemy of our country, and we must be prepared at the sword's point to defend that liberty and country!"

Then rose up those that had been already robbed, princes and bishops, and accused the sovereign of Germany. Their hearts kindled more and more under the recital, till at length the multitude arose as one man, and with lifted hands swore to lay down their lives for freedom. This threatened outbreak Henry met by insult and renewed injustice. Hildebrand heard, as news he had expected, of the attack on Goslar by sixty thousand excited men; of the king's flight to Hartzberg; of the siege of that fortress; of the demands of the besiegers that the castles throughout their land should be destroyed; of Henry's farther flight in the night-time, through woodland paths where he had often chased the deer, over mountains and across rivers, drawing not his bridle for four days. The enthusiastic, noisy rising of the Thuringians, and the more silent discontent of the Swabians and Franconians, were all talked of in the Vatican; even the secret determination of the diet of Gerstungen to dethrone Henry, and substitute Rodolph of Swabia, was whispered at the pope's table. But Gregory himself was not there to hear these later news. Since midsummer of 1073, he had been journeying, receiving embassies from Constantinople and elsewhere, trying to obtain of the Greek Church submission to Rome, regulating Italy, interfering in the Church quarrels of Africa, and writing to France the letter which we have already quoted, threatening Philip. He turned over in his mind the affairs of the Empire, all which he was duly informed of, as we have said, by the very best authority, — probably by Rodolph himself. Long and earnestly he meditated on his proper course as the representative of God on earth, while he journeyed through the whispering valleys of the Apennines, under the clear December moon. And much did he need wisdom; for in Germany every thing seemed verging to chaos.

In the dry clear cold of that winter of 1073-74, Henry, bent upon effecting the reduction of the Saxons, had gone forth from Worms, his soldiers covered with bucklers whereon were painted the great deeds of their forefathers. Over the crackling earth, across the bending ice-bridges, they plodded on hungrily, not half liking the business they were on. Bread was scarce; the mill-wheels, covered with ice, refused to turn. The days passed in murmurs; at night, supernatural arches and columns in the clear sky shook men's souls. The Saxons, on their part, were pressed with hunger too; the rude masses said to their lords, that they must make peace, fight, or go home; freeze and starve any longer they would not. The king's friends grew ever colder, — the Saxon boors waxed fiercer; negotiations and threats, threats and promises, passed back and forth through the mountains. Spring was coming, and the boors must be at home; so it was "fight or treat at once." Henry treated. He gave up his forts; promised to right all wrongs, to restore all stolen goods, to forgive the rebels, and to behave more like a king and a Christian. The streets of his old court city, Goslar, were filled with shouting multitudes; the windows beamed with beauty; the young, handsome, daring king had yielded to his subjects' just demand, and the civil war was over. Peace and plenty, joy and virtue, must reign thenceforward. With smiling face, half angry and half pleased, the monarch rode through the happy throng, confirmed to the citizens their old grants, gave them new ones,

"And all went merry as a marriage bell."

But the golden age had not come. The king had promised to give up all his castles; but he could not bear to do so; his pet château at Hartzberg he must keep, if it were only for the sake of the church there, founded by Charlemagne. Instantly the applauding voices sank into threatening growls; his life was in danger. He must yield, then; and he did yield, so far as to destroy the outer walls. This calmed the multitudes, but only for a season. Henry left Saxony for the Rhine, and, as he crossed the frontier, grinding his teeth, he vowed never to return thither till he could do so as a master, and ride his rebel subjects with boot and spur. He said this, or was reported to have said it. Every man at Goslar told it to his neighbour, and from the city the news of the threatened tyranny spread up the wooded hillsides, and reached the peasant in his field, and the hunter in his mountain covert. The garrison at Hartzberg mourned the absence of the merry king, almost a week gone; lazily they paced the court-yards, or clambered over the fragments of the razed outer-wall, and whispered of the day when the hill would wear a prouder crown than ever. Night came;

the forest-moanings were mingled with the sound of peasants' horns and distant voices. The knights of the castle listened in doubt and fear. Doubt soon fled; for nearer and nearer came the sounds of a great multitude, pressing on without order, without a leader, without military music or knightly array. The wild, fierce Saxon peasantry, in their blind wrath, are upon them. By fire or force, every thing goes down; church and altar, the royal sepulchre and the martyrs' relics, the golden chalice and the lawn robe, are doomed to the same destruction by the raging offspring of the old pagan manslayers. A few hours, and the mountain stands as bare as God made it.

Let us pass to Cologne, — the rich, happy city of the Rhine, where old Anno, the king-stealer, still presided in 1074. In the late troubles, he had taken part against Henry; but the people of Cologne loved the prodigal monarch. They also had a grudge against their archbishop, who was of a somewhat hasty and overbearing temper. A Westphalian bishop, a friend of his, had come up to spend a church festival with Anno in the spring of this year. The festival was over, and the bishop proposed to return home. He wished a boat for this purpose, and the archbishop, having none at hand, sent his men to find one. They seized one belonging to a rich merchant, which was filled with goods, throwing out the goods without leave or ceremony. Of this the merchant's son got word, and in his young haste, followed by the house-servants, he went and demanded the instant restitution of his father's bark. The prelate's servants refused it; words were soon followed by blows, and a crowd gathering, the tumult swelled rapidly.

The archbishop, who was sitting at the table with his friend from Westphalia, hearing of the difficulty, sent word that the young law-breakers who had made the trouble should suffer at the next session of court. This was putting out the fire with oil; the young merchant instantly advocated open resistance. Worms had driven out her bishop, why not Cologne her archbishop? they were both enemies of the noble, generous young Henry! Men armed themselves, the shops were closed prematurely, window-shutters were carefully bolted, the great thoroughfares were deserted, and the by-ways filled. As evening came on, the masses moved toward the episcopal palace in silent determination. Anno, with the parting cup in his hand, his head half bent in salutation to his guest, heard the muffled sounds, and paused. All around the table listened with open ears, when, as from a military engine, arrows and stones, flung from a thousand stout arms, broke through every window, wounding and killing those within. Horror and despair dispersed those who were about the festal board, and the prelate with his friends fled to the church of St. Peter, which he barricaded. The palace was stripped, its treasures cast to the mob, the wine-casks were staved, so that the cellars were flooded, and men were drowned in them. The chapel was ransacked, the altars overturned, and holy vessels and vestments were no more respected by the mad citizens of Cologne than by the mad boors of Saxony. For three days the tumult continued, and the former quiet city scarcely knew itself. Anno, meanwhile, had with difficulty escaped from the church in which he had taken refuge; he had thrown himself upon the country, where his friends were found; and not a week had passed, before the burghers saw coming near an army which they knew they could not resist, — an army composed of men marching against the sacrilegious enemies of the Holy Church. The despairing citizens attempted no defence; the violators of the chapels were excommunicated, the leaders of the mob were blinded or beaten, and while the forces of the prelate began an indiscriminate plunder, six hundred of the richest citizens fled in one night to the king. The rich, bustling city became a lifeless solitude. Such were the scenes which Germany presented in 1074.

Upon such a Germany, filled with violence and misrule, with married priests and simoniacal nobles, a land of disorder, ruled by a king who could create only disorder, Gregory looked anxiously, and with doubt as to the course which his duty required of him. In that year, 1074, he met his first council; simony and marriage among the clergy were denounced in the strongest terms, and in connection with the condemnatory canons the doctrine was promulgated, that every Christian owed a stronger allegiance to the Roman than to his own peculiar bishop. The canons were instantly sent to Italy, Germany, and France, and every means were brought to bear upon the higher ecclesiastics to induce them to enforce the penalties of simony and incontinence. Legates from Rome also beset the German king, while his mother, Agnes, poured her remonstrances into his unwilling ears. The bishops of Bremen and Bamberg were suspended, until they should appear at Rome, and prove themselves innocent of the charges of simony; and Germany at large advised that the decrees of the Church should be obeyed. But it was easier to give this notice than to obtain obedience. When the Archbishop of Mayence attempted to carry out the canons relative to marriages, he was resisted by bishops, clergy, and people, and nearly lost his life in the tumult. But Gregory paused not a moment; to bishops, princes, archbishops, and the king himself, his letters were unceasing, and the constant burden was, — "Fear not, despair not; extinguish simony and enforce celibacy, and God will uphold you." The Crusade, long lying near his heart, he also wrote of, and prepared the way, in the minds of men, for that great enterprise.

Turning from Henry to Philip of France, he dealt that prince the hardest blows, so far as words can strike. He distinctly informed both king and people, that, "with God's help, he would deliver the kingdom of France from his oppression," unless he radically changed. In England and Spain, also, his letters and legates asserted the supremacy of Rome.

But the great moral evils of the Church were not yet done away; never had they been more prominent. Was Gregory, then, wholly defeated and disappointed? We think not. He must have known that mere words could not overturn the corruption of ages; what good, then, in using them? They attracted men's minds to the subject, raised a papal party everywhere, and gave courage and a voice to the heretofore silent advocates of reform. His words were seeds; they fell, and were apparently lost; but they were lost in human bosoms, where in silence they germinated, and made possible that perfect papal despotism which they taught, and which later generations witnessed.

Into the details of events in the year 1075 we cannot enter; with one exception, they were like those of the previous year. Gregory pressed his canons unceasingly, the priests and nobles resisted, legates and letters passed to and fro, from January till August. Henry and the Saxons were again at war, and at length he was victorious. Then his true purposes and character showed themselves; thus far he had been pliant and yielding; now he became fiercely opposed to Hildebrand. He stopped not at the grossest simony, and cared not for the most barefaced injustice. Yet, at this very time, he had the impudence to ask of Gregory the deposition of the bishops who had opposed him. At the same moment that the emperor thus appealed to the Holy See, the Saxons did the same; and the pope saw that the hour was at hand when he must cease speaking and act. One more letter he wrote, to tell the monarch, that, unless he obeyed the orders of the Church, he should be excommunicated. Then followed legates summoning him to Rome to clear himself of the crimes charged, under pain of an instant separation from the Church of Christ. Henry's hot blood leaped at the insult; with flashing eyes he expelled the legates, and summoned an immediate council at Worms. Hither flocked all the discontented; the houses were crowded with priests' families, and buyers and sellers of holy offices; the streets echoed with curses upon the monk of Cluny, the carpenter's son who dared outlaw a monarch. The pope was accused of every crime, even of murder and necromancy. In the council, the most violent charges were made against him; and at length, a messenger took horse to cross the Alps, bearing a letter from Henry to the Romans, calling on them to expel the false monk Hildebrand from the papal throne.

The messenger reached Rome, entered the synod where Gregory sat on high, and called upon him to come down from the place he had usurped. The Romans could scarce believe their senses; the prefect drew his sword, but the pope shielded the bold speaker with his own body. He calmed the tumult, showed the gathering crowd the necessity of cool determination, explained the inevitable contest that was before them, and, taking from the person of the messenger the letters which he bore, read them aloud. Couched in the most insulting terms, they raised the fury of the listeners almost beyond control; and when Gregory told them how mildly he had treated Henry, until he showed himself utterly inimical to the Holy Church, — when, with tearful eyes, he described his own struggles, his efforts to keep peace, his kind remonstrances, his fatherly admonitions, his long-suffering and patience, — the whole assembly rose and demanded in the name of God's justice the instant promulgation of the anathema against the perjured and tyrannical king of Germany. Gregory stood forth, calm and resolute, with uplifted hand and upturned eyes, appealing to Heaven. One short prayer he uttered, while the stillness of death sank down upon the assembly.

"Blessed and holy Peter," the calm, deep voice began, "hear

thy servant whom thou hast brought up and delivered from the hands of wicked men, who have hated me because I have been faithful to thee. Thou art my witness, thou and the blessed Virgin, that the Roman Church has called me, despite myself, to govern her, and that I had rather end my life in exile than usurp thy chair by unworthy means. But finding myself, by thy goodness and not my own merit, thy successor, I cannot but believe that it is thy will that all Christians should obey me, God having given me, as in thy place, power to bind and to loose upon the earth.

"In that faith, for the honor and safety of the Church, in the name of the all-powerful God, Father, Son, and Holy Ghost, and by thy authority, I forbid Henry, son of the Emperor Henry the Third, who through unheard-of pride has placed himself against thy Church, to govern the kingdoms of Germany and Italy; I absolve all Christians from the oath which they have taken or may take to serve him, and I forbid all men to obey him as king. And since he has refused to act as a Christian, and has persisted in living with evil, excommunicated men, in thy name I load him with curses, that the world may know that thou art Peter, and that upon this Rock the Son of the living God has built his Church, and that the gates of hell shall not prevail against it."

The deep voice of Hildebrand, so earnest, solemn, and collected, ceased; but the silence of the hundred and ten bishops remained unbroken; they dared not move. And when this solemn act was followed by the excommunication of archbishops, abbots, counts, and nobles, almost without number, they trembled at the boldness of their master; in Upper Italy he left but two bishops undeposed.

Such were the labors of the Synod of 1076; they cast a thunderbolt among the nations. All Germany, all Western Europe, was divided; no ears could be longer closed to the quarrel; every peasant with his plough, every wife with her distaff, must thenceforth be for Pope or Emperor. At first, men were against the newly asserted spiritual power; but had not Christ given Peter all power, and was not the Roman bishop Peter's successor? The dim, wavering forms of superstition became the ready allies of Hildebrand.

Sounds were heard in the night-air; sights of horror passed across the sky; the adherents of Henry died fearful deaths. Then rose the Saxons again; every day saw the mere temporal prince weaker, every day the undefinable dread grew stronger and spread wider. Walls would not shut it out, dungeons would not hold it; the curse of the Church, the anathema of God, like a terrible ghost, haunted men. In the midst of their revels, while they pledged the king, the clinking of the goblets was mingled with the echo of God's voice forbidding them; they dreamed of the excommunication, they woke to hear it reiterated. Every day, Henry lost adherents. Nor were the deserters merely those who were urged by superstition. Germany was of old ruled by its several princes; these the great emperors had subjected, and made the imperial power all-powerful. The emperor and the princes were opposed, and the latter defeated. They now saw, by a union with the pope, the means of rising again in the political scale, and overthrowing the central force which had subjected both Church and feudal sovereigns. Thus they were led to incline strongly in favor of Gregory's pretensions, and the Diet of 1076 was willing, in connection with the pope, to depose the excommunicated king.

Henry, who, with all his hot-headed inconstancy, could act with decision when necessity called, and who saw himself literally deserted, determined to submit, and to obtain the pope's forgiveness. We need not dwell upon the particulars of his journey to Canossa. All have heard of his climbing the snowy Alps, with danger and difficulty feeling his way along the precipices and among the glaciers, and sliding in a sled of hide, lowered carefully by peasant hands, down to the plains of Lombardy. All have been told of his three days' waiting, bareheaded and barefooted, in the bitter cold, for admission to the presence of the carpenter's son; and all know how hardly he obtained forgiveness at last. And when he did obtain it, it amounted to nothing. He was not reinstated in his regal rights, and had disgusted and cast off, by his humiliation, those that had clung to him. His very guards called aloud for a new emperor; the common people scoffed at him; the cities would not receive the mean-spirited monarch; encamped in the fields, he found himself shivering and starving in the midst of a universal hiss of contempt. Who can tell the rage of that proud, inconstant, undisciplined soul? He knew not where to turn, or how to give his anger and agony vent. Foiled in an attempt to make Gregory his prisoner, he turned, like a loose lion, upon Germany. His character seemed changed; with unlooked-for energy and decision he gathered an army, swept like a tempest through Swabia, Franconia, and Bavaria, leaving behind him a desert, nor ever ceased his mad career of revenge, until, seven years after his miserable humiliation at Canossa, he entered Rome in triumph.

We need not dwell upon those years. They offer us nothing but the rage of the emperor, the immovable courage of Hildebrand, and the devotion of the Countess Matilda to the Holy See; of the first two our readers know enough; of Matilda we cannot say sufficient to give any just idea of her peculiar and noble character.

The year 1085 opened amid a chaos in Germany and Italy; war, famine, pestilence, and floods made all men bow in misery and fear. Gregory, from his stronghold in Salerno, looked down upon the crooked, narrow, lava-paved streets of his last refuge, and off upon the blue gulf, dimpled by wandering winds. How beautiful the works of God looked to the worn combatant! — so calm, so pure, so divine! His mind turned to the world of man, rent and blood-stained, and his heart was sick within him. What had he accomplished towards that regeneration of Europe which he had so long dreamed of? Were his aims attained? Was the Church free, pure, united, acknowledged ruler of rulers? He felt within him the failing of his overtasked nature; his heart beat languidly; his time had nearly come, and how had he sped with his work? Never, perhaps, had there been a period of greater confusion and discord within and without the Church, and seldom less purity or union. As for the supremacy of Rome, — alas! the chief of bishops, betrayed by Romans, pursued by Germans and Italians thirsting for his blood, at variance with France, Spain, and England, was dying a forsaken exile. Had Hildebrand's sick heart failed him then, it would not have been strange; but he looked at his crucifix, at the image of his forsaken, dying, and yet victorious Master, and grew strong; for that told him how little the final triumph of a moral truth can be judged of from immediate success or failure. "And I, too," he murmured to himself, in words which, a few weeks later, were the last upon his lips, — "and I, too, have loved justice and hated iniquity, and I die an exile." The future, in which all his great principles triumphed, was hidden to him; but he knew that God ruled, that the great thoughts which by his struggles he had made familiar to men, rested not on his strength, but on an eternal basis; and that, though he was passing away, the Omnipotent remained as the world's ruler; — he knew that he had sown the seed, and that God would give the harvest.

The mild May weather lent daily new beauty to the outer world, and the languid eyes of the monk of Cluny loved to dwell upon the deepening verdure. Sometimes his soul mingled again with its old ardor in the contests that were raging; he called his attendant bishops to remind them once more never to own any one pope who was not chosen according to the canons. Then his mind went back to the green valleys of the Apennines, to the shepherds' huts and the snow-fed rills of spring-time; and it passed thence to the heaven he was approaching. Again he murmured, "I have loved justice and hated evil, therefore I die in exile." The aged bishop, who had risen from the pleasant window as he heard the voice, bent over him and said: "Not so, Holy Father, you cannot die in exile; for God has given you all nations for a heritage, and the ends of the earth for a dominion." The calm, grave lips moved not in reply; Gregory was not there; the overburdened heart had ceased to beat; the wise, fearless, immovable Hildebrand had gone into the presence of his God. Hildebrand had gone, but his words and struggles, as sown seed, remained; and soon Europe saw his victorious enemy, Henry the Fourth, sink on a door-step and die of cold and hunger, because Rome had cast him off; she saw a strong-minded Frederick, Emperor of the West, holding a pope's stirrup-iron; she saw France and England quail beneath papal interdicts; — in short, she saw, long after the dust of Hildebrand had mingled with the earth, each one of Hildebrand's ideas made practice; she saw the Church independent, united, free from simony and priest-marriages, and the ruler of rulers. The visions of the Cluny arbors were realized; Europe again was one.

III.

SAINT LOUIS OF FRANCE.*

Every student of history knows that a few periods only are worthy of careful and continued attention; if these are well understood, the times between them are also; but if they remain in darkness, the whole tale of the world's doings remains a puzzle and a mystery. And this is equally true, whether we read for mere amusement, or to learn the principles of national growth, or to become acquainted with the heroes and the monsters of our race. Hampdens and Washingtons appear at such epochs; and at such also come into view the Mirabeaus, the Robespierres, and the Benedict Arnolds, to show us how vast a depth of evil lies in us. But in studying such periods, we are apt to fall into the error of dwelling chiefly upon the rapid and violent changes which close them, rather than upon the quiet, mighty agencies which brought those changes to pass. Among all the histories of the French Revolution that have been written, we do not know of one which clearly, fully, and vividly traces, from the time of Louis the Fourteenth, those influences which caused the final outburst, and also those which gave to that outburst its peculiar character. Even the development of the causes of our own Revolution has not been at-

* *Michelet's History of France.* Translated by G. H. Smith, F. G. S. New York: Appleton & Co. Vol. I. 1846. 8vo.

From the North American Review for April, 1846.

tempted, independent of the various colonial affairs which had little or no connection with it. It is usual, indeed, to preface the account of any great change by a view of things before the change took place; and occasionally by a statement of all that has happened since man was created; or even, as in the case of Professor Rafinesque's Annals, prefixed to Marshall's History of Kentucky, by a suggestion of various matters which took place long before Adam was fashioned from clay; but in most such cases, the introduction is hurried, vague, and unimpressive. We may notice, as examples of what we mean, the account drawn up by Scott, and that given by Alison, of France before the meeting of the States General in 1789. But the error of which we speak as common among historical students is especially seen, we think, in the almost total neglect of the period in which the feudal yielded to the monarchical spirit, and when, though without volcano-bursts, the religious, moral, social, political, and industrial state of Western Europe underwent so vast a change. To speak of that period as a whole, except in the most general, and therefore most useless manner, would evidently be beyond the limits of a review; but we may, perhaps, turn the thoughts and inquiries of some of our readers to the era in question, by an account of one who bore a leading, though unconscious, part in changing the government of baronial force and priestly rule for that of regal law. We refer to Louis the Ninth, St. Louis, the champion of the Church, who yet undermined her power; the respecter of all feudal rights and obligations, who nevertheless destroyed the life of feudalism.

Louis was born April 25, 1215. It was in the midst of the war against the Albigenses. A week before his birth, his father, prince of France, followed by bishops, counts, and knights innumerable, reached Lyons on his way to Languedoc, through which devoted land he marched unresisted, levelling, as he went, the walls of Toulouse and Narbonne.

Six weeks after the birth of St. Louis, John of England met his barons at Runnymede, and grudgingly gave them their Magna Charta. Seven months after his birth, Innocent the Third, under whom the theocracy founded by Hildebrand attained its height, met the fourth Lateran Council, the most numerous of the ancient assemblies of the Western Church, and among whose seventy canons was that which for the first time made confession obligatory. When Louis had lived through thirteen months, his father, who had passed to England, claiming its crown, was feasting among the barons of John, and listening to the shouts of welcome sent up by the citizens of London. A few months more, and the little boy, scarce two years old, was but learning his earliest prayers at the knees of Blanché of Castile when his father's reverses began; and Blanche heard that her husband was worsted in England, and condemned at Rome. The old, unscrupulous Philip Augustus dared not aid his suffering son, so hard did the priests threaten; but the young, devout, priest-led Blanche was not to be led or driven, when all that was dear to her was at stake; she gathered her knights, provided her vessels, and sent her reinforcements to the aid of her lord; but, alas! even then English seamen were to be feared, and Blanche's little fleet was defeated, and the prince was obliged to surrender.

And now had Louis reached his ninth year; gentle, thoughtful, and filled with a sense of duty, such as rarely falls to the share of human beings, and especially to those of regal education, the little boy grew up under the influence of his mother's devotional, but independent spirit. In July of that year, 1223, his grandfather Philip died, and the claimant of the English throne, under the name of Louis the Lion, became monarch of France, and our young saint his heir-apparent. Louis the Lion was by no means worthy of his name, which was, in truth, not given him from any supposed resemblance to the king of beasts, nor even through flattery, but was bestowed upon him just before his death, to help in the fulfilment of an ancient prophecy. He was weak in body, mind, and soul, and far more truly priest-ridden than either his wife or son, though far less pious than either. And yet in him were united for the first time the races of Capet and Charlemagne; and as the streets of Paris after his consecration, hung as they were with the richest cloths and most beautiful garlands, resounded to the songs of Troubadours and the music of the dancers, men felt they knew not what strange hope of a king who should be one indeed; not a suzerain only, but a sovereign; a follower of the great Charles, as well as his descendant; a monarch who would curb the cruel power of the barons, and enable the honest and industrious to live in peace. Alas for their hopes! The first request made by his barons to the new king was for a discharge of all the debts which they owed the Jews, the money-lenders, and their request was granted. For three years Louis the Lion reigned, quarrelling with and conquering the English and the Albigeois; and died, at length, of a fever resulting from the fatigues and exposures of his last campaign against the heretics of the South. St. Louis was not yet quite twelve years old. It did not require much sagacity to foresee that a regency of nine years would try the value and strength of those additions which Philip Augustus and his predecessors had made to the kingly power. The claims of the late monarchs were by no means pleasing to the turbulent feudal nobles, and Louis and Blanche saw no less plainly than the barons that the minority of their son would be a time of contest. The last acts of the expiring king, with a view to the future, were to bind all about him by an oath to obey and consecrate his son as their monarch, and to confide him to the care of his mother.

Blanche was at Paris when she heard of the death of her husband. She felt strong in her self-confidence that it was necessary, not only that she should have the education of her son in her hands, but also that she should have the regency of the kingdom; and yet the fact that she was a Spaniard was as much against her as her sex, in the eyes of the French nobility; so that she knew her chance of being what she wished was small, unless secured by management. On two men of influence she believed she could rely, the papal legate, and Thibaud, Count of Champagne. The latter was one of the most noted men of the day, as well as the most powerful vassal of the crown. A poet, a knight, a gallant, and a determined upholder of his feudal rights, he had quarrelled with the late king, nay, was even by the lovers of scandal in later times openly accused of having procured his death, and yet was looked to by his widow as one in whom she might trust for support. It is hard to say why this was so. The students of Paris, who in after days hated Thibaud and Blanche both, attributed it to a criminal passion; but the tale is clearly unsupported. It may have been that the queen knew the vanity and the weakness of the count, and felt sure that he would desert the barons as soon as he could serve his own purposes better by doing so. Certain it is, that he was weak enough to make men think him wicked. He had already, before the king's death, bound himself to Peter Mauclerc of Brittany, the Count de la Marche, step-father of Henry the Third of England, and others, to uphold the rights of the feudal vassals against the growing power of the crown. He was not present at the consecration of the young king; indeed, the king's uncle, Philip the Rude, threatened to have the gates of Rheims shut in his face if he appeared before them, so insulting had been his conduct to the late monarch; and he was regarded as the chief of the malcontents. He even went so far as to collect men and arms, as if he intended open rebellion. Then, suddenly, to the astonishment of all but the queen, Thibaud left the party of the nobles, and at Tours, in February, 1227, did homage to the king, and became his true subject and defender. And he needed a defender; Philip the Rude probably meant to make himself regent at a fitting opportunity, and with him upon the one hand, and Philip "the evil clerk" of Brittany upon the other, poor Blanche and her young saint would have been close beset. By her alliance with the Count of Champagne, therefore, she secured a powerful friend, and only drove into open enmity a secret foe. The discontented nobles, finding themselves thus weakened by the desertion of Thibaud, resolved upon seizing the person of the young king, and withdrawing him from his mother's influence; and in an attempt which they made to do so they might have succeeded, had not the burghers of Paris, who justly dreaded the power of the great lords, flocked out to Montlhery, where Louis then was, with arms in their hands, and borne him with shouts and songs to his capital. It was an incident to affect the mind of a child like Louis; his barons, his peers, were seeking to imprison him, to tear him from the mother whom he so much loved and reverenced, and the common people rose and became his deliverers.

From that time Blanche remained in substance, if not in name, the regent of the kingdom; and woman and foreigner as she was, she ruled it as no native-born man-monarch had ever done. But she did not govern without opposition. The whole baronial power stood antagonist to her and her supporter, Thibaud. Against him they warred, on the pretence that he was the murderer of Louis the Lion; and in 1229 they ravaged his county of Champagne, and raised up a counter claimant to all his estates. In 1230, worn out and defeated, he was forced to take refuge in Paris, and to bind himself to go upon the crusade, as a kind of expiation for his alleged, but never proved or acknowledged, crime of king-killing. He was a strange man, this Troubadour count, and the influence of Blanche over him was also strange. Before his defeat above referred to, the barons had tried to bribe him back to their party, and old Peter, the priest-hater of Brittany, had agreed to give him, as a third wife, his daughter. Thibaud entered into an agreement to rejoin them. The marriage-day was fixed, the bride was decked, the priest ready, when the groom, already on his way to the altar, received a note from Blanche requiring him to abandon the plan and break off the proposed alliance ; and, without a moment's hesitation, he obeyed. But though the regent had the Duke of Brittany and all his friends in the North to contend with, she was by no means unobservant of the opportunity which offered itself in the South to add greatly to the royal power ; and after forwarding the persecutions in Languedoc, through 1228, she succeeded, by a treaty made the following April, in securing to the crown the ultimate possession of that beautiful land. Raymond the Seventh, by the terms of that treaty, gave up his kingdom, and his daughter paid to the crown twenty thousand marks of silver, broke down the walls and filled the ditches which defended Toulouse, destroyed the fortifications of thirty other towns and strongholds, bound his subjects by oath to take arms against him if he shrunk from the conditions of the treaty, and bound himself to do battle with the Count de Foix and others, his old friends and allies. The volume of the history of Languedoc closes with the seventh Raymond.

Nor was Blanche, while thus successful in the South, less fortunate in her contest with Peter the Breton, whom, in 1231, she brought to terms, and so closed her civil wars, having placed the monarchy of France on a firmer basis than it had rested upon for two centuries and a half; for to be unresisted under a woman-regent was more than to be bowed to under Philip Augustus. From that time until 1236, when Louis reached his twenty-first year, the internal history of the kingdom is nearly a blank.

And with the majority of St. Louis little or no change took place in the affairs of France, although there commenced a more general stir in those of Europe at large. It was the midst of the contest between the second Frederick of Germany, and Honorius the Third, Gregory the Ninth, and Innocent the Fourth. The second of these prelates then occupied the papal throne, a stern, fearless old man of ninety years, whom reverses could not vanquish, but only kill, — a worthy opponent of the strong-minded monarch of Germany. In 1227, within six months after the time of his elevation to the papacy, Gregory had excommunicated Frederick, because he did not depart, as was expected, on the crusade; in 1228, the monarch was denounced anew, because, unforgiven, he dared to set sail for the Holy Land, and fight for the Holy Sepulchre. The Templars, Hospitallers, and Teutonic knights were called on to oppose this wilful champion of Christendom. Jerusalem, because he obtained possession of it, was laid under an interdict, and the fearless emperor was forced to crown himself, no priest daring even to say mass. Returning to Italy, Frederick wrung a repeal of the excommunication from Gregory by force of arms; but the bitter blood was not sweetened. In 1239, the pope again launched his thunderbolt, and the war of extermination went on, until the successes of his antagonist laid the worn head of the Church, now ninety-four years old, upon his bed of death, in 1241.

Meanwhile, in 1237, came Baldwin, the Latin claimant of the throne of Constantinople, with the true Crown of Thorns in its casket under his arm, asking for money to aid him in recovering his kingdom. For a time he contrived to obtain assistance from certain Venetian money-lenders, with whom he placed the relic as collateral security; but he was not satisfied to leave it thus, and wished to prevail upon some pious monarch to purchase his treasure. France already possessed one undoubted original of the same relic; but Blanche and Louis were given to the feelings of the times, and the young king readily agreed to the proposition of the displaced emperor. One difficulty at first, however, seemed insurmountable ; — to deal in relics, by the rules of the Church, was simony. But there were clever heads and hair-splitting advocates then, no less than now, and it was soon seen that all trouble would be avoided by this simple contrivance. Baldwin should present the Crown to his pious friend Louis as a free gift and gage of love ; while the French monarch, not to be outdone in generosity, should, out of pure affection, bestow upon the somewhat needy emperor such a sum of money as would be a fair equivalent. In December, 1238, two Dominicans started with full purses for Constantinople,* there to exchange presents ; and, returning after six months' absence, met, in the heat of August, the pious king of France dressed in a simple tunic, or shirt, and barefooted, walking out from Paris to receive and carry upon his own shoulders the inestimable gift of Baldwin to the cathedral of Notre Dame. It was a sight to be noted, and most characteristic of the day, that procession of bishops and nobles, common people and children, all uncovered and with bare feet, chanting litanies as they followed their saintly king, with his long locks and bended head, bearing, in company with his brother Robert, the chest of the Sacred Crown.

But soon affairs of wider interest and a more stirring character than the reception of relics, and the building of chapels to contain them, were presented to the mind of the son of Blanche. In 1227, Genghiz Khan died ; before 1237, all Europe was troubled by the fear of the new swarm from Central Asia, which was fast inundating Russia, Poland, Hungary, and already with angry murmurs hovered on the confines of the Empire. The Saracens, most exposed to the devouring hosts of Tartars, sent embassies to Christendom to ask aid against a common foe ; the Old Man of the Mountain by his messengers offered fraternity to the rulers

* Or Venice; see Gibbon.

of France and England. On all sides was great trembling, but from none came signs of success to the West. Frederick called on his fellow-monarchs to aid him; but they were deaf; and his old enemy, the pope, never ceased to denounce and condemn him. The politicians of England and France refused any help to the Saracens, or the Christians of the East; as to the infidels, they said, "Let the dogs worry and kill one another"; for their brethren they could afford to pray, but by no means to fight, and day by day the Tartar hordes came on. But as yet the sound of their coming was distant. Blanche, indeed, heard it, and wept, lest all the faithful were to be borne from the earth. "Courage, my mother," said her son; "if we conquer, we drive these wretches to perdition; if the victory is theirs, they but open heaven's gates for us."

Other sounds, and nearer, of trouble and confusion drew, for a time, the thoughts of Louis from the enemies of his faith. The old feudal spirit was dormant, not dead, and Louis was called upon to renew the contest which his mother had waged during his boyhood. It was in the spring or summer of 1241 that Louis invited his nobles of the West to meet him at Saumur in Anjou, where he wished to present to them his brother Alphonso, who had married the daughter of Raymond the Seventh, and whom the king proposed to invest with the counties of Poitou and Auvergne. The monarch was not unaware of the feeling which prevailed among the Western barons in favor of the claims of England to that portion of his dominions. Philip Augustus had gained by force or diplomacy much of that country to the French crown; and the English affirmed, that, when Louis the Lion was caught in their island, as in a mouse-trap, in 1217, he had sworn, as one condition of his release, to restore all his father's conquests in Poitou and thereabouts. When, therefore, the Lion's son met at Saumur old Peter the priest-hater of Brittany, with his heir, and the Count de la Marche, whose wife was mother to the king of England, with others of doubtful sentiments, we may be assured that he looked round upon his guests, as they sat solemn in their silks and cloths of gold, with some uneasiness. Not that Louis was a coward; no braver heart ever beat; but he said to himself, as he looked forward to the prospect of a civil war to grow out of the investiture he proposed to make, — "Perhaps my father took that oath of restitution, and I am bringing on bloodshed by upholding injustice." Sad and doubting, the conscientious king sat in the midst of his black-browed peers. The feasting at Saumur was over at length, and all took horse for Poictiers, where his brother was to receive his counties, and the homage of his vassals. Among these vassals was Hugh de la Marche, and he, like Louis, rode sad and doubting. But by degrees his doubts cleared up, and he determined on flat rebellion. Too weak to come to blows at once, but resolved never to acknowledge Alphonso as his suzerain, and in due time to assert the alleged rights of the English monarch, he left Louis, assembled his followers, and, stationing himself at his château of Lusignan, offered no violence, but effectually prevented, by his show of force, the king's return from Poictiers to Paris. Louis the Saint found himself trapped, as his father had been in England; one by one, all his nobles left him; and after a fortnight's forced stay at Poictiers, he was obliged to make terms of some kind with his vassal, in order to get home again. It was clear that feudalism was not yet dead.

Had any doubt as to that fact remained, however, it would have been impossible to question it after the following Christmas. At that epoch, Alphonso, young and hopeful, Count of Poitou and Auvergne, and in his wife's right presumptive heir to the beautiful domains of Toulouse, called together his vassals at his capital, Poictiers, to hold high festival, and complete the solemn act of feudal investiture. From far and near men and women flocked to the ancient capital of the Pictones; its crooked, steep streets were filled with vine-dressers from the borders of the Vienne, with nobles and squires, dames and damsels, clerks and monks. The great cathedral, which had been two centuries in progress, and was nearly completed, echoed the solemn music of the season; in the Gothic castle all was preparing for feast and merriment. Alphonso received, as they arrived, knight and baron, and to each assigned his dwelling, already prepared at the expense of the new count, who was to pay all costs. And among the rest came Hugh de la Marche and Isabel his wife, mother of England's weak monarch; they, too, were welcome, — especially so, perhaps, as their coming seemed to promise all harmony, and with due honor and ceremonious respect were they received. Gloomy still, but in no degree doubting, was the great vassal of Alphonso. Since his secession, after the meeting at Saumur, he had employed his time well. Silently messengers had passed from him to England, — to Navarre, over which Blanche's friend, the Troubadour Count Thibaud of Champagne, was then king, — to Toulouse, where Raymond sat in smothered anger, ready enough to war against his daughter's husband, or any one else, — and over the Pyrenees, through the autumn-snows, to the kings of Aragon and Castile. Bonds holding them all together, in opposition to the king of France, had been silently knit while the leaves were falling; and now, when the bare branches glittered like silver with the hoar-frost, the lord of La Marche had come to defy his superior in the first flush of his pride, and before the face of all his vassals. The day for rendering the act of homage was at hand; — "To-morrow, and the ceremony which assures me my rank and counties is complete"; — so thought Alphonso, as he passed from group to group in the public place by the castle. But why these groups gathering toward nightfall in these short December days? If Alphonso asked that question within himself, a quick reply came from without. Hugh de la Marche stands before him, a page holding his battle-horse; near by, Isabel sits upon her palfrey, amid armed retainers. "I have been deceived," says the haughty vassal, in his most arrogant tone; "never, never, I swear to you, will I hold myself your man. Against all right you have usurped this county of Poitou, the birthright of Richard of Cornwall, who has been fighting for you in Palestine while you have been robbing him here." Turning on his heel without more words, he sprang into his saddle, struck the spurs into his steed, and, rejoining his wife, rode toward the southern gate. Alphonso stood stupefied; he was recalled to his senses by the bursting of flames from the house where the rebel had been lodged; he had fired it in the moment of departure. The young noble saw in the conflagration a symbol of coming war. War, indeed, was already declared by the act of the Count de la Marche.

That war occupied the next year. We need not enter into its details, although it was the last of the feudal wars; it is enough to say that Hugh de la Marche was forced on his knees to beg forgiveness; that Henry, the Incapable, of England, was utterly worsted, and nearly taken prisoner; and that the Spanish kings attended to their own affairs, leaving their neighbour Raymond to shift for himself, which he did, by submission. The gentle French monarch dealt with his rebels as leniently when conquered, as he had vigorously when in arms. From Raymond he required only adherence to Blanche's treaty of 1229; and when his lords wished him to put to death De la Marche's son, who was taken prisoner while commanding at Fontenay, his answer was, "No; he has done no wrong in obeying his father." There is another anecdote of this war worthy of remembrance. Richard of Cornwall, brother to Henry the Third, and son of Isabella of La Marche, had done good service to some French knights in Palestine. During the reverses of Henry, he sent his brother, dressed in his Palestine pilgrim's dress, and with a staff in place of a sword, to ask of Louis a cessation of hostilities. When the French knights, many of whom had been in the Holy Land, heard that Cornwall was thus approaching their camp, the memory of his gallantry came strongly on their hearts; and in the truest spirit of chivalry, they went out to the verge of the English lines, and received as an honored guest the brother and son of their leading enemies, formed an escort for him, and brought him to the throne of their monarch. He, too, forgot the foe in the crusader, took the prince by the hand, treated him as a brother, and granted the armistice requested.

St. Louis, as we have said, by this war of 1242 finished those contests of the crown with its vassals which had been going on since the time of his ancestor, Louis the Fat. But it was not by warfare that he was to aid in breaking down the strongholds of feudalism. The vassals might have been beaten time and again, and yet the *spirit* of feudalism, still surviving, would have raised up new champions to contend against the crown. St. Louis struck at the spirit of the Middle Age, and therein insured the downfall of its forms and whole embodiment. He fought the last battles against feudalism, because, by a surer means than battling, he took, and unconsciously, the life-blood from the opposition to the royal authority. Unconsciously, we say; he did not look on the old order of things as evil, and try to introduce a better; he did not selfishly contend for the extension of his own power; he was neither a great reformer, nor a (so-called) wise king. He undermined feudalism, because he hated injustice; he warred with the Middle Age, because he could not tolerate its disregard of human rights; and he paved the way for Philip-le-Bel's struggle with the papacy, because he looked upon religion and the Church as instruments for man's salvation, not as tools for worldly aggrandizement. He is, perhaps, the only monarch on record who

7*

failed in most of what he undertook of active enterprise, who was under the control of the prejudices of his age, who was a true conservative, who never dreamed of effecting great social changes, — and who yet, by his mere virtues, his sense of duty, his power of conscience, made the mightiest and most vital reforms.

One of these reforms was the abolition of the trial by combat. Soon after the Poitou war, when poor old De la Marche, his gray locks bowed to the dust, was moaning his folly and his fortune, one of his vassals, who had sworn deadly enmity to him, accused the old man of unknown felonies, and dared him to the combat. His son wished to fight in his stead; but the ungenerous Alphonso insisted upon the appearance of his ancient enemy and insulter, in person. Against this sentence there was one cry of protest, and Louis, whose attention was called to the matter, interfered, and forbade the contest.

But though the king, as we have said, was the conqueror in his Poitou campaign, he returned from that region an invalid. A great part of his army had been made unwell by want of proper food, by foul air, and impure water. The king himself passed from one phase of disease to another, until at length, in November, 1244, a dysentery settled upon him. Sick, and each day more sick, — from mouth to mouth, from town to town, the sad news spread. The churches echoed with the prayers and vows of priests and people, pleading for their king; for their noble, just, sympathizing king. Around Pontoise, where the sufferer lay, were knots of country folks, and of Parisians who had walked out so far, — all busy with the same sad questioning. No good news for them; sick, and each day more sick, — so the word goes. And at last they say he is dead. Men look heavenward; where is there hope for them now, unless in heaven? Then comes a rumor that the tale was not true, and the monarch lives. Again comes a rumor that he is not only living, but has assumed the cross. How was it? Let us see what Joinville relates, and imagine the little points he omits. The sickness grew ever worse, he tells us, and no hope was left. Just breathing, the good king lay, wasted in body, resigned and fearless in soul. In his clear, calm mind he revolved, as we guess, the progress of the infidel arms, the neglect and deadness of Christendom on behalf of the land of Jesus. In his sick chamber, in subdued tones, they talked of the Tartar conquests, and of the barbarities of the Karismians in Palestine; — the sick man heard, but spoke not. They spoke to him, and he could not answer; scarce any pulse, scarce any breath; his kind eyes closed! so he lies, sinking away. Blanche, his mother, and Margaret, his wife, worn with watching and weeping, have left him to the two hired nurse-women. One of them from time to time bends over him; more and more deathlike grows his calm countenance; the smile of the departing soul hovering there, not yet fixed. "Does he live still?" reverently asks the other waiting-woman. The more eager of the two, who has been impatiently watching for the moment of death, listens, touches his wrist, holds a morsel of down to his nostrils, clasps her hands, and with upturned eyes answers, "Alas! it is all over." Her companion springs to the bedside, holds back the sheet with which the first would have covered his face, and tries in her turn to discover how life and death stand with him; patiently she listens, and patiently she presses his arm, — stands a moment, her pallid lips parted, then cries with swimming lids, "He lives, and *will* live to confound the enemies of the Lord." His vital power, just at the ebb, begins to swell again as he heard, in his living death-trance, her glad cry, her bold prophecy; his heart beats stronger, his lungs play again; by and by his voice comes, and his first words are, "Bring me the red cross." The last of the crusaders assumes the badge of his Master!

It is not our purpose to follow Louis either in his first or second crusade. If the great work of his life was not to be done by fighting at home, still less was it to be accomplished by battles in Egypt or Tunis. His mission was other and greater than he dreamed of, and his service to Christendom was wholly unlike that which he proposed to himself. Of his Eastern labors and sufferings we can give but the leading dates, with here and there an anecdote worthy of recollection, as illustrating either the character of the man or of his times. In November, 1244, he took the cross; but it was June of 1248 before he was able to leave Paris to embark upon his cherished undertaking. During the interval, he labored unceasingly to rouse all Europe to the necessity of union on behalf of the Holy Land, and in opposition to the infidels, who threatened, unless met by united Christendom, to plant their horse-tails upon the cathedrals of Paris and of Rome. He even, by what we should call a trick, enlisted his nobles as crusaders, and the act is worthy of notice as illustrating the moral tone of the age; for, be it remembered, it was the act of one of the most truthful and conscientious of men. At Christmas it was usual for the king to give to the gentles in his service new dresses. Louis invited his followers to meet him on that day at an early mass before it was yet light. They came willingly, and each as he entered received a dress at the door, given in the king's name, and which he was requested to wear at the ceremony. All of course complied. On bended knees, with bowed heads, around the altar, they listened to the services of the church, in the dim waxen twilight. By and by the rays of the morning struggled through the darkness and the censer-smoke, and for the first time friend looked toward, and smiled on, friend. And in all faces there was surprise; some looked blank, some fearful, some merry; what meant all this dumb show? It meant this. On each shoulder stood, indelible, the red cross. And as the secret became evident, and they awoke to the truth, that, with their new cloaks, the pious monarch had bound them to the crusade, anger, grief, trouble, joy, and wonder, in varied combinations, spoke from the silent faces of the group of courtiers, in the midst of whom stood silently the grave, calm, kindly king.

But of all the efforts which Louis was called on to make in order to bring about the desired union of Christendom, the most difficult and the least successful was his attempt to reconcile the emperor of Germany, who was a kind of royal Luther, with the unforgiving Innocent the Fourth, who, after a long vacancy of the papal throne, had succeeded to Gregory the Ninth. Innocent was a man of capacity and immense stubbornness. The contest between pope and emperor was such that nothing but death could end it; they had been friends, but now were foes; and what enmity so deadly as that between old comrades? In December, 1250, Frederick died; and the head of the church, then at Lyons, whither he had been driven in the struggle, returned to Rome, singing hymns of joy, and at once proclaimed a crusade, not against Turks or Tartars, but against the successor of his ancient enemy.

Meanwhile, in France, all was made ready for the departure of the champions of the cross. But their chief was destined to be yet further tried. With ceaseless sighs and prayers, his mother and wife beset him, telling him his mind was disturbed at the moment he took the vow to go to Palestine, and that he was no more bound thereby. Gently the pious king replied to their urgency; but still they urged their suit that he would stay, and brought the bishop of Paris to support their pleas. "It may be so," said Louis mildly. Hope glowed in their affectionate, unheroic eyes. "I was not in a state to act wisely, you say." "You were not, surely." "Behold, then, I tear my cross from my shoulder." They leaped for joy. "And am I now well? Can

I judge wisely now?" "Most wisely, beloved son and lord." "Well, then,"—and we may think the unruffled monarch could scarce suppress a smile, though his peace-loving eyes kindled with the hope of yet warring for God,—"well, then, I now resume the cross;—and no food shall pass my lips till I am bound anew sworn soldier of my Lord."

On the twenty-fifth of August, 1248, the devoted crusader embarked for Cyprus. Having passed the winter there, on the fifth of June, 1249, he landed in Egypt, which was to be conquered before Palestine could be safely attacked. On the seventh of June, Damietta was entered, and there the French slept and feasted, wasting time, strength, and money, until the twentieth of the following November. Then came the march southward; the encampment upon the Nile; the terrors of the Greek fire; the skirmishes which covered the plain with dead; the air heavy with putridity and pestilence; the putrid water; the fish fat with the flesh of the dead; sickness, weakness, retreat, defeat, captivity. On the sixth of April, 1250, Louis and his followers were prisoners to the Mussulmans; Louis might have saved himself, but would not quit his followers; he had been faithful thus far, and would be till death. And when he had procured his freedom, he would not yet leave the East for his own land. He thought of the prisoners in the hands of the Mamelukes, he remembered the Christians of the Holy Land, and determined to remain where he could best serve the suffering. On the eighth of May, 1250, Louis was a freeman, and it was not until the twenty-fifth of April, 1254, that he set sail to return to his native shores, where Blanche, who had been regent during his absence, had some months since yielded up her breath.

On the seventh of September, he entered Paris, sad and worn. All met him with joy and honor, but with eyes abased he walked without a smile through the streets of his capital. Ten years had passed, and what had been done? Poor king! bowed with self-reproaches, he little knew that during those ten years he had done, though none saw it, and he knew nothing of it, a vast work, — a work to make his reign ever memorable; he had founded a throne in the hearts of his subjects, and had made himself, through their affections, omnipotent as the leader of the great crusade against the abuses of the Middle Age. Every wounded knight that had come from Egypt, every freed captive, every soldier that retired from service, had told with enthusiasm of the sanctity and the humanity of their king. A knight, a devotee, a kind and just man, he met at one point or another the wishes and prejudices of every class; but especially, by his sympathy with the masses, and his readiness to consider their generally neglected welfare and rights, he won upon the body of his people, and laid the foundation for that strong feeling which not only led at last to his canonization, but made every ordinance of his life at once bind them as subjects, and control them as the word of a true hero. The shepherd-crusade of 1251, which had degenerated into a mere rabble-swarm of thieves and rogues, began in a love for the captive monarch; and the feeling which prompted that hasty and evil movement, a feeling in favor of Louis, as a contrast, if not an antagonist, to the proud, luxurious, and selfish prelates and nobles, continued after his return from captivity. And scarce had he landed, before he began that course of legislation which continued until once more he embarked upon the crusade.

In captivity, under suffering, treated with imperfect justice, and at the mercy of tyrannical masters, we may easily believe that Louis had revolved in his mind once and again the injustice done in his own realm, and to his own people. In his lonely hours of distress and sickness, how natural was it for such a soul to conceive of a complete revisal and reform in those judicial processes which he was conscious wrought so much wrong; and especially, to so true a soul, how natural the determination to begin by righting the wrongs done by himself and his ancestors! True and noble soul, indeed! full of prejudices, and superstitions, and errors, it may be; — but how free from the mass of those errors and evils which beset the men who then breathed, walked, wept, laughed, and did work in the world! Where shall we look among rulers for a parallel in point of disinterested heroism, unless to our own Washington?

In his first legislative action, Louis proposed to himself these objects, — to put an end to judicial partiality, to prevent needless and oppressive imprisonment for debt, to stop unfounded criminal prosecutions, and to mitigate the horrors of legalized torture. In connection with these general topics, he made laws to bear oppressively upon the Jews, to punish prostitution and gambling, and to diminish intemperance.

But the wish which this rare monarch had to recompense all who had been wronged by himself and forefathers was the uppermost wish of his soul. He felt that to do justice himself was the surest way to make others willing to do it. Commissioners were sent into every province of the kingdom to examine each alleged case of royal injustice, and with power in most instances to make instant restitution. He himself went forth to hear and judge in the neighbourhood of his capital, and as far north as Normandy. The points which weighed mainly, however, on the mind of Louis were not the private wrongs which were to be set aright, but those international difficulties whence grew ceaseless war in Christendom, the victories of the infidels, and scandal to the name of the Prince of Peace. France was embroiled on the one hand with England, on the other with Aragon. Neither of these powers was sufficiently strong to wring any thing from her; and as to the justice of the matters, — each party in the contest honestly conceived itself to have a clear claim to the disputed territory. Here, then, was a case for heathen patriotism to struggle with Christian justice in the mind of the stronger monarch. It may be they did struggle, but not long. The self-forgetting crusader looked on justice and generosity as nobler virtues than mere heathen patriotism; he saw, with his heart and conscience, if not his mind, that whoso begins by loving his country more than right will end by loving himself more than his country. With England and with Aragon, during the year 1258, he concluded treaties, in opposition to swarms of wise, selfish advisers, whereby peace and concession were substituted for obstinacy and war.

Such were the first acts of our crusader, when he came to his home once more. Can we wonder that men already, in their speechless hearts, canonized him? And when, a little after, it was again noised abroad that the king lay deadly ill, and every hour's news were listened for with faces ready to weep, or beam with joy, — how heart-touching to hear men tell one another at the street-corners, and in the butchers' shops, and by the dusty road-side, or in the crisp harvest-field, — how the dear king had called his young heir, now sixteen, to his bedside, and had said to him, — "Fair son, I pray you to make the people of your kingdom love you; for I would rather a Scotchman from Scotland should come and govern the people of my realm well and justly, than that you, child of my loins, should rule them in evil." Poor Louis! he rose from his sick-bed; but his son lay down in his stead, and rose no more.

And as he grew yet older, the spirit of generosity grew stronger daily in his bosom. He would have no hand in the affairs of Europe, save to act, wherever he could, as peacemaker. Many occasions occurred where all urged him to profit by power and a show of right, a naked legal title, to possess himself of valuable fiefs; but Louis shook his head sorrowfully and sternly, and did as his inmost soul told him the law of God directed. And with all this, we say again, he had no spark of radicalism in him; nay, he was eminently conservative. He reverenced the old feudal customs, and never, by direct means, warred against them. He wrought in opposition to the *infinite* evils of feudalism, its *God*-antagonism, — not against its *conventional* mischiefs, its impolicy, and awkward semiorganization. When his friend Joinville, in 1248, would not take the oath taken by those who held directly from the crown, because his immediate lord was the Count of Champagne, Louis may have smiled at the feudal foolery of his faithful follower, but deemed him none the less a friend. Many reformers are like the wolf, which tears the cast-off coat of the flying victim, and loses its prey; Louis, like all heart-directed Christian laborers for humanity, struck at the living fugitive, not the dead garment that was left behind.

And how did he strike? We have already referred to his earlier laws on behalf of right; let us now look farther.

Feudalism rested on physical force. Its gospel was given in three words, — "Might makes right." Upon this idea all feudal relations depended, all feudal laws (if we may use such a word) were founded. In a double sense, it was a system of *feuds*. Its legislation rested on arbitrary will; its judicial proceedings on strong limbs, able to work out the judgments of God; its executive functions were confided to men-at-arms. The despotism of baronial ignorance and obstinacy, the judicial combat, and private warfare, formed the three divisions of feudal, legal, and political science. Against these Louis the Ninth labored. His clear soul knew that the determinations of the church, from the time of Hildebrand and earlier, against these things were not mere ecclesiastical censures, but were expressions of the deepest feelings of man's nature. And though the church in practice had fallen far short of the theory of her great leaders on this and countless other points, — though in her bosom, too, were despots, tempters of God, and lovers of blood, — the great truth which lay in the action of those leaders was evident to the seeing eyes of the just monarch of France. In October, 1245, before he went upon his sad Egyptian pilgrimage, he had issued an ordinance, the purpose of which was to counteract the old Germanic, barbarian, and so feudal, feeling, that a wrong done one was not to be revenged by injury to the wrong-doer, but must be washed out by vengeance taken on his innocent kindred. He that slew his brother's murderer did but take the place of the hangman or headsman; he must slay one who did not deserve slaying, and so place himself on an equality with the offender. This, within limits, Louis forbade; if a man must have blood, he should take the blood of the wrong-doer. Next came a law by which either party liable to be involved in a private warfare might, by going to a feudal superior, prevent the resort to force; the other party, in short, was bound to keep the peace, and if he did not keep it, he was hung. But these steps, though large ones, were not enough to satisfy the conscientious lawmaker; and in January, 1257, by the advice and consent of his council, he utterly forbade all private warfare whatsoever. True, his prohibition did not stop it entirely and at once; but from the moment he promulgated this last edict, we may be sure that all who reverenced its author, all who loved quiet, all who saw the evils of overruling physical force, all who recognized the immense moral mischief of the old system, united in upholding the ordinance of Louis, and founding the reign of modern law. The husbandman whose corn-fields were trampled to mire, the merchant whose goods roving bands of armed men seized by the way, the mechanic whose shop was searched for arms and accoutrements, the priest who was insulted by the lawless soldiery, the newly seen law-student whose scraps from the Pandects were torn from him by unlettered squires, — all the lower, all the middle, and a large part of the female half of the higher class, — were agreed upon the vital question, "Shall this private redress of wrongs continue?" With one voice they answered, "No"; and though for more than a century the baronial power withstood king, commons, and women, it each day grew weaker, and drew nearer to its last death-struggle.

But the use of force in the executive department was a less evil, and a more manageable one, than its use in courts of justice; and for a plain reason; an all-prevailing superstition sanctioned the latter; the judicial combat was an appeal to God, and in those "ages of faith," the masses — not the church — smiled on every such appeal. Nor was it superstition and popular feeling alone which upheld the judgment by force of arms; the interest of the armed aristocracy was no less urgent in its support. So long as a good lance, a trusty steed, and a strong arm could insure a man God's voice in his favor, — that is, so long as might could make right, — all who were trained to the battle-field as their true sphere feared nothing; they dared in any cause meet any one in battle, and the combat was a reference of all questions to strength and skill. How many lonely nights of prayer, meditation, and heart-sick doubt the kindly Louis spent in Egypt, Syria, and France, considering, with full eyes and damp brow, how he might cure the evil, he was conscious of, not even the faithful Joinville can reveal to us; they will be numbered in the last day, at the footstool of the Great King. All that we learn is this, that in 1260, not arbitrarily, but as before, by advice and consent of a parliament or council, he forbade peremptorily all use of the "battles of justice" within his own feudal domains, ordaining in their place proof by witnesses. Especially he forbade the battles between a party to the trial and his judge, which in those old feudal times of force served instead of writs of error and bills of exceptions; and in room thereof, he ordered an appeal or reference of the whole proceedings to the king's own tribunal. These two steps, — the substitution of witnesses in place of an appeal to God by battle between parties, and the creation of an appeal to himself, when either party was dissatisfied with his judge, instead of another call to Heaven, — these two steps, although for the time confined to his own domains, did more to destroy that form of organized barbarism which we call feudalism, than all the contests and victories of Louis the Fat and Philip Augustus. Any baron with a bull's or boar's head could guess who was victor in a listed field; but when he was set down to read papers (leaving out of view the probability that he could not read at all, and must employ a scribe or lawyer to read for him), — when, we say, this Front-de-bœuf was set down to read documents, weigh evidence, split hairs, and logically work out conclusions, his patience could nowise bear the trial, and he was glad enough to refer the whole matter to a legist, a lawyer, an antibaron, who strove week by week and hour by hour to effect the great work of modern days, — the subordination of physical, brute force to intellectual, human acumen. Will the hour ever come, when both these shall yield to the power of Divine goodness?

Nor was the appeal to the king's court less important than the use of testimony in place of swords and lances. It did, indeed, far more than any thing else to increase the power of the throne, and especially its moral power, its position in the eyes of mankind. We say, more than any thing else; but in this we regard the right to declare a case to be a "royal case" as a form of appeal. There had been for some reigns back a growing disposition to refer certain questions to the king's tribunals, as being regal, not baronial questions. Louis the Ninth gave to this disposition distinct form and value, and, under the influence of the baron-hating legists, he so ordained, in conformity with the Roman law, that, under given circumstances, almost any case might be referred to his tribunal. This, of course, gave to the king's judgment-seat and to him more of influence than any other step ever taken had done. It was, in substance, an appeal of the people from the nobles to the king, and it threw at once the balance of power into the royal hands.

And how did he use this power? Less like a king than a father. Under the oak-trees at Vincennes behold him sitting, — his learned counsellors, Pierre de Fontaines and Geoffroy de Vellettes, near by, — waiting rather to arbitrate than judge between those who came to his tribunal. How patiently he listens! How anxiously he examines all proofs! How kindly he points out the middle way, overlooked by both disputants, which will conduct to justice! Can we still wonder that such a man, in such times, was soon to become a saint in the estimation of men? But neither he, nor any other mortal, could perform the whole duty required; and it became necessary to make the occasional sitting of the king's council or parliament, which exercised certain judicial functions, permanent; and to change its composition, by diminishing the feudal and increasing the legal or legist element. Thus everywhere, in the barons' courts, the king's court, and the central parliament, the Roman, legal, organized element began to predominate over the German, feudal, barbaric tendencies, and the foundation-stones of modern society were laid.

But the just soul of Louis and the prejudices of his Romanized counsellors were not arrayed against the old Teutonic barbarism alone, with its endless private wars and judicial duels; they stood equally opposed to the extravagant claims of the Roman hierarchy. Rome had commenced the work of uniting Christendom; had labored, and effectually, against the democracy of nobles, the feudal system; the crusades were the fruit, as chivalry was the flower, of the union between the German element and the church. But in destroying in some respects feudal disintegration, Rome had left it in other respects untouched; her strength lay in the disagreements of kings and nobles; and where she produced union, it was always in subjection, not to Christianity, but to the Western church. The great plans of Hildebrand hinged upon the ultimate omnipotence on earth of the see of St. Peter; all temporal power must bow to spiritual, and at the head of all spiritual powers in this world was the successor of the great Apostle of the keys. Against this first form of modern unity there had been struggles numberless; — one familiar to all English readers is the contest of Henry Plantagenet and Thomas à Becket; — but the first calm, deliberate, consistent opposition to the centralizing power of the great see was that offered by its truest friend and most honest ally, Louis of France. From 1260 to 1268, step by step was taken by the defender of the liberties of the Gallican church, until, in the year last named, he published his "Pragmatic Sanction," his response, by advice of his wise men, to the voice of the nation, the Magna Charta of the freedom of the church of France, upon whose vague articles the champions of that freedom could write commentaries, and found claims, innumerable. The provisions of this charter are nowise remarkable; the fifth protects France to some extent against the exactions of Rome; but otherwise there was nothing in the Pragmatic Sanction of 1268 which the popes had not time and again countenanced. And yet this ordinance of Louis has been the sheet-anchor of that Gallic independence in ecclesiastical matters which, we suspect, will yet shake off Papacy for Catholicism, and demonstrate that there may be a church free, on the one hand, from sectarianism, on the other, from despotism.

But the legislation of Louis did not stop with antagonism to the feudal system and to the unauthorized claims of the church; it provided for another great grievance of the Middle Age, that lying and unequal system of coinage which was a poison to honest industry and commercial intercourse. Eighty barons struck money as they pleased, and changed their coinage as the fit took them, or interest prompted. In each barony that coin only was current which the lord had his clipping from. And as alterations of the money were of incalculable evil, and the subjects of each coiner prayed for permanence in the value of each class of pieces, the lords wisely — as the world goes — took pay from the sufferers as a bribe not to vary the standard, and then — in the same spirit of wisdom — varied it as they pleased, and sweated their pounds very nearly to ounces. These things, evil and unjust, did not escape the eye of our conscientious king. As early as 1247, he began his changes by shutting out foreign coin, and making the royal coin everywhere receivable, and everywhere the standard. Having once assumed this ground, he had only to preserve the king's coin at one unvaried value, and all others were forced to bring their moneys to the same value, or they were driven from the market. By these simple means did the good monarch and his long-headed advisers — a sound heart working by a hundred keen wits — cause, for a time at least, uniformity where had been diversity, make it for the interest of the knavish to become honest, and ultimately secure the general prevalence of the issue from the regal mint, as men found that it never changed, while the baronial money-moulders were for ever striving to overreach their neighbour burghers and the thick-headed Flemish merchants. The old gospel had been, as we have said, "Might makes right"; the new commercial glad tidings were fast growing in favor, — the saying, that "Honesty is the best policy." Through thick world-vapors the sun of Christianity comes slowly up.

But among the laws of Louis bearing upon commercial interests were many which would not suit our liberal, free-thinking, free-trade age. His first reforms included, as we have seen, provisions against the Jews; and in after days, Christian-Jews as well, Lombards and others, came under his condemnation. Why? Partly because of the old

Jewish provision against usury ; partly because Aristotle and the philosophy of the Middle Age forbade the fertility of money ; and partly, also, because, in the days of St. Louis, money was not so used by most of those who paid usury as to make it a fair subject of usury. The Jews and Lombards, when money first took its modern omnipotent position, and could no longer be come at by the strong hand, *were* mostly usurers in the worst sense, and wrung "the forfeit of the bond," though it were the pound of flesh, from the panting, dying debtor, who had at first borrowed but as a means of staving off some earlier leech, some other Shylock.

However, while the feeling of our day will and must protest against Louis's strong provisions in opposition to usury, it is entitled to record its vote in favor of the general tendency of his commercial regulations. They were calculated to raise the trading, and ultimately the laboring classes, to their true position in the eyes of the public ; they were incomplete, perhaps evil ; but surely they were a step beyond the old iron feudalism ; and if our age be, as we claim, in advance of the Middle Age, then was the legislation of St. Louis superior to that of his predecessors. Philip Augustus had done much to break down the baronial power ; but in doing this, he warred as chief of the barons, and nothing that he did was calculated any more to abolish the woes and wrongs of feudalism than the subjection of the barons of conquered England by William the Victor and Henry Plantagenet. Louis, on the other hand, unconsciously, through sheer love of right, and aided, urged on, guided, by those who had whetted their intellects on the Pandects and the history of Roman despotism, sapped the foundations of Teutonic law and Papal unity, — two things which he reverenced ; — and laid the basis of modern despotism, — a thing he dreamt not of, and would have hated. England was saved from this eddy of absolutism against individualism, partly by the strong hold which the early Norman monarchs had over the nobles in the midst of a conquered but unquiet people, and partly by the formation of a middle, Cedric-the-Saxon class, which were neither Robin-Hood outlaws, and so short-lived, nor easy Athelstanes, with bull-necks bowed for the yoke. England withstood the transition from feudal lawlessness to modern, industrial law, by the power of her country gentry, and their offspring in the cities and boroughs, — all of good, substantial, German make; France — impulsive, mercurial, Celtic, Romanized France — gave up Teuton barbaric freedom, and put on the straight-jacket of revived imperial rule, as easily as her Gallic ancestors had bent to the sword of Cæsar. Rome conquered Gaul, but never Germany; the lawyers of the time of Louis the Ninth — the spiritual progeny of ancient Rome — re-conquered the dwellers in the Gallic provinces, but were repulsed by the tough Teutonic Hampdens and Cromwells of the isle of Hengist and Horsa.

And now the great work of Louis was completed; the barons were conquered, the people protected, quiet prevailed through the kingdom, the national church was secured in her liberties. The invalid of Egypt, the sojourner of Syria, had realized his dreams and purposes of good to his own subjects, and once again the early vision of his manhood, the recovery of Palestine, haunted his slumbering and his waking hours. And from that land, so dear to him, came news of greater and greater terror and interest to the Christian world; the Mamelukes were exterminating its inhabitants. In 1267, the king of France convened his nobles at Paris. He sent to Joinville to be present; but the worthy seneschal excused himself on the ground that he had an ague; the king, however, would not listen to excuses, and assuring him he had physicians who could cure any ague, prevailed on his old comrade to appear at the capital, though why he was summoned he knew not. On the twenty-fifth of May, however, all was explained. In the great hall of the Louvre, Louis, bearing the Crown of Thorns in his reverent hands, met his nobles, and announced to them his purposes. Weak almost to fainting, too weak to sit a horse or ride even in a carriage, worn to a shade by fasts, penances, and vigils, — but with an eye expressive of the undaunted and tireless soul that upheld him, he, first of all, resumed the cross; then his three sons bound themselves to the crusade; and then, unable to resist so firm and self-forgetting a spirit, lords and knights, many a one. But though all admired the disinterested heroism of Louis, not a few blamed his rashness. The pope tried to dissuade him; Joinville opposed him; his councillors pointed out the danger to his kingdom; his family wept at the prospect of his loss; his clergy grumbled at the idea of increased taxes. But the hero of the cross had not taken his resolve rashly, and no slight obstacles could stop him; he felt his end drawing near, and his heart ached to beat its last in the service of Jesus. Through three years, calmly, consistently, and with a prescience that he should not return, he prepared all within and without his kingdom for his departure; provided for his children; began his paper of instructions to his successor; and named those who were to act as regents. At length the appointed time came; with bare feet he made his last visits to Notre Dame, to the tomb of St. Denis, assumed the staff and wallet of the pilgrim, and bowed before the holy relics in adoration.

On the sixteenth of March, 1270, he left Paris for the seashore; on the first of July, he sailed from France. The sad, sad story of this his last earthly doing need not be here repeated. Led, we scarce know why, to sail to Tunis; without wishing it, involved in an unjust and useless war with the Moors; delayed by the tardiness of his able but abominable brother, Charles of Anjou; and seeing daily his army melt away beneath the heat of the climate, thirst, hunger, pestilence, and the Moorish arrows, — it was but too certain that the last of the crusaders was drawing near his end. From his resting-place, the castle of Carthage, Louis could look out upon the burning sands of the shore, the molten sea, the sky of burnished brass; he could watch the southern winds sweep the sharp dust of the desert into the camp of his followers; could behold the African horsemen hovering around his devoted troops, destroying every straggler. Leaning with his thin, feeble hands upon the battlements, he looked toward the bay where floated the ship in which his favorite son lay sick, stricken by the plague which was consuming so many; which even then had fastened upon the king's own blood. With tearful, anxious, yet patient and confiding eyes, he watched the vessel just moving in the roll of the bay under that August sun, and prayed to God and Jesus that his son might live, and his brother quickly come. His prayer was not granted; on the third of August, the Count of Nevers died; on the eleventh, his death was told to his father; on the morning of the twenty-fifth, the fleet of Charles of Anjou had not yet appeared. Meanwhile the poison in the veins of the monarch had through twenty-one days been working, and none yet knew whether he would live or die. From his sick-bed he had sent messages of comfort and resignation to the sick around him; on his bed of weakness and pain he had finished those advices to his successor which should be engraved in adamant, and given to every king and king's son to grow better by. "Hold to justice," such are some of his words, — "be inflexible and true, turning neither to the right hand nor the left, and sustain the cause of the poor until justice be done him. If any one has to do with thee, be for him and against thyself. Beware of beginning war, ... and if it be begun, spare the church and the innocent. Appease all quarrels that thou canst. Procure good officers, and see that they do their duty. Keep thy expenses within bounds."

So passed the closing hours of the French king. During the night of the twenty-fourth of August, he asked to be taken from his bed, and laid, unworthy sinner that he was, on a bed of ashes. His request was complied with; and so he lay, his hands crossed, his eyes fixed upon the suffering form of his Saviour, until some three hours after the next midday. Those who sat by, and saw how breath failed him, drew the curtains of the window to admit the slight breeze that curled the waters of the bay, and looked out, carelessly, into the August afternoon. Afar off, a fleet was just coming in sight, the long-expected fleet of Anjou. With beating hearts they knelt and told the royal invalid on his couch of ashes; but his ear was deaf, his eye lifeless, his jaw fallen.

Make ready your spices to embalm his body, poor thread-bare garment that it is! And issue your bulls to embalm his memory as a saint, for as such already his name is aromatic in the mouths of men! Truly a saint; not faultless, — neither was Peter; not intellectually omnipotent, — neither was John; not an overturner, — he would render Cæsar's dues to Cæsar, God's to God. We have said he was no radical; perhaps we erred; there is no truly radical, root-reaching reform that does not flow from the infinite in man's heart and conscience; the finite, in his mind, is much, but always superficial, not radical. Glory to Louis the Ninth! glory to all who have reformed as their Master did, from the centre outward! Let him be Saint Louis, the Holy Louis, the divinely enlightened Louis! And let us of Protestantism weep that it is so hard for us to raise our true and noble men, our heroes and earthly saviours, our Eliots, Hampdens, and Cromwells, Washingtons and Jays, into saints also, for ever to be revered.

IV.

THE FOUNDER OF THE JESUITS.*

THE Jesuits! It is a word of terror which M. Michelet and his friend utter in the ears of their countrymen, — of terror even to many of their Catholic brethren. Nor is the dread of this long slumbering, but now reawakening, body confined to France. Jesuitism is spreading, and silently acquiring strength, in the United States; for good or for evil, it is gaining ground among us; and many, whose eyes are open to the fact, see in our future history *auto-da-fes* and inquisitions, and Protestantism destroyed by a new St. Bartholomew. Under these circumstances, we have thought that a sketch of the founder of Jesuitism, of his purposes and constitutions, might be interesting and even useful.

It was in the year 1491, that the word spread from the ancestral castle up into the valleys of Guipuzcoa, that another son was born to the noble house of Ogner and Loyola. Already had Don Bertram seven sons and three daughters, before the birth of Ignatius, the last born of the family. And what a world was that upon which his eyes first opened! In Germany, a little, fair-haired Martin Luther, eight years old, was gathering fagots with his mother in the woods of Mansfield. In Florence, a polished, treacherous Lorenzo de

---

* *Des Jésuites.* Par MM. MICHELET et QUINET. Paris: 1843. From the North American Review, for October, 1844.

Medici, worn out with gout and intrigue, was preparing to take to his death-bed, and sue, without success, to the haughty, unhappy monk Savonarola, for absolution. In Rome, a Roderic Borgia, the incarnation of evil, was looking forward to the day when, as Alexander the Sixth, he should preside over the Christian Church. In Spain itself, the Moor was fighting his last battles, and breathing his last sigh, and Columbus was standing ready to prove with his life the truth of his bold speculations. Ignatius had not yet walked alone, or mastered his first word, before Granada yielded, Lorenzo died, Columbus sailed, and the Holy College, guarded by armed men, chose the vilest churchman of Christendom as its supreme head.

Six years of his life passed by, and the youngest son of Loyola, handsome, intelligent, proud, ambitious, was already destined to the life of a courtier, and given as a page to Ferdinand the Catholic, when that same overbearing monk, Savonarola, who had refused absolution to the chief of Florence unless he would restore freedom to his country, and all that he had usurped from them to his neighbours, stood forth against the abominable Borgia, and on the birthday of his Saviour proclaimed it as a revelation made to him from God, that he was not to obey the corrupt see of Rome. Men looked on admiring, and fancied the day of retribution had come. Not yet; this was but the first blush of its morning, and their admiration and fancy died with the unhappy Dominican, whose weak recantations, a year later, were mingled with the hissing of his blood on the coals which were consuming him. The day was not yet; the great champions were not ready; the little Martin was now a stout scholar of fifteen, singing for bread at Magdeburg and Eisenach; Ignatius, a boy of seven, was waiting on his most Catholic Majesty.

Years pass away; vast events, to our eyes vague and ghost-like, flit across the stage of European history. Spain and France — mighty burglars — agree to enter, and divide the booty of Naples; they enter it, quarrel, and Spain remains mistress. Charles is born, heir to Austria, and Aragon, and Burgundy, and Castile. Cæsar Borgia rages like a wolf through the whole centre of Italy. Venice, that mighty monster of the sea, contends with Turkey, France, the Emperor, the Pope, the Duke of Ferrara, the Marquis of Mantua, and Ferdinand of Aragon; and yet, though the ocean is red with her blood, lives and fights on. The Pope Borgia dies, — dies of his own poison-cup, prepared for another, but seized on thoughtlessly by himself after riding on a warm day; he and Cæsar both drink; the latter outlives it, being plunged by his physicians into the warm and reeking entrails of a mule; but the father is too gross, and dies, and the armed head of Julius fills his place.

Amid all this confused hubbub, Luther sits quietly at Erfurt, studying his Thomas Aquinas, his Cicero and Virgil, but above all, when once found, David, and Isaiah, and John, and Paul, and Jesus. Quietly he sits there, his half-muttered exclamations of delight hardly audible in that world of contest and dispute; and yet within him is preparing matter with noise enough in it to make all Europe rock. Little Charles of Spain, heir to so many thrones, a lad of some three years old, never once suspects, as he plays with his golden tassels, that so much trouble for his future life is preparing in the centre of Germany. But so it was ordained; by study, by sickness, by the murder of his friend, by the lightning of heaven, Luther is led on, forced on, till we see him, in the night-time, knocking for admission at the hermit-house of St. Augustine. The Saint admits him, bestows his own name upon him, and, to uproot the pride of his heart, sends him forth to beg bread of his old friends. He is not merely in Augustine's house, and bearing the name of Augustine; but the writings of the old African become, by intense study through ten years, first at Erfurt, then at Wittenberg, his key to the Bible, to life, and to his own heart. The greatest doctor of the Roman Church becomes, in Luther's hands, its deadliest enemy.

We look elsewhere, and find that the boy Ignatius had chafed at his pacific duties as a page, and, under Don Antonio Manrique, has long since become a soldier. When Luther went to Wittenberg, Ignatius was a lad of seventeen, gay, brave, and gallant; when Luther struck his first blow at the Church theology, Loyola was a daring and devoted soldier of twenty-five. Handsome and vain, without any other moral guide than honor and good feeling, beloved by his followers, admired by the courtiers, with a taste for poetry, and absorbed in the pursuits of war and pleasure, there is hardly a man in Europe who seems less likely to do battle with the bull-necked Augustinian of Saxony. Five years more pass by, and, in 1521, the monk stands before the Imperial Diet at Worms, the eyes of Europe fastened upon him; far off, looking down from the towers of Pampeluna on the pleasant plain about it, and across to the steep mountains which rise on every side, the soldier, unseen by Europe, waits the coming of the French army under Esparre. There are few troops in the town, and they are determined to surrender. Ignatius, a mere looker-on, without command, scolds and persuades to no purpose; he retires into the citadel, followed by one soldier. The commander of the citadel also wishes to surrender, and Loyola opposes him. A conference is held with the French, and Loyola, to break it off, becomes violent and insulting; the French, angry at his conduct, leave the meeting; and now they must fight. As a volunteer, he leads the van, and is the soul of the little garrison. The French guns have thrown down the wall, and Ignatius is in the gap; hot, and fierce, and obstinate is the contest. Suddenly, the self-made leader falls, his right leg broken by a cannon ball, his left torn by a splinter. The contest is over, and the flag of France waves above the high walls and narrow streets of the capital of Navarre.

There were two castles in Europe, which, in that year, 1521, held strong men, engaged in fierce internal struggles; the one was the Waldburg, overlooking the blue mountains and the Thuringian plains; the other, Loyola, from which, perhaps, across the vales and hill-sides, the eye might catch a glimpse of the sea of Biscay. In the former sat Luther, doubting, dyspeptic, "uttering cries like a woman in travail"; his mind and pen never resting, his great heart corroding in solitude, the enemy of God and man torturing and mocking him. In vain he sang the songs he had sung at Eisenach; in vain he leaned against the oak and listened to the nightingale; in vain he gave his whole soul to the task of reviving a vase of violets which the snow had caused to droop, and wept like a child over one that defied his power. His soul was at ease only in the busy struggle of the world, and in his "Patmos" did but grow more bitter against all opponents. In the other castle lay Ignatius, lame, sick, hopelessly deformed. His broken limb had been set unskilfully, and he caused it to be fractured again; a bone projected near the knee, and he made the surgeons cut it off, scoffing at the agony; the leg was still too short, and he stretched himself on the rack to lengthen it. It was all in vain; he was hopelessly deformed. How bitter to the young courtier, the handsome soldier, were those words,—hopelessly deformed! The light of life was eclipsed, and the music of praise was silenced for ever.

Thin and pale, with lips grown white from suffering, and eyes too proud to weep, but dull with dead hopes, Loyola lay waiting the administration of the eucharist. It was the vigil of the festival of St. Peter and St. Paul, and the medical attendants said he could hardly live till morning. The priest came, and the mysterious wafer was given to the dying man. But before his dying sight still flitted the forms of enemies he had slain, and ladies he had loved; he had eaten of the body of Christ, but was far from being filled with his spirit. The night wore on; the relatives, one by one, retired; with failing vision Ignatius watched the fantastic figures on the tapestry, as they moved with the mountain wind, until, to his faint brain, they seemed like living men. Old, familiar faces smiled or scowled on him; at moments he remembered the rite just administered, and then he thought of the holy men whose festival was to come on the morrow. Again he lost all consciousness, and then, recovering himself, asked if it was death or sleep. Such intervals became more and more frequent; he was then passing away, and with cold lips he tried to fashion a prayer to Jesus, to Paul, to Peter. His lips ceased moving, his eyes closed; the watchers by his side, worn out, dozed in silence. The wind stirring the forest boughs, and the tread of the sentinel, were the only sounds heard in the castle. At that hour, to the unconverted soldier, whose heart beat so wearily, appeared the majestic form of an old man, whose quick, kind eye filled with tears as he gazed upon him. "I am Peter," said the old man, "and I am sent of God to heal and save thee." He touched Ignatius with his hand, and then, turning, passed the watchers, who waked not, though his garments swept their feet, — and disappeared. Daylight stole over the Pyrenees, and the watchers of Loyola wakened like guilty men, and crept to the bed-side to see if he still lived. Calmly breathing, with placid brow, and cheeks no longer drawn by pain, the Heaven-rescued man slept as one to whom health has come again. His heart was no longer weary, no longer wholly given to the world; the Apostle had driven out disease, and planted the germ of that faith which was to develop into Jesuitism.

The germ, — it was but the germ, — and the great enemy, tired of buzzing about Luther's ears in vain, strove hard to root out what the Apostle had planted. The lame, but now convalescing man, as he lay there hour after hour, day after day, thinking of the future, grew nervous and impatient, and longed to be amused. They searched the castle for novels; there was not one that he had not read again and again. Those old chivalric romances had been his Bible for many a day; his faith, and thence his life, had been shaped by them; from them he had drawn that spirit of gallantry and war, which had sustained him thus far, and was, under new forms, to sustain him through yet greater contests, and to lead him to greater victories. They brought him "The Lives of the Saints," St. Benedict, St. Dominic, and St. Francis; these, at least, he had never read. How he turned the book over, and glanced it through in utter despair, is not written, but is none the less sure. Then the remembrance of his dream, or of the actual visit of St. Peter, — he knew not which to think it, — came over him, and his eye caught the account of the miraculous conversion of St. Francis. He read it through with care, read it again, and a third time. He thought of his own past life, of his miraculous cure, of the impossibility that he should thenceforth be a soldier, of the conquests which the holy men, whose written lives lay before him, had effected, of the work yet to be done, of the field yet white with the harvest. His eye kindled with a new hope, his hollow cheek flushed with the fever of a new ambition, and turning to the beginning of the volume which a few hours before seemed so tedious, he read it with his heart. Then rose the curtain from that dark future over which he had brooded so long; he saw God's purposes in his wounds and sickness; he knew why he had been torn from the war-saddle, and stripped of his manly beauty. He was a chosen vessel; God had great objects in store for him; he might regain the Holy Land, the Lord's sepulchre, Calvary, and Bethlehem, not, like the old crusaders, with an arm of flesh, but by the omnipotence of spiritual power. Who can tell what visions passed before the mind of the warm-blooded Spaniard, as, with many struggles and relapses, — by prayer, and reading, and silent thought, — he became the soldier of Christ; threw up his allegiance to Charles and to Spain, and bound himself to God and the whole earth; quenched for ever his cherished love "for a noble lady of the court of Castile," and devoted himself to her who is indeed greater than countess or duchess, even to Mary the Virgin?

His friends saw the change, and guessed the cause. His brother urged him to remember his renown, his warlike genius, and "to do nothing foolish." Ignatius answered little, discussed nothing, promised nothing, wavered not at all. He, who had been stretched on a rack to lengthen his leg, would not be easily turned aside from the redemption of a world. He was now well, and one day proposed to ride over to Navarreta to see Manrique, his instructer and companion in arms. With two servants he quitted his home; how calm outwardly, how full of fire within, we may imagine. We can almost see him turning his horse, as he ascends the last hill that overlooks Loyola, and while his servants on their mules jog along under the oaks and chestnuts, we can observe his lips move as he bids farewell for ever to home, friends, wealth, fame, and pleasure, and with iron will bind himself to poverty, chastity, pain, self-denial, and reproach. He visited Manrique, sent back his servants, and pursued his way alone across the peninsula to Montserrat.

There was at that time in the monastery of Montserrat a Frenchman, John Chanones, who had been long a man of the world and distinguished in it; but the Holy Spirit had called him, and he sat on the mountain, chief-confessor of the pilgrims who flocked thither. One evening, there came to him a man richly dressed, with the manner of a knight, and, though thin and feeble in appearance, wholly unlike the common people who thronged to his confessional. The holy father listened to his words, which were those of an agonized soul. His confession would be long and trying; he had written it, he said, that he might omit nothing, and asked leave of the priest to commence on the morrow. He did so, and for three days upon his knees, interrupted only by his own sighs and lamentations, did Ignatius pour into that sympathizing ear the tale of his sins, his sufferings, his conversion, his purposes, his temptations, and his fears. Well versed himself in the dangers of the world, the confessor listened with feeling, and answered with wise words. He showed Loyola how Satan slips into the very act of conversion, and prompts the half-saved soul to spiritual pride; he pointed out the true life for the penitent to pursue, and the dangers he would need especially to guard against; he sketched for him the varying features of the Evil One, so that he might know them even when they came before him in the guise of an angel's countenance.

Strengthened and purified, Ignatius left his weary post on the third evening, and going forth, sought out the meanest beggar of the place, and bestowed upon him his rich apparel, clothing himself in the coarse gown and simple sandals of a common pilgrim. His sword, however, was still by his side, retained there, that, in due time, it might be dedicated to his holy mistress. That night, the devotee who rose, as the clock tolled twelve, to pray before the altar of the Virgin, was startled to find there a man pacing to and fro, as the young candidate for knighthood was accustomed to do before admission to his order. In a pilgrim's dress, but with the bearing of a soldier, and carrying in his hand a knight's sword sheathed, this solitary figure walked there before the altar, or knelt, or stood gazing upward, muttering prayers, or talking in low tones to himself, from midnight till early morning. He then hung the sword upon a pillar near the shrine, for the last time dedicated himself to the service of Our Lady, received the communion, and on foot, with bare head, sought concealment in the hospital of

Manresa, until the port of Barcelona should be opened, and the way to the Holy Sepulchre lie clear before him.

Meanwhile, the great warfare with the flesh and the Devil was to be maintained; so he girt himself with an iron chain, put on a shirt of hair, fasted on bread and water, or, if he ate herbs, sprinkled them with ashes, slept upon the ground, and thrice a day applied the scourge to his flesh. Seven hours of every twenty-four he spent upon his knees in prayer; to wound his pride, he begged from door to door; and to confound that personal vanity which had so long ruled him, he made himself revolting to the sight, so that the children stoned him in the streets. But at this very time, a report spread in the village, that the loathsome beggar was a grandee of Spain, and men began to look on him with altered eyes, and met him as if he had been a saint. The Great Tempter came, too, and whispered, that, if he would only return, changed and sanctified as he was, to his old haunts, the court and camp, he would be able to reform and regenerate them. But Ignatius knew the features of the deceiver, and, plying his scourge with redoubled force, shouted, "Away from me, Satan!" and for a time he fled. Then he came again, in a new form, and despondency stole over the heart of the weakened devotee; but again he was recognized and foiled. A third time he came, and whispered in a voice of kindness words of comfort. Why should this penitent fear to die? Was he not saintly in his sufferings and self-mortification? Was he not approved and beloved of God and Jesus? Angels seemed to descend and invite him to paradise. But the enthusiast was even here a match for the tempter. He called to mind all his sins anew, exaggerated them, dwelt on them, made men sit by him and recite them in his ears, until the false heaven and the fallen angels vanished.

Words cannot picture the mental condition of Ignatius Loyola during that period of his life. We may call him fanatical, mad, hypocritical, perhaps; but call him what we will, he was training his nature to endurance and labor such as few men have ever encountered. To form any just opinion of what he was, however, we should study his "Spiritual Exercises," composed chiefly at this time, in 1522. In them shines forth the most marvellous compound of extravagance and good sense, of the wildest enthusiasm and the calmest wisdom, of intense, heart-rending passion, and deliberate meditation. His life was a similar compound. He united then, in a manner which has characterized his order to this day, overwhelming impulses with the coolest judgment, manifested in adapting means to ends.

The parallel between Loyola as he was in 1522, and Luther as he was when at Erfurt, sixteen years earlier, which has been run by Ranke and D'Aubigné, we regard as entirely unjust; for when we consider, that Luther's struggles with himself arose from the action of conscience and intellect, were waged by means of his intellect, and terminated in a doctrine, — while Loyola's came from conscience and a past life of wrong-doing, went on by the instrumentality of imagination and feeling, and resulted in a new life, we see no ground for any comparison between the two. Luther's whole process, which, we repeat, led him to a doctrine, and not to the Reformation, was characterized by those features, both good and evil, which distinguish Protestantism, and Loyola's by those which are peculiar to Catholicism; and any parallel between the two men is but a comparison of the two faiths which they embodied, and addresses itself to prejudice, and not to fair judgment.

At length the plague ceased, and the port of Barcelona was opened. Loyola embarked for Italy, followed by the prayers and blessings of thousands; for he had become known far and wide, had preached and exhorted to the conversion of many, and was already sainted in hundreds of warm and pure hearts. He went to Rome to receive the

Pope's blessing, thence to Venice to embark, and on the 31st of August, 1523, landed at Jaffa. When Ignatius reached the Holy Land, with his heart burning to convert the infidel Turks, and rescue the sepulchre of Jesus from pollution by rescuing those who polluted it from Mohammed, Luther, on his part, was just commencing, in defiance of the Elector, now trembling under the hand of death, his warfare upon the mass, "the sacrilege of Tophet." "Ketha," not yet his, and, indeed, hardly over the tremor which she felt as she left, with her companions, the monastery of Nimptsch, looked on admiring from the house of the burgomaster of Wittenberg. Luther triumphed; the dean, frightened by the reformer's bulls, ordained the cessation of the great Catholic sacrifice in the church of All Saints, on Christmas day, 1524. The monastery, too, at that time, was no longer a home for monks, but had become the property of the University; and Catharine Bora was beginning to think, that she might yet be the wife of the great reformer.

Luther triumphed, but not so Loyola. His bright dreams of converting the heathen were all dispelled by the absolute command of the Pope's representative in Jerusalem, that he should return forthwith to Europe. The Franciscan little knew to what a proud heart he spoke; his easy eye saw nothing of the struggle in the enthusiast's breast, as he bent without one word to the authority of the Church, resigned his new ambition, crushed his new hopes, and forgot his disappointments in a long, last gaze upon the miraculous footprints of Jesus on the Mount of Olives. Five months after he landed at Jaffa, Ignatius was again in Europe; and when Luther, on the 11th of June, 1525, went up with his bride to the house of Amsdorff to receive the nuptial benediction, Ignatius was studying Latin among little children in the grammar school of Barcelona. He had been led to think, as he returned from Palestine, that, to convert others, he must himself become wiser, a linguist and a theologian;

and there he sat, with difficulty mastering the rules of Latin syntax, while the heart of Europe stood still with dismay at the Insurrection of the Peasants. There he sat, studying, contending with the Evil One, who for ever drove out his Latin verbs with Spanish prayers; or waited on the sick in the hospitals; or preached to those of evil lives; or won to the Church the innocent who were yet beyond its fold; a saint in the eyes of many, and gifted with divine power, but among the last one would even then have selected to meet the triumphant monk who had worsted popes, emperors, and kings.

At the end of two years, he went to Alcala to study philosophy, followed by three disciples, to whom a fourth was added at that place. And he studied philosophy, not in Aristotle and Thomas Aquinas, — who were not much more to his taste than to Luther's, — but in the highways and hovels, in prisons and by the side of dying men, now among the dissolute students, and now amid a group of little children; he studied and he taught, and to such purposes that men thought him a magician, or at least a heretic. The ears of the Inquisition were at that time wide open, for the din of the Lutheran battle drove away sleep; even Spain was menaced, and every suspected man was watched with countless eyes. The abominable practices of Loyola and his disciples, which consisted mainly in doing ten times as much good as the priests, looked very like heresy, and quietly, but speedily, inquisitors from Toledo passed to Alcala. The whole life of Ignatius was examined, but neither magic or heresy was found in it; and in silence the terrible inquirers sped back again, only requiring of the accused, through the Vicar-General, to go no more barefoot, — no very severe sentence for that tribunal.

But Satan, who had so long been trying to corrupt Loyola, all to no purpose, was bent upon trying what danger and suffering could do; and it was not long before a new accusation arose, of such a character as caused the Vicar-General to cast him into prison, where he lay many weeks, and when proved wholly innocent, he was released with the injunction, that he should give up preaching under penalty of excommunication. This was on the 1st of June, 1527. The sufferings of poor Loyola were now complete. Six years ago, all worldly honor and power were torn from him, and he gave them up without a sigh; two years later, the haughty Franciscan of Palestine demanded the abandonment of hopes and plans that were deep in his heart, and he abandoned them instantly; and now he is bidden, by one who speaks almost with divine authority, to give up what he had so long believed the voice of the Almighty required him to exercise.

It was a trial even for a saint's faith and patience. With reverence he remonstrated, and was sharply answered, that he should not preach novelties. "I did not think," said he, raising his calm, devout countenance, and looking the Vicar-General full in the face, "I did not think, that to preach Jesus Christ was a novelty among you. I appeal to the Archbishop." If Luther, who, far off in Germany, was at that moment, perhaps, struggling in great agony with temptation, sickness, and despair, had been near when Loyola spoke those words, he would assuredly have welcomed him as a fellow-laborer.

The Archbishop of Toledo, to whom he appealed, advised him to go to Salamanca, which he accordingly did. But Satan was there before him, and no sooner did he commence teaching the people than he was once more cast into prison, where he stayed twenty-two days. As no fault could be found in him, however, by his judges, save that he preached rather too well, they were forced to set him free, though forbidding him to preach even orthodox doctrines, until he had read a course of divinity. Here again, as at Alcala, the voices of God and of the Church seemed opposed; in vain did the enthusiast try to reconcile them; obey he dared not, and disobedience would but expose him to the dungeon again, and close his lips and his mission. But Loyola was not a Hamlet, to waste his life in trying to reconcile opposing duties. He cut the knot he could not loose, and turning his back on Spain, in mid winter, alone, — for his disciples, too, left him at this juncture, — he passed the Pyrenees in safety, through storms, and snow, and bands of robbers, and early in February, 1528, stood looking down on the tall houses and narrow streets of Paris, from the heights of Montmartre. Thirty-seven years of his life had now passed, and seven of his regenerated existence; — and there he stood, alone, without a friend in the vast city below him, with but a little money, given him by some compassionate people in Barcelona, and in the character of a mere student; for his only object in Paris was to procure a proper education. Strangers from England and from Italy brushed by him as he meditated, and talked of the application which it was rumored Henry was about to make to the Pope for a divorce from Catharine; of the reported alliance between the English king and Francis against the Emperor; of the devastation of Rome since its fall the May previous; and of the horrors of its pillage, which, after nine months' occupation by the Spaniards and Germans, had not even then ceased. Their words fell on Loyola's ear, but made no impression. His mind was filled with the single thought of becoming the spiritual regenerator of the immense multitude moving at his feet; his projected life of poverty, labor, and religious instruction became more and more clearly revealed to him, and, before he returned to the Hospital of St. James for the night, the work of the morrow, of many morrows, was determined for him. Placing the little fund he had in a companion's hands for safe keeping, he begged his bread from door to door; he pursued his study of Latin at Montaigne College; and having obtained a hold upon some young

Spaniards, proceeded with them through the "Spiritual Exercises," described by him six years before, and persuaded them to sell all they had, to give their money to the poor, and to beg with him enough to support life. But these young men had friends, who looked on all this as madness, and tried to persuade them to come back to common sense; failing in this, they seized and withdrew them by force from the company of Ignatius, and denounced him, as a dangerous seducer of youth, to Ori, the inquisitor, who ordered him to appear and explain his conduct.

But Loyola had for a time left Paris. The friend to whom he had confided his money had proved a rogue, and having spent part, had run away with the remainder. He reached Rouen, there fell sick, and was at last brought to great want and suffering. In this emergency, he wrote to Loyola, and at the moment that the inquisitor summoned the Spanish enthusiast before him as a criminal, he was toiling on his way to Rouen to aid the poor wretch who had robbed him; and before he returned to stand his trial, at the call of the representative of the dread tribunal, he had, by asking alms, obtained enough to procure the repentant wrong-doer a passage to Spain. He returned, was tried, and acquitted.

During seven years, Loyola remained in Paris. His life there was one of poverty, struggle, patient toil, and earnest study. It was the life that had been revealed to him during that first evening on Montmartre; to which hill he frequently retired for prayer and meditation. Into the details of that life we have not room to enter. To reclaim the sinful was one of his chief aims, and no suffering, no labor, deterred him from it. Having long tried to turn one from licentiousness by reason and persuasion, he at length placed himself one evening by the side of the road along which the offender was to pass, plunged to the neck in a half-frozen pond; and as the young man came near, there was heard, as from the earth, a voice picturing God's punishment for sin. Startled by such sounds in the partial darkness, the youth trembled and stopped. "It is I," said Ignatius; and, as the terrified and conscience-stricken man crept to the water's edge and peered through the gloom at him, he continued, "And here will I suffer, O sinner, for your sins! Go, gratify your lust."

But his darling purpose was the realization of that dream which for ten years had haunted him, — the reclaiming of Palestine; and he proceeded to enlist disciples to aid him in the work. Through six long, silent years he labored, and for every year could count one convert. It was in February, 1528, that he reached Paris; in August, 1534, in the subterranean chapel of Montmartre, Ignatius, Xavier, Laynez, Salmeron, Bobadilla, Rodriguez, and Faber, bound themselves to the conversion of the infidels of Palestine, or, if they were not permitted to go thither, then to go whithersoever the Vicar of Jesus should send them.

But while, with the enthusiasm of Jesuits, they bound themselves by that memorable vow, with the calm good sense of Jesuits, also, they deferred the execution of their purpose for two years and a half, in order to complete their studies. When Loyola himself went to Spain, early in 1535, it was with the understanding, that his disciples would meet him in Venice, in 1537.

This act of Ignatius, his separation from his disciples for two years, and return home after an absence of fourteen years, we regard as one of the most characteristic of his life. It shows his coolness, his confidence, his power over his companions, his justice, and his self-command, in the clearest manner. Any but a master-mind, which, after so many years of fruitless toil, found itself on the brink of apparent success, would have urged immediate action, and have watched the new converts with jealous eyes, lest they should have forgotten all the past in dreams of the future.

Loyola delayed the execution of his cherished scheme, left his disciples to the snares and dangers of Paris and the world, and turned his steps homeward, to repair, before he left Europe for ever, the wrongs of his youth in his native neighbourhood. He reached that neighbourhood, and took up his abode at a hospital in Aspeytia, near by the castle of his fathers. To that castle, however, he was asked in vain. In vain was he tempted by rich meats, sent from it to his hospital; he distributed them among the poor. He preached on the open hill-side to the thousands that flocked to hear him; he founded charities; he broke up the gaming-houses; he stripped, by his eloquence, the rich ornaments of the women from their heads; and publicly asking pardon of one to whom, when young, he had done a wrong, gave him two farms as a partial compensation for what he had suffered. It was no wonder that such a man, in that age and land, was able "to do what he pleased"; and was followed, almost worshipped, as a miracle-working saint. Having in this manner bidden farewell to his birthplace, about the end of 1535 he repaired to Venice, there to await his companions.

They came, earlier than was anticipated by some weeks on the 8th of January, 1537. This they did because of the war then raging between France and the Emperor. When they reached the place of embarkation, though they found their leader there prepared to set forward to the Holy Land the way was barred by the contest between the Turks and Christians, which continued through that year. Loyola, we say, was ready to go forward; during the year which he had passed in Venice, new views had, probably, been unfolded to him; but he had not in the least abandoned his determination to aim first at the rescue of that land where Jesus taught and died. During that year, he had become acquainted, had lived and labored, with Gianpietro Caraffa, afterwards Paul the Fourth, the chief of the Theatines, and one of the most eloquent, violent, self-willed, self-sacrificing, in short, thoroughly *Roman* Catholic, rulers by whom the Universal Mother was ever governed. From him Loyola caught something, but not much; and even in receiving this, he refused so much more, that he made the future Pope his enemy; so openly his enemy, that, when the missionaries for Palestine thought proper to ask the ruling pontiff for his blessing on their enterprise, it was judged best by Ignatius, that he should not be one of those who were to ask it. That blessing, through the good offices of Peter Ortiz, who represented the injured Catharine of England at the court of Rome, was given; and those who were yet laymen having been ordained as priests, they waited for the new year to open the way to Palestine. If it was not open by the close of the year, then their vow bound them to follow the Pope's behests. They waited, not in idleness and luxury, but in hospitals, prisons, and hermit-cells. Labor and suffering, self-denial and self-sacrifice, were not words and resolutions, but acts, with those men.

But they waited in vain; the path was closed, and now another career opened before them. It was at Vicenza that Ignatius met his companions, who had been scattered through various cities on their deeds of mercy. Forty years of constant effort and exposure had matured the expression of that calm, commanding countenance, upon which not a shade of disappointment or regret could be seen, as he announced the failure of the great purpose of his life. When he bade the castle of Loyola farewell in 1522, tears stood upon his cheek; when he abandoned Palestine, his lip trembled; when tyrannized over at Alcala and Salamanca, his eye flashed fire; but years had done their work, and in the spirit of true faith and resignation, he now pointed out to his followers the way which God had opened for them. It was not Palestine, but the whole wide world, that was to be their field; it was not the Mohammedans, but all heretics, all pagans, all sinners, whom they were to convert and bring into the fold of the Saviour. As he spoke, the visions of his youth returned upon Loyola; he saw again, as at Manresa, the opposing camps of Jesus and Satan; he heard again that voice of divine melody, which had so often given him strength in his trials, and saw Mary herself smile upon him. "Brothers," he said, with the calmness of confirmed strength, "brothers, we are 'The Company of Jesus'; he is our Captain, and, battling under him, we will drive back the heretics of Germany, and carry the gospel to the farthest East, and to the new-found heathen of the West." They listened as to a prophet; they felt the presence of Jesus in the midst of them, sanctioning the words of their elder brother; they received the spirit of faith which enabled them to fulfil the prophecy.

Ignatius, Laynez, and Faber went at once to Rome, to offer the services of the Company to the Pope. The others divided themselves among the Universities of Italy, to aid the youth in the pursuit of heavenly wisdom. They bound themselves to live in hospitals, and upon alms; to receive no money; to preach with apostolic plainness; to teach children; to aid all men; and to obey one another in turn.

The chief and his two companions were received with kindness at Rome; their works had gone before them. Ignatius became the spiritual director of some aged and distinguished men; the others were appointed to teach in the University. From that time, Rome became the residence of the founder of the Jesuits; sometimes in disgrace, sometimes persecuted, once tried, and through perjury almost condemned, he still labored to assist the suffering, and to perfect the outline of that order which it was now agreed should be founded by the members of the Company of Jesus. The spirit had been breathed into them at Vicenza, the form was taken at Rome; and after long examinations and debates, after prayer and fasting on the part of the comrades, and struggles to resist them on the part of those who feared all change, it was at last approved by the Holy Father on the 27th of September, 1540. In that year, the cause of Luther received two wounds: the bigamy of Philip of Hesse, half-sanctioned by the Reformers; and the foundation of the "Society of Jesus."

The order being sanctioned, a general was to be chosen, and rules or constitutions were to be formed. It could not be that any other than Loyola would be chosen general, and though he resisted the choice, it was clear that his resistance must yield. At length, on Easter day, 1541, he acquiesced in the unchanging wish of his followers. On the following Friday, this now triumphant enthusiast, who for twenty years had labored for that day, walked with his little band through the streets of Rome, visited the seven churches, received and gave the communion, took the vows of poverty, chastity, and obedience, and bound himself and his brethren to go wherever the Pope should order, and to teach little children the Christian doctrine. To this last duty Ignatius at once devoted himself, and through forty days the church of Santa Maria de Strata was filled with curious and awe-struck listeners; — the noble, the rich, the beautiful, learned divines, and venerable teachers, were there, catching with eagerness the broken Italian of the Spanish saint, as he expounded the catechism to the children about his knees. Some sneered, but for the most part men and women wept, or smiled through their tears, as they heard the heart-felt, heart-reaching accents of him who had studied divinity so profoundly in the great school of life.

Nor did the active benevolence of Loyola prove less when he possessed power, than when he was borne down by poverty and weakness. He still visited the prison, the sick-bed, and the poor man's hovel; he labored to convert the Jews, to reclaim the vicious, and to ward off danger from those yet uncorrupted. He founded institutions and asylums in pursuance of his designs; but the two great objects of his life thenceforward were, to complete the Constitutions of his society, and to fulfil the weighty duties which devolved upon him as its first general.

The Constitutions of Loyola are worthy of deep study; they unfold his plans, and reveal his spirit. They should be investigated by every student of associated action, and in many points we believe they are worthy of imitation. Let us examine them a little. The purpose of his order was, to fight the battles of Jesus, and to conquer the enemy of Christ and man. His followers were to do this first in themselves, and then in others; remembering, that every blow struck for another's salvation helped to secure their own, provided the act was done in the spirit of Christian love. To attain these two ends, self-sanctification and the good of others, Ignatius saw that there was needed less of solitary contemplation, and more of active labor and benevolence, than was to be found in the other orders of Christendom. He saw, too, that the true field for action was education, in its widest sense; and that the instruction and edification of the young especially was the best method of securing a hold upon the adult population of the world. With equal clearness, he perceived the immense advantage to be gained by occupying those portions of the world, which as yet lay in heathen darkness. The faith of the Western Church was truth to him; the cause of that Church was the cause of Christ; and to spread its power was to spread the power of the gospel. In farther India, in remote Peru, he would lay foundations broad and deep for the Church to rest upon securely, even when, in Europe, the earth rocked under her. With these two great instruments, the education of the young and the conversion of the heathen world, he would combine the power derived through the confessional, and the moral influence growing out of self-sacrificing charity. Aided by these, he knew his followers might preach to good purpose, and lay hold of the springs of life in their hearers. But how could men be found capable of such labors as were to be required even of the privates in that Company of Jesus? They were to be *made;* to be made at once perfectly obedient and perfectly self-sustaining. They were not to be machines, but men, — and yet men acting with the unity, the regularity, the unconsciousness, of the various parts of a machine. They were to give up every thing to the great purposes of the order, and were to pursue those purposes with the devotion due to individual ends. They were to annihilate themselves, and yet develop every faculty and taste to the utmost. They were to combine the characters of the religious recluse, the devoted missionary, the finished scholar, the polished gentleman, and the Christian man of the world; to respect no claims, to regard no rules, which interfered with the purposes of the order; for these were God's purposes, far above all other claims and human regulations.

Such was the problem before Ignatius, to make such men. He and his successors solved it; they made men who, in union, could do more for good or evil than any others the world has ever seen; and who did more good when the true purpose was in view, and more evil when a false one usurped its place. They attained success, first, by choosing the right material, and rejecting every one who might begin, but could not go through, the trial. Whoever entered the order was tried like the musket at the armory, and only those who were beyond all question were kept. Secondly, he who entered the society was to abandon every thing beyond it; to hold no converse with the world, except under a superior's eye; to hate father, and mother, and all, for the sake of Jesus. Thirdly, the whole course of education for the order was calculated, like that of a military school, to secure perfect obedience, — that peculiar loss of individuality which is seen among soldiers, with whom the corps is every thing, and the man is nothing. Fourthly, exercises were contrived which caused each member to learn his own resources and rely upon them, — to cultivate and know every power he possessed. The Jesuits were like an army drilled to the last degree in unity of action, and yet so that every man among them could sustain the duties of a partisan warrior. And fifthly, the discipline which was to develop the youth into a Jesuit continued until the habits of life were fixed and hardened, not to be changed.

But Loyola saw that all must not be of one rank, or bound to the same duties. He established, therefore, four grades; first, professed fathers, bound to live by alms, and to go on missions; secondly, spiritual coadjutors, without individual property, but provided for by college revenues; these were the instructers; thirdly, the scholars, or Jesuits in the process of development; and fourthly, the temporal coadjutors, who retained their property, and assisted without recompense in the administration of the society. At the centre of this body sat the general, receiving, as through electric telegraphs, news from every quarter; a despot, whose will seemed almost omnipotent, whose eye was on every member in the farthest isles of the Indian sea, and yet who was himself watched and ruled, and who was absolute only within the prescribed circle of his power. If he went beyond that circle, he was warned; and if the warning was disregarded, he might be deposed.

Such are the outlines of those Constitutions, which, with prayer and praise, and, as he believed, under the inspiration of God, Ignatius drew up; which he submitted to the chief men of the society, and left to be approved by the first general congregation that should meet. Into the history of the order we do not propose to enter; but one remark is worthy of a place here, — that the evils of Jesuitism did not appear until the Constitutions had been practically changed, the plan of Loyola violated, and the balance of power overthrown.

Ignatius lived fifteen years at the head of the society which he had founded. He died in 1556, at the age of sixty-five. Luther had died just ten years before. In the latter portion of Loyola's life, we see a man calm and firm as Washington, ruling with the energy and the success of a narrow, but mighty, mind. Obedience was his watchword; he who had obeyed others required others to obey him, absolutely and wholly. He required not only that the conduct and will should comply, but that the mind should deem that course true and right which the superior determined to be true and right. He withstood popes, cardinals, and kings, when they came within his province, as resolutely as Luther, and with far more dignity. He would not allow his followers to receive any high office in the Church, but required devotion, entire devotion, to the order they had joined. Novelties he hated and abjured; he was the man of the past, of the ages of blind faith, passive obedience, and pattern excellence; as Luther was the man of the future, of the ages of destruction, and doubt, and disobedience, and progress. Rapidly and widely Loyola saw his order spread. At his death, it existed in fourteen provinces; hundreds of its members were laboring in India, America, and Africa, and millions of souls were under its sway. In the very year that he died, it became fixed at Cologne, at Ingolstadt, and at Prague; and the Protestants, on the field where the Reformation had triumphed, saw themselves surrounded by papal forces far different from the lazy monks whom Luther, and Erasmus, and Hutten warred against.

Then the enthusiast prepared himself to die in triumph. God had granted his prayer, had rolled back the tide of heresy, and won new lands for Christendom. We can see him on that night of the 30th of July, when all had left him, and when, filled with the conviction that his end was close at hand, he bent for the last time before his Maker, giving thanks for the victory which Jesus had secured to his faithful soldiers. And as he looked back and scanned the life of which he was so soon to give an account, his idle youth, his laborious manhood, his successful old age, did Ignatius find himself a hypocrite? Never, we believe, did a man's heart acquit him more entirely of that crime than did Loyola's. He saw his folly, his waste of time, his ill-directed enthusiasm; but he knew that he had sincerely, heartily, laboriously, striven to advance the cause of the Church; and as the body failed, and the remembrance of that other death-night in the ancestral castle, when Peter had appeared to him, rose upon his soul, the calm, stern old man became a visionary youth again. The mountains of his boyhood rose about him; the pebbly brooks he had sat by, reading romances, again gurgled in his ear. The unknown maiden, to whose service he had mentally devoted himself, came by upon her palfrey; his heart was yet young, and far purer than when Peter healed him by a touch. Then, death stood by him, a dreaded and ghastly form from below; now, it was an angel stooping from above to receive him. In his excited mind, the bubbling brook, the maiden's laugh, changed to the hymns of blessed spirits, and the form of his early lady-love became that of his true Mistress, before whose altar he had hung up his sword.

Day broke over the Eternal City. It was scarce sunrise, when the fathers came to visit their superior. The color had left his lips, his pulse just moved, but his eye was calm and full of light. They put cordials to his mouth, but he would not taste them. They would have sent for the physicians; but he, by gesture, forbade them. They knelt by his bed-side, they heard the death-rattle, and they marked the life leaving the eye. One word his faint lips fashioned, and faintly it echoed through the room, as if spirits had repeated it; it was the name of his Great Captain, "Jesus"; before the echo ceased, Ignatius Loyola had passed to another world.

What, then, was this man? He was one based upon sincerity, above all things; narrow and stationary, fanciful and fanatical, a deep faith still worked in every thing he did and wrote. He was not a man of vast intellect, but of vast energy and courage, and who, without convincing men, obliged them to yield by force of will and nerve of character. His institution was not the result of long meditation and profound ambition, but sprang from circumstances, from the inability of the Companions to reach Palestine, and the experience of their leader during that winter in Venice spent with Caraffa. Its success came from the sincerity of the men who formed it. Less true and devoted, they would have received the honors of the Church; they would have refused such utter devotion to their order; they would have rebelled against the despotic power of the general.

The Constitutions of the Jesuits were less the result of the wisdom of thought, than of the wisdom of devotedness. Laynez was a man of thought, and did much toward perfecting the Constitutions; but their great features were from the soldier Ignatius. The truth of this view will be seen in the history of the order; for when selfishness took the place of self-sacrifice, the Constitutions were changed, the general was stripped of power, and the order was forgotten by its members, as it no longer served to forward their individual ends; the honors of the Church were received, worldliness took the place of sincerity, and Jesuitism was without power.

Lastly, Loyola was a conservative, attached to the past. Forms he was ready enough to violate; but the substance of old things, the excellencies of the middle time, he clung to with desperation; and lest he should lose them, he clung also to its follies and its evils. He was a man of one idea, and this idea was, like that of Hildebrand, to bring all things, temporal and spiritual, physical and intellectual, into submission to the will of God, and to the Roman Church. This design may be ascribed to ambition; but look at the life of Loyola up to the year 1538, and where are there plans which show ambition? Yet he had then been laboring sixteen years. And what shall we say of the institution which he founded? The end proposed was one of the highest which man can entertain; for what can be higher than the sanctification of the human race and the spread of Christianity? Though we think Loyola's Christianity was but gross superstition, this judgment cannot affect our estimate of his design. It may be said, also, that the means proposed for gaining the end were admirable, for their efficiency has been attested by their success.

And what may be done by Protestants in this country to stop the growth of Jesuitism? Shall they try to preach or write it down? To vote or burn it down will hardly be openly advocated as the true method. To us the proper course seems to be this; to found better schools, and to seek out more self-sacrificing laborers, more earnest missionaries, more persuasive preachers. Let Protestantism quit scolding, and live out a better Christianity than Romanism and Jesuitism, and these latter cannot succeed. But if they form the church militant, while Protestantism continues to be only the church termagant, the power and the growth will be theirs.

V.

EARLY FRENCH TRAVELLERS IN THE WEST.*

WE need say nothing here of the services which Mr. Sparks has rendered to American history. His Lives of Ledyard and Morris and Washington; his editions of the writings of Washington and Franklin, and of the Diplomatic Correspondence; and his collection of American Biographies, which has now reached the tenth volume, are all known through this country and in Europe. He has done more than any other one man to preserve for posterity the undoubted records of our early history; and we trust a long life may be granted him, wherein to pursue his labors; for, with the advance already gained in a knowledge of the details of past times, his labors are becoming every year more and more valuable.

Among his various publications, the series of American Biographies ranks high in interest and utility; through it, many have been made known to the world, who might otherwise have found no historian; and we hope he may be able to continue it through many more volumes. Among those persons, who but for this work might have remained without

---

* *The Life of Father Marquette.* By JARED SPARKS. (Library of American Biography. Vol. X.)

From the North American Review, for January, 1839.

their deserved celebrity, is Father Marquette, whose brief story is now before us. His Journal, giving an account of the discovery of the great Mississippi Valley, was published in France in 1681, and a poor translation of it was given in the Appendix to Hennepin's volumes, printed in London in 1698; but all knowledge of his doings slept in these dusty works, and in a few pages of Charlevoix's "New France," until Mr. Sparks drew up an abstract of the original Journal, for the second edition of Butler's "History of Kentucky." This abstract he has now somewhat altered and enlarged, and put into a wider circulation, through his "Biography." It is curious and interesting; and as Marquette's discovery is but little known, and the labors of those that followed him but slightly appreciated, we have thought it worth while to give our readers a sketch of the progress of the French in the knowledge and settlement of the Mississippi valley.

The advantages of water communication were never more perfectly shown, than in the rapid progress of the French in Canada, when first settled. During the years in which John Eliot was preaching to the savages of Natick and Concord, the Jesuits were lifting their voices upon the farthest shores of Lake Superior; while a journey from Boston to the Connecticut was still a journey through the heart of the wilderness, Allouez and Dablon had borne the cross through that very "Mellioki" (Milwaukie) region, to which our speculators have just reached.* With strong hearts those old monks went through their labors; sleeping, in mid winter, under the bark of trees for blankets, and seasoning their only food, "Indian corn, grinded small," with "little frogs gath-

* In the library of Harvard College is a map, published in Paris by N. Sanson d'Abbeville, in the year 1656, in which are given portions of Lakes Superior and Michigan; the southern part of the map is the north of Florida, as discovered by Fernando de Soto, and as it is drawn in the map accompanying the History of his Adventures by Garcilaso de la Vega.

ered in the meadows." * They were very different men from "the apostle" of the Puritans; but, to all appearance, were as pure, and as true, and as loving; the Miamis were "so greedy to hear Father Allouez, when he taught them," says Marquette, "that they gave him little rest, even in the night."

Among those who were foremost in courage and kindness, was Marquette himself; a modest, quiet man, who went forward into unknown countries, not as a discoverer, but as God's messenger; who thought all his sufferings and labor fruitful, because among "the Illinois of Perouacca," he was able to baptize one dying child; and who took such a hold of the hearts of those wild men, through the inspiration of love, that for years after his death, when the storms of Lake Michigan swept over the Indian's frail canoe, he called upon the name of Marquette, and the wind ceased and the waves were still.†

In the year 1671, this Jesuit missionary led a party of Hurons to the point of land which projects from the north, at the strait between Lakes Michigan and Huron, and there founded the old settlement of Michillimackinac.‡ Here, and along the neighbouring shores, he labored with noiseless diligence until 1673, when the Intendent-general of the colony, M. Talon, a man of great activity and enterprise, and who was upon the point of closing his career in Canada, determined that the close should be worthy of his character, and called upon Marquette to be the leader of a small party, which was to seek for that great river in the West, of which the Indians had so often spoken.§ The representative of the government in this undertaking was M. Joliet, a substantial

* Hennepin, *Nouvelle Découverte.*

† Charlevoix's *Letters,* 2d, p. 97. London Ed. 1761. — *Nouvelle France,* Vol. VI. p. 21. Paris Ed. 1744.

‡ Charlevoix's *History of Canada,* (*Nouvelle France,*) Vol. II. p. 239.

§ *Ibid.,* Vol. II. p. 248.

citizen of Quebec, and with them went five other Frenchmen.*

Upon the 13th of May, 1673, this little band of seven left Michillimackinac in two bark canoes, with a small store of Indian corn and jerked meat, wherewith to keep soul and body in company, bound they knew not whither.

The first nation they visited, one with which our reverend Father had been long acquainted, being told of their venturous plan, begged them to desist. There were Indians, they said, on that great river, who would cut off their heads without the least cause; warriors who would seize them; monsters who would swallow them, canoes and all; even a demon, who shut the way, and buried in the waters, that boiled about him, all who dared draw nigh; and, if these dangers were passed, there were heats there that would infallibly kill them. "I thanked them for their good advice," says Marquette, "but I told them that I could not follow it; since the salvation of souls was at stake, for which I should be overjoyed to give my life."

Passing through Green Bay, from the mud of which, says our voyager, rise "mischievous vapors, which cause the most grand and perpetual thunders that I ever heard," they entered Fox River, and toiling over stones which cut their feet, as they dragged their canoes through its strong rapids, reached a village where lived in union the Miamis, Mascoutens, and "Kikabeux" (Kickapoos). Here Allouez had preached, and behold! in the midst of the town, a cross, (*une belle croix*,) on which hung skins, and belts, and bows, and arrows, which "these good people had offered to the great Manitou, to thank him because he had taken pity on them during the winter, and had given them an abundant chase."

* Marquette's *Journal*, Vol. I. p. 8. In this place he says, I told them that he (Joliet) "estoit envoyé de la part de Monsieur, notre Gouverneur, pour découvrir des nouveaux pays, et moy de la part de Dieu, pour les éclairer des lumières du Saint Evangile."

Beyond this point no Frenchman had gone; here was the bound of discovery; and much did the savages wonder at the hardihood of these seven men, who, alone, in two bark canoes, were thus fearlessly passing into unknown dangers.

On the 10th of June, they left this wondering and well-wishing crowd, and, with two guides to lead them through the lakes and marshes of that region, started for the river, which, as they heard, rose but about three leagues distant, and fell into the Mississippi. Without ill-luck these guides conducted them to the portage, and helped them carry their canoes across it; then, returning, left them "alone amid that unknown country, in the hand of God."

With prayers to the mother of Jesus they strengthened their souls, and then committed themselves, in all hope, to the current of the westward-flowing river, the "Mescousin" (Wisconsin); a sand-barred stream, hard to navigate, but full of islands covered with vines, and bordered by meadows, and groves, and pleasant slopes. Down this they floated with open eyes, until, upon the 17th of June, they entered the Mississippi, "with a joy," says Marquette, "that I cannot express."

Quietly floating down the great river, they remarked the deer, the buffaloes, the swans, — "wingless, for they lose their feathers in that country," — the great fish, one of which had nearly knocked their canoe into atoms, and other creatures of the air, earth, and water, but no men. At last, however, upon the 21st of June, they discovered upon the bank of the river the foot-prints of some fellow-mortals, and a little path leading into a pleasant meadow. Leaving the canoes in charge of their followers, Joliet and Father Marquette boldly advanced upon this path toward, as they supposed, an Indian village. Nor were they mistaken; for they soon came to a little town, toward which, recommending themselves to God's care, they went so nigh as to hear the savages talking. Having made their presence known by a loud cry, they were graciously received by an embassy of four old men, who presented them the pipe of peace, and told them, that this was a village of the "Illinois." The voyagers were then conducted into the town, where all received them as friends, and treated them to a great smoking. After much complimenting and present-making, a grand feast was given to the Europeans, consisting of four courses. The first was of hominy, the second of fish, the third of a dog, which the Frenchmen declined, and the whole concluded with roast buffalo. After the feast they were marched through the town with great ceremony and much speech-making; and, having spent the night, pleasantly and quietly, amid the Indians, they returned to their canoes with an escort of six hundred people. The Illinois, Marquette, like all the early travellers, describes as remarkably handsome, well-mannered, and kindly, even somewhat effeminate. The reverend Father tells us, that they used guns, and were much feared by the people of the South and West, where they made many prisoners, whom they sold as slaves.

Leaving the Illinois, the adventurers passed the rocks upon which were painted those monsters of whose existence they had heard on Lake Michigan, and soon found themselves at the mouth of the Pekitanoni, or Missouri of our day; the character of which is well described; muddy, rushing, and noisy. "Through this," says Marquette, "I hope to reach the Gulf of California, and thence the East Indies." This hope was based upon certain rumors among the natives, which represented the Pekitanoni as passing by a meadow, five or six days' journey from its mouth, on the opposite side of which meadow was a stream running westward, which led, beyond doubt, to the South Sea. "If God give me health," says our Jesuit, "I do not despair of one day making the discovery." Leaving the Missouri, they passed the demon, that had been portrayed to them, which was indeed a dangerous rock in the river, and came to the

Ouabouskigou, or Ohio, a stream which makes but a small figure in Father Marquette's map, being but a trifling water-course compared to the Illinois. From the Ohio, our voyagers passed with safety, except from the mosquitoes, into the neighbourhood of the "Akamscas," or Arkansas. Here they were attacked by a crowd of warriors, and had nearly lost their lives ; but Marquette resolutely presented the peace-pipe, until some of the old men of the attacking party were softened, and saved them from harm. "God touched their hearts," says the pious narrator.

The next day the Frenchmen went on to "Akamsca," where they were received most kindly, and feasted on corn and dog till they could eat no more. These Indians cooked in and eat from earthen ware, and were amiable and unceremonius, each man helping himself from the dish and passing it to his neighbour.

From this point Joliet and our writer determined to return to the North, as dangers increased toward the sea, and no doubt could exist as to the point where the Mississippi emptied, to ascertain which point was the great object of their expedition. Accordingly, on the 17th of July, our voyagers left Akamsca; retraced their path, with much labor, to the Illinois, through which they soon reached the Lake; and "nowhere," says Marquette, "did we see such grounds, meadows, woods, buffaloes, stags, deer, wildcats, bustards, swans, ducks, parroquets, and even beavers," as on the Illinois river.

In September the party, without loss or injury, reached Green Bay, and reported their discovery; one of the most important of that age, but of which we have now no record left except the narrative of Marquette, Joliet (as we learn from an abstract of his account, given in Hennepin's second volume, London, 1698,) having lost all his papers while returning to Quebec, by the upsetting of his canoe. Marquette's unpretending account, we have in a collection of voyages by Thevenot, printed in Paris in 1681.* Its general correctness is unquestionable; and, as no European had claimed to have made any such discovery at the time this volume was published, but the persons therein named, we may consider the account as genuine.

Afterwards Marquette returned to the Illinois, by their request, and ministered to them until 1675. On the 18th of May, in that year, as he was passing with his boatmen up Lake Michigan, he proposed to land at the mouth of a little stream running from the peninsula, and perform mass. Leaving his men with the canoe, he went a little way apart to pray, they waiting for him. As much time passed, and he did not return, they called to mind that he had said something of his death being at hand, and anxiously went to seek him. They found him dead; where he had been praying, he had died. The canoe-men dug a grave near the mouth of the stream, and buried him in the sand. Here his body was liable to be exposed by a rise of water; and would have been so, had not the river retired, and left the missionary's grave in peace. Charlevoix, who visited the spot some fifty years afterward, found that the waters had forced a passage at the most difficult point; had cut through a bluff, rather than cross the lowland where that grave was. The river is called Marquette.†

While the simple-hearted and true Marquette was pursuing

---

* This work is now very rare.

† Charlevoix's *Letters*, Vol. II. p. 96. *New France*, Vol. VI. p. 20. — Marquette spells the name of the great western river, "Mississipy"; Hennepin made it "Meschasipi"; others have written "Meschasabe," &c. &c. — There is great confusion in all the Indian oral names; we have "Kikabeaux," "Kikapous," "Quicapous;" "Outtoauets," "Outnovas;" "Miamis," "Oumamis;" and so of nearly all the nations. Our "Sioux," Charlevoix tells us, is the last syllable of "Nadouessioux," which is written, by Hennepin, "Nadoussion" and "Nadouessious," in his "*Louisiana*," and "Nadouessans" in his "*Nouvelle Découverte*."

his labors of love in the West, two men differing widely from him, and each other, were preparing to follow in his footsteps, and perfect the discoveries so well begun by him and his shadowy compeer, the Sieur Joliet. These were Robert de la Salle and Louis Hennepin.

La Salle was a native of Normandy, and was brought up, as we learn from Charlevoix,* among the Jesuits; but, having lost, by some unknown cause, his patrimony, and being of a stirring and energetic disposition, he left his home, to seek fortune among the cold and dark regions of Canada. This was about the year 1670. Here he mused long upon the pet project of those ages, a short-cut to China and the East; and — gaining his daily bread we know not how — was busily planning an expedition up the great lakes, and so across the continent to the Pacific, when Marquette returned from the Mississippi. At once the hot mind of La Salle received from his and his companion's narrations, the idea that, by following the Great River northward, or by turning up some of the streams which joined it from the westward, his aim might be certainly and easily gained. Instantly he went towards his object. He applied to Frontenac, then governor-general of Canada, laid before him an outline of his views, dim but gigantic, and, as a first step, proposed to rebuild of stone, and with improved fortifications, Fort Frontenac upon Lake Ontario, a post to which he knew the governor felt all the affection due to a namesake. Frontenac entered warmly into his views. He saw, that, in La Salle's suggestion, which was to connect Canada with the Gulf of Mexico, by a chain of forts upon the vast navigable lakes and rivers which bind that country so wonderfully together, lay the germ of a plan which might give unmeasured power to France, and unequalled glory to himself, under whose administration he fondly hoped all would be realized. He advised

* Charlevoix's *New France*, Paris Edition of 1744, Vol. II. p. 263.

La Salle, therefore, to go to the king of France, to make known his project, and ask for the royal patronage and protection; and, to forward his suit, gave him letters to Seignelay, who had succeeded his father, the great Colbert, as minister of marine.

With a breast full of hope and bright dreams, the penniless adventurer sought his monarch; his plan was approved by the minister to whom he presented Frontenac's letter; La Salle was made a Chevalier; was invested with the seignory of Fort Catarocouy or Frontenac, upon condition he would rebuild it; and received from all the first noblemen and princes assurances of their good-will and aid. His mission having sped so well, on the 14th of July, 1678, La Salle, with his lieutenant, Tonti, an Italian, and thirty men, sailed from Rochelle for Quebec, where they arrived upon the 15th of September; and, after a few days' stay, proceeded to Fort Frontenac.*

Here was quietly working, in no quiet spirit, the rival and co-laborer of La Salle, Louis Hennepin, a Franciscan friar, of the Recollet variety; a man full of ambition to be a great discoverer; daring, hardy, energetic, vain, and self-exaggerating, almost to madness; and, it is feared, more anxious to advance his own holy and unholy ends than the truth. He had in Europe lurked behind doors, he tells us, that he might hear sailors spin their yarns touching foreign lands; and he profited, it would seem, by their instructions. He came to Canada, some three years before La Salle returned from his visit to the court, and had to a certain extent prepared himself by journeyings among the Iroquois, for bolder travels into the wilderness. Having been appointed by his religious superiors to accompany the expedition which was about to

* Charlevoix's *New France*, Vol. II. p. 264, 266. What La Salle was about from the close of 1673, when Joliet returned, till July, 1678, Charlevoix tells us only in the most general terms.

start for the extreme west under La Salle, Hennepin was in readiness for him at Fort Frontenac, where he arrived, probably, some time in October, 1678.*

The Chevalier's first step was to send forward men to prepare the minds of the Indians along the lakes for his coming, and to soften their hearts by well-chosen gifts and words; and also, to pick up peltries, in which, under the king's patent, he had the almost, if not entirely exclusive, right to trade in those quarters. For, it must be understood, that our hero, having had nothing in the outset, was forced to look throughout to his own good management, in order to raise funds wherewith to carry on his operations; a thing not always done with ease; indeed, few mortals seem to have been more dunned than he; and, at one time, Hennepin tells us,

---

* Hennepin's *New Discovery*, Utrecht Edition of 1697, p. 70.—Charlevoix's *New France*, Vol. II. pp. 266.

It may be as well here, once for all, to give the names of the lakes and rivers as they appear in the early travels.

Lake Ontario, was also Lake Frontenac.

Lake Erie, was Erike, Erige, or Erie, from a nation of Eries destroyed by the Iroquois; they lived where the State of Ohio now is (Charlevoix's *New France,* Vol. II. p. 62); it was also Lake of Conti.

Lake Huron, was Karegnondi in early times (*Map of* 1656); and also, Lake of Orleans.

Lake Michigan, was Lake of Puans (*Map of* 1656); also, of the Illinois, or Illinese, or Illinouacks; also Lake Mischigonong, and Lake of the Dauphin.

Lake Superior, was Lake *Supérieur*, meaning the Upper, not the Larger lake,—also, Lake of Condé.

Green Bay, was Baie des Puans.

Illinois river, in Hennepin's *Louisiana*, and Joutel's *Journal*, is River Seignelay; and the Mississippi River, in those works, is River Colbert; and was by La Salle called River St. Louis.

Ohio river, was Ouabouskigou, Ouabachi, Ouabache, Oyo, Ouye, Belle Rivière.

Missouri river, was Pekitanoni, Rivière des Osages, and Massourites; and by Coxe is called Yellow River.

his property was actually under execution.* He therefore began operations by sending forward a party to collect skins, from which he might realize enough to cover his winter's expenses, which promised to be somewhat heavy. First, Fort Catarocouy was to be altered and repaired; then Lake Ontario was to be crossed; a new fort was to be built upon Lake Erie, and a bark of unexampled magnitude for those seas established thereon, to carry forward the trade which he hoped to set on foot; and some twenty or forty men to be kept alive and hammering, while all these things were doing; for all which purposes he had we know not what funds, but unhappily small ones at the best. However, La Salle was a man with a large heart in his bosom; he had drawn for himself a grand outline, — the discovery, conquest, fortification, possession, and commercial union, of that immense country which lies along the greatest lakes and rivers of the world, from Ontario to Superior, from the falls of Niagara to the Gulf of Mexico; and small obstacles were to him none at all.

Cheerfully he sent forward his pioneers, therefore, to seek for him beaver skins and other valuables; and, upon the 18th of November, 1678, embarked with his followers in a little vessel of ten tons, to cross Lake Ontario. This, says one of his chroniclers, was the first ship that ever sailed upon that fresh water sea. The wind was strong and contrary, and four weeks nearly were passed in beating up the little distance between Kingston and Niagara. Having forced their brigantine as far toward the Falls as was possible, our travellers landed; built some magazines with difficulty, for at times the ground was frozen so hard that they could drive their stakes, or posts, into it only by first pouring

---

* *New Discovery*, p. 102. We follow Hennepin, whose early *Journal* has not been disputed; it is the same in his *Louisiana* and his *New Discovery*.

upon it boiling water; and then made acquaintance with the Iroquois of the village of Niagara, upon Lake Erie. Not far from this village La Salle founded a second fort, upon which he set his men to work; but, finding the Iroquois jealous, he gave it up for a time, and merely erected temporary fortifications for his magazines; and then, leaving orders for a new ship to be built, he returned to Fort Frontenac, to forward stores, cables, and anchors for his forthcoming vessel.

Through the hard and cold winter days, the lake lying before them "like a plain paved with fine polished marble," some of his men hewed and hammered upon the *Griffin*, as the great bark was to be named, while others gathered furs and skins, or sued for the good-will of the bloody savages amid whom they were quartered; and all went merrily until the 20th of January, 1679. On that day, the Chevalier arrived from below; not with all his goods, however, for his misfortunes had commenced. The vessel in which his valuables had been embarked was wrecked through the bad management of the pilots; and, though the more important part of her freight was saved, much of her provision went to the bottom, which caused the carpenters, who were working upon somewhat thin diet, to groan and even grumble. And, worse than this, those who were jealous of La Salle's monopoly, and apparent good luck, had stirred up the Iroquois, some of whom, feigning drunkenness, attacked the blacksmith of the expedition, and would have killed him, had not he, Nicol-Javie-like, caught a red-hot bar from the fire, and put them to flight. But Hunger and Hate had a strong soul to deal with in our Chevalier; he pushed every thing forward, while Father Hennepin did his share by preaching, and all seemed on the road to success. During the winter, also, a very nice lot of furs was scraped together, with which, early in the spring of 1679, the commander returned to Fort Frontenac to get another outfit; while Tonti was sent forward to scour the lake coasts, muster together the men who had been sent before, collect skins, and see all that was to be seen. In thus coming and going, buying and trading, the summer of this year slipped away, and it was the seventh of August before the *Griffin* was ready to sail. Then, with *Te-Deums*, and the discharge of arquebuses, she began her voyage up Lake Erie, while the Iroquois looked on in horror and amazement, which they hastened to communicate to the Dutch at "Nouvelle Jorck."*

Over Lake Erie, through the strait beyond, across St. Clair, and into Huron, the voyagers passed most happily. In Huron they were troubled by storms, dreadful as those upon the ocean, and were at last forced to take refuge in the road of Michillimackinac. This was upon the 28th of August. At this place, which is described as one "of prodigious fertility," La Salle remained till the middle of September, founded a fort there, and sent men therefrom in various directions to spy out the state of the land. He then fell down to Green Bay, the "Baie des Puans," of the French; and, finding there a large quantity of skins and furs collected for him, he determined to load the *Griffin* therewith, and send her back to Niagara, and so stop the mouths of some of his many creditors, who were becoming noisy. This was done with all promptness; and, upon the 18th of September, she was despatched under the charge of a pilot, supposed to be competent and trustworthy, while the Norman himself, with fourteen men, proceeded down Lake Michigan, paddling along its shores in the most leisurely manner; Tonti, meanwhile, having been sent to hunt up stragglers, with whom he was to form the main body at the bottom of the lake.

From the 19th of September till the 1st of November, the time was consumed by La Salle in his voyage down the

* Hennepin.

sea in question. On the day last named, he arrived at the mouth of the river of the Miamis ; a spot the position of which is thus clearly described by one claiming to have been there: " This country," says he, meaning that of the Miamis, " is bounded to the east by Virginia and Florida, and on the other side by the Iroquois and Illinois." * At the mouth of this stream La Salle built the fort of the Miamis.

What river this " of the Miamis " was, has been a little questioned. Butler, in his " History of Kentucky," having no original account before him, pronounces it the Fox River of Green Bay, — an obvious mistake ; † Peck says, it is supposed to have been the Chicago ; ‡ and upon a first view of Hennepin's map, one would think it the Calumet, which runs into Lake Michigan from the southwest. A little examination, however, makes it clear that it was the St. Joseph's. Hennepin describes it as coming from the southeast, (the English translation makes it south*west*, perhaps that the text and map may correspond,) and says the Illinois rises a short distance, not from its source, but from its main stream ; and to this the map corresponds exactly. Now, no stream from Lake Michigan has a branch of the Illinois rising near its main current except the St. Joseph's, near which the Kaukakee rises ; whence we conclude, that the Miamis river was the former, and the Illinois the latter stream. To render this the more certain, we have the maps of Joutel, La Hontan, Coxe, and some anonymous English ones of that time, all of which represent the Miamis river in the place occupied by the St. Joseph's ; and that of Charlevoix, made in 1744, which gives us the Fort of the Miamis, on the river " St. Joseph's " ; which we must regard as decisive.

We have, then, La Salle and his little band driving pali-

* *An Account of M. De La Salle's Last Expedition and Discoveries.* New York Historical Collections, Vol. II. p. 233.

† *History of Kentucky*, Introduction, 2d edition, p. xviii.

‡ *Gazetteer of Illinois*, p. 103.

sades near the mouth of the St. Joseph's of Lake Michigan, upon the 1st of November, 1679. They were sounding the entrance of the river, too, to learn its bars and shoals, that they might warn therefrom their long-delayed *Griffin*, which ought now to be near at hand; and scouring parties were abroad in the forest for game, and for information touching the country, and their further course. And game was indeed wanting, for nothing could be had but bear's flesh, very fat and oily, for the bears had been feeding upon grapes till they were full; and this, being too rank for digestion, made the men dyspeptic and desponding. Winter began to moan in the woods, too; and the *Griffin* was still missing; "why?" men asked, and the answers which suggested themselves were far from comforting. The Iroquois might have sacked her, or creditors seized her; or her timbers, hard wrought as they had been, might have found a hard bed upon some rocky shore. Nevertheless, La Salle, nothing fearing, stuck up bear-skins upon long poles on all the shallows; and Father Hennepin preached perseverance, courage, and hope; and, by and by, Tonti dropped in to their relief, not with news of the missing ship, nor even with all the missing people, but with a canoe-full of good dry venison, most relishing to oil-deluged stomachs.

It was clear to La Salle, that he was in an awkward position; his vessel gone, no one knew how nor whither, and winter close upon him. If the rivers froze before he could get to the south, ruin and starvation were like to be his fire-side comforters. So he made up his mind at once to push on without waiting for the *Griffin*.

On the 3d of December, therefore, having mustered all his men, he placed a garrison of ten in his Fort of the Miamis, and with the remainder, thirty working men and three monks, started again upon his "great voyage and glorious undertaking." *

---

* Charlevoix, *New France*, (Vol. II. p. 269,) tells us, that La Salle

By a short portage they passed to the Illinois, and "fell down the said river by easie journeys, the better to observe that countrey." This country consisted, in the main, of quaking bogs, where with great difficulty could a man find footing; all which answers to that about the Kaukakee. Through this swamp our adventurers floated on leisurely, sometimes in great straits for food, and, about the last of December, reached a village of the Illinois Indians containing some five hundred cabins, but, at that moment, no inhabitants. The Sieur La Salle, being in great want of bread-stuffs, took advantage of this absence of the Indians to help himself to a sufficiency of maize, of which large quantities were found hidden in holes under the huts or wigwams. This village was, as near as we can judge, not far from the spot marked on our maps as Rock Fort, in La Salle county, Illinois. The corn being got aboard, the voyagers betook themselves to the stream again, and toward evening on the 4th of January, 1780, fell into a lake, which must have been the lake of Peoria, where they caught "some excellent fish," wherewith to season their corn. While the prospect of a good supper was filling all minds, unluckily bands of savages appeared, one on each bank of the river, and they found their evening meal was likely to be a stomach full of fighting, instead of fried fish. But, as it soon seemed, the Indians were as much and as disagreeably surprised as the whites; and, when all were waiting the onset, "contented themselves," as we are told, "to ask us who we were; being naturally inclined to peace." The Frenchmen having answered this appropriate question in a satisfactory manner, the Illinois received them, "not as savages use to do, but as men well-bred and civilized." Indeed, they brought out for

---

returned from the fort of the Miamis to Fort Frontenac; but Hennepin, and the journal published as Tonti's, agree that he went on, and tell a more consistent story than the historian.

the new comers, "beef and stag, and all sorts of venison and fowls," which politeness the Europeans, (in a most typical manner,) repaid by bumpers of brandy, and discharges of fire-arms; and the feast lasted three whole days, the white and red men fraternizing and embracing in a manner most entirely French; so that, says the writer from whom we quote, "we discovered in the Illinois a great humanity, and a good disposition to civil society."* This tribe, if we may credit the early writers, had really something very French in them; they were "flatterers, complaisant, cunning, and dexterous." Hunting was their great delight, and their habits were effeminate and dissolute; yet they knew the character of their conduct, and paid a kind of homage to virtue by preserving appearances.

In the midst of this nation, La Salle determined to build another fort, for he found that already some of the neighbouring tribes were trying to disturb the good feeling which existed; and, moreover, some of his own men were disposed to complain. A spot upon rising ground, near the river, was accordingly chosen about the middle of January, and the fort of *Crèvecœur* (Broken Heart), commenced; which doleful name was expressive of the very natural anxiety and sorrow, which the pretty certain loss of his *Griffin*, and his consequent impoverishment (for there were no insurance offices then), the danger of hostility on the part of the Indians, and of mutiny on the part of his own men, might well cause him.

Nor were his fears by any means groundless. In the first place, his discontented followers, and afterwards emissaries from the Mascoutens, tried to persuade the Illinois that he was a friend of the Iroquois, their most deadly enemies; and that he was among them for the purpose of enslaving them.

---

* *Last Discoveries of La Salle*, published with Tonti's name. See *post* as to authority.

But La Salle was an honest and fearless man, and as soon as coldness and jealousy appeared on the part of his hosts, he went to them boldly and asked the cause, and by his frank statements preserved their good feeling and good will. His disappointed enemies, then, or at some other time, for it is not very clear when,* tried poison; and, but for "a dose of good treacle," La Salle might have ended his days in his Fort Crèvecœur.

Meanwhile the winter wore away, and the prairies were getting to look green again; but our discoverer heard no good news, received no reinforcement; his property was gone, his men were fast leaving him, and he had little left but his own strong heart. The second year of his hopes, and toils, and failures was half gone, and he farther from his object than ever; but still he had that strong heart, and it was more than men and money. He saw that he must go back to Canada, raise new means, and enlist new men; but he did not dream, therefore, of relinquishing his projects. On the contrary, he determined that, while he was on his return, a small party should go down to the Mississippi and explore that stream toward its sources; and that Tonti, with the few men that remained, should strengthen and extend his relations among the Indians.

For the leaders of the Mississippi exploring party, which was to consist of eight, he chose M. Dacan and Father Louis Hennepin; and, having furnished them with all the necessary articles, started them upon their voyage on the last day of February, 1680.

And here we must stop our narrative, and indulge our readers with a little criticism. One of the historians of La

---

* Charlevoix says, it was at the close of 1679; Hennepin, that they did not reach the Illinois, till January 4th, 1680. We have no means of deciding, but follow Hennepin, who is particular as to date, and was present.

Salle's progress so far, and the one whom we have chiefly followed, has been the worthy Recollet, Father Louis Hennepin. This same personage was the historian of the expedition to which, as we have just stated, he was attached. In the narrative of this expedition as first printed, generally known as his "Louisiana," he claimed to have done what was ordered, that is, to have gone from the mouth of the Illinois *up* the Mississippi; but some years after, claimed to have gone *down* the Father of Waters, and discovered its mouth, and published the journal of his voyage, in the volume known as his "New Discovery." The authenticity of this journal was doubted, of course; but the friar said, that La Salle was so jealous lest he should forestall him in his discoveries, that he dared not publish that journal in France, where his first account was put forth. People still shook their heads at Father Louis, however, and have continued to shake them to this day. Mr. Sparks, in the work before us, denies Hennepin's claim entirely, and so have many other historical scholars; but we are not aware of any thorough critical statement of the grounds which exist for thinking the reverend Father so great a liar.* As we have no doubt that he was distinguished in that line, we will ask our reader's patience while we state them.

And, in the first place, we would remark, that the long-existing desire which Hennepin had felt to be a discoverer, and which seems to have been a passion with him, gives us a motive for his claim to be a discoverer, which, though no argument against his veracity, adds weight to the circumstantial evidence upon which we have to rely for a conviction. Another circumstance worthy of note for the same reason, is the importance which the Recollet assumes to himself throughout his narrative. La Salle is sent from be-

* Partial statements may be found in the *Journal* of Andrew Ellicott, Philadelphia, 1803, and in Stoddard's *Sketches of Louisiana.*

low with provisions for the ship which "*we*" were building; all the forts are joint work; all plans are joint plans; for his "we" does not refer to the party, but to La Salle and himself; evidently they appear in his eyes to be joint commanders. This mode of self-glorification reaches its height at the point where La Salle determines to send men to the Mississippi, while he returns to Canada; for not only does Father Louis make the whole thing result from a consultation between himself and the commander, but he entirely drops poor M. Dacan, who, from the narrative claiming to be by Tonti, and the history of Charlevoix, appears to have been the head of the band; does not mention his name even; but makes himself sole commander, historian, and lieutenant, having under him two canoe-men. And a strong evidence of looseness in his ideas of truth-telling is to be found in the fortieth chapter of his "New Discovery," where he assures us, that Joliet had often informed him, that he had never been farther west than the land of the Hurons and Ottawas (Outtawaats). Now there is falsity here somewhere, and far more reason to think that it came from Hennepin than from Joliet.

Turning to the Journal, the veracity of which is in question, we are at once struck by the mode in which it is interpolated into the midst of the first published volume on Louisiana. For the "New Discovery" is not a new work, but is, in the main, a reprint of the "Louisiana," as far as the close of the thirty-sixth chapter, the last sentence of which begins the new Journal; the paragraph preceding, which in the "Louisiana" had been followed by the second paragraph of the forty-fourth chapter of the "New Discovery," being in substance repeated at the beginning of that forty-fourth chapter, in order to keep up the old connection. Looking a little farther, we find, that in this interpolating no change of dates has been made, to suit the altered circumstances. In the

"Louisiana"* we are told, that on the 29th of February, 1680, Hennepin and his comrades left Fort Crèvecœur; that on the 7th of March they met with the Tamaroa Indians, about two leagues from the mouth of the Illinois; that the ice in the Mississippi detained them at the mouth of the stream they had descended, until the 12th of March; that they then began to sound and examine the Mississippi, which, with its tributaries, is described at some length; and finally, that, upon the 11th of April, they were taken by the savages, two hundred miles above the Illinois. In the "New Discovery" the same account is given as to the time of leaving the Fort, the events of the 7th of March, and the delay until the 12th, in consequence of ice; then comes the interpolated journal, and it begins by saying, that on the 8th they started to go down the Mississippi. Then follow the events of the 9th, 10th, and 11th of March; and all this is related without any perception apparently, that the story contradicts itself. But the close of the inserted Journal is worse than the beginning; for we are told, that, upon the 1st of April, the voyagers left the mouth of the Mississippi upon their return to the north, that, upon the 9th of that month, they reached the Arkansas, and upon the 12th were taken by the savages one hundred and fifty leagues above the Illinois river; and then follow the events of the 13th! So fearless is Father Hennepin, that he does not hesitate to insert into his old account a new one, which informs us, that he and two men paddled a canoe upon the Mississippi, at the rate of sixteen or eighteen miles an hour, for sixty hours without cessation. His first account is not in any point incredible so far as we have examined it, and, in respect to dates and distances, is quite reasonable. According to that we have him going up the Great River at the rate of five leagues a day, about the usual distance made by canoe-men, including stoppages, as

* We use the Amsterdam edition, of 1688.

we learn from Charlevoix; but when, in the thirty days which passed between our Reverend narrator's leaving the Illinois, and his seizure by the Indians, we have to go with him over eight hundred and twenty leagues (according to his own account), that is, twenty-seven a day, it makes our souls faint.

Nor is the substance of the inserted Journal down the Mississippi any more in its favor than are its dates. It was published in Utrecht in 1697, the very year in which the account claiming to be written by Tonti was printed in Paris. This last-named work, whatever may be its authenticity (of which more anon), was written by one well acquainted with the facts of La Salle's journey; and when we find, as we do, a strong resemblance between Hennepin's story and Tonti's, and also discover that the former contains nothing, not so much as the name of any tribe, which the latter does not, while it omits some things and names which the latter contains, we cannot but suspect that our Recollet copied his tale from the narrative just published under Tonti's name. Where, for instance, Tonti tells us that the Indians were absent from their town in 1683, Hennepin says they were so in 1680. Where Tonti found a village with dead bodies in the wigwams, Hennepin did also three years before. Where La Salle was received with ceremony and kindness, Father Louis had been so. Where the former heard only the drums of a nation, and saw nothing of them, the latter also heard their drums. In short, all of Hennepin's Journal, except what relates to his own actions, may have been taken from Tonti's, the general accuracy of which is confirmed by all contemporary accounts; and, though we have no means of knowing which was published earliest in the year 1697,* we have, upon the whole, little doubt that Tonti's was,

* The printing of Tonti's, we see by the original edition, was finished January 21st.

and that Father Louis quietly helped himself therefrom, and in his haste omitted to preserve the due consistency of time.

Here we are, therefore, upon the banks of the Illinois, without an historian of personal experience to guide us beyond this 1st of March, 1680. Hennepin, whom we have followed (under Charlevoix's eye, however,) thus far, is off upon his own travels northward; and Tonti, whose aid we fondly hoped for, vanishes utterly. In this strait we have no resource left us but to follow the historian of New France, on whom alone we henceforth rely.

A few words, however, should be given to our old, but false friend, the Recollet, who, with his two canoe-men, to say nothing of the mysterious M. Dacan and four nameless shadows, was, upon the 11th or 12th of April, taken by the Indians. This seizure was made somewhere near Black River, and they were forthwith carried into unknown regions in the north, going as high, at any rate, as the Falls of St. Anthony, which Father Louis named.* They, or some of them, returned to Canada in a year from that time, coming by the route pursued by Marquette when going; and, in 1683, we have the Friar in Paris, publishing his "Louisiana." After that time, he made no stir in America; but continued to put forth his "Voyages in France and Holland," and is soon lost to our sight.

Once more, then, we turn to that not undeserving person, our Chevalier; who remained, when Dacan was sent away, at Fort Crèvecœur. Here, to what end we know not, he stayed till the following November, as though he had been a man of fortune and leisure; and then started for Canada again, leaving Tonti and his men among the Illinois. Upon his way up the river, he was struck by the advantages of a high rock upon the bank, and at once determined to have a fort there. He accordingly laid one out, and, sending the

---

* See Schoolcraft's *Travels;* and Long's *Second Expedition.*

plan to Tonti by some stragglers, desired him to complete it. This the lieutenant tried to do; but had scarce struck spade into the earth, when those he had left at Fort Crèvecœur revolted, and he was forced to return thither at once, or all would be lost; so the new fort on the hill remained unfinished. This new fort was afterwards called Fort St. Louis, and was the place under Tonti's command when La Salle returned to France. It was, as far as we can judge, at the spot called in our day, Rock Fort, La Salle county, Illinois.

The truth was, these French among the Indians led too easy a life altogether, and became too much attached to it to be willing to make new forts or defend old ones; so that our lietenant found himself left with seven or eight men. This was at the close of 1680; and with this diminutive garrison, to which a stray Frenchman, or a spoiled Indian, now and then joined himself, Tonti worried along till September, 1981,* when, to his surprise and horror, there came in sight a large body of Iroquois warriors, irritated, not wearied, by their long journey across the wilderness. Of the various doings with these savages, the self-constituted M. Tonti gives a full account, while Charlevoix only tells us, that the Italian tried to act as mediator between the Iroquis and Illinois, for whom, and not for the French, the visit seems to have been intended, but tried to little purpose, the New York savages being very unappeasable. The end of the matter, however, by all accounts, was, that Tonti found himself under the necessity of abandoning the Illinois, and quietly creeping back to Canada with five men. This was in the middle of September, 1681; and in October he reached Lake Michigan, upon the shores of which he remained through the winter.

* Charlevoix says 1680, but La Salle did not go back till November, 1680.

La Salle, meanwhile, had returned to Canada, as we have said; there he busied himself in his old way, raising recruits, gathering funds, and building vessels wherewith to carry on the trade upon which he must live; and, in the spring of 1682, we find him once more upon the Illinois, manning Crèvecœur, finishing Fort St. Louis, and in one way or another killing time until August, when once more he must back to Fort Frontenac, and muster all his forces for his Second Voyage.

This second voyage commenced upon the Illinois river, in January, 1683;* but, as there was much ice to impede our voyagers, it was the 2d of February when they reached the Mississippi, and the 9th of April when they came to its mouth; that is, it took them twice as long to go down the Mississippi as it did Hennepin (on paper) to go and come again. Of this passage Charlevoix gives us no details; but the professed Tonti is more generous, and displays for our entertainment and edification, the banks of the Illinois river, "covered over with pomegranate-trees, orange-trees, and lemon-trees"; the "Chicacha" Indians, with "faces flat like plates, which is reckoned among them for a stroke of beauty"; the "crocodiles" which come "into the world but like a chicken, being hatched of an egg"; the Indian women of the Tacucas, to one of whom he gave a pair of "cizars," who in return squeezed his hand so hard as to give him reason to think, that those women "might easily be

---

* The Introduction to Joutel's *Journal* (p. xx.) tells us, that even then, in 1714, the second voyage of La Salle was variously represented as in 1682 and 1683, and Charlevoix writes it as in 1682; but, by examining his dates, it is made evident that he dropped a year; and the Journal of Tonti, in the main facts of which, whoever wrote it, we have great confidence, makes 1683 the year; we therefore adopt that. In our 99th Number (p. 417), it was stated, on Charlevoix's authority, that La Salle reached the Mississippi in 1682. This we may here correct; and also a misprint in our 94th Number, p. 64, where the year of this discovery is printed 1681.

tamed by us, and taught the politer arts of conversation"; and, also, the pearl oysters of the Natchez, the shells of which "you may see on a fair day open themselves to receive the dew of heaven; which dew breeds the first seeds of the pearl within the shells."

It is grievous to think, that all these details must be put aside as not legitimate, even if true; and nothing be left us of La Salle's second voyage but the barren date of his arrival at the seashore, and the yet more unsatisfactory statement, that he returned to Quebec some time in 1683 (it is by no means clear when, for Charlevoix has his dates tangled), and that afterwards he embarked for France on the 9th of November, 1683, as we learn from the Baron Hontan. To these husks is plain history unhappily confined.*

One other and very familiar thing we find on record; trouble in Canada; the governor and the intendant quarrelling, and both recalled; the Indians threatening; and a new governor appointed, M. de la Barre, who began his administration by accusing La Salle of being a rogue, a rioter, a fomenter of discord, and a general nuisance in the colony.†

But La Salle had, fortunately, a most able advocate in France, for he was there in person; and the whole nation

---

* Charlevoix's dates stand thus: The summer of 1679 was spent in preparing to get off the *Griffin;* she was finished in August; on the 28th of February, 1680, Dacan left Crèvecœur; La Salle stayed there till *November* (1680 of course); *not long after* came the Iroquois, and Tonti was forced away, *September* 11th, 1680 (Tonti's narrative says 1681); a year passes, and in February, 1682, the Mississippi is reached; on the 15th of May (1682), La Salle falls sick coming up the Mississippi, and does not reach Quebec till the spring of 1683, and embarks some months after. But Tonti's account (so called) is clearer; a year is passed in Crèvecœur after La Salle leaves it; the Mississippi is reached in 1683; in May, 1683, La Salle falls sick, and in September of that year reaches Michillimackinac, and in a month or more sails for France; to bring him out right Charlevoix has to keep him sick a year.

† Charlevoix's *New France*, Vol. II. p. 286.

being stirred by the story of the new discoveries, of which Hennepin had published his first account some months before La Salle's return, our hero found ears open to drink in his words, and imaginations warmed to make the most of them. The minister, Seignelay, desired to see the adventurer, and he soon won his way to whatever heart that man had; for it could not have required much talk with La Salle to have been satisfied of his sincerity, enthusiasm, energy, and bravery. The tales of the new governor fell dead, therefore, and the king listened to the prayer of his subject, that a fleet might be sent to take possession of the mouth of the Mississippi, and so that great country of which he told them be secured to France. The king listened; and soon the town of Rochelle was busy with the stir of artisans, ship-riggers, adventurers, soldiers, sailors, and all that varied crowd which in those days looked into the dim West for a land where wealth and life were to be had for the seeking.

Of this third voyage of La Salle, let us be thankful that we have a full and true history. We no longer follow the fame and not truth loving Hennepin, the ghost of a Tonti, or the somewhat inaccurate and second-hand Charlevoix. We have now as our guide and comforter the worthy Monsieur Joutel, a commander and actor in that same expedition; a man of accuracy and unquestioned truth, and whose volume, as translated into English, and published in London by A. Bell, at the "Cross Keys and Bible," Cornhill, in 1714, now lies before us.

On the 24th of July, 1684, twenty-four vessels sailed from Rochelle for America, four of which were for the discovery and settlement of the famed Louisiana. These four carried two hundred and eighty persons, including the crews; there were soldiers, artificers, and volunteers, and also "some young women." There is no doubt that this brave fleet started full of light hearts, and vast, vague hopes; but, alas! it had scarce started when discord began; for La Salle and the commander of the fleet, M. de Beaujeu, were well fitted to quarrel one with the other, but never to work together. In truth, our hero seems to have been nowise amiable, for he was overbearing, harsh, and probably selfish to the full extent to be looked for in a man of worldly ambition. However, in one of the causes of quarrel which arose during the passage, he acted, if not with policy, certainly with boldness and humanity. It was when they came to the Tropic of Cancer, where, in those times, it was customary to baptize all green hands, as is still sometimes done under the Equator. On this occasion, the sailors of La Salle's little squadron promised themselves rare sport and much plunder, grog, and other good things, the forfeit paid by those who do not wish a seasoning; but all these expectations were stopped, and hope turned into hate, by the express and emphatic statement on the part of La Salle, that no man under his command should be ducked, whereupon the commander of the fleet was forced to forbid the ceremony.

With such beginnings of bickering and dissatisfaction the Atlantic was slowly crossed, and, upon the 20th of September, the island of St. Domingo was reached. Here certain arrangements were to be made with the colonial authorities; but, as they were away, it became necessary to stop there for a time. And a sad time it was. The fever seized the newcomers; the ships were crowded with sick; La Salle himself was brought to the verge of the grave; and, when he recovered, the first news that greeted him, was that one of his four vessels, the one wherein he had embarked his stores and implements, had been taken by the Spaniards. The sick man had to bestir himself thereupon to procure new supplies; and, while he was doing so, his enemies were also bestirring themselves to seduce his men from him, so that what with death and desertion, he was like to have a small crew at the last. But energy did much; and, on the 25th of November, the first of the remaining vessels, she that was "to carry the light," sailed for the coast of America. In her went La Salle, and our writer, Joutel.

For a whole month were our disconsolate sailors sailing, and sounding, and stopping to take in water and shoot alligators, and drifting in utter uncertainty, until, on the 28th of December, the mainland was fairly discovered. But "there being," as Joutel says, "no man among them who had any knowledge of that Bay," it was not strange, that they went feeling and trembling like one that in the dark seeks for a door; and so, feeling and stumbling, and ever fearful of knocking their noses by venturing too near the wall, they went past the very Mississippi-door which they sought; and in a most useless and melancholy manner, quarrelling and bickering, wore away the whole month of January, 1685. At last, La Salle, out of patience, determined to land some of his men, and go along the shore towards the point where he believed the mouth of the Mississippi to be, and our friend Joutel was appointed one of the commanders of this exploring party. They started on the 4th of February, and travelled eastward (for it was clear that they had passed the door), during three days, when they came to a great river which they could not cross, having no boats. Here they made fire-signals, and, on the 13th, two of the vessels came in sight; the mouth of the river, or entrance of the bay, for such it proved to be, was forthwith sounded, and the barks sent in to be under shelter. But, sad to say, La Salle's old fortune was at work here again; for the vessel which bore his provisions and most valuable stores, was run upon a shoal by the grossest neglect, or, as Joutel thinks, with malice prepense; and, soon after, the wind coming in strong from the sea, she fell to pieces in the night, and the bay was full of casks and packages, which could not be saved, or were worthless when drawn from the salt water. From this untimely fate our poor adventurer rescued but a small half of his second stock of indispensables.

Who can help pitying this unlucky La Salle? Full of genius, he plans one of the grandest of modern operations, — the union of Canada with the Gulf of Mexico. Full of energy, dogged perseverance, undaunted courage, he tries to execute his plan; at every step he meets some difficulty; his own men, his fellow-countrymen, the Iroquois, the very elements throw blocks in his way, and he falls again and again. But from each fall he rises with new strength. Having nothing at the outset, he builds vessels, and raises and equips men; when the vessels are lost, he builds others; when the men desert, he musters new recruits; and so, during four long years, battles with Fortune unweariedly, and at length makes known the Mississippi from the Falls of St. Anthony to the mouth. And now, when it would seem that his future might be easier, and his fortune milder, again, all things conspire against him; two outfits are lost before his enterprise is under way; one company of followers has mostly deserted him, and now another threatens to do likewise. But was it indeed Fortune that for ever heaped evil on his head? Not wholly; we see enough of La Salle, dim as his features are to us, to see that loveliness was no trait of his. He bound none to him by the only indissoluble cord, affection. Men stood aloof, or worked with, not for him; from fear, or selfish ambition, never (unless somewhat in Tonti's case) from that personal reverence and love, which bound men to Washington; and of his misfortunes a large proportion came from the ill-will of his enemies.

But leaving such thoughts, let us look at our friend the Chevalier's condition in the middle of March, 1685. Beaujeu, with his ship, is gone, leaving his comrades in the marshy wilderness, with not much of joy to look forward to. They had guns and powder and shot; eight cannon, too, "but not one bullet," that is, cannon-ball, the naval gentlemen having refused to give them any. And here are our lonely settlers, building a fort upon the shores of the Bay of

St. Louis, as they called it, known to us as the Bay of St. Bernard. They build from the wreck of their ship, we cannot think with light hearts; every plank and timber tells of past ill luck, and, as they look forward, there is vision of irritated savages (for there had been warring already), of long search for the *Hidden River*,* of toils and dangers in its ascent when reached. No wonder, that "during that time several men deserted." So strong was the fever for desertion, that of some who stole away and were retaken, it was found necessary to execute one, while the others were condemned "to serve the king ten years in that country"; a mode of punishment, which may be termed nominal, probably, it being a sort of forced enlistment on the part of our Chevalier.

And now La Salle prepares to issue from his nearly completed fort, to look round and see where he is. He has still a good force, some hundred and fifty people; and, by prompt and determined action, much may be done between this last of March and next autumn. In the first place, the river falling into the Bay of St. Louis is examined, and a new fort commenced in that neighbourhood, where seed is planted also; for the men begin to tire of meat and fish, with spare allowance of bread, and no vegetables. But the old luck is at work still. The seed will not sprout; men desert; the fort goes forward miserably slow; and at last, three months and more gone to no purpose, Joutel and his men, who are still hewing timber at the first fort, are sent for, and told to bring their timber with them in a float. The float or raft was begun "with immense labor," says the wearied historian, but all to no purpose, for the weather was so adverse, that it had to be all taken apart again and buried in the sand. Empty-handed, therefore, Joutel sought his superior, the effects being left at a post by the way. And he came to a

* So the Spaniards called the Mississippi.

scene of desolation; men sick, and no houses to put them in; all the looked-for crop blasted; and not a ray of comfort from any quarter.

"Well," said La Salle, "we must now muster all hands, and build ourselves 'a large lodgment.'" But there was no timber within a league; and not a cart nor a bullock to be had, for the buffaloes, though abundant, were ill broken to such labor. If done, this dragging must be done by men; so, over the long grass and weeds of the prairie-plain, they dragged some sticks, with vast suffering. Afterwards the carriage of a gun was tried; but it would not do; "the ablest men were quite spent." Indeed, heaving and hauling over that damp plain, and under that July sun, might have tried the constitution of the best of Africans; and of the poor Frenchmen thirty died, worn out. The carpenter was lost; and, worse still, La Salle, wearied, worried, disappointed, lost his temper and insulted the men. So closed July; our Chevalier turned carpenter, marking out the tenons and mortises of what timber he could get, and growing daily more cross. In March we thought much might be done before autumn, and now autumn stands but one month removed from us, and not even a house built yet.

And August soon passed too, not without results, however; for the timber that had been buried below was got up, and a second house built, "all covered with planks and bullock's hides over them."

And now once more was La Salle ready to seek the Mississippi. First, he thought he would try with the last of the four barks with which he left France; the bark *La Belle*, "a little frigate, carrying six guns," which the King had given our Chevalier to be his navy. But, after having put all his clothes and valuables on board of her, he determined to try with twenty men to reach his object by land. This was in December, 1685. From this expedition he did not return until March, 1686, when he came to his fort again, ragged, hatless, and worn down, with six or seven followers at his heels, his travels having been all in vain. It was not very encouraging; but, says Joutel, "we thought only of making ourselves as merry as we could." The next day came the rest of the party, who had been sent to find the little frigate, which should have been in the bay. They came mournfully, for the little frigate could not be found, and she had all La Salle's best effects on board.

The bark was gone; but our hero's heart was still beating in his bosom, a little cracked and shaken, but strong and iron-bound still. So, borrowing some changes of linen from Joutel, toward the latter end of April he again set forth, he and twenty men, each with his pack, "to look for his river," as our writer aptly terms it. Some days after his departure, the bark *La Belle* came to light again; for she was not lost, but only ashore. Deserted by her forlorn and diminished crew, however, she seems to have been suffered to break up and go to pieces in her own way, for we hear no more of the little frigate.

And now, for a time, things went on pretty smoothly. There was even a marriage at the fort; and "Monsieur le Marquis de la Sablonière" wished to act as groom in a second, but Joutel absolutely refused. By and by, however, the men, seeing that La Salle did not return, "began to mutter." There were even proposals afloat to make way with our friend Joutel, and start upon a new enterprise; the leader in which half-formed plan was one Sieur Duhaut, an unsafe man, and inimical to La Salle, who had, probably, maltreated him somewhat. Joutel, however, learned the state of matters, and put a stop to all such proceedings. Knowing idleness to be a root of countless evils, he made his men work and dance as long as there was vigor enough in them to keep their limbs in motion; and in such manner the summer passed away, until in August La Salle returned. He had been among the Indians in the north of Mexico, and also toward the Mississippi, had traded with them, and brought home five horses; but, of the twenty men he had taken with him, only eight returned, some having fallen sick, some having died, and others deserted. He had not found "his river," though he had been so far in that direction; but he came back full of spirits, "which," says our writer, "revived the lowest ebb of hope." He was already, too, to start again at once, to seek the Mississippi, and go onward to Canada, and thence to France, to get new recruits and supplies; but "it was determined to let the great heats pass before that enterprise was taken in hand." And the heats passed, but with them our hero's health, so that the proposed journey was delayed from time to time until the 12th of January, 1687.

On that day started the last company of La Salle's adventurers, seventeen in number. Among them went the discontented Duhaut; and all took their "leaves with so much tenderness and sorrow as if they had all presaged that they should never see each other more." They went northwest along the bank of the river on which their fort stood, until they came to where the streams running toward the coast were fordable, and then turned eastward, as in that direction they hoped to find the Mississippi. From the 12th of January till the 15th of March did they thus journey across that southern country, crossing "curious meadows," through which ran "several little brooks of very clear and good water," which, with the tall trees, all of a size, and planted as if by a line, "afforded a most delightful landskip." They met many Indians too, with whom La Salle established relations of peace and friendship. Game was abundant, "plenty of foul, and particularly of turkeys," was there, which was "an ease to their sufferings"; and so they still toiled on in shoes of green bullocks' hide, which, dried by the sun, pinched cruelly, until, following the tracks of the buffaloes, who choose by instinct the best ways, they had come to a pleasanter country than they had yet passed through, and were far toward the long-sought Father of Waters.

On the 15th of March, La Salle, recognizing the spot where they then were as one through which he had passed in his former journey, and near which he had hidden some beans and Indian wheat, ordered the Sieurs Duhaut, Hiens, Liotot the surgeon, and some others, to go and seek them. This they did, but found that the food was all spoiled, so they turned toward the camp again. While coming campward they chanced upon two bullocks, which were killed by one of La Salle's hunters, who was with them. So they sent the commander word that they had killed some meat, and that, if he would have the flesh dried, he might send horses to carry it to the place where he lay; and, meanwhile, they cut up the bullocks, and took out the marrow-bones, and laid them aside for their own choice eating, as was usual to do. When La Salle heard of the meat that had been taken, he sent his nephew and chief confidant, M. Moranget, with one De Male, and his own footman, giving them orders to send all that was fit to the camp at once. M. Moranget, when he came to where Duhaut and the rest were, and found that they had laid by for themselves the marrow-bones, became angry, took from them their choice pieces, threatened them, and spoke harsh words. This treatment touched these men, already not well pleased, to the quick; and, when it was night, they took counsel together how they might best have their revenge. The end of such counselling, where anger is foremost, and the wilderness is all about one, needs scarce to be told; "we will have their blood, all that are of that party shall die," said these malcontents. So, when M. Moranget and the rest had supped and fallen asleep, Liotot the surgeon took an axe, and with few strokes killed them all; all that were of La Salle's party, even his poor Indian hunter, because he was faithful; and, lest De Male might not be with them (for him they did not kill), they forced him to stab M. Moranget, who had not died by the first blow of Liotot's axe, and then threw them out for the carrion-birds to feast on.

This murder was done upon the 17th of March. And at once the murderers would have killed La Salle, but he and his men were on the other side of a river, and the water for two days was so high they could not cross; so they sat, eating of their bullocks, and meditating what they had done and must yet do. There was, beyond doubt, less sweetness in those marrow-bones which they had won so dearly, than they had hoped for.

La Salle on his part was growing anxious too; his nephew so long absent, what meant it? and he went about asking if Duhaut had not been a malcontent; but none said, Yes. Doubtless there was something in La Salle's heart, which told him his followers had cause to be his foes. It was now the 20th of the month, and he could not forbear setting out to seek his lost relative. Leaving Joutel in command, therefore, he started with a Franciscan monk and one Indian. Coming near the hut which the murderers had put up, though still on the opposite side of the river, he saw carrion-birds hovering near, and, to call attention if any were there, fired a shot. There were keen and watching ears and eyes there; the gun told them to be quick, for their prey was in the net; so, at once, Duhaut and another crossed the river, and, while the first hid himself among the tall weeds, the latter showed himself to La Salle at a good distance off. Going instantly to meet him, the fated man passed near to the spot where Duhaut lay hid. The traitor lay still till he came opposite; then, raising his piece, shot his commander through the brain, "so that he dropped down dead on the spot, without speaking one word."

Thus fell La Salle, on the threshold of success. No man had more strongly all the elements that would have borne him safe through, if we except that element which insures affection. "He had a capacity and talent," says Joutel, one of his staunchest friends, "to make his enterprise successful; his constancy, and courage, and extraordinary knowledge in arts and sciences, which rendered him fit for any thing, together with an indefatigable body, which made him surmount all difficulties, would have procured a glorious issue to his undertaking, had not all those excellent qualities been counterbalanced by too haughty a behaviour, which sometimes made him insupportable, and by a rigidness toward those that were under his command, which at last drew on him an implacable hatred, and was the occasion of his death."

La Salle died, as far as we can judge, upon a branch of Trinity River.*

And now, the leader being killed, his followers toiled on mournfully, and in fear, each of the others,—Duhaut assuming the command,— until May. Then there arose a difference among them as to their future course; and, by and by, things coming to extremities, some of La Salle's murderers turned upon the others, and Duhaut and Liotot were killed by their comrades. So blood is still washed out by blood, and there is ever a stain behind. This done, the now dominant party determined to remain among the Indians, with whom they then were, and where they found some who had been with La Salle in his former expedition, and had deserted. These were living among the savages, painted, and shaved, and naked, with great store of squaws and scalps. But our good Monsieur Joutel was not of this way of thinking; he and some others still wished to find the Great River and get to Canada. At last, all consenting, he did, with six others, leave the main body, and take up his march for the Illinois, where he hoped to find Tonti, who should have been all this while at Fort St. Louis. This was in May, 1687.

---

* Map in Charlevoix, Vol. III., where the spot is marked.

With great labor this little band forced their heavy-laden horses over the fat soil, in which they often stuck fast; and, daring countless dangers, at length, upon the 24th of July, reached the Arkansas, where they found a post containing a few Frenchmen, who had been placed there by Tonti. Here they stayed a little while, and then went forward again, until, upon the 14th of September, they reached Fort Louis, upon the Illinois. At this post Joutel remained until the following March, — that of 1688, — when he set off for Quebec, which city he reached in the last of July, just four years having passed since he sailed from Rochelle.*

Thus ended La Salle's third and last voyage, producing no permament settlement; for the Spaniards came, dismantled the fort upon the Bay of St. Louis, and carried away its garrison, and the Frenchmen who had been left elsewhere in the southwest intermingled with the Indians, until all trace of them was lost.

And so ended our adventurer's endeavours, in defeat. Yet he had not worked and suffered in vain. He had thrown open to France and the world an immense and most valuable country; had established several permanent forts, and laid the foundation of more than one settlement there. Peoria, Kaskaskia, Cahokia, to this day, are monuments of La Salle's labors; for, though he founded neither of them, (unless Peoria was built upon the site of Fort Crèvecœur,) it was by those whom he brought into the West, that these places were peopled and civilized. He was, if not the discoverer, the first settler of the Mississippi Valley, and as such deserves to be known and honored.

* We have followed throughout Joutel alone; Charlevoix vouches for him (*New France*, Vol. III. 56). Hennepin gives a second-hand account, drawn from the monks of his order who were with La Salle, which in most points agrees with Joutel's. That given in the *Journal* under Tonti's name is wholly different, and is also professedly second-hand from Cavalier.

And now, having buried the gentle Marquette and stout Sieur La Salle, what little interest there may have been in our sketch of western travel in old times is passed away. For, dim as have been the features of these our adventurers, those that succeed to them are ghosts indeed; and our interest in a tale is ever in proportion to the flesh and blood that walk and speak in it; whence novels chain our attention more than history, though there is no doubt, that the events of the true ever surpass in wonder those of the fictitious story.

We have now, among our foremost personages in this shadowy band, the genuine Tonti. Tonti, left by La Salle when he sailed for France, after reaching the Gulf of Mexico, in 1683, remained as commander of that Rock Fort of St. Louis, which he had begun in 1680, and which he now finished. Here he stayed, swaying absolutely the Indian tribes, and acting as viceroy over the unknown and uncounted Frenchmen who were beginning to wander through that beautiful country, making discoveries of which we have no records left. In 1685, looking to meet La Salle, he went down to the mouth of the Mississippi; of which going we have a full account in his apocryphal *Relation*, and an undoubted proof in a letter from him to La Salle, dated April 20th, 1685, written at the village of the Quinipissas, and mourning that they had not met at the mouth of the Mississippi, as had been expected.* Alas! at the very moment that the faithful Tonti was writing his regrets, his friend and commander was looking, with heavy heart, at his men as they toiled together building, from the wreck of his vessel, the fated fort upon the Bay of St. Louis!

Finding no signs of his old comrade, Tonti turns northward again, and reaching his fort on the Illinois, finds work

* Given in Charlevoix, Vol. III. 383.

to do; for the Iroquois, long threatening, were now in the battle-field, backed by the English, and Tonti, with his western-wild allies, was forced to march and fight. Engaged in this business, he appears to us at intervals in the pages of Charlevoix; in the fall of 1687 we have him with Joutel, at Fort St. Louis; in April, 1689, he suddenly appears to us at Crèvecœur, revealed by the Baron La Hontan; and again, early in 1700, D'Iberville is visited by him at the mouth of the Mississippi. After that we see him no more; and the *Biographie Universelle* tells us, that, though he remained many years in Louisiana, he finally was not there; but of his death or departure thence no one knows. So vaguely lives and dies the Chevalier Tonti, an Italian by birth, and an old soldier. He had lost his hand by a grenade, at some famous siege of those times, and was, upon the whole, noted in his generation.

Next in sequence, we have a glimpse of the abovenamed Baron La Hontan, discoverer of the Long River, and, as that discovery proves, drawer of a somewhat long bow. By his volumes, published *à la Haye*, in 1706, we learn, that he too warred against the Iroquois in 1687 and 1688; and, having gone so far westward as the Lake of the Illinois, thought he would contribute his mite to the discoveries of those times. So, with a sufficient escort, he crossed, by Marquette's old route, Fox River and the Wisconsin, to the Mississippi; and, turning up that stream, sailed thereon till he came to the mouth of a river, called *Long River*, coming from the West. This river emptied itself (as appears by his map) nearly where the St. Peter's does in our day. Upon this stream, one of immense size, our Baron sailed for eighty and odd days, meeting the most extensive and civilized Indian nations of which we have any account, that is to say, in those regions; and, after his eighty and odd days' sailing, he got less than half-way to the head of this great river, which was, indeed, not less than two thousand miles long, and, as he learned from the red men, who drew him a map of its course above his stopping-point, led to a lake, whence another river led to the South Sea; so that at last the great problem of those days was solved, and the wealth of China and the East thrown open by the Baron de la Hontan.* And why, we might ask the Baron, did you not go and bathe in that South Sea, instead of floating down the Long River again, and paddling up the comparatively inconsiderable Missouri? Probably this question was asked in those days, for we find the Baron's story much doubted and denied, though he was not, like La Salle, an adventurer, but a man in authority, governor of Newfoundland in after days, and well known at home and abroad. Poor Baron, he was, and is well known; but it is as the foolish inventor of a lie, which, lifting him for the moment above his level, made his fall to earth again, deadly. And so he passes.†

And now our sketch becomes dimmer than ever. "La Salle's death," says Charlevoix, in one place, "dispersed the French who had gathered upon the Illinois;" but in another, he speaks of Tonti and twenty Canadians, as established among the Illinois three years after the Chevalier's fate was known there.‡ This, however, is clear, that about 1700 or 1705, the reverend Father Gravier began a mission among the Illinois, at the spot, as the historian of New France says,

---

* *Voyages de La Hontan*, Vol. I. p. 194.

† See the Preface to Schoolcraft's *Travels*, and Long's *Journey up the St. Peter's*. These men knew the whole ground over which La Hontan says he went; and yet we have at times thought that the Baron may have entered the St. Peter's when filled with the back waters of the Mississippi, and heard from the Indians of the connection by it and the Red River with lake Winnipeg, and the communication between that lake and Hudson's Bay, by Nelson River, and, looking westward all the while, turned Hudson's Bay into the South Sea.—See map in Long's *Second Expedition up the St. Peter's*, and La Hontan's maps.

‡ *New France*, Vol. III. pp. 395, 383.

where Fort St. Louis had been; or, as we would suppose from the letter of Father Gabriel Maret, dated at Cascasquias, November 9th, 1712, somewhere in the neighbourhood of that settlement.* At any rate, Gravier, and Marest his fellow-laborer, succeeded in gathering a little flock of converted Indians about them, and laid the corner-stone of that permanent French settlement in Illinois, the remains of which astonish the traveller at this day. In 1750, as we are told by one of the missionaries, Vivier, then laboring "aux Illinois," there were in that country five French villages, containing one hundred and forty families, and three villages of colonized natives, numbering not less than six hundred.†

An attempt was also made to build up a settlement at the point where the Ohio and Mississippi join, at all times a favorite spot among planners of towns, and at this moment, if we mistake not, in the process of being made into a town. The first who tried this spot was the Sieur Juchereau, a Canadian gentleman, assisted by Father Mermet, who was to Christianize the Mascoutens, of whom a large flock was soon gathered.‡ But these savages were less docile, pliable, and French, than the Illinois, and with superstitious ardor placed all faith in their magicians or jugglers. Our worthy Father Mermet thought his first step should be to corner and confound these pseudo-priests, so, in the presence of the assembled colony, he opened an argument with one of them, one whose god was the Buffalo. With cunning questions, the wise European puzzled his antagonist, and forced him, at length, to own publicly and directly, that it was not the beast, Buffalo, to which he bowed, but that Spirit which had charge of the beast, and which was unseen, unknown; nay, still

---

* *Lettres Edifiantes*, (original edition,) Vol. XI.

† Idem., Vol. XXVIII. p. 36.

‡ Charlevoix, Vol. III. p. 393. — *Lettres Edifiantes* (selected). Paris Edition of 1809, Vol. VII. p. 127.

further, the unwise juggler was led to acknowledge, that the Spirit of the Buffalo was worshipful because it was good, and that this was known by the excellency of its charge, the beast in question. "Ah ha!" said the wily schoolman, "now I have you; for if the excellency of the animal signifies that of its Spirit, and therefore is worshipful, then must you own that the Spirit of man, who is better than any other animal, is better than any other spirit; and therefore you must worship God." Nothing could be more logical, and no logical "must" more imperative. But the poor wild men laughed at demonstration, and went on worshipping the Buffalo; for he, and not the God of Father Mermet, had been kind to them; *he had made the buffaloes, which had supplied them with meat and clothing!* Would not our good Father have done well to try the argument, that he and they were worshipping one Being, the Giver of good gifts?

But the attempt of our Canadian gentleman and his reverend assistant failed. Sickness came, and, as the savages were ready to believe the white man's God *stronger* than theirs, they (very likely at the suggestion of Father Mermet himself) looked on the epidemic as the effect of his wrath, kindled by their conduct. So, after trying without success to kill his minister, our missionary, and then to appease him by a procession and prayers, they at last deserted the low and sickly land, and took to their woods and free life again.

Of the date of these doings we find no mention; but from Vivier's letter, already quoted, it is clear that, previous to 1750, no settlement existed upon the Ohio or any of its branches, as he enumerates all then in being. The cause of this is not clear, as Hennepin was aware of the existence of "a great river, called Hoio, which passes through the country of the Iroquois," in 1673 or 1674. Indeed, we are told the route from the Lakes by that great river had been explored in 1676;* and in Hennepin's volume of 1698 is a short journal, professing to be that sent by La Salle to Count Frontenac, in 1683, which mentions the Maumee and Wabash as the most direct road from Canada to the Mississippi. And yet, though we hear of journeying by this way, there is no record of any attempt at a settlement above the mouth of the Ohio before 1750.†

In thus running over the progress of things in Illinois, we have far outrun all dates and times, and must turn back and make known to our readers the doings of the successor of La Salle in the attempt to find the mouth of the Mississippi, Monsieur D'Iberville.

This officer, who from 1694 to 1697 distinguished himself not a little by battles and conquests among the icebergs of the "Baye d'Udson" or Hudson's Bay,‡ having, in the year last named, returned to France, proposed to the minister to try, what had been given up since La Salle's sad fate, the discovery and settlement of Louisiana by sea. The Count of Pontchartrain, who was then at the head of marine affairs, was led to take an interest in the proposition; and, upon the 17th of October, 1698, D'Iberville took his leave of France, handsomely equipped for his expedition, and with two good ships to forward him in his attempt.§

Of this D'Iberville we have no very clear notion, except that he was a man of judgment, self-possession, and prompt action. Gabriel Marest presents him to us in the "Baye d'Udson," his ships crowded and almost crushed by the ice, and his brother, a young, bright boy of nineteen, his favorite brother, just killed by a chance shot from the English

---

* *Hist. Gén. des Voyages*, Vol. XIV. p. 758.

† The details of this subject may be presented by us in another paper.

‡ *New France*, Vol. III. pp. 215, 299. — *Lettres Edifiantes*, Vol. X. p. 280.

§ *New France*, Vol. III. p. 377.

fort which they were besieging; — and there the commander stands on the icy deck, the cold October wind singing in the shrouds, and his dead brother waiting till their lives are secured before he can receive Christian burial, — there he stands, "moved exceedingly," says the missionary, — but giving his orders with a calm face, full tone, and clear mind. "He put his trust on God," says Father Gabriel, "and God consoled him from that day; the same tide brought both his vessels out of danger, and bore them to the spot where they were wanted." *

Such was the man who, upon the 31st of January, 1699, let go his anchor in the Bay of Mobile. Having looked about him at this spot, he went thence to seek the great river called by the savages, says Charlevoix, "Malbouchia," and by the Spaniards, "la Palissade," from the great number of trees about its mouth. Searching carefully, upon the 2d of March our commander found and entered the Hidden River, whose mouth had been so long and unsuccessfully sought. As soon as this was done, one of the vessels returned to France to carry thither the news of D'Iberville's success, while he turned his prow up the Father of Waters. Slowly ascending the vast stream, he found himself puzzled by the little resemblance which it bore to that described by Tonti and by Hennepin. So great were the discrepances, that he had begun to doubt if he were not upon the wrong river, when an Indian chief sent to him Tonti's letter to La Salle, on which, through fourteen years, those wild men had been looking with wonder and awe. Assured by this that he had indeed reached the desired spot, and wearied probably by his tedious sail thus far, he returned to the Bay of Biloxi, between the Mississippi and the Mobile waters, built a fort in that neighbourhood, and having manned it in a suitable manner, returned to France himself.†

---

* *Lettres Edifiantes*, Vol. X. p. 300.

† *New France*, Vol. III. p. 380, *et seq.*

While he was gone, in the month of September, 1699, the lieutenant of his fort, M. De Bienville, went round to explore the mouths of the Mississippi, and take soundings. Engaged in this business, he had rowed up the main entrance some twenty-five leagues, when, unexpectedly and to his no little chagrin, a British corvette came in sight, a vessel carrying twelve cannon, slowly creeping up the swift current. M. Bienville, nothing daunted, though he had but his leads and lines to do battle with, spoke up, and said, that, if this vessel did not leave the river without delay, he had force enough at hand to make her repent it. All which had its effect; the Britons about ship and stood to sea again, growling as they went, and saying, that they had discovered that country fifty years before, that they had a better right to it than the French, and would soon make them know it. This was the first meeting of those rival nations in the Mississippi Valley, which, from that day, was a bone of contention between them till the conclusion of the old French war. Nor did the matter rest long with this visit from the corvette. Englishmen began to creep over the mountains from Carolina, and, trading with the Chicachas, or Chickasaws of our day, stirred them up to acts of enmity against the French.

When D'Iberville came back from France, in January, 1700, and heard of these things, he determined to take possession of the country anew, and to build a fort upon the banks of the Mississippi itself. So, with due form, the vast valley of the West was again sworn in to Louis, as the whole continent through to the South Sea had been previously sworn in by the English to the Charleses and Jameses; and what was more effectual, a little fort was built, and four pieces of cannon placed therein. But even this was not much to the purpose ; for it soon disappeared, and the marshes about the mouth of the Great River were again, as they had ever been, and long must be, uninhabited by men.

And now we must turn aside for a time, and let our readers know something of these English claims and attempts.

"King Charles the First, in the fifth year of his reign (1630), granted unto Sir Robert Heath, his attorney-general, a patent of all that part of America," which lies between thirty-one and thirty-six degrees north latitude, from sea to sea. Eight years afterwards, Sir Robert conveyed this very handsome property to Lord Maltravers, who was soon, by his father's death, Earl of Arundel. From him, by we know not what course of conveyance, this grant, which formed the Province of Carolana (not Carolina), came into the hands of Dr. Daniel Coxe, who was, in the opinion of the attorney-general of England, true owner of that Province in the year of D'Iberville's discovery, 1699.*

In support of the English claim, thus originating, we are told by Dr. Coxe, that, from the year 1654 to the year 1664, one "Colonel Wood in Virginia, inhabiting at the Falls of James River, above a hundred miles west of Chesapeake Bay, discovered at several times, several branches of the great rivers, Ohio and Meschasebe." Nay, the Doctor affirms, that he had himself possessed, in past days, the Journal of a Mr. Needham, who was in the Colonel's employ, which Journal, he adds, "is now in the hands of," &c. The Doctor also states, that about the year 1676, he had in his keeping a Journal, written by some one who had gone from the mouth of the Mississippi, up as far as the Yellow or Muddy River, otherwise called Missouri; and he says, this Journal, in almost every particular, was confirmed by the late travels. And still further, Dr. Coxe assures us, that, in 1678, "a considerable number of persons went from New England upon discovery, and proceeded so far as New

---

* *A Description of the English Province of Carolana*, &c., by Daniel Coxe, Esquire. London, 1722. pp. 113, *et seq.*

Mexico, one hundred and fifty leagues beyond the river Meschasebe, and, at their return, rendered an account to the government at Boston;" for the truth of all which he calls Governor Dudley, who was still living, as witness. Nor had he been idle himself; "apprehending that the planting of this country would be highly beneficial," he tried to reach it first from Carolina, then from "Pensilvania, by the Susquehannah river," and "many of his people travelled to New Mexico." He had also made discoveries through the great river Ochequiton, or, as we call it, Alabama; and "more to the northwest, beyond the river Meschasebe," had found a "very great sea of fresh water, several thousand miles in circumference," whence a river ran into the South Sea, about the latitude of forty-four degrees, and "through this," he adds, "we are assured the English have since entered that great lake."

These various statements are, it must be owned, somewhat startling; but, leaving them undisturbed for the present, we can see clearly the bearing of what follows, namely, that the Doctor, in 1698, fitted out two vessels, well armed and manned, one of which (when, we hear not) entered the Mississippi and ascended it above one hundred miles, and then returned,—wherefore, is not specially stated. This was, doubtless, the corvette which M. Bienville turned out of what he considered French domains; as Charlevoix tells us, that the vessel, which Bienville met, was one of two which left England in 1698, armed with thirty-six guns, the same number which Daniel Coxe, the Doctor's son, tells us, were borne by his father's vessels. The English, having thus found their way to the Meschasebe, wished to prosecute the matter, and it was proposed to make there a settlement of the French Huguenots, who had fled to Carolina; but the death of Lord Lonsdale, the chief forwarder of the scheme, put an end to that plan, and we do not learn from Coxe, whose work appeared in 1722, that any further attempts were made by England, whose wars and woes nearer home kept her fully employed.

And now, what are we to say to those bold statements by Coxe; statements contained in his memorial to the King in 1699, and such as could hardly, one would think, be tales *à la Hontan?* Colonel Wood's adventures are recorded by no other writer, so far as we have read; for, though Hutchins, who was geographer to the United States when the western lands were first surveyed, refers to Wood, and also to one Captain Bolt, who crossed the Alleghanies in 1670, his remarks are very vague, and he gives us no one to look to, as knowing the circumstances. Of the Boston expedition we know still less; the story is repeated from Coxe by various pamphlet writers of those days, when Law's scheme had waked up England to a very decided interest in the West; but all examinations of contemporary writers, and the town records, have as yet failed to lend a single fact in support of this part of the Doctor's tale.

But what makes us suspect the whole, is his account of discoveries to the northwest which were never made, and which account, in all probability, was taken direct from the author of the Long River. We must own, therefore, that we are disposed to doubt all Dr. Coxe's statement relative to English travellers upon the Mississippi, and to think that he was guided and spurred on, in his undertaking of 1698, by the two spurious narratives of Hennepin and Tonti, published in 1697.

Resuming our sketch of French endeavours, we have next to record the project of our friend D'Iberville to found a city among the Natchez, which nation he visited in 1700, — a city to be named, in honor of the Countess of Pontchartrain, *Rosalie.* Indeed, he did pretend to lay the corner-stone of such a place, though it was not till 1714 that the fort called *Rosalie* was founded, where the city of Natchez is standing at this day.

Having thus built a fort at the mouth of the Great River, and begun a settlement upon a choice spot above, D'Iberville once more sought Europe, having, before he left, ordered M. Le Sueur to go up the Mississippi in search of a copper mine, which that personage had previously got a clue to, upon a branch of the St. Peter's river;* which order was fulfilled, and much metal obtained, though at the cost of great suffering. Mining was always a Jack-a-lantern with the first settlers of America, and our French friends were no wiser than their neighbours. The products of the soil were, indeed, scarce thought valuable on a large scale, it being supposed that the wealth of Louisiana consisted in its pearl-fishery, its mines, and the wool of its wild cattle.† In 1701 the commander came again, and began a new establishment upon the river Maubile, one which superseded that at Biloxi, which thus far had been the chief fort in that southern colony. After this, things went on but slowly until 1708; D'Iberville died on one of his voyages between the mother country and her sickly daughter, and after his death little was done. In 1708, however, M. D'Artagnette came from France as commissary of Louisiana, and, being a man of spirit and energy, did more for it than had been done before. But it still lingered; and, under the impression that a private man of property might do more for it than the government could, the King, upon the 14th of September, 1712, granted to Crozat, a man of great wealth, the monopoly of Louisiana for fifteen years, and the absolute ownership of whatever mines he might cause to be opened.

Crozat relied mainly upon two things for success in his speculation; the one, the discovery of mines; the other, a lucrative trade with New Mexico. In regard to the first,

---

* Charlevoix, Vol. IV. pp. 162, 164. In Long's *Second Expedition*, p. 318, may be seen a detailed account of Le Sueur's proceedings, taken from a manuscript statement of them.

† Charlevoix, Vol. III. p. 389.

after many years' labor, he was entirely disappointed; and met with no better success in his attempt to open a trade with the Spaniards, although he sent to them both by sea and land.

His agent in the land enterprise was the Sieur Juchereau, probably the same that tried with Mermet to colonize and convert the Mascoutens. He, with great labor and hazard, found his way to the Viceroy of Mexico, who dwelt in the city of that name; but, no sooner had he presented himself to the Spanish grandee, than he was seized and cast into prison, where he lay three months. At length, some French officers, who were in the Spanish service, prevailed upon the Viceroy to let him come into free air again; and, as he was thrown into the company of that personage, the Spaniard's heart was touched by the noble and honest character of the Sieur Juchereau, and he took him kindly by the hand, and made him eat at his own table. As they thus came closer in contact, the Spaniard ever found the more to love and admire in his prisoner. He began to try to persuade him to leave the French service, and remain where he was; and the French officers added their persuasions. It was no slight temptation to a man like the Sieur Juchereau, without property or prospect; but he was a true man, and declined all offers. "Well," said the Spaniard, when all other argument failed, "are you not already half Spanish? Do you not love a Spanish maiden at Fort St. Jean? Will not the hope of gaining her hand win you over?" "I cannot deny," answered the gallant Frenchman, "that I love the damsel, though I have no hope of winning her." "But you shall win her," said the Viceroy. "Hearken! for two months you may think of my offer; then join us, and you shall be wedded to the lady of your love, and made an officer in our ranks." The two months slowly pass; and now how is it with our Sieur Juchereau? "I cannot desert my king," is his constant answer. The Viceroy, more touched than ever, gives him his liberty; places in his hands a purse with a thousand piastres in it, "to defray," he said, "his wedding expenses, for he still hoped Doña Maria would persuade him;" and, with a firm and melancholy face, the Frenchman turns northward.

A few days' travel brings him to the Fort St. Jean, where he finds Don Pedro de Velascas, the father of the damsel, plunged in grief, because certain of the Indian tribes within his jurisdiction had determined to remove elsewhere, which he knew would call down upon him the anger of his superiors, and probably cost him his life. Juchereau, hearing how things stood, offered his services, to go to the savages, and try to persuade them to stay. "But they will kill you!" cries the astonished Don Pedro. "I have no fear," replies the Sieur; and on the morrow, with his friend Jallot, a surgeon, he mounts and seeks the red men, who had already left their old homes. On their swift horses, the fearless Frenchmen make rapid progress, and soon overtake the moving multitude; and, with his white handkerchief held aloft as a flag of friendship, the Sieur asks a conference with the chiefs. Long skilled in Indian ways, and, above all, true as the sun, he soon persuades the wild men that they are acting unwisely; he appeals to their love of their old homes; paints the dangers of the course they are taking; and guarantees them good treatment, if they will but go back. The chiefs consult, hesitate, listen, and consult again; and the next day, Don Pedro, looking anxiously abroad, sees the two Europeans return with all the Indians at their back. And now was Doña Maria won indeed; not by battle, but by peace-making; and soon the little Spanish frontier town was all astir to celebrate the nuptials of the fair daughter of its governor, and her true Christian knight.*

But, happy as the Sieur Juchereau's mission had been for

---

* Charlevoix, Vol. IV. p. 170.

himself, it had done nothing for his employers; for the Viceroy's last words had been, "I can allow no trade between Mexico and Louisiana." Crozat, therefore, being disappointed in his mines and his trade, and having, withal, managed so badly as to diminish the colony, at last, in 1717, resigned his privileges to the King again. Then was formed Law's famous West India Company, who sent out settlers in 1717 and 1718, in one of which years New Orleans was laid out.* This company was to have had a monopoly of the commerce of the Mississippi for twenty-five years; but, at the end of fourteen, they were very glad to resign to the King in their turn. During these years, the history of Louisiana is mostly a detail of quarrels with Spaniards, English, Choctaws, and Natchez; all which we have not room to write here, even if we had the inclination. It may be found in the work of Du Pratz, who was an eminent man in the colony, from 1718 to 1734, or in the pages of Charlevoix. Passing by the battles and conspiracies of these times, and of the next nineteen years, we leave our imperfect sketch at the middle of the century, as then began a new era, the struggle of the French and British for the region beyond the Alleghanies.

In 1749, there were no other French settlements in the West, than those upon the Illinois, already referred to; that at New Orleans, including its various dependences, where, according to Vivier, were twelve hundred persons; and some small posts among the Arkansas and Alibamons.

In closing, we cannot but express a hope, that some of our Historical Societies will reprint from Thevenot the original French *Journal* of Marquette, from the Paris edition of 1683 (if it can be had); Hennepin's *Louisiana;* Joutel's *Journal* (from the French, if it can be found, if not, from the English); the most interesting of the *Lettres Edifiantes*

* Charlevoix, Vol. IV. p. 196, says, 1717; Du Pratz says, 1718.

relating to the West; and any other valuable original accounts now extant; — together with lithographic fac-similes of the map of 1656; of that of 1660, in Du Creux's work on Canada (*Hist. Canadensis*, *a* P. F. Creuxio; Paris, 1664); of Marquette's; of Hennepin's, of 1683; of Joutel's; of Coxe's, and Charlevoix's. We would also suggest the appointment of committees to examine and report upon works of doubtful authenticity, such as Hennepin's *New Discovery*, Tonti's *Journal*, and La Hontan's *Account of the Long River;* thus placing, in an accessible and permanent form, what, in our pages, must soon pass out of view, even supposing our researches and hints to be of value to the historical reader.

VI.

ENGLISH DISCOVERIES IN THE OHIO VALLEY.*

It is not our purpose to review the Journal of the old traveller in the Northwest, though it is curious and interesting; but to give within the proper limits, an outline of the history of the Ohio valley from 1744 to 1774, a period which has been generally despatched in two pages, but might, if well explored, fill a volume. In our last number but one, we sketched, with a few rapid strokes, the progress of French discovery in the valley of the Mississippi. The first travellers reached that river in 1673, and when the new year of 1750 broke upon the great wilderness of the West, all was still a wilderness, except those little spots upon the prairies of Illinois, and among the marshes of Louisiana, of which we gave a list in that sketch. It is true, that some have told us that St. Vincent's, or Vincennes, upon the Wabash, was settled before the middle of the last century. Volney thought

* 1. *Travels through the Interior Parts of North America, in the Years* 1766, 1767, *and* 1768. By J. Carver, Esquire, Captain of a Company of Provincial Troops, during the late War with France. The third Edition. To which is added, some Account of the Author, and a Copious Index. London: printed for C. Dilly, H. Paine, and J. Phelps. 1780.

2. Carver's *Travels in Wisconsin.* From the Third London Edition. New York: Harper & Brothers. 1838.

From the North American Review, for July, 1839.

he found evidence of its settlement in 1735,* and Bishop Bruté, the present Catholic bishop of Indiana, speaks of a missionary station at Vincennes in 1700, and of the death of a M. de Vincennes, who was sent to protect the post, in 1735.† We cannot, however, discover any early authority to support the traveller or the bishop. Charlevoix, whose History comes down to about 1735, makes no mention either in that, or in his Journal, of any such missionary station as that referred to by Bishop Bruté, nor is any point upon his map of the Wabash marked as a settlement; and the M. de Vincennes whose death he mentions, was killed at the South. Vivier, who names the settlements of the West in 1750, says nothing of Vincennes, although he was giving to his religious superiors an account of the missionary stations.‡ In a volume of *Mémoires* on Louisiana, compiled from the minutes of M. Dumont, and published in Paris in 1753, but probably written in 1749, though we have an account of the Wabash or St. Jerome, its course and origin, and the use made of it by the traders, not a word is found touching any fort, settlement, or station on it; § and Vaudreuil, then governor of Louisiana, and afterwards of Canada, as quoted by Pownall, mentions, even in 1751, Fort Massac upon the Ohio, and Fort Miamis on the Maumee, but says nothing of a post on the Wabash.|| Nor is this negative evidence all; for, in a pamphlet published in London in 1755, called "The Present State of North America," which is accompanied with a map giving all the French forts and stations, we have a particular account of the settlement of Vincennes.

---

* Volney's *View*, p. 336.

† Butler's *Kentucky*. Intro. xviii. Note. 2d edition.

‡ *North American Review*, Vol. XLVIII. p. 98.

§ *Mémoires Historiques sur la Louisiane*, &c. &c.

|| Pownall's *Memorial on Service in North America*, &c., drawn up in 1756. It forms an Appendix to his "Administration of the Colonies;" 4th edition. London. 1768.

This work states, that in 1750 a fort was founded there, and that in 1754, three hundred families were sent to settle about it.*

In 1749, therefore, when the English first began to move seriously about sending men into the West, there were, we think, only the Illinois and lower country settlements; the present States of Ohio, Indiana, and Kentucky, being still in the possession of the Indians, though forts may have been founded at Sandusky and the mouth of the Maumee.

Having seen on what the French claim to the West rested, namely, discovery and occupancy; we now, before proceeding to the quarrel which arose for the possession of that Eden-like land, shall give, as well as we can, the grounds of the British claims to it.

---

* *Present State of North America*, p. 65. — See this settlement referred to by Governor Morris of Pennsylvania, 1754, in Sparks's *Franklin*, Vol. III. page 285.

The French forts mentioned in this work as north of the Ohio, were,

Two on French Creek (Rivière des Bœufs).
Du Quesne.
Sandusky.
Miamis on Maumee.
St. Joseph's on the St. Joseph's of Lake Michigan.
Pontchartrain at Detroit.
Missilimacanac.
Fox River of Green Bay.
Crèvecœur, } on the Illinois.
Rock Fort, or Fort St. Louis, } on the Illinois.
Vincennes.
Mouth of the Wabash.
Cahokia.
Kaskaskia.
Mouth of the Ohio.
Mouth of the Missouri.

At the mouth of the Scioto (called in the work just named, the "Sikoder") the French had a post during the war of 1756; see Rogers's *Journal*, London, 1765; Post's *Journal* in Proud's *Pennsylvania*, Vol. II. App. p. 117.

England, from the outset, claimed from the Atlantic to the Pacific, on the ground that the discovery and possession of the seacoast was a discovery and possession of the country; and, as is well known, her grants to Virginia, Connecticut, and other colonies were through to the South sea. It was not upon this, however, that Great Britain relied in her contest with France; she had other grounds, namely, actual discovery, and purchase or title of some kind from the Indian owners.

Her claim on the score of actual discovery was poorly supported, and little insisted on; the statements given by Coxe, as to Colonel Wood and others, will be found in our last volume.* Beside those, we have it from tradition, that in 1742, John Howard crossed the mountains from Virginia, sailed in a canoe made of a buffalo skin down the Ohio, and was taken by the French on the Mississippi; † and this tradition is confirmed by a note, contained in a London edition of Du Pratz, printed in 1774, in which the same facts as to Howard are substantially given as being taken from the official report of the Governor of Virginia, at the time of his expedition. But this expedition by Howard, even if true, could give England no claim to the West, for he made no settlement, and the whole Ohio valley had doubtless long before been explored by the French traders; it is, however, worthy of remembrance, as the earliest visit by an Englishman to the West, which can be considered as distinctly authenticated. Soon after that time, traders undoubtedly began to flock thither from Pennsylvania and Virginia. In 1748, Conrad Weiser, an interpreter, was sent from Philadelphia with presents to the Indians at Logstown, an Indian town upon the Ohio, between Pittsburg and the Big Beaver creek, and we find the residence of English traders

---

* Vol. XLVIII. pp. 103, 104.

† Kercheval's *Valley of Virginia*, p. 67.

in that neighbourhood referred to as of some standing, even then.*

But the great ground whereon the English claimed dominion beyond the Alleghanies, was, that the Six Nations † owned the Ohio valley, and had placed it, with their other lands, under the protection of England. As early as 1684, Lord Howard, governor of Virginia, held a treaty with the Six Nations, at Albany, when, at the request of Colonel Dungan, the governor of New York, they placed themselves under the protection of the mother country.‡ This was again

---

* Butler's *History of Kentucky*, Vol. I. 2d edition (Introd. xx.), gives the adventures of one Salling in the West, as early as 1730; but his authority is a late work (*Chronicles of Border Warfare*), and the account is merely traditional, we presume; Salling is named in the note to Du Pratz, as having been with Howard in 1742. There are various vague accounts of English in the West, before Howard's voyage. Keating, in Long's *Expedition*, speaks of a Colonel Wood, who had been there, beside the one mentioned by Coxe. In a work called "The Contest in America between England and America. By an Impartial Hand. London, 1757," we find it stated, that the Indians at Albany, in 1754, acknowledged that the English had been on the Ohio for *thirty* years. And in a memorial by the British ministry, in 1755, they speak of the West as having been cultivated by England for "*above twenty years*." (Sparks's *Franklin*, Vol. IV. p. 330.

† When we first hear of the great northern confederacy, there were five tribes in it; namely, Mohawks, Oneidas, Onondagas, Cayugas, and Senecas. Afterwards the Tuscaroras were conquered and taken into the confederacy, and it became *the Six Nations*. Still later, the Nanticokes and Tuteloes came into the union, which was, however, still called *the Six Nations*, though sometimes *the Eight United Nations*. This confederacy was by the French called the "Iroquois," by the Dutch "Maquas," by the other Indians "Mengive," and thence, by the English, "Mingoes." These varied names have produced countless errors and endless confusion. Thus, on the first page of Butler's *History*, we are told of the *Iroquois or Mohawks;* and the Mingoes of the Ohio are almost always spoken of as a tribe. We have used the terms "Six Nations," and "Iroquois," and now and then "Mingoes," always meaning the whole confederacy.

‡ *Plain Facts*, &c., Philadelphia, 1781, pp. 22, 23.

done in 1701; and upon the 14th of September, 1726, a formal deed was drawn up, and signed by the chiefs, by which their lands were conveyed to England, in trust, "to be protected and defended by his Majesty, to and for the use of the grantors and their heirs." * If, then, the Six Nations had a good claim to the western country, there could be little doubt that England was justified in defending that country against the French; particularly as France, by the treaty of Utrecht, had agreed not to invade the lands of Britain's Indian allies, or something to that effect.† But this claim of the New York savages has been disputed. Very lately, General William H. Harrison has attempted to disprove it, and show, that the Miami confederacy of Illinois and Ohio could not have been conquered by the Iroquois.‡ We shall not, at present, enter into the controversy; but will only say, that to us the evidence is very strong, that, before 1680, the Six Nations had overrun the western lands, and were dreaded from Lake Michigan to the Ohio, and west to the Mississippi. In 1673, Allouez and Dablon found the Miamis upon Lake Michigan, fearing a visit from the Iroquois; § and from this time forward we hear of them in that far land from all writers, genuine and spurious. || We cannot doubt, therefore, that they did overrun the lands claimed by them, and even planted colonies in what is now Ohio; but that they had any claim, which a Christian nation should have recognized, to most of the territory in question, we cannot for a moment think, as for half a century at least it had been under the rule of other tribes, and, when the differences between France and England began, was, with the exception of the lands just above

---

* This may be found at length in Pownall's *Administration of the Colonies*, 4th edition, London, 1768, p. 269.

† Sparks's *Franklin*, Vol. IV. p. 329.

‡ See Harrison's *Historical Address*, 1837.

§ Charlevoix, Vol. II. Paris ed., 1744, p. 252.

|| See Charlevoix, La Hontan, Hennepin, Tonti, &c.

the head of the Ohio, the place of residence and the hunting-ground of other tribes.*

But some of the western lands were also claimed by the British, as having been actually purchased. This purchase was said to have been made at Lancaster, Pennsylvania, in 1744, when a treaty was held between the colonists and the Six Nations relative to some alleged settlements that had been made upon the Indian lands in Pennsylvania, Virginia, and Maryland; and to this treaty we now turn, — thankful that we have a very good and graphic account of it, written by Witham Marshe, who went as secretary with the commissioners for Maryland, and from whom we draw largely in illustration of the times, and the mode of treating with the Indians.

After many days' journey, diversified with villanous bacon and eggs, and fine tongues and hams, "sorry rum and water, called *bumbo*," and generous wine, the Maryland commissioners reached Lancaster upon the 21st of June, before either the governor of Pennsylvania, the Virginia commissioners, or the Indians had arrived; though all but the natives came that evening. Having got a good dinner, "to their great comfort," and engaged beds, they went out to look at the town, which had then been settled about sixteen years. They found it well laid out, but very dirty, and inhabited by a mixture of Dutch, Scotch, Irish, English, and Israelites. Most of the houses were of wood, two stories high, and much as they are now, but dirtier. The water was bad, and in dry weather the air was hot and dusty; and before the houses were heaps of dirt filled with vermin. The market was good, and provisions "prodigiously cheap." It being summer, the commissioners suffered much from the "Dutch fleas," and

* "In 1744, when the Lancaster treaty was held with the Six Nations, some of their number were making war upon the Catawbas." — *Marshe's Journal*, Mass. Hist. Coll., Vol. VII. pp. 190, 191.

their auxillaries; so much, indeed, that many preferred the court-house floor.

The next forenoon wore wearily away, and all were glad to sit down, at one o'clock, to a dinner in the court-house, which the Virginians gave their friends, and from which not many were drawn, even by the coming of the Indians, who came, to the number of two hundred and fifty-two, with squaws and little children on horseback, and with their fire-arms, and bows, and arrows, and tomahawks, and, as they passed the court-house, invited the white men with a song to renew their former treaties. On the outskirts of the town, vacant lots had been chosen for the savages to build their wigwams upon, and thither they marched on with Conrad Weiser, their friend and interpreter,* while the Virginians "drank the loyal healths," and finished their entertainment. After dinner they went out to look at their dark allies, who had few shirts among them, and those black from wear, and who were very ragged and shabby; at all which the well-clad and high-fed colonists bit their lips, but feared to laugh. That afternoon the chiefs and commissioners met at the court-house, "shaked hands," smoked a pipe, and drank "a good quantity of wine and punch." The next day, being Saturday, the English went "to the Dunkers' nunnery," and the Indians drank, and danced, and shrieked. Monday, the speaking began, to the satisfaction of all parties, and ended merrily with dancing, and music, and a great supper. On Tuesday and Wednesday, also, speeches were made, varied by dances, in which appeared some very disagreeable women, who "danced wilder time than any Indians." On Thursday the goods were opened, wherewith the Maryland people wished to buy the Indian claim to the lands on which settlements had been made. These goods were narrowly

---

* For some idea of Weiser, see Proud's *History of Pennsylvania*, Vol. II. p. 316, where a long letter by him is given.

scanned by the red men, but at last taken for £220 Pennsylvania money, after which they drank punch. Friday, the Six Nations agreed to the grant desired by the Marylanders, and punch was drunk again; and, on Saturday, a dinner was given to the chiefs, "at which," says Marshe, "they fed lustily, drank heartily, and were very greasy before they finished." At this dinner, the Indians bestowed on the governor of Maryland the name of Tocaryhogon, meaning "Living in the honorable place." After this came much drinking, and when that had gone forward some time, the Indians were called on to sign the deed which had been drawn up, and the English again "put about the glass pretty briskly." Next, the commissioners from Virginia, supported by a due quantity of wine and bumbo, held their conference with the Indians, and received from them "a deed releasing their claim to a large quantity of land lying in that colony;" and upon this it was that a claim to the western lands was founded, as we learn from the pamphlet called "Plain Facts," for Marshe gives us no particulars. From this pamphlet* it would seem, that the Indians were persuaded to give a deed "recognizing the King's right to all lands that are, *or by his Majesty's appointment shall be*, within the colony of Virginia." For this they received £200 in gold, and a like sum in goods, with a promise that, as settlements increased, more should be paid, which promise was signed and sealed. We need make no comment upon this deed, nor speculate upon the probable amount of bumbo which produced it. The commissioners from Virginia, at

* "*Plain Facts, being an Examination, &c., and a Vindication of the Grant from the Six United Nations of Indians to the Proprietors of Indiana* vs. *the Decision of the Legislature of Virginia.* pp. 29-39. Philadelphia: R. Aitken. 1781. See also Sparks's *Washington*, Vol. II. p. 480. — As a general rule we have little faith in party pamphlets; but the one just quoted, so far as we can judge, is accurate as to its main facts.

this treaty of Lancaster, were Colonel Thomas Lee and Colonel William Beverly.*

On the 5th of July, every thing having been settled satisfactorily, the commissioners left "the filthy town" of Lancaster, and took their homeward way, having suffered much from the vermin and the water, though when they used the latter would be a curious inquiry.

Such was the treaty of Lancaster, upon which, as a corner-stone, the claim of the colonists to the West, by purchase, rested; and upon this, and the grant from the Six Nations, Great Britain relied in all subsequent steps.

As settlements extended, and the Indians murmured, the promise of further pay was called to mind, and Wieser was sent across the Alleghanies to Logstown, in 1748,† with presents, to keep the Indians in good humor; and also to sound them, probably, as to their feeling with regard to large settlements in the West, which some Virginians, with Colonel Thomas Lee, the Lancaster commissioner, at their head, were then contemplating.‡ The object of these proposed settlements was not the cultivation of the soil, but the monopoly of the Indian trade, which, with all its profits, had till that time been in the hands of unprincipled men, half civilized, half savage, who penetrated to the lakes of Canada and competed everywhere with the French for skins and furs; three such "impudent Indian traders" as once took possession of our Secretary Marshe's bed at Lancaster, and were with difficulty driven out. It was now proposed in Virginia

---

* Marshe's *Journal*. † *Plain Facts*, pp. 40, 119, 120.

‡ Sparks's *Washington*, Vol. II. p. 478. Scarce any thing was known of the old Ohio Company, until Mr. Sparks's inquiries led to the note referred to; and even now so little is known, that we cannot but hope some Historical Society will prevail on Mr. Mercer of Virginia, who holds the papers of that Company, to allow their publication. No full history of the West can be written, until the facts relative to the great land companies are better known.

to turn these fellows out of their good berth beyond the mountains, by means of a great company, which should hold lands and build trading-houses, import European goods regularly and export the furs of the West in return to London. Accordingly, after Weiser's conference with the Indians at Logstown, which was favorable to their views, Thomas Lee, with twelve other Virginians, among whom were Lawrence and Augustine, brothers of George Washington, and also Mr. Hanbury of London, formed an association which they called the "Ohio Company," and in 1748, petitioned the King for a grant beyond the mountains. This petition was approved by the monarch, and the government of Virginia was ordered to grant to the petitioners half a million of acres within the bounds of that colony, beyond the Alleghanies, two hundred thousand of which were to be located at once. This portion was to be held for ten years free of quitrent, provided the company would put there one hundred families within seven years, and build a fort sufficient to protect the settlement; all which the company proposed, and prepared to do at once, and sent to London for a cargo suited to the Indian trade, which was to come out so as to arrive in November, 1749.

But the French were not blind all this while. They saw, that, if the British once obtained a strong-hold upon the Ohio, they might not only prevent their settlements upon it, but must at last come upon their lower posts, and so the battle be fought sooner or later. To the danger of the English possessions in the West, Vaudreuil, the French governor, had been long alive. Upon the 10th of May, 1744, he wrote home representing the consequences that must come from allowing the British to build a trading-house among the Creeks;* and, in November, 1748, he anticipated their seiz-

* Pownall's *Memorial on Service in America*, as before quoted. Vaudreuil came out as Governor of Canada in 1755. — *Massachusetts Historical Collections*, Vol. VII. p. 105. See also Holmes's *Annals*, Vol. II. p. 23.

ure of Fort Prudhomme, which was upon the Mississippi below the Ohio.* Nor was it for mere sickly missionary stations that the governor feared; for, in the year last-named, the Illinois settlements, few as they were, sent flour and corn, the hams of hogs and bears, pickled pork and beef, myrtle-wax, cotton, tallow, leather, tobacco, lead, iron, copper, some little buffalo wool, venison, poultry, bear's grease, oil, skins, and coarse furs, to the New Orleans market. Even in 1746, from five to six hundred barrels of flour went thither from Illinois, convoys annually going down in December with the produce.† Having these fears, and seeing the danger of the late movements of the British Gallisonière, then governor of Canada, determined to place, along the Ohio, evidences of the French claim to, and possession of, the country; and for that purpose, in the summer of 1749, sent Louis Celeron, with a party of soldiers, to place plates of lead, on which were written out the claims of France, in the mounds, and at the mouths of the rivers.‡ Of this act, William Trent, who was sent out in 1752 by Virginia, to conciliate the Indians, heard while upon the Ohio, and mentioned it in his Journal; and within a few years, one of the plates, with the inscription partially defaced has been found near the mouth of the Muskingum. Of this plate, the date upon which is August 16th, 1749, a particular account was sent, by De Witt Clinton, to the American Antiquarian Society, in whose second volume (p. 535-541) the inscription may be found at length. By this step, the French, perhaps, hoped to quiet

* Pownall's *Memorial*. † Ibid.

‡ Sparks's *Washington*, Vol. II. p. 430. — Atwater's *History of Ohio*, 1st edition, p. 109. — *Transactions of the American Antiquarian Society*, Vol. II. pp. 535-541. De Witt Clinton received the plate mentioned in the text from Mr. Atwater, who says it was found at the mouth of the Muskingum, though marked as having been placed at the mouth of Venango (Tenangue) river (French Creek, we presume).

the title to the river "Oyo"; but it produced not the least result. In that very year, we are told, a trading-house was built by the English upon the great Miami, at the spot since called Loramie's Store;* while, from another source we learn, that two traders were, in 1749, seized by the French upon the Maumee. At any rate, the storm was gathering; the English company was determined to carry out its plan, and the French were determined to oppose them.

During 1750, we hear of no step, by either party; but in February, 1751, we find Christopher Gist, the agent who had been appointed by the Ohio Company to examine the western lands, upon a visit to the Twigtwees or Tuigtuis, who lived upon the Miami River, one hundred and fifty miles from its mouth.† In speaking of this tribe, Mr. Gist says nothing of a trading-house among them (at least in the passage from his Journal quoted by Mr. Sparks), but he tells us, they left the Wabash for the sake of trading with the English; and we have no doubt, that the spot which he visited was at the mouth of Loramie's Creek, where, as we have said, a trading-house was built about or before this time. Gist says, the Twigtwees were a very numerous people, much superior to the Six Nations, and that they were formerly in the French interest. Wynne speaks of them as the same with the Ottawas; but Gist undoubtedly meant the great Miamis confederacy; for he says, that they are not one tribe, but "many different tribes, under the same form of government."‡ Upon this journey Gist went as far down the Ohio

---

* *Contest in America, by an Impartial Hand.* Once this writer speaks of this post as upon the Wabash, but he doubtless meant that on the Miami.

† Sparks's *Washington*, Vol. II. p. 37.

‡ See Harrison's *Discourse*, already quoted. — Franklin (Sparks's *Franklin*, Vol. IV. p. 71) speaks of the Piankeshaws, a tribe of the Twigtwees; and again, of the Miamis or Twigtwees (Ibid., Vol. III. p. 72).

as the Falls, and was gone seven months, though the particulars of his tour are still unknown to us; his journal, with the exception of one or two passages published by Mr. Sparks, still resting in manuscript.

Having thus generally examined the land upon the Ohio, in November Gist commenced a thorough survey of the tract south of the Ohio and east of the Kanawha, which was that on which the Ohio Company proposed to make their first settlement. He spent the winter in that labor. Meanwhile no treaty of a definite character had yet been held with the western Indians; and, as the influence both of the French and of the independent English traders, was against the company, it was thought necessary to do something, and the Virginia government was desired to invite the chiefs to a conference at Logstown, which was done.

All this time the French had not been idle. They not only stirred up the savages, but took measures to fortify certain points on the upper waters of the Ohio, from which all lower posts might be easily attacked, and, beginning at Presqu'Ile, or Erie, on the lake, prepared a line of communication with the Alleghany. This was done by opening a wagon-road from Erie to a little lake lying at the head of French Creek, where a second fort was built, about fifteen miles from that at Erie. When this second fort was fortified we do not clearly learn; but some time in 1752, we believe.* But lest, while these little castles were quietly rising amid the forest, the British also might strengthen themselves too securely to be dislodged, a party of soldiers was sent to keep the Ohio clear; and this party, early in 1752, having heard of the trading-house upon the Miamis, and, very likely, of the visit to it by Gist, came to the

* Washington's *Journal*, of 1753. — Mante, in his *History of the War*, says, early in 1753; but there was a post at Erie when the traders were taken, before June, 1752.

Twigtwees and demanded the traders, as unauthorized intruders upon French lands. The Twigtwees, however, were neither cowards nor traitors, and refused to deliver up their friends.* The French then attacked the trading-house, which was probably a block-house, and, after a severe battle, in which fourteen of the natives were killed, and others wounded, took and destroyed it, carrying the traders away to Canada as prisoners, or, as one account says, burning some of them alive. This fort, or trading-house, was called by the English writers Pickawillany.†

Such was the fate of the first British settlement in the Ohio valley, of which we have any record. It was destroyed early in 1752, as we know by the fact, that its destruction was referred to by the Indians at the Logstown treaty in June. What traders they were who were taken, we do not know with certainty. Some have thought them agents of the Ohio Company; but Gist's proceedings about the Kenhawa do not favor the idea, neither do the subsequent steps of the company; and in the "History of Pennsylvania," ascribed to Franklin, we find a gift of condolence made by that Province to the Twigtwees for those slain in defence of the traders among them, in 1752, which leads us to believe that they were independent merchants from that colony. Blood had now been shed, and both parties became more deeply interested in the progress of events in the West.

---

* Sparks's *Franklin*, Vol. IV. p. 71. — Vol. III. p. 230. — *Plain Facts*, p. 42. — *Contest in North America*, &c., p. 36. — *Western Monthly Magazine*, 1833. — This fort was always referred to in the early treaties of the United States with the Indians; see *Land Laws*. — Several other captures beside this are referred to by Franklin and others. The attack on Logstown, spoken of by Smollett and Russell, was doubtless this attack on the Miamis post. Smollett, *George II.*, Chap. IX. See also Burk's *Virginia*, Vol. III. p. 170.

† A memorial of the King's ministers, in 1755, refers to it as "Pickawillanes, in the centre of the territory between the Ohio and the Wabash." — Sparks's *Franklin*, Vol. IV. p. 330.

The English, on their part, determined to purchase from the Indians a title to the lands they wished to occupy, by fair means or foul; and, in the spring of 1752, Messrs. Fry, Lomax, and Patton were sent from Virginia to hold a conference with the natives at Logstown, learn what they objected to in the treaty of Lancaster, of which it was said they complained, and settle all difficulties.* On the 9th of June, the commissioners met the red men at Logstown: this was a little village, seventeen miles and a half below Pittsburg, upon the north side of the Ohio.† It had long been a trading-point, but had been abandoned by the Indians in 1750.‡ Here the Lancaster treaty was produced, and the sale of the western lands insisted upon; but the chiefs said, "No; they had not heard of any sale west of the warrior's road, which ran at the foot of the Alleghany ridge." The commissioners then offered goods for a ratification of the Lancaster treaty; spoke of the proposed settlement by the Ohio Company; and used all their persuasions to secure the land wanted. Upon the 11th of June, the Indians replied. They recognized the treaty of Lancaster, and the authority of the Six Nations to make it, but denied that they had any knowledge of the western lands being conveyed to the English by said deed; and declined, upon the whole, having any thing to do with the treaty of 1744. "However," said the savages, "as the French have already struck the Twigtwees, we shall be pleased to have your assistance and protection, and wish you would build a fort at once at

---

* *Plain Facts*, p. 40. — Sparks's *Washington*, Vol. II. p. 480.

† Croghan, in his *Journal* says, that Logstown was *south* of the Ohio. (Butler's *Kentucky*, App.) The river is itself nearly north and south at the spot in question; but we always call the Canada side the north side, having reference to the general direction of the stream.

‡ Bouquet's *Expedition*. London, 1766. p. 10. — Logstown is given on the map accompanying this volume.

the Fork of the Ohio."* But this permission was not what the Virginians wanted; so they took aside Montour, the interpreter, who was a son of the famous Catherine Montour,† and a chief among the Six Nations, being three fourths of Indian blood, and persuaded him by valid arguments (of the kind which an Indian most appreciates, doubtless), to use his influence with his fellows. This he did; and, upon the 13th of June, they all united in signing a deed confirming the Lancaster treaty *in its full extent*, consenting to a settlement southeast of the Ohio, and guaranteeing that it should not be disturbed by them.‡ By such means was obtained the first treaty with the Indians in the Ohio valley.

All this time the two powers beyond the Atlantic were in a professed state "of profound peace"; and commissioners were at Paris trying to out-manœuvre one another with regard to some of the disputed lands in America,§ though in the West all looked like war. We have seen how the English outwitted the Indians, and secured themselves, as they thought, by their politic conduct. But the French, in this as in all cases, proved that they knew best how to manage the natives; and, though they had to contend with the old hatred felt toward them by the Six Nations, and though they by no means refrained from strong acts, marching

* *Plain Facts*, p. 42.

† For a sketch of this woman, see *Massachusetts Historical Collections*, First Series, Vol. VII. p. 189, or Stone's *Life of Brant*, Vol. I. p. 339. She had two sons, Andrew and Henry. The latter was a captain among the Iroquois, the former a common interpreter, apparently. Andrew was taken by the French in 1749. Which of them was at Logstown we are not told; but, from his influence with the Indians, it was probably Henry.

‡ *Plain Facts*, pp. 38–44. The Virginia commissioners were men of high character, but treated with the Indians according to the ideas of their day.

§ See Smollett, *George II.*, Chapters VIII. and IX.

through the midst of the Iroquois country, attacking the Twigtwees, and seizing the English traders, nevertheless they did succeed, as the British never did, in attaching the Indians to their cause. As an old chief of the Six Nations said at Easton, in 1758; "The Indians on the Ohio left you because of your own fault. When we heard the French were coming, we asked you for help and arms, but we did not get them. The French came, they treated us kindly, and gained our affections. The Governor of Virginia settled on our lands for his own benefit, and, when we wanted help, forsook us." *

So stood matters at the close of 1752. The English had secured (as they thought) a title to the Indian lands southeast of the Ohio, and Gist was at work laying out a town and fort there on Shurtees (Chartier's) Creek, about two miles below the Fork.† Eleven families also were crossing the mountains to settle at the point where Gist had fixed his own residence, west of Laurel Hill, and not far from the Youghiogany. Goods too had come from England for the Ohio Company, which, however, they could not well, and dared not, carry beyond Will's Creek, the point where Cumberland now stands, whence they were taken by the traders and Indians; and there was even some prospect of a road across the mountains to the Monongahela.

On the other hand, the French were gathering cannon and stores upon Lake Erie, and, without treaties or deeds for land, were gaining the good-will of even inimical tribes, and preparing, when all was ready, to strike the blow. Some of the savages, it is true, remonstrated. They said they did not understand this dispute between the Europeans, as to which of them the western lands belonged to, for they did

---

* *Plain Facts*, p. 55. —Pownall's *Memoir on Service in North America.*

† Sparks's *Washington*, Vol. II. pp. 433, 482, and map, p. 38.

not belong to either. But the French bullied when it served their turn, and flattered when it served their turn, and all the while went on with their preparations, which were in an advanced state early in 1753.*

In May of that year, the governor of Pennsylvania informed the Assembly of the French movements, a knowledge of which was derived, in part at least, from Montour, who had been present at a conference between the French and Indians relative to the invasion of the West.† The assembly thereupon voted six hundred pounds for distribution among the tribes, besides two hundred for the present of condolence to the Twigtwees, already mentioned. This money was not sent, but Conrad Weiser was despatched in August to learn how things stood among the Ohio savages.‡ Virginia was moving also. In June, or earlier, a commissioner was sent westward to meet the French, and ask how they dared invade his Majesty's province. This messenger went to Logstown, but was afraid to go up the Alleghany, as instructed.§ Trent was also sent out with guns, powder, shot, and clothing for the friendly Indians; and then it was, that he learned the fact already stated, as to the claim of the French, and their burial of medals in proof of it. While these measures were taken, another treaty with the wild men of the debatable land was also in contemplation; and in September, 1753, William Fairfax met their deputies at Winchester, Virginia, where he concluded a treaty, with the particulars of which we are unacquainted, but on which, we are told, was an indorsement, stating that such was their feeling, that *he had not dared to mention to them either the*

* See in Washington's *Journal* the Speech of Half-king to the French commander, and his answer. — Sparks's *Washington*, Vol. II. p. 431.

† Sparks's *Franklin*, Vol. III. p. 219.

‡ Ibid., p. 230.

§ Sparks's *Washington*, Vol. II. p. 430.

*Lancaster or the Logstown treaty;** a most sad comment upon the modes taken to obtain those grants.

Soon after this, no satisfaction being obtained from the Ohio, either as to the force, position, or purposes of the French, Robert Dinwiddie, then Governor of Virginia, determined to send to them another messenger, and selected a young surveyor, who, at the age of nineteen, had received the rank of major, and whose previous life had inured him to hardship and woodland ways, while his courage, cool judgment, and firm will, all fitted him for such a mission. This young man, as all know, was George Washington, who was twenty-one years and eight months old, at the time of the appointment.† With Gist as his guide, Washington left Will's Creek, where Cumberland now is, on the 15th of November, and, on the 22d, reached the Monongahela about ten miles above the Fork. Thence he went to Logstown, where he had conferences with the chiefs of the Six Nations living in that neighbourhood. Here he learned the position of the French upon the *Rivière aux Bœufs*, and the condition of their forts. He heard also that they had determined not to come down the river till the following spring, but had warned all the Indians, that, if they did not keep still, the whole French force would be turned upon them; and that, if they and the English were equally strong, they would divide the land between them, and cut off all the natives. These threats, and the mingled kindness and severity of the French, had produced the desired effect. Shingiss, king of the Delawares, feared to meet Washington, and the Shannoah (Shawanee) chiefs would not come either.‡

The truth was, these Indians were in a very awkward po-

---

* *Plain Facts*, p. 44.

† Sparks's *Washington*, Vol. II. pp. 428-447.

‡ Shingiss, or Shingask, was the great Delaware warrior of that day, and did the British much mischief. — See Heckewelder's *Narrative*, p. 64.

sition. They could not resist the Europeans, and knew not which to side with; so that a non-committal policy was much the safest, and they were wise not to return by Washington (as he desired they should) the wampum received from the French, as that would have been equivalent to breaking with them.

Finding that nothing could be done with these people, Washington left Logstown on the 30th of November, and, travelling amid cold and rain, reached Venango, an old Indian town at the mouth of French Creek, on the 4th of the next month. Here he found the French, with their wine, and self-confidence, and other comfortable things; and here, through the rum, and the flattery, and the persuasions of his enemies, he very nearly lost all his Indians, even his old friend the Half-king. Patience and good faith conquered, however, and, after another pull through mires and creeks, snow, rain, and cold, upon the 11th he reached the fort at the head of French Creek. Here he delivered Governor Dinwiddie's letter, took his observations, received his answer, and upon the 16th set out upon his return journey, having had to combat every art and trick, "which the most fruitful brain could suggest," in order to get his Indians away with him. Flattery, and liquor, and guns, and provision were showered upon the Half-king and his comrades, while Washington himself received bows, and smirks, and compliments, and a plentiful store of creature-comforts also.

From Venango, Washington and Gist went on foot, leaving their Indian friends to the tender mercies of the French. Of their hardships and dangers we need say nothing; every schoolboy knows them.* In spite of them, however, they

* Three out of five men who went with Washington, were so badly frost-bitten as to become unable to go on.—Sparks's *Washington*, Vol. II. p. 55.

reached Will's Creek, on the 6th of January, well and sound. During the absence of the young messenger, steps had been taken to fortify and settle the point formed by the junction of the Monongahela and Alleghany; and, while upon his return, he "met seventeen horses, loaded with materials and stores for a fort at the Fork of the Ohio," and, soon after, "some families going out to settle." These steps were taken by the Ohio Company; but, as soon as Washington returned with the letter of St. Pierre, the commander on French Creek, and it was perfectly clear that neither he nor his superiors meant to yield the West without a struggle, Governor Dinwiddie wrote to the Board of Trade, stating, that the French were building another fort at Venango, and that in March twelve or fifteen hundred men would be ready to descend the river with their Indian allies, for which purpose three hundred canoes had been collected; and that Logstown was then to be made head-quarters, while forts were built in various other positions, and the whole country occupied. He also sent expresses to the governors of Pennsylvania and New York, calling upon them for assistance; and, with the advice of his council, proceeded to enlist two companies, one of which was to be raised by Washington, the other by Trent, who was a frontier man. This last was to be raised upon the frontiers, and proceed at once to the Fork of the Ohio, there to complete in the best manner, and as soon as possible, the fort begun by the Ohio Company; and, in case of attack, or any attempt to resist the settlements, or obstruct the works, those resisting were to be taken, or if need were, killed.*

While Virginia was taking these strong measures, which were fully authorized by the letter of the Earl of Holdernesse, Secretary of State,† written in the previous August,

---

* Sparks's *Washington*, Vol. II. pp. 1, 431, 446. — Sparks's *Franklin*, Vol. III. p. 254.

† Sparks's *Franklin*, Vol. III. p. 251, where the letter is given.

and which directed the governors of the various provinces, after representing to those who were invading his Majesty's dominions the injustice of the act, to call out the armed force of the province, and repel force by force; — while Virginia was thus acting, Pennsylvania was discussing the question, whether the French were invading his Majesty's dominions, — the governor on one side, and the Assembly on the other,* — and New York was preparing to hold a conference with the Six Nations, in obedience to orders from the Board of Trade, written in September, 1753.† These orders had been sent out in consequence of the report in England, that the natives would side with the French, because dissatisfied with the occupancy of their lands by the English; and simultaneous orders were sent to the other provinces, directing the governors to recommend their Assemblies to send commissioners to Albany to attend this grand treaty, which was to heal all wounds. New York, however, was more generous when called on by Virginia, than her neighbour on the south, and voted, for the assistance of that colony, five thousand pounds currency.‡

It was now April, 1754. The fort at Venango was finished, and all along the line of French Creek troops were gathering; and the wilderness echoed the strange sounds of a European camp, — the watchword, the command, the clang of muskets, the uproar of soldiers, the cry of the sutler; and with these were mingled the shrieks of drunken Indians, won over from their old friendship by rum and soft words. Scouts were abroad, and little groups formed about the tents or huts of the officers, to learn the movements of the British. Canoes were gathering, and cannon were painfully hauled here and there. All was movement and activity

---

* Sparks's *Franklin*, Vol. III. pp. 254–263.

† *Plain Facts*, pp. 45, 46. — Sparks's *Franklin*, Vol. III. p. 253.

‡ *Massachusetts Historical Collections*, 1st Ser., Vol. VII. p. 73.

among the old forests, and on hill-sides, covered already with young wild flowers, from Lake Erie to the Alleghany. In Philadelphia, meanwhile, Governor Hamilton, in no amiable mood, had summoned the Assembly, and asked them if they meant to help the King in the defence of his dominions; and had desired them, above all things, to do whatever they meant to do, quickly. The Assembly debated, and resolved to aid the King with a little money, and then debated again and voted not to aid him with any money at all, for some would not give less than ten thousand pounds, and others would not give more than five thousand pounds; and so, nothing being practicable, they adjourned upon the 10th of April until the 13th of May.*

In New York, a little, and only a little better spirit, was at work; nor was this strange, as her direct interest was much less than that of Pennsylvania. Five thousand pounds, indeed, was voted to Virginia; but the Assembly questioned the invasion of his Majesty's dominions by the French, and it was not till June that the money voted was sent forward.†

The Old Dominion, however, was all alive. As, under the provincial law, the militia could not be called forth to march more than five miles beyond the bounds of the colony, and, as it was doubtful if the French were within Virginia, it was determined to rely upon volunteers. Ten thousand pounds had been voted by the Assembly; so the two companies were now increased to six, and Washington was raised to the rank of lieutenant-colonel, and made second in command under Joshua Fry. Ten cannon, lately from England, were forwarded from Alexandria; wagons were got ready to carry westward provisions and stores through the heavy spring roads; and everywhere along the Potomac

---

* Sparks's *Franklin*, Vol. III. pp. 264, 265.

† *Massachusetts Historical Collections*, 1st Ser., Vol. VII. pp. 72, 73, and note.

men were enlisting, — or weighing the Governor's proclamation, which promised to those that should serve in that war, two hundred thousand acres of land on the Ohio, — or, already enlisted, were gathering into grave knots, or marching forward to the field of action, or helping on the thirty cannon and eighty barrels of gunpowder, which the King had sent out for the western forts. Along the Potomac they were gathering, as far as to Will's Creek ; and far beyond Will's Creek, whither Trent had come for assistance, his little band of forty-one men were working away, in hunger and want, to fortify that point at the Fork of the Ohio, to which both parties were looking with deep interest. The first birds of spring filled the forests with their song; the red-bud and dogwood were here and there putting forth their flowers on the steep Alleghany hill-sides, and the swift river below swept by, swollen by the melting snows and April showers; a few Indian scouts were seen, but no enemy seemed near at hand; and all was so quiet, that Frazier, an old Indian trader, who had been left by Trent in command of the new fort, ventured to his home at the mouth of Turtle Creek, ten miles up the Monongahela. But, though all was so quiet in that wilderness, keen eyes had seen the low entrenchment that was rising at the Fork, and swift feet had borne the news of it up the valley; and, upon the 17th of April, Ensign Ward, who then had charge of it, saw upon the Alleghany a sight that made his heart sink, — sixty bateaux and three hundred canoes, filled with men, and laden deep with cannon and stores. The fort was called on to surrender; by the advice of the Half-king, Ward tried to evade the act, but it would not do; Contrecœur, with a thousand men about him, said "Evacuate," and the ensign dared not refuse. That evening he supped with his captor, and the next day was bowed off by the

Frenchman, and, with his men and tools, marched up the Monongahela. From that day began the war.*

Of the early events of this war in Virginia we need say nothing. It was but recently that they were detailed upon our pages. The march towards Red Stone Creek, the affair with Jumonville, the battle of the Great Meadows, with the sufferings and perseverance of the troops, the troubles of Washington, and the conduct of the French, must be fresh in the minds of those who read our last October number.† But while these things were doing at the south, while the captors of the works at the Fork were, at a better point, raising other works (called Fort Du Quesne, after the governor of Canada), with "walls two fathoms thick," and, by means of presents, were gaining the good-will of the savages, and making themselves acquainted with the woods and hills in all directions, there was much doing also in Pennsylvania and New York.

In Pennsylvania, the governor and Assembly scolded each other much in the old way; but the latter sanctioned the choice of commissioners that had been made by the former to attend the Albany treaty, and even granted a present for the Indians.‡ This proposed meeting at Albany was not, however, merely for the purpose of holding a conference with the Six Nations; for it was now suggested to form a

---

* Sparks's *Washington*, Vol. II. The number of French troops was probably overstated, but to the captives there was a round thousand. Burk, in his History of Virginia, speaks of the taking of Logstown by the French; but Logstown was never a post of the Ohio Company as he represents it, as is plain from all contemporary letters and accounts. Burk's ignorance of Western matters is clear in this, that he says the French *dropped down* from Fort Du Quesne to Presqu'Ile and Venango; they, or part of them, did drop down the Ohio, but surely not to posts, one of which was on Lake Erie, and the other far up the Alleghany!

† *North American Review*, Vol. XLVII. pp. 350, *et seq.*

‡ Sparks's *Franklin*, Vol. III. p. 276.

union among the colonies to manage Indian affairs and provide for the common defence; and, though this suggestion was vague, and no provincial legislature but that of Massachusetts instructed its delegates with regard to it, it was undoubtedly in the minds of all. Franklin, who was one of the commissioners from Pennsylvania, had sketched a Plan of Union before reaching Albany.*

The day appointed for the meeting of the commissioners was the 14th of June, but it was the 18th or 19th before they got together. There were present delegates from New Hampshire, Massachusetts, Rhode Island, Connecticut, New York, Pennsylvania, and Maryland.† Virginia did not send any, for she was interested in immediate action, and, hoping to have with her against the French both the Six Nations and the Southern Indians (Cherokees, &c.), who had hitherto been at enmity, she proposed a treaty at Winchester in May, where all differences might be settled, and the opposing tribes united. Her plan, however, entirely failed, because so few of the natives attended. At Albany things went not much better; the attendance was small, and those who came were cross and bold. Hendrick, the Mohawk Sachem, told the Congress very plain truths, such as that the French were men, and they women; to which the Congress, on their part, listened gravely, and gave the presents which had been confided to them; but of the treaty we hear little, save that it was a renewal of existing ones.‡ The commissioners, however, were moving in the matter of union, upon the necessity of which they all agreed, and appointed a committee, one from each colony, to draw up a plan. From among those presented to this committee it selected Frank

* Sparks's *Franklin*, Vol. III. pp. 22, 276.

† Ibid. — *Massachusetts Historical Collections*, First Series, Vol. VII. p. 76. — *Plain Facts*, pp. 47 - 50.

‡ Smollett's *George II.*, Chap. IX.

lin's, which, upon the 10th or 11th of July, was adopted by the convention. It is not our purpose to give any sketch of this well-known paper, nor to trace its fate. It is enough to say, that it was universally rejected in America and England. It was at, or near this time, also, that Franklin drew up his plan for settling two barrier colonies upon the Ohio River, one at the mouth of the Scioto, the other below French Creek; a plan which, like the Albany plan of union, produced no result.

It was now the fall of 1754. Fort Cumberland had been built on Will's Creek, the North Carolina troops had been disbanded from want of money, and the Virginia frontiers were defended by some companies from New York and South Carolina, which were in the pay of the King, together with a few Maryland and Virginia volunteers. Virginia herself had, meantime, changed her military establishment; and, having raised forty thousand pounds at home and abroad, had increased her six companies to ten, and degraded all her higher officers to the rank of captain; a step, which, among other results, led to the resignation of his place by Washington, who retired for the time to Mount Vernon.*

In Pennsylvania, Morris, who had succeeded Hamilton, was busily occupied with making speeches to the Assembly and listening to their stubborn replies; † while in the North the Kennebec was fortified, and a plan talked over for attacking Crown Point on Lake Champlain the next spring; ‡ and in the South things went on much as if there were no war coming. All the colonies united in one thing, however, — in calling loudly on the mother country for help. During this same autumn the pleasant Frenchmen were securing the

* Sparks's *Washington,* Vol. II. pp. 63, 64, &c.

† Sparks's *Franklin*, Vol. III. p. 282.

‡ *Massachusetts Historical Collections*, Vol. VII. p. 88.

West, step by step; settling Vincennes, gallanting with the Delawares, and coquetting with the Iroquois, who still balanced between them and the English. The forests along the Ohio shed their leaves, and the prairies filled the sky with the smoke of their burning; and along the great rivers, and on the lakes, and amid the pathless woods of the West, no European was seen, whose tongue spoke other language than that of France. So closed 1754.

The next year opened with professions, on both sides, of the most peaceful intentions, and preparations on both sides to push the war vigorously. France, in January, proposed to restore every thing to the state it was in before the last war, and to refer all claims to commissioners at Paris; to which Britain, upon the 22d, replied, that the West of North America must be left as it was at the treaty of Utrecht. On the 6th of February, France made answer, that the old English claims in America were untenable; and offered a new ground of compromise, namely, that the English should retire east of the Alleghanies, and the French west of the Ohio. This offer was long considered, and at length agreed to by England on the 7th of March, *provided* the French would destroy all their forts on the Ohio and its branches; to which, after twenty days had passed, France said, "No."* While all this negotiation was going on, other things also had been in motion. General Braddock, with his gallant troops, had crossed the Atlantic, and, upon the 20th of February, had landed in Virginia, commander-in-chief of all the land forces in America; and in the North all this while there was whispering of, and enlisting for, the proposed attack on Crown Point; and even Niagara, far off by the Falls, was to be taken, in case nothing prevented. In France, too, other work had been done than negotiation; for at Brest and Rochelle ships were fitting out, and troops

* *Plain Facts*, pp. 51, 52.— *Secret Journals*, Vol. IV. p. 74.

gathering, and stores crowding in. Even old England herself had not been all asleep, and Boscawen had been busy at Plymouth, hurrying on the slow workmen, and gathering the unready sailors.* In March, the two European neighbours were smiling and doing their best to quiet all troubles; in April they still smiled, but the fleets of both were crowding sail across the Atlantic; and, in Alexandria, Braddock, Shirley, and their fellow-officers were taking counsel as to the summer's campaign.

In America four points were to be attacked; Fort Du Quesne, Crown Point, Niagara, and the French posts in Nova Scotia. On the 20th of April, Braddock left Alexandria to march upon Du Quesne, whither he was expressly ordered, though the officers in America looked upon it as a mistaken movement, as they thought New York should be the main point for regular operations. The expedition for Nova Scotia, consisting of three thousand Massachusetts men, left Boston on the 20th of May; while the troops which General Shirley was to lead against Niagara, and the provincials which William Johnson was to head in the attack upon Crown Point, slowly collected at Albany.

May and June passed away, and midsummer drew nigh. The fearful and desponding colonists waited anxiously for news; and, when the news came that Nova Scotia had been conquered, and that Boscawen had taken two of the French men of war, and lay before Louisburg, hope and joy spread everywhere. July passed away, too, and men heard how slowly and painfully Braddock made progress through the wilderness, how his contractors deceived him, and the colonies gave little help, and neither horses or wagons could be had, and only one Benjamin Franklin sent any aid; † and

* Sparks's *Washington*, Vol. II. p. 68. — *Massachusetts Historical Collections*, Vol. VII. p. 89. — Smollett, *George II.*, Chap. X.

† Sparks's *Washington*, Vol. II. p. 77, &c. — Sparks's *Franklin*, Vol. VII. p. 94, &c.

then reports came that he had been forced to leave many of his troops, and much of his baggage and artillery, behind him; and then, about the middle of the month, through Virginia there went a whisper, that the great general had been defeated and wholly cut off; and, as man after man rode down the Potomac confirming it, the planters hastily mounted, and were off to consult with their neighbours; the country turned out; companies were formed to march to the frontiers; sermons were preached; and every heart and every mouth was full. In Pennsylvania the Assembly were called together to hear the "shocking news"; and in New York it struck terror into those who were there gathered to attack the northern posts. Soldiers deserted; the bateaux-men dispersed; and when at length Shirley, since Braddock's death the commander-in-chief, managed with infinite labor to reach Oswego on Lake Ontario, it was too late and stormy, and his force too feeble, to allow him to do more than garrison that point, and march back to Albany again.* Johnson did better; for he met and defeated Baron Dieskau upon the banks of Lake George, though Crown Point was not taken, nor even attacked.

Although the doings of 1755 could not be well looked on as of a very amicable character, war was not declared by either France or England, until May of the following year; and even then France was the last to proclaim the contest which she had been so long carrying on, though more than three hundred of her merchant vessels had been taken by British privateers. The causes of this proceeding are not very clear to us. France thought, beyond doubt, that George would fear to declare war, because Hanover was so exposed to her attacks; but why the British movements, upon the sea particularly, did not lead to the declaration on her

* For a full account of Shirley's Expedition, see the paper in *Massachusetts Historical Collections*, Vol. VII.

part, is not easily to be guessed. Early in 1756, however, both kingdoms formed alliances in Europe; France with Austria, Russia, and Sweden; England with the Great Frederic. And then commenced forthwith the Seven Years' War, wherein most of Europe, North America, and the East and West Indies all partook and suffered.

Into the details of that war we cannot enter; not even into those of the contest in North America. We can but say, that, though during 1756 it was proposed to attack Crown Point, Niagara, and Fort Du Quesne, neither was attacked; for Montcalm took the forts at Oswego, which he destroyed to quiet the jealousy of the Iroquois, within whose territory they were built, and this stroke seemed to paralyze all arms. One bold blow was made by Armstrong at Kittaning, on the Alleghany, in September,* and the frontiers of Pennsylvania for a time were made safe; but otherwise the year in America wore out with little result.

During the next year, 1757, nothing took place, but the capture of Fort William Henry, by Montcalm, and the massacre of its garrison by his Indians; a scene, of which the readers of Cooper's novels need scarce be reminded. This, and the near destruction of the British fleet by a gale off Louisburg, were the leading events of this dark season; and no wonder that fear and despair sank deep into the hearts of the colonists. Nor was it in America alone, that Britain suffered during that summer. On the continent Frederic was borne down; in the Mediterranean she had been defeated, and all was dark in the East; and, to add to the weight of these misfortunes, many of them came upon Pitt, the popular minister.†

But the year 1758 opened under a new star. On sea and land, in Asia, Europe, and America, Britain regained what

---

* Holmes's *Annals*, Vol. II. p. 73. — Burk's *Virginia*, Vol. III. p. 221.

† He returned to office, June 29th, 1757.

had been lost. The Austrians, Russians, and Swedes, all gave way before the great Captain of Prussia, and Pitt sent his own strong, and hopeful, and energetic spirit into his subalterns. In North America Louisburg yielded to Boscawen; Fort Frontenac was taken by Bradstreet; and Du Quesne was abandoned upon the approach of Forbes through Pennsylvania. From that time, the post at the Fork of the Ohio was Fort Pitt.

In this last capture, as more particularly connected with the West, we are now chiefly interested. The details of the gathering and the march may be seen in the letters of Washington, who, in opposition to Colonel Bouquet, was in favor of crossing the mountains by Braddock's road, whereas Bouquet wished to cut a new one through Pennsylvania. In this division, Bouquet was listened to by the general; and late in the season a new route was undertaken, by which such delays and troubles were produced, that the whole expedition came near proving a failure. Braddock's road had, in early times, been selected by the most experienced Indians and frontier men as the most favorable whereby to cross the mountains, being nearly the route by which the national road has been since carried over them. In 1753, it was opened by the Ohio Company. It was afterward improved by the Provincial troops under Washington, and was finished by Braddock's engineers;* and this route was now to be given up, and a wholly new one opened, probably, as Washington suggested, through Pennsylvania influence, that her frontiers might thereby be protected, and a way opened for her traders. The hardships and dangers of the march from Raystown to Fort Du Quesne, where the British van arrived upon the 25th of November, may be seen slightly pictured in the letters of Washington and the second Journal of Post,†

* Sparks's *Washington*, Vol. II. p. 302.

† Proud's *Pennsylvania*, Vol. II. Appendix.

and may be more vividly conceived by those who have passed through the valley of the upper Juniata.*

But, turning from this march, let us look at the position of things in the West, during the autumn of 1758. We have said, that in the outset the French did their utmost to alienate the Six Nations and Delawares from their old connection with the British; and so politic were their movements, so accurate their knowledge of Indian character, that they fully succeeded. The English, as we have seen, had made most foolish and iniquitous attempts to get a claim to the Western lands, and by rum and bumbo had even obtained written grants of those lands; but when the rum had evaporated, the wild men saw how they had been deceived, and listened not unwillingly to the French professions of friendship, backed as they were by presents and politeness, and accompanied by no attempts to buy or wheedle land from them.† Early, therefore, many of the old allies of England joined her enemies; and the treaties of Albany, Johnson Hall, and Easton,‡

---

* While upon this march, General Forbes was so sick that he was carried in a close litter, and to this the officers went to receive their orders. An anecdote was afterwards told of some inimical Indian chiefs, who came to the army on an embassy, and who, observing that from this close litter came all commands, asked the reason. The British officers, thinking the savages would despise their General, if told he was sick, were at first puzzled what answer to make; but in a moment one of them spoke out, and said, that in that litter was their General, who was so fierce and strong that he felt it necessary to bind himself, hand and foot, and lie still until he came to the enemy's country, lest he should do the ambassadors, or even his own men a mischief. The red men gave their usual grunt, and placed some miles of forest between themselves and this fierce chieftain as soon as possible.

† See Post's *Journals;* Pownall's *Memoir, on Service in North America.*

‡ Many treaties were made between 1753 and 1758, which amounted to little or nothing. See *Massachusetts Historical Collections*, Vol. VII. p. 97. — Sparks's *Franklin*, Vol. III. pp. 436, 450, 471, &c. —

did little or nothing toward stopping the desolation of the frontiers of Pennsylvania, Maryland, and Virginia. The Quakers always believed, that this state of enmity between the Delawares and themselves, or their rulers, might be prevented by a little friendly communion; but the persuasions of the French, the renegade English traders, and the low Irish Catholics, who had gone into the West, were great obstacles to any friendly conversation on the one side, and the common feeling among the whites was an equal difficulty on the other. In the autumn of 1756, a treaty was held at Easton with the Pennsylvania Delawares,* and peace agreed to. But this did not bind the Ohio Indians even of the same nation, much less the Shawanese and Mingoes; and though the Sachem of the Pennsylvania savages, Teedyuscung, promised to call to his western relatives with a loud voice, they did not, or would not hear him; the tomahawk and brand still shone among the rocky mountain fastnesses of the interior. Nor can any heart but pity the red men. They knew not whom to believe, nor where to look for a true friend. The French said they came to defend them from the English; the English said they came to defend them from the French; and between the two powers they were wasting away, and their homes disappearing before them. "The kings of France and England," said Teedyuscung, "have settled this land so as to coop us up as if in a pen. This very ground that is under me was my land and inheritance, and is taken from me by fraud." Such being the feeling of the natives, and success being of late nearly balanced between the two European

---

Proud's *Pennsylvania*, Vol. II. App.; Friendly Association's *Address*, and Post's *Journals*. There were two Easton treaties; one with the Pennsylvania Delawares, in 1756, the other with all the Indians, in 1758. — See also, in Proud's *Pennsylvania*, Vol. II. p. 331, an inquiry into the causes of quarrel with the Indians, and extracts from treaties, &c.

* Sparks's *Franklin*, Vol. VII. p. 125.

powers, no wonder that they hung doubting, and knew not which way to turn. The French wished the Eastern Delawares to move west, so as to bring them within their influence;* and the British tried to persuade them to prevail on their western brethren to leave their new allies and be at peace.

In 1758, the condition of affairs being as stated, and Forbes's army on the eve of starting for Fort Du Quesne, and the French being also disheartened by the British success elsewhere, and their force at Du Quesne weak, — it was determined to make an effort to draw the western Indians over, and thereby still further to weaken the force that would oppose General Forbes. It was no easy matter, however, to find a true and trustworthy man, whose courage, skill, ability, knowledge, and physical power, would fit him for such a mission. He was to pass through a wilderness filled with doubtful friends, into a country filled with open enemies. The whole French interest would be against him, and the Indians of the Ohio were little to be trusted. Every stream on his way had been dyed with blood, every hill-side had rung with the death-yell, and grown red in the light of burning huts. The man who was at last chosen was a Moravian, who had lived among the savages seventeen years, and married among them; his name Christian Frederic Post. Of his journey, sufferings, and doings, we have his own journal, though Heckewelder tells us, that those parts which redound most to his own credit, he omitted when printing it. He left Philadelphia upon the 15th of July, 1758; and, against the protestations of Teedyuscung, who said he would surely lose his life, proceeded up the Susquehannah, — passing "many plantations deserted and laid waste." Upon the 7th of August, he came to the Alleghany opposite French Creek, and was forced to pass under the very eyes of the

* Heckewelder's *Narrative*, p. 53.

garrison of Fort Venango, but was not molested. From Venango, he went to "Kushkushkee," which was on or near Big Beaver Creek. This place, he says, contained ninety houses and two hundred able warriors. At this place Post had much talk with the chiefs, who seemed well disposed, but somewhat afraid of the French. The great conference, however, it was determined should be held opposite Fort Du Quesne, where there were Indians of eight nations. The messenger was at first unwilling to go thither, fearing the French would seize him; but the savages said, "they would carry him in their bosom, he need fear nothing," and they well redeemed this promise. On the 24th of August, Post, with his Indian friends, reached the point opposite the Fort; and there immediately followed a series of speeches, explanations, and agreements, for which we must refer to his Journal. At first he was received rather hardly by an old and deaf Onondago, who claimed the land whereon they stood as belonging to the Six Nations; but a Delaware rebuked him in no very polite terms. "That man speaks not as a man," he said; "he endeavours to frighten us by saying this ground is his; he dreams; he and his father (the French) have certainly drunk too much liquor; they are drunk; pray let them go to sleep till they are sober. You do not know what your own nation does at home, how much they have to say to the English. You are quite rotten. You stink. You do nothing but smoke your pipe here. Go to sleep with your father, and when you are sober we will speak to you."

It was clear that the Delawares, and indeed all the Western Indians, were wavering in their affection for the French; and, though some opposition was made to a union with the colonists, the general feeling, produced by the prospect of a quick approach by Forbes's army, and by the truth and kindness of Post himself, was in favor of England. The Indians, however, complained bitterly of the disposition which the whites showed in claiming and seizing their lands. "Why did you not fight your battles at home, or on the sea, instead of coming into our country to fight them?" they asked, again and again; and were mournful when they thought of the future. "*Your* heart is good," they said to Post, "*you* speak sincerely; but we know there is always a great number who wish to get rich; they never have enough; look! we do not want to be rich, and take away what others have." "The white people think we have no brains in our heads; that they are big, and we a little handful; but remember, when you hunt for a rattlesnake you cannot find it, and perhaps it will bite you before you see it." When the war of Pontiac came, this saying might have been justly remembered.

At length, having concluded a pretty definite peace, Post returned toward Philadelphia, setting out upon the 9th of September; and, after the greatest sufferings and perils from French scouts and Indians, reached the settlements uninjured.

At Easton, meantime, had been gathering another great council, at which were present "the eight United Nations (the Iroquois), and their confederates"; with all of whom, during October, peace was concluded. Of the particulars of this treaty we know nothing; from a note in Burk's "History of Virginia," * we find that the Iroquois were very angry at the prominence of Teedyuscung; but further than this, and that peace was made, and notice of it sent to the Western Indians, we hear not a word of this final peacemaking. With the messengers to the West, Post was sent back, within five weeks after his return. He followed after General Forbes, from whom he received messages to the various tribes, with which he once more sought their chiefs; and was again very instrumental in preventing any junction

* Vol. III. p. 239.

of the Indians with the French. Indeed, but for Post's mission, there would in all probability have been gathered a strong force of Western savages to waylay Forbes and defend Fort Du Quesne; in which case, so adverse was the season and the way, so wearied the men, and so badly managed the whole business, that there would have been great danger of a second "Braddock's field"; so that our humble Moravian friend played no unimportant part in securing to his British Majesty again the key to Western America.

With the fall of Fort Du Quesne, all direct contest between the French and British in the West ceased. From that time Canada was the only scene of operations, though garrisons for a while remained in the forts on French Creek. In 1759, Ticonderoga, Crown Point, Niagara, and at length Quebec itself, yielded to the English; and on the 8th of September, 1760, Montreal, Detroit, and all Canada, were given up by Vaudreuil, the French governor.

But the French had not been the only dwellers in Western America; and when they were gone, the colonists still saw before them clouds of dark and jealous warriors. Indeed, no sooner were the Delawares quiet in the north, than the Cherokees, who had been assisting Virginia against her foes, were roused to war by the thoughtless and cruel conduct of the frontier men, who shot several of that tribe because they took some horses which they found running at large in the woods. The ill-feeling bred by this act was eagerly fostered by the French in Louisiana; and while Amherst and Wolfe were pushing the war into Canada, the frontiers of Georgia, the Carolinas, and Virginia were writhing under the horrors of Indian invasion. This Cherokee war continued through 1760, and into 1761, but was terminated in the summer of the last-named year by Colonel Grant. We should be glad to enter somewhat at large into the events of it, as then came forward two of the most remarkable chiefs of that day, the Great Warrior, and the Little Carpenter (Attakullakulla); but our limits will not permit this, and we must refer our readers to the second volume of Thatcher's "Indian Biography."

Along the frontiers of Pennsylvania and Northern Virginia, the old plantations had been, one by one, reoccupied since 1758, and settlers were slowly pushing farther into the Indian country, and traders were once more bearing their burdens over the mountains, and finding a way into the wigwams of the natives, who rested, watching silently, but narrowly, the course of their English defenders and allies. For it was, professedly, in the character of defenders, that Braddock and Forbes had come into the West; * and, while every British finger itched for the lands as well as the furs of the wild men, with mistaken hypocrisy they would have persuaded them that the treasure and the life of England had been given to preserve her old allies, the Six Nations, and their dependents, the Delawares and Shawanese, from French aggression. But the savages knew whom they had to deal with, and looked at every step of the cultivator with jealousy and hate.

In 1760, the Ohio Company once more prepared to pursue their old plan, and sent to England for such orders and instructions to the Virginia government as would enable them to do so.† During the summer of that year, also, General Monkton, by a treaty at Fort Pitt, obtained leave to build posts within the wild lands, each post having ground enough about it whereon to raise corn and vegetables for the use of the garrison.‡ Nor, if we can credit one writer, were the settlements of the Ohio Company, and the forts, the only in-

---

* Sparks's *Franklin*, Vol. IV. p. 328. — Post's Journals show how full of jealousy the Indians were; see there also Forbes's letter, sent by him.

† Sparks's *Washington*, Vol. II. p. 482. — *Plain Facts*, p. 120, where a letter from the Company, dated September 9th, 1761, is given.

‡ Dated August 20th. *Plain Facts*, pp. 55, 56.

roads upon the hunting-grounds of the savages; for he says, that in 1757, by the books of the Secretary of Virginia, three millions of acres had been granted west of the mountains. Indeed, we know that in 1758 she tried by law to encourage settlements in the West; and the report of John Blair, Clerk of the Virginia Council, in 1768 or 1769, states, that most of the grants beyond the mountains were made before August, 1754.* At any rate, it is clear that the Indians early began to murmur; for, in 1762, Bouquet issued his proclamation from Fort Pitt, saying that the treaty of Easton, in 1758, secured to the red men all lands west of the mountains as hunting-grounds; wherefore he forbids all settlements, and orders the arrest of the traders and settlers who were spreading discontent and fear among the Ohio Indians.†

But if the Ohio Indians were early ill-disposed to the English, much more was this the case among those lake tribes, who had known only the French, and were strongly attached to them; the Ottaways, Wyandots, and Chippeways. The first visit they received from the British was after the surrender of Vaudreuil, when Major Robert Rogers was sent to take charge of Detroit.‡ He left Montreal on the 13th of September, 1760, and on the 8th of October reached Presqu'Ile, where Bouquet then commanded. Thence he went slowly up Lake Erie, having despatched by land forty bullocks as a supply, when near or at Detroit, which place he summoned to yield itself upon the 19th of November. It was, if we mistake not, while waiting for an answer to this summons, that he was visited by the great Ottawa chieftain, Pontiac, who demanded how the English dared enter his

* *Contest in North America, by an Impartial Hand*, p. 36. — *Secret Journals*, Vol. III. p. 187. — *Plain Facts*, Appendix.

† *Plain Facts*, p. 56. — See Heckewelder's *Narrative*, p. 64.

‡ See his *Journal*, London, 1765. Also, his *Concise Account of North America*, London, 1775.

country; to which the answer was given, that they came, not to take the country, but to open a free way of trade, and to put out the French, who stopped their trade. This answer, together with other moderate and kindly words spoken by Rogers, seemed to lull the rising fears of the savages, and Pontiac promised him his protection.

Beleter, meantime, who commanded at Detroit, had not yielded; nay, word was brought to Rogers on the 24th, that his messenger had been confined, and a flag-pole erected, with a wooden head upon it, to represent Britain, on which stood a crow picking the eyes out, — as emblematic of the success of France. In a few days, however, the commander heard of the fate of the lower posts, and, as his Indians did not stand by him, on the 29th he yielded. Rogers remained at Detroit until December 23d, under the personal protection of Pontiac, to whose presence he probably owed his safety. From Detroit the Major went to the Maumee, and thence across the present State of Ohio to Fort Pitt; and his Journal of this overland trip is the first which we have of such a one in that region. His route was nearly that given by Hutchins,* in Bouquet's "Expedition," as the common one from Sandusky to the Fork of the Ohio. It went from Fort Sandusky, where Portland now is, crossed the Huron River, then called Bald Eagle Creek, to "Mohickon John's Town," upon what we know as Mohican Creek, the northern branch of White Woman's River, and thence crossed to Beaver's Town, a Delaware town on the west side of the "Maskongam Creek," opposite "a fine river," which, from Hutchins's map, we presume was Sandy Creek. At Beaver's Town were one hundred and eighty warriors, and not less than three thousand acres of cleared land. From there the track went up Sandy Creek and across to the Big Beaver, and up

* Thomas Hutchins, afterwards Geographer of the United States, was, in 1764, assistant engineer on Bouquet's expedition.

the Ohio, through Logstown, to Fort Pitt, which place Rogers reached January 23d, 1760, precisely one month having passed while he was upon the way.

In the spring of the year following Rogers's visit (1761), Alexander Henry, an English trader, went to Missilimacanac for purposes of business, and he found everywhere the strongest feeling against the English, who had done nothing by word or act to conciliate the Indians. Even then there were threats of reprisals and war. Having, by means of a Canadian dress, managed to reach Missilimacanac in safety, he was there discovered, and was waited on by an Indian chief, who was, in the opinion of Thatcher, Pontiac himself. This chief, after conveying to him the idea, that their French father would soon awake and utterly destroy his enemies, continued: —

> "Englishman! Although you have conquered the French, you have not yet conquered us! We are not your slaves! These lakes, these woods, these mountains, were left to us by our ancestors. They are our inheritance, and we will part with them to none. Your nation supposes that we, like the white people, cannot live without bread, and pork, and beef. But you ought to know that He, the Great Spirit and Master of Life, has provided food for us upon these broad lakes and in these mountains."

He then spoke of the fact, that no treaty had been made with them, no presents sent them; and while he announced their intention to allow Henry to trade unmolested, and to regard him as a brother, he declared that with his king the red men were still at war.*

Such were the feelings of the Northwestern savages immediately after the English took possession of their lands; and these feelings were in all probability fostered and increased by the Canadians and French. Distrust of the British was

---

* *Travels* of Alexander Henry in Canada, from 1760 to 1776. New York. 1809. — Thatcher's *Indian Biography*, Vol. II. pp. 75, *et seq.*

general; and, as the war between France and England still went on in other lands, there was hope among the Canadians, perhaps, that the French power might be restored in America. However this may have been, it is clear that disaffection spread rapidly in the West, though of the details of the years from 1759 to 1763 we know hardly any thing.*

Upon the 10th of February, 1763, the treaty of Paris was concluded, and peace between the European powers restored. Then once more men began to think seriously of the West. Pamphlets were published upon the advantages of settlements on the Ohio. Colonel Mercer was chosen to represent the old Company in England, and try to have their affairs made straight, for there were counter-claims by the soldiers who had enlisted, in 1754, under Dinwiddie's proclamation; and on all hands there were preparations for movement. But even at that moment there existed through the whole West a conspiracy or agreement among the Indians, from Lake Michigan to the frontiers of North Carolina, by which they were with one accord, with one spirit, to fall upon the whole line of British posts and strike every white man dead. Chippeways, Ottawas, Wyandots, Miamis, Shawanese, Delawares, and Mingoes for the time laid by their old hostile feelings, and united under Pontiac in this great enterprise. The voice of that sagacious and noble man was heard in the distant north, crying, "Why, says the Great Spirit, do you suffer these dogs in red clothing to enter your country and take the land I have given you? Drive them from it! Drive them! When you are in distress, I will help you."

That voice was heard, but not by the whites. The unsuspecting traders journeyed from village to village; the soldiers in the forts shrunk from the sun of the early summer, and dozed away the day; the frontier settler, singing in

* Thatcher's *Indian Biography*, Vol. II. p. 86.

fancied security, sowed his crop, or, watching the sunset through the girdled trees, mused upon one more peaceful harvest, and told his children of the horrors of the ten years' war, now, thank God! over. From the Alleghanies to the Mississippi the trees had leaved, and all was calm life and joy. But through that great country, even then, bands of sullen red men were journeying from the central valleys to the lakes of the Eastern hills. Bands of Chippeways gathered about Missilimacanac. Ottawas filled the woods near Detroit. The Maumee post, Presqu'Ile, Niagara, Pitt, Ligonier, and every English fort was hemmed in by mingled tribes, who felt that the great battle drew nigh which was to determine their fate and the possession of their noble lands.* At last the day came. The traders everywhere were seized, their goods taken from them, and more than one hundred of them put to death. Nine British forts yielded instantly, and the savages drank, "scooped up in the hollow of joined hands," the blood of many a Briton. The border streams of Pennsylvania and Virginia ran red again. "We hear," says a letter from Fort Pitt, "of scalping every hour." In Western Virginia, more than twenty thousand people were driven from their homes. Detroit was besieged by Pontiac himself, after a vain attempt to take it by stratagem; and for many months that siege was continued in a manner, and with a perseverance, unexampled among the Indians. Even a regular commissariat department was organized, and bills of credit issued. It was the 8th of May when Detroit was first attacked, and upon the 3d of the following December it was still in danger. As late as March of the next year, the inhabitants were "sleeping in their clothes, expecting an alarm every night." †

---

* See Henry's *Narrative.* — Thatcher's *Indian Biography*, Vol. II. p. 83.

† Ibid.

Fort Pitt was besieged also, and the garrison reduced to sad straits from want of food. This being known beyond the mountains, a quantity of provision was collected, and Colonel Bouquet was appointed to convey it to the head of the Ohio, having assigned him for the service the poor remains of two regiments, which had but lately returned from the war in Cuba. He set out toward the middle of July, and upon the 25th reached Bedford. From that post, he went forward by Forbes's road, passed Fort Ligonier, and upon the 5th of August was near Bushy Run, one of the branches of Turtle Creek, which falls into the Monongahela ten miles above Fort Pitt. Here he was attacked by the Indians, who, hearing of his approach, had gathered their forces to defeat him, and during two days the contest continued. On the 6th, the Indians, having the worst of the battle, retreated; and Bouquet, with his three hundred and forty horses, loaded with flour, reached and relieved the post at the Fork.*

It was now nearly autumn, and the confederated tribes had failed to take the three most important fortresses in the West, Detroit, Pitt, and Niagara. Many of them became disheartened; others wished to return home for the winter; others had satisfied their longing for revenge. United merely by the hope of striking and immediate success, they fell from one another when that success did not come; jealousies and old enmities came in; the league was broken; and Pontiac was left alone, or with few followers.

In October, also, a step was taken by the British government, in part for the purpose of quieting the fears and suspicions of the red men, which did much, probably, toward destroying their alliance. A proclamation was issued, forbidding the grant, by any governor, of Western lands, and the purchase or settlement of those lands by individ-

---

* Holmes's *Annals*, Vol. II. p. 121. — Sparks's *Washington*, Vol. II., Map, at p. 38.

uals.* To assist the effect of this proclamation, it was determined to make two movements in the spring and summer of 1764; General Bradstreet being ordered into the country upon Lake Erie, and Bouquet into that upon the Ohio. The former moved to Niagara early in the summer, and there held a grand council with twenty or more tribes, all of whom sued for peace; and, upon the 8th of August, the army reached Detroit.† Bouquet, meanwhile, collected troops at Fort Pitt, and in the autumn marched across from Big Beaver to the Upper Muskingum, and thence to the point where the White Woman's River comes into the main stream. There, upon the 9th of November, he concluded a peace with the Delawares and Shawanese, and received from them two hundred and six prisoners, eighty-one men and one hundred and twenty-five women and children. He also received, from the Shawanese, hostages for the delivery of some captives, who could not be brought to the Muskingum at that time. These hostages escaped, but the savages were of good faith, and upon the 9th of May, 1765, the remaining whites were given up to George Croghan, the deputy of Sir William Johnson, at Fort Pitt. Many anecdotes are related in the account of the delivery of the captives to Bouquet, going to show that strong attachments had been formed between them and their captors; and West's pencil has illustrated the scene of their delivery. But we have little faith in the representations of either writer or painter.‡

Pontiac, the leading spirit in the past struggle, finding his attempts to save his country and his race at that time hope-

* *Land Laws*, p. 84. — Sparks's *Franklin,* Vol. IV. p. 374.

† Henry's *Narrative*. Henry was with Bradstreet.

‡ "An Historical Account of the Expedition against the Ohio Indians in the Year 1764, under the Command of Henry Bouquet, Esquire, &c. Published from Authentic Documents, by a Lover of his Country. London. 1766." This volume was first printed in Philadelphia.

less, left his tribe and went into the West, and for some years after was living among the Illinois, attempting, but in vain, to bring about a new union and new war. He was in the end killed by a Peoria Indian. So far as we can form a judgment of this chieftain, he was, in point of talent, nobleness of spirit, honor, and devotion, the superior of any red man of whom we have any account. His plan of extermination was most masterly; his execution of it equal to its conception. But for the treachery of one of his followers, he would have taken Detroit early in May. His whole force might then have been directed in one mass, first upon Niagara, and then upon Pitt, and in all probability both posts would have fallen.* Even disappointed as he was at Detroit, had the Six Nations, with their dependent allies, the Delawares and Shawanese, been true to him, the British might have been long kept beyond the mountains; but the Iroquois — close upon the colonies, old allies of England, and under the influence of Sir William Johnson as they were, and disposed, as they ever proved themselves, to claim and sell, but not to defend, the West — were for peace after the King's proclamation. Indeed, the Mohawks and leading tribes were from the first with the British; so that, after the success of Bradstreet and Bouquet, there was no difficulty in concluding a treaty with all the Western Indians; and late in April, 1765, Sir William Johnson, at the German Flats, held a conference with the various nations, and settled a definite peace.† At this meeting two propositions were made; the one to fix some boundary line, west of which the Europeans should not go; and the savages named, as this line, the Ohio or Alleghany and Susquehannah; but no definite agreement was made, Johnson not being empowered to act. The

* Thatcher's *Indian Biography*, Vol. II. Our knowledge of Pontiac and his war is very limited. We hope something more may come to light yet.

† *Plain Facts*, p. 60.

other proposal was, that the Indians should grant to the traders who had suffered in 1763, a tract of land in compensation for the injuries then done them, and to this the red men agreed.*

With the returning deputies of the Shawanese and Delawares, George Croghan, Sir William Johnson's sub-commissioner, went to the West for the purpose of visiting the more distant tribes, and securing, so far as it could be done, the allegiance of the French who were scattered through the Western valleys, and who were stirring up the savages to warfare, as it was believed. The Journal of his voyage may be found in the Appendix to Butler's "History of Kentucky" (2d edition), together with his estimate of the number of Indians in the West; a very curious and valuable table, though, of course, vague and inaccurate.

So stood matters in the West during this year, 1765. All beyond the Alleghanies, with the exception of a few forts, was a wilderness until the Wabash was reached, where dwelt a few miserable French, with some fellow-vagabonds† not far from them upon the Illinois and Kaskaskia. The Indians, a few years since undisputed owners of the prairies and broad vales, now held them by sufferance, having been twice conquered by the arms of England. They, of course, felt both hatred and fear; and, while they despaired of saving their lands, and looked forward to unknown evils, the deepest and most abiding spirit of revenge was roused within them. They had seen the British coming to take their hunting-grounds upon the strength of a treaty which they knew not of. They had been forced to admit British troops into their country; and, though now nominally protected from settlers, that promised protection would be but

* *Plain Facts*, p. 60. — Butler's *History of Kentucky*, 2d ed., p. 479, *et seq.*

† Croghan's *Journal*, and those of all travellers of that time, so represent them.

an incentive to passion, in case it was not in good faith extended to them.

And it was not in good faith extended to them by either individuals or governments. During the very year that succeeded the treaty of German Flats, settlers crossed the mountains and took possession of lands in Western Virginia and along the Monongahela. The Indians, having received no pay for these lands, murmured, and once more a border war was feared. General Gage, commander of the King's forces, was applied to, probably through Sir William Johnson, and issued his orders for the removal of the settlers; but they defied his commands and his power, and remained where they were.* And not only were frontier men thus passing the line tacitly agreed on, but Sir William himself was even then meditating a step which would have produced, had it been taken, a general Indian war again. This was the purchase and settlement of an immense tract south of the Ohio River, where an independent colony was to be formed. How early this plan was conceived we do not learn, but, from Franklin's letters, we find that it was in contemplation in the spring of 1766.† At that time Franklin was in London, and was written to by his son, Governor Franklin of New Jersey, with regard to the proposed colony. The plan seems to have been, to buy of the Six Nations the lands south of the Ohio, a purchase which it was not doubted Sir William might make, and then to procure from the King a grant of as much territory as the company, which it was intended to form, would require. Governor Franklin, accordingly, forwarded to his father an application for a grant, together with a letter from Sir William, recommending the plan to the ministry; all of which was duly communicated to the proper department. But at that time

* *Plain Facts*, p. 65.

† Sparks's *Franklin*, Vol. IV. p. 233, *et seq.*

there were various interests bearing upon this plan of Franklin. The old Ohio Company was still suing, through its agent, Colonel George Mercer, for a perfection of the original grant. The soldiers claiming under Dinwiddie's proclamation had their tale of rights and grievances. Individuals, to whom grants had been made by Virginia, wished them completed. General Lyman, from Connecticut we believe, was soliciting a new grant similar to that now asked by Franklin; and the ministers themselves were divided as to the policy and propriety of establishing any settlements so far in the interior, — Shelburne being in favor of the new colony, Hillsborough opposed to it.

The company was organized, however, and the nominally leading man therein being Mr. Thomas Walpole, a London banker of eminence, it was known as the Walpole Company. Franklin continued privately to make friends among the ministry, and to press upon them the policy of making large settlements in the West; and, as the old way of managing the Indians by superintendents was just then in bad odor in consequence of the expense attending it, the cabinet council so far approved the new plan as to present it for examination to the Board of Trade, with members of which Franklin had also been privately conversing.

This was in the autumn of 1767. But, before any conclusion was come to, it was necessary to arrange definitely that boundary line, which had been vaguely talked of in 1765, and with respect to which Sir William Johnson had written to the ministry, who had mislaid his letters, and given him no instructions. The necessity of arranging this boundary was also kept in mind by the continued and growing irritation of the Indians, who found themselves invaded from every side. This irritation became so great during the autumn of 1767, that Gage wrote to the Governor of Pennsylvania on the subject. The Governor communicated his letter to the Assembly on the 5th of January, 1768, and representations were at once sent to England, expressing the necessity of having the Indian line fixed. Franklin, the father, all this time, was urging the same necessity upon the ministers in England; and about Christmas of 1767, Sir William's letters on the subject having been found, orders were sent him to complete the proposed purchase from the Six Nations, and settle all differences. But the project for a colony was for the time dropped, a new administration coming in which was not that way disposed.

Sir William Johnson having received, early in the spring, the orders from England relative to a new treaty with the Indians, at once took steps to secure a full attendance.* Notice was given to the various colonial governments, to the Six Nations, the Delawares, and the Shawanese, and a congress was appointed to meet at Fort Stanwix during the following October. It met upon the 24th of that month, and was attended by representatives from New Jersey, Virginia, and Pennsylvania; by Sir William and his deputies; by the agents of those traders who had suffered in the war of 1763; and by deputies from all of the Six Nations, the Delawares, and the Shawanese. The first point to be settled was the boundary line which was to determine the Indian lands of the West from that time forward; and this line the Indians, upon the 1st of November, stated should begin on the Ohio, at the mouth of the Cherokee (or Tennessee) River; thence go up the Ohio and Alleghany to Kittaning; thence across to the Susquehannah, &c.; whereby the whole country south of the Ohio and Alleghany, *to which the Six Nations had any claim*, was transferred to the British. One deed, for a part of this land, was made on the 3d of November to William Trent, attorney for twenty-two traders, whose goods had been destroyed by the Indians in 1763. The tract conveyed by this was be-

---

* For an account of this long-lost treaty see *Plain Facts*, pp. 65–104, or Butler's *Kentucky*, 2d edition, pp. 472–488.

tween the Kenhawa and Monongahela, and was by the traders named Indiana. Two days afterward, a deed for the remaining Western lands was made to the King, and the price agreed on paid down.* These deeds were made upon the express agreement, that no claim should ever be based upon previous treaties, those of Lancaster, Logstown, &c.; and they were signed by the chiefs of the Six Nations, for themselves, their allies and dependents, the Shawanese, Delawares, Mingoes of Ohio, and others; but the Shawanese and Delaware deputies present did not sign them.

Such was the treaty of Stanwix, whereon rests the title by purchase to Kentucky, Western Virginia, and Pennsylvania. It was a better foundation, perhaps, than that given by previous treaties, but was essentially worthless; for the lands conveyed were not occupied or hunted on by those conveying them. In truth, we cannot doubt that this immense grant was obtained by the influence of Sir William Johnson, in order that the new colony, of which he was to be governor, might be founded there. The fact, that such an extent of country was ceded voluntarily, — not after a war, not by hard persuasion, but at once and willingly, — satisfies us that the whole affair had been previously settled with the New York savages, and that the Ohio Indians had no voice in the matter.

But the grant was made. The white man could now quiet his conscience when driving the native from his forest home, and feel sure that an army would back his pretensions. A new company was at once organized in Virginia, called the "Mississippi Company," and a petition sent to the King for two millions and a half of acres in the West. Among the signers of this were Francis Lightfoot Lee, Richard Henry Lee, George Washington, and Arthur Lee. The gentleman

* There were also given two deeds of lands in the interior of Pennsylvania, one to Croghan, and the other to the proprietaries of that colony.

last named was the agent for the petitioners in England. This application was referred to the Board of Trade on the 9th of March, 1769, and after that we hear nothing of it.*

Meantime more than one bold man had ventured for a little while into the beautiful valleys of Kentucky, and on the 1st of May, 1769, there was one going forth from his "peaceable habitation on the Yadkin River in North Carolina," whose name has since gone far and wide over this little planet of ours, he having become the type of his class. This was Daniel Boone. He crossed the mountains, and spent that summer and the next winter in the West.† But, while he was rejoicing in the abundance of buffalo, deer, and turkeys among the cane-brakes, longer heads were meditating still that new colony, the plan of which had been lying in silence for two years and more. The Board of Trade was again called on to report upon the application, and Lord Hillsborough, the President, reported against it. This called out Franklin's celebrated "Ohio Settlement," a paper written with so much ability, that the King's Council put by the official report, and granted the petition, a step which mortified the noble lord so much that he resigned his official station.‡ The petition now needed only the royal sanction, which was not given until August 14th, 1772; but in 1770, the Ohio Company was merged in Walpole's, and, the claims of the soldiers of 1756 being acknowledged both by the new company and by government, all claims were quieted. Nothing was ever done, however, under the grant to Walpole, the Revolution soon coming upon America.§ After the Revolution, Mr. Walpole and his associates petitioned Congress respecting their lands, called by them "Vandalia," but could

* *Plain Facts*, p. 69. — Butler's *Kentucky*, p. 475.

† Boone's *Narrative*, which may be found in Carey's *Museum*, Vol. II. p. 324.

‡ Sparks's *Franklin*, Vol. IV. p. 302.

§ Sparks's *Washington*, Vol. II. p. 483, *et seq.* — *Plain Facts*, p. 149.

get no help from that body. What was finally done by Virginia with the claims of this and other companies, we do not find written, but presume their lands were all looked on as forfeited.

During the years in which Franklin, Pownall, and their friends, were trying to get the great Western land company into operation, actual settlers were crossing the mountains all too rapidly; for the Ohio Indians "viewed the settlements with an uneasy and jealous eye," and did "not scruple to say, that they must be compensated for their right, if people settled thereon notwithstanding the cession by the Six Nations." * It has been said, also, that Lord Dunmore, then governor of Virginia, authorized surveys and settlements on the Western lands, notwithstanding the proclamation of 1763; but Mr. Sparks gives us a letter from him, in which this is expressly denied.† However, surveyors did go down even to the Falls of the Ohio, and the whole region south of the Ohio was filling with white men. The futility of the Fort Stanwix treaty, and the ignorance or contempt of it by the fierce Shawanese, are well seen in the meeting between them and Bullitt, one of the early emigrants, in 1773.‡ Bullitt, on his way down the Ohio, stopped, and singly sought the savages at one of their towns. He then told them of his proposed settlement, and his wish to live at peace with them; and said, that, as they had received nothing under the treaty of 1768, it was intended to make them presents the next year. The Indians considered the talk of the Long Knife, and the next day agreed to his proposed settlement, provided he did not *disturb them in their hunting south of the Ohio;* a provision wholly inconsistent with the Stanwix deed.

Among the foremost speculators in Western lands at that

* Washington's "Journal to the West, in 1770." Sparks's *Washington*, Vol. II. p. 531.

† *Ibid.*, p. 378.

‡ Butler's *Kentucky*, p. 20.

time was George Washington. He had always regarded the proclamation of 1763 as a mere temporary expedient to quiet the savages, and, being better acquainted with the value of Western lands than most of those who could command means, he early began to buy beyond the mountains. His agent in selecting lands was Crawford, afterwards burnt by the Ohio Indians. In September, 1767, we find Washington writing to Crawford on this subject, and looking forward to the occupation of the Western territory; and in 1773, being entitled, under the King's proclamation of 1763, (which gave a bounty to officers and soldiers who had served in the old French war,) to ten thousand acres of land, he became deeply interested in the country beyond the mountains, and had some correspondence respecting the importation of settlers from Europe. Indeed, had not the Revolutionary war been just then on the eve of breaking out, Washington would in all probability have become the leading settler of the West, and all our history been changed.*

But though that Revolution retained him east of the mountains, it did not come quick enough to prevent such preparations for strong settlements in the West, while yet nominally British, as secured a population there when America cast off her allegiance. And here again we see the adaptation that exists in human affairs; for, had there been no Western settlements when the war began in earnest, the power of Britain operating from Canada, in connection with the whole body of Indians, must have changed, and might have materially changed, the event of that strife. No human being knows how far the struggles of Boone, Logan, and their companions, together with the genius of Clark, affected the issue of the Revolution; but it is clear, that their influence on it was not slight.

And these frontier men, during the years from 1769 to

---

* Sparks's *Washington*, Vol. II. pp. 346-387.

1774, were quietly passing into the rich valleys of Kentucky, and scouring her woods for game. The Indians saw "the pen," in which, as Teedyuscung said, they were crowded, growing more and more narrow. Their hunting-grounds were the hunting-grounds of the whites, and even their homes were scarce sacred from the European's claims. Settlers were swarming upon the Wabash.* Nor was this all; for, as the emigrants became stronger, they became bolder, and the red men were insulted by them. And so wrong followed wrong. The savages stole the horses of the settlers, and the settlers took vengeance as they could. A white family was murdered, and their fellow-whites fell upon the nearest native town, and destroyed it, careless if its indwellers were guilty or innocent. These things were known, and the savages became jealous and angry. Parties collected, and war was threatened. The whites kept even pace with their foes in hatred, and far outdid them in treachery. The well-known murders on the Ohio, near Yellow and Captina Creeks, took place. Logan's family was destroyed, and this old friend of the whites was made their deadly foe. Next fell the traders who were among the Indians, and the revenge wreaked upon them spoke of long-smothered and now desperate passion. One, who was killed near the town of White Eyes, the peace-chief of the Muskingum Delawares, was cut in pieces, and his remains hung upon the bushes. The Delaware went out, collected, and buried them; but the next day they were disinterred, and scattered far and wide. White Eyes, however, again collected them, and in a secret place gave them burial.

War was now fully declared; and the Senecas, led on by Logan, with the Shawanese, headed by Comstock, poured down upon the settlements of Western Virginia, with all the

* See Gage's Proclamation, April 8th, 1772, in *Land Laws*, Appendix.

ferocity of wild men whose passions were fully up, and who felt their cause to be a just one. For a few months the contest was most bloody. But the Virginians were now comparatively at home in the West; and troops were soon mustered and led to the Kenhawa. At the mouth of this river, in October, 1774, was fought the well-known battle of Point Pleasant, described by every writer on Western history, and even given at some length by Mr. Stone in his "Life of Brant"; in consideration of which we omit all details of it, and also of the march by Lord Dunmore and General Lewis, through Ohio, upon the Scioto towns. There was held the treaty, at which Logan's famous speech was made; and there Comstock, one of the most fearless and masterly red men of whom we have any record, submitted to the power of the whites.

This war of 1774, known sometimes as Logan's war, sometimes as Dunmore's, was the last conflict of the British with the Western Indians; for, even while Dunmore was marching into the Western country, he was doubting the stability of the British power in America, and probably hastened on a peace with the savages because he saw the necessity of a quick return to the sea-coast. The peace made by him, however, did not prevent the Shawanese of the Miami valley from waging war upon the Kentucky settlers. In truth, from the spring of 1774 to the peace of Wayne in August, 1795, there was not any cessation in the warfare between the whites and the Indians. Lord Dunmore, it is true, states his treaty with the Shawanese to have contained an agreement on their part to hunt south of the Ohio; but, unluckily, this was made in the valley of the Scioto and not that of the Miami, where dwelt no small part of the nation.* We have

* See, as to Dunmore's war, Doddridge, Heckewelder's *Narrative*, Butler's *Kentucky*, Jefferson's *Notes on Virginia*, Virginia *Gazette*, 1775, referred to by Butler.

not followed, and do not care to follow, the first wanderers in Kentucky through their perils and adventures, though there is much of interest in them. The first house built by the white man in that region was not erected until two months after the battle of Lexington;* and, as we do not propose to carry this sketch beyond the opening of the Revolution, the settlement of the lands south of the Ohio does not now come within our reach. But, some time before Dunmore's war, there had been a settlement made north of the Ohio, which we cannot omit to speak of, though so isolated was it in its purposes and character, that we have thus far said nothing of it.

Our readers will remember the bold and calm Moravian, Christian Frederick Post, who journeyed to the Big Beaver Creek in 1758, and won the Delawares to peace. This same man, in 1761, thinking the true faith might be planted among those Western tribes, journeyed out to the Muskingum, and, upon the banks of that stream, about a mile from Beaver's Town, built himself a house.† The next season, that is, in the spring of 1762, he again crossed the mountains in company with the well-known Heckewelder, who went out as his assistant. The Indians having consented to his living among them, and teaching their children to read and write, Post prepared to clear a few acres whereon to raise corn. The chiefs hearing of this called him to them, and said they feared he had changed his mind, for, instead of teaching their children, he was clearing land; which if he did, others might do, and then a fort be built to protect them, and then the land claimed, and they be driven off, as had always, they said, been the case. Post replied, that a teacher must live, and, as he did not wish to be a burden on them, he proposed to raise his own food. This reply the

* Butler's *Kentucky*, p. 28.

† Heckewelder's *Narrative*, p. 59.

Indians considered, and told him, that, as he claimed to be a minister of God, just as the French priests did, and as these latter looked fat and comely though they did not raise corn, it was probable that the Great Spirit would take care of him as he did of them, if he wished him to be his minister; so they could only give him a garden spot. This Captain Pipe stepped off for him, and with this he had to shift as well as he could.

These proceedings were in 1762, and while they show the perfect perception which the Indians had of their dangers, and of the English tactics, explain most clearly the causes of the next year's war.

Post continued to till his little garden spot and teach his Indian disciples through the summer of 1762, and in the autumn accompanied King Beaver to Lancaster, in Pennsylvania, where a fruitless treaty was concluded with the whites. Returning from this treaty in October, he met Heckewelder, who had been warned by his red friends to leave the country before war came, and was forced back upon the settlements.

From this time until the autumn of 1767, no Moravians visited the West. Then, and in the following spring, Zeisberger went to the Alleghany, and there established a mission, against the will, however, of the greater part of the savages, who saw nothing but evil in the white man's eye.* The fruits would not ripen, the deer would not stay, they said, where the white man came. But Zeisberger's was a fearless soul, and he worked on, despite threats and plots against his life; and not only held his place, but even converted some of the leading Indians. Among these was one who had come from the Big Beaver, for the purpose of refuting the Moravians; and, this man being influential, the missionaries were in 1770 invited to come to the Big Beaver,

* Heckewelder's *Narrative*, p. 98.

whither they went in April of that year, settling about twenty miles from its mouth. Nor did the kindness of the Indians stop here. The Delawares of the Muskingum, remembering perhaps what Post had done among them ten years before, invited the Christian Indians of Pennsylvania to come and live on their river; and in this invitation the Wyandots joined. The proposition was long considered, and at last agreed to; and on the 3d of May, 1772, Zeisberger, with twenty-seven of his native disciples, founded Shoenbrun, upon the Muskingum, — the first true Christian settlement made within the present State of Ohio, and the beginning of that which was destroyed by the frontier men ten years afterward, in so cruel and cowardly a manner. To this settlement, in the course of the next year, the Christian Indians of the Susquehannah, and those of the Big Beaver, removed. Though endangered by the war of 1774, it was not injured, and, when our Revolution began, was the only point beyond Pittsburg where the English were dwelling and laboring.

And here we must close this meagre and dim outline of the history of the Ohio valley. We have attempted little else than a sketch of those events which were connected with that valley, because of Louisiana and Canada we have histories and annals, but of the course of things in the Ohio country, no continuous record whatever. Let us now, for a moment, look back and glance at the events already spoken of.

From 1670 to 1750, the French were silently founding their towns in the West, unsuspected and unopposed by the natives. A few English traders were straying into the country, and the Indian tribes heard of proposals to settle their lands, on the part of the British; while the Iroquois, claiming the whole Ohio valley, but occupying only a very small part of it, had, previous to the year 1750, been by degrees becoming familiarized to the idea of selling those claimed lands to the white men, to whom, by the treaty of 1744, they did actually sell some of them. About 1750, the Indians found their homes about to be invaded by both English and French. Hoping to prevent the evils apprehended, they first (1752) called on the English to keep out the French, and then were persuaded to join the French (1755). The war followed (1756). The French were driven out (1758); and the English built forts in the Indian country to defend them from the return of their late allies (1760). By 1762, settlers began to annoy and alarm the natives, who feared the English wanted rather to have their lands, than to defend them; and they made a gigantic effort to free themselves from their oppressors (1763). They were conquered (1764), and more English were put among them, though their lands were guaranteed to them (1765). In a few years those lands were once more invaded, and another war threatened (1766, 1767). Then the hunting-grounds of the Shawanese, Delewares, and Miamis were bought of the Iroquois (1768), and whites began to flock into them, against the protests of the occupants (1770, &c.). These whites injured the savages (1773). Once again war came (1774), and once again the savages were conquered (1774). There we leave the parties; the Indians overcome, but full of hate, and jealousy, and a determination to defend their rights; the Europeans claiming that beautiful country under fraudulent and void deeds, and holding it by the right of might.

Against the French the English had no claim, save as defenders of the Indians under the old deed of the Six Nations. Against the Indians they had no claim at all. The simple truth with respect to the British possessions in the West, in 1775, was this; that Britain had conquered France, and had conquered the Indians, and had, to what territory she occupied, the right of conquest, and no other.

VII.

THE PIONEERS OF KENTUCKY.*

We wish, if we can, to shake ourselves free from books, and cities, and the present time, and go with our readers into the grim and green wilderness, and look at the pioneers as they press so boldly, yet cautiously, forward, and build their cabins in the shade of the noble forests which cover the hunting-grounds of the Cherokee and the Shawanese.

The spring of 1769 rose calmly over those broad woodlands. Not a cabin, not a wigwam, lay hidden in those budding valleys; not a white man's foot profaned their ancient silence. Elsewhere there was noise enough. Boston merchants, and Virginia burgesses, and British ministers, all scolding at once about the right of trial in the colonies, and the non-importation of English goods; traders swearing and Indians yelling, from the Ohio to Lake Erie. The western slopes of the Alleghanies swarmed with emigrants. On the Wabash and the Illinois, red, white, and mongrel men made the prairies hideous with their orgies. In the South, and along the Mississippi, the Anglo-Saxons were already crowding the Frenchman and the Spaniard. But in the midst of all this busy life, in the centre of this whirlpool of humanity, lay a virgin land, unknown to the white, uninhabited by

---

* From the North American Review, for January, 1846.

the red man, — the Dark and Bloody Ground, — the hunter's paradise; the home of the buffalo and the elk. Englishmen had sailed up and down the "Belle Rivière" for twenty years; they had built trading stations in the centre of Ohio; they knew the Miami, and the Scioto, and the Maumee by heart; they had formed great companies to colonize the West. But the peerless forests of that neutral ground, where the Indians of the North and South met to chase the bison together, or to engage in deadly conflict, had been scarce ever entered by the pioneers of the West, the roaming traders.

The reason is plain enough; there were no dwellers there, none to trade with. Of one band, a dim and shadowy company, and of one only, we hear, as having entered Kentucky before 1769. In 1767, John Finley, — with others, we cannot doubt, — having crossed the mountains by the Cumberland Gap, instead of following the old beaten path of business to the Cherokees and other Southern savages, turned northward, along an Indian track known as the Warrior's Road, which led from the Cumberland Ford over the broken country lying upon the eastern branches of the Kentucky River, on to the mouth of the Scioto. John was a business man, and saw a good chance for speculation by buying up the Indians' peltries on the spot where they took them; and it seems that he drove a good trade, and was pleased with the country; so that he left, promising himself a speedy return and further profits. Slowly over that rugged region Finley and his comrades toiled back to Carolina; and the tales they told of the game that filled those new lands buzzed far and wide among the long-legged, fearless hunters that ranged the eastern slope, and the steep valleys of the Appalachian range.

Among these hunters was one Daniel Boone, who, with his wife and children, lived in the upper valley of the Yadkin; a man in the prime of life, thirty-six years of age, —

for he was born in the same year with Washington, 1732.* He was a quiet man, who had known poverty, and after many changes was poor still. A born hunter Daniel was, and fond of nothing but hunting, — a man who preferred to roam the mountain, and sleep in a cavern or camp by a gushing spring, to the dull farm life and the home fireside. We say he was a born hunter; he possessed the instinct of the bee, and could go to his own dwelling in a bee-line from any point to which his wanderings might carry him. Fatigue, hunger, and exposure he could bear like an Indian. Strong, but light, active as a deer, courageous, but cautious, kind, silent, thoughtful, he was the very man to act the part of pioneer. And to him, among others, came rumors of the new lands which the traders had visited, and his heart burned within him. He sought out Finley, and from his own lips learned that of a truth there was a country where buffalo swarmed like flies in summer, and where the wild turkey and the deer were scarce worth wasting powder upon. How he meditated on the tales he had heard, how he discussed the wisdom of an excursion to the Far West with Mrs. Boone, and how she vanquished him in argument, but could not change his heart one hair's breadth, how he climbed the mountains and thought of the distant Eden, and slept by the brook-side and dreamed of it, — all these things our readers must imagine as they best can. Little doubt can exist that the year before Boone's journey began was a year of hesitation, and hope, and doubt, and deep thought. But the temptation was too strong for him. The winter of 1768 – 69 wore away, and listlessly Daniel performed his spring duties on the farm, and sighed as he thought how the year was passing by. March passed, and April glided

* Or 1735. See Rev. J. M. Peck's *Memoir of Daniel Boone*, in Sparks's *American Biography*. This date was obtained from the children of Colonel Boone's sisters, by L. C. Draper, Esq., of Baltimore. — Ed.

on, and still he lingered. But at length Finley prepared to return to the place he had before visited, and renew his trade with the savages; and, on the 1st of May, throwing aside plough and hoe, Daniel tightened his belt, put a new edge to his knife, shouldered his rifle, bade his wife and little ones good by, and, in company with five comrades, started "in quest of the country of Kentucky."

Finley led the way; by the Negro Mountain, over range after range of rugged hills, through the Cumberland Gap, northward by the ford, on and on they toiled toward the Red River, a branch of the Kentucky, running from the eastern highlands. Rain poured upon the little band of pioneers; the paths were most rough and toilsome; and as days came and went, — one week, two, three, — and still steep hills and narrow valleys, gushing streams and tangled woods, alone met their eyes, they began to think more highly of having a roof within a hundred miles of one, and a change of clothes once a month in rainy weather. But they had put their hands to the plough, and might not look back. Five weeks had gone and the sixth was entered upon, when Finley began to recognize the neighbourhood; the hills were less abrupt; the forest was more open; cane-brakes began to appear; now and then small herds of buffalo were seen; and at length, upon the 7th of June, the wet, weary sojourners stopped, built themselves a cabin, dried their clothes, cleaned their guns, talked over their plans by the blazing fire, and fell asleep by its embers.

They talked over their plans, but what they were we know not. Nothing can well be more barren than the preposterous paper prepared by John Filson from Boone's account of himself; and yet that paper is our only source of exact information as to the events of much of the pioneer's life. From it we learn, that, from June 7th to the 22d of December, 1769, the band of adventurers hunted with great success, and that, upon the last-named day, Boone and one of his companions were suddenly attacked by Indians and made prisoners; whereupon the other four took to their heels and got back to the settlements as soon as possible. This is all that we know; but in accordance with the habit of more eminent historians, it may be proper, in the absence of facts, to introduce some suppositions. We would suggest, therefore, that, during the six months and a half spent before the attack of the savages, Finley and his fellows had been trading with the Indians as on his former visit. That six white men could scour the choice hunting-grounds of the natives, undiscovered, for half a year, is not to be believed, and probably friendly relations during that time existed between the white and red men. But how these relations were disturbed we know not. Very probably some of Boone's comrades were knaves and cheated their simple customers; or it may have been jealousy of the strangers, who, from mere passing traders, seemed changing into residents and claimants of the lands, that led the Indians to the act of violence recorded by Boone.

But whatever may have caused the natives to assume a hostile attitude toward the new-comers, certain it is that from that 22d of December, 1769, they always maintained it, till the power of the invaders was too great to be longer resisted, and Wayne wrung from them the treaty of Greenville. Boone and his companion were their first prisoners, and remained in durance for seven days. During that time they avoided showing any sign of hoping, or even of wishing, to escape, and thus succeeded in throwing their captors off their guard, so that, after a week of confinement, they were able to set themselves free. Boone does not tell us that he used this time in noticing the ways and stratagems of the Indians; but we cannot doubt that he did so, and thus prepared himself more effectually to baffle them at their peculiar art and mystery. Indeed, we have often thought that he continued so long in captivity for the very purpose of making himself acquainted with those customs and tricks, which he had never before, probably, had so good an opportunity of learning. When free, he and his friend soon found their way back to the camp where they had spent the summer; but behold! it was deserted. It was no part of Boone's plan, however, after he had once entered so deeply into the dangers and delights of the wilderness, to leave them on the first show of danger; and he, with Stewart, his companion in captivity, continued to hunt as before, only using greater precautions against being once more surprised by the savages.

While Daniel was thus daring the perils of the extreme frontier, his brother, Squire Boone, a man of equal skill and spirit, was on his way from the settlements to join him. Following the Warrior's Road, he came at last, in company with one other man, to the camp near the Red River, and there found his predecessors still alive and full of hope and courage. Whether he brought out any messages from Mrs. Daniel to her husband — orders to return, or the like — history fails to notice; but if the bearer of any such requests, he bore them to no purpose, for the wanderer had no thought of going back to the plough while he could live so comfortably by the rifle. These four then commenced their winter campaign; but not many weeks had passed before Stewart was killed by the Indians, an event which probably induced the new-comer, Squire Boone's companion, to return to Carolina; and thus the brothers were left alone in the great forest of Kentucky. It was early in the year 1770 that they were thus left, and until March, 1771, they remained by themselves, with the exception of the months of May and June, 1770, when Squire Boone returned to the borders of the civilized world to provide a supply of powder and shot, while Daniel, without even a dog for company, hunted, travelled, ate, slept, meditated, and enjoyed his leisure.

It is impossible for men who have grown up in our tame civilization to enter into the feelings of one so situated. Many hundred miles from all to whom he could look for aid, in a boundless wood filled with subtle and cruel enemies, dependent upon his gun, yet with a scanty supply of ammunition, without a comrade or the hope of one, — and still contented and cheerful, nay, very happy. Every day he changed his position; every night he slept in a different place from the one he had occupied the night before; constantly in danger, he was forced to be constantly on his guard; but freedom, the love of nature, the excitement of peril, and the pleasures of the chase, appear to have repaid him for all his trials, toils, and watchfulness. One circumstance, which helps us to explain Boone's security while among the bands of roaming savages, and, as we should suppose, in hourly dread of losing his life, was this; the forests of Kentucky at that early period were filled with a species of nettle, which being once trodden on retained for a long time the impression of the foot; even a turkey might with ease be tracked in it. This weed, the Indians, numerous and fearless, took no pains to avoid, while the solitary hunter never touched it; it thus became to him a sure and easy means of knowing the presence, position, and numbers of his enemies, without betraying his own whereabouts. The surface of the country was as if covered with snow for the feet of his foes, but naked for his own.

Probably most of his time was spent about the valleys of the Kentucky and Licking. In the former was the choice region where he afterwards settled; in the latter he sought for salt, and was able also to kill any number of buffalo he desired. One that has not seen them cannot realize the exquisite beauty of the forests near Lexington and Versailles. Free from all rugged undergrowth, but filled originally with the slender, graceful cane; carpeted by a turf like that of an English park, and with scarce a dry leaf to be seen; the trees tall and stately, and of the most beautiful varieties; the surface slightly rolling, with springs bursting from every hill-side, and clear brooks singing along every valley, — these forests are the pride of the West. And these, when Boone first entered them, were swarming with game of every kind, bird and beast. No wonder he thought Kentucky an Eden. We can almost forgive Filson, who fills these noble woods with blossoms and fruit at the close of December.

The Licking valley possessed none of the charms of that of the Kentucky, but it contained an invaluable treasure in the mineral spring at the Blue Licks, now a fashionable watering-place. The hills of the Licking are steep and rugged; near the Blue Licks they are barren and stony; stripped of all herbage and of every bush, and beaten to macadam by the tramping, for ages, of immense herds of buffalo, elk, and mammoth. The spring itself is somewhat saline, that is, impregnated with common salt; but it also contains many other mineral ingredients. It is a favorite water throughout the West and Southwest, the planters buying it in barrels, and drinking it in the morning as a preservative against bilious diseases. To the early settlers this spring had a threefold value; it supplied them with salt, it was their grand medicine-chest, and it attracted immense quantities of game. From it in various directions went off great buffalo tracks, like turnpikes, along which the animals of the forest were for ever coming and going; while about the spring itself, in the open valley, were sometimes gathered ten or twenty thousand bisons at a time. Such, at least, was the calculation of their numbers made by Simon Kenton, who lived near by, and was there very frequently. One obstacle alone interfered with the enjoyment of this unlimited supply of game; in consequence of the bare character of the hills about the spring, it was impossible to approach the animals without exposing one's self to an enemy in the surrounding forest. But the nature of the hills and valleys, abrupt and varied, afforded excellent opportunities for concealment, and for the exercise of that skill and cunning upon which the hunters prided themselves.

We once heard an anecdote strikingly illustrative of this skill, which, if we remember right, came from Boone himself to our informant. Boone had approached the Licking from the west at the same time that Simon Kenton had reached the borders of the valley from the east. Each paused to reconnoitre, before he left the covert of the woods; and each ascertained the presence of another human being in the neighbourhood. Then commenced a process on the part of each for learning who the other was without revealing himself; and such wás their mutually baffling power of concealment, that forty-eight hours passed before either could satisfy himself that the other was not an Indian and a foe.

About this spring, and through the region extending thence to the point where Boonesborough was afterwards built, Daniel hunted during nearly two months that his brother was absent. On the 27th of June they were safely reunited, and again pursued their adventures together.

But we must for a time leave them to wander, while we notice the entrance, at that very period, into the South of Kentucky, of a band known as the Long Hunters. It was led by Colonel James Knox, and consisted, at the outset, of forty hunters, only nine of whom crossed the whole Appalachian range; and while the Boones were wandering solitary over the sunny slopes about the Elkhorn, these men explored the wild and broken region lying upon the northern borders of Tennessee. But little is known even now of the vast country lying along the western slope of the Alleghanies from Kentucky to Georgia. The people of the interior of Africa have been more fully described, and the depths of the Himalaya range more thoroughly investigated. The whole region is as rugged as well can be, where there are neither volcanoes nor alpine peaks. You travel from two to three hundred miles, through a district destitute even of a cart-road, and where a wheeled vehicle was never seen. Three of the country towns of Kentucky are approachable only by bridle-paths. In many parts, even horses cannot find footing. An informant, who tried to penetrate without a guide to the falls of the Cumberland, told us he was forced to leave his saddle and find his way on foot, sometimes on all fours. At one point, he came to a little settlement, and, knocking at a door to ask for food, was astonished to find himself, when it was opened, clasped in the arms of a stout mountain maiden; not remembering ever to have seen her before, he knew not what to think of the civility, till he learned that it was twelve years since she had seen any one except the half-dozen persons who lived near by, and a stranger was to her too great a rarity, too exquisite a luxury, to escape an enthusiastic welcome.

Into this most rough and inhospitable tract Colonel Knox and his companions forced their way in pursuit of the buffalo, and from the length of time they were absent from their homes, they obtained, in the traditions of the West, their name of the Long Hunters. In that same year, 1770, George Washington also visited the Ohio for the second time, going as far down as the Great Kanawha, to examine lands in that vicinity to which he had claims. The journal of his trip may be found in the appendix to the second volume of Mr. Sparks's great work; one fact alone therein mentioned is of much import to us in relation to Western history; that fact is the growing impatience of the Indians at the gradual encroachments of the whites on the lands south of the Ohio. To those lands England had obtained a nominal title by the treaty of Fort Stanwix, made two years before; but from what Washington saw, it is clear that the Mingoes and Shawanese of the West were not disposed to yield their hunting-lands at the bidding of the proud Iroquois of New York, and already the exasperation which resulted in Dunmore's war had shown itself in various ways.*

But of Washington and Knox the Boones knew nothing. Having stayed as long as they dared in the neighbourhood of the Kentucky River, they went southward toward the Cumberland, and there continued their strange, dangerous, but exciting life, until March, 1771, when they returned home.

From 1771 till 1773, the beauties and excellences of the West were in a great degree lost sight of. In England there was enough of discussion and bad blood relative to the great valley of the Mississippi; but in Carolina, Boone leaned upon his plough, and through Virginia and Pennsylvania the frontier men moved lazily or not at all. Why this was so we have no means of ascertaining; but all the meagre records of Western history yet accessible give us no hint of any important steps taken in the settlement of the land until 1773. In that year, by the Ohio River, went on their labors the McAfees, Thomas Bullitt, Hancock, Taylor, James Douglas, Colonel Floyd, and others less known to provincial fame; while Boone, poorer than any of them, but now world-famous, hitched his team and gathered his cattle, and took his wife and household gods, and began his journey of emigration by the same Cumberland route which he had taken on his first expedition.

But it was not destined that he should yet become a "residenter" of the Eden he was bound to. He had sold his farm, reconciled his helpmate to her new lot, had shaken hands twice over with all the neighbours, — for every body loved him, — and on the 25th of September had set his face Kentucky-ward. He had climbed the Blue Ridge and the Iron Mountains, crossed the valley of the Clinch, and had

---

* See, on this whole subject, *North American Review*, Vol. XXXV. pp. 1 – 20.

won his way over Powell's Ridge, and was drawing nigh to the last great barrier, the Cumberland range, with five families from the Yadkin besides his own, and forty men who had joined him in Powell's valley, when, upon the 10th of October, unlooked for as thunder from a clear sky, a band of Indians poured upon the rear of the little emigrant army a deadly fire. Women shrieked, children squalled, the cattle broke and ran, horses reared and plunged, the young men drew their rifles to their shoulders, and the old "treed" instantly. A few moments decided the matter; the whites were victors; but six dead men, and one badly injured, gave them an idea of the nature of frontier life. Among the dead was Daniel Boone's oldest son. A council of the survivors was at once called, and though, we presume, only men were present thereat, we doubt not that women and children were represented. Anxiety was in every face; the hostile conduct of the savages, their evident preparation to resist all further invasion of their hunting-grounds, the loss of cattle, the fears of wives and daughters, the probability of a universal massacre if they went forward, — all concurred in recommending an immediate retreat; and Daniel found himself unwillingly obliged to resign his paradise on the very day that he was called to weep the death of his son. They turned on their track, and retrod their steps to Clinch River, a distance of forty miles. Alas for our woodman! Another year of quiet, stupid repose and farm labor seemed destined to try his patience. Dozing in security under his stoop by the westward flowing stream, he sighed for the howl of the wolf, and the stealthy, scarce-leaf-rustling tread of the Shawanese.

He dozed, but dreamed not how rapidly, since he left them, his fellow white men had desecrated the solemn forest-temples he had wandered and worshipped in. All that summer of 1773 had Mammon been sending his pioneers into the wilderness, — surveyors and speculators. Gallant men many of them were, and they loved dearly the life of danger they led. Far superior to Boone in the power of planning, in grasp of intellect, in education, fortune, and demeanour, there were still few or none of them his equals in forest-craft and a simple love of forest-life. They measured out, with cool, scientific, money-loving eyes, the glorious valleys and greensward woods, at sight of which Boone's lids had run over with tears of delight. They laid out towns where he had fancied the buffalo and deer would congregate for ever; and though already the fierce mutterings of the tribes beyond the Ohio reached their ears, and they knew a contest to be inevitable, they lingered, rod and chain in hand, on the pleasant banks of the Elkhorn, or by the cave-born rivulets that feed the Kentucky.

Meanwhile, the long-smothered hatred of the Indians was burning towards a clear flame. Injury upon injury inflicted by the unprincipled land-jobbers, who swarmed along the Ohio from Wheeling downward, made every savage heart beat with darker blood; and when, toward the close of April, 1774, those massacres took place in which Logan's family wholly perished, human nature — not to say Indian nature — could stand it no longer; the tomahawk and the scalping-knife grew bright in every wigwam. From afar Boone heard the coming tempest, and longed to join in the war-dance; for he hated an Indian as heartily as he loved an Indian life. He longed, but without prospect, until one day, behold! riding down the valley in a foam, a messenger from Virginia, from Governor Dunmore, seeking one Boone, Daniel Boone, a woodman that had been in the West. All flocked to the door to hear the strange news. Boone sent for by a governor! Think of it! And for what? To go westward to the falls of the Ohio and thereabouts, and conduct in the surveying parties who were lounging and measuring in that region; for the gleam of steel was all along the border. Daniel looked at his wife, drew a long breath, took down his rifle with the air of one whose mind is made up, though he does not say so, cast a second glance at his helpmate, who could not say nay when a governor and earl was the asker, and accepted the proposition.

Accordingly, on the 6th of June, 1774, in company with one Michael Stoner, he started upon his perilous journey, reached the surveyors in safety, and in safety reconducted them to the settlements; the distance gone over being, by Boone's calculation, about eight hundred miles, and the time taken, two months. This trip, or "tour," as Mr. Filson calls it, exhibited the completeness of Boone's woodcraft to so great advantage as to lead to his after employment, first by Governor Dunmore, and next by a company which was proposing to settle the West on a large scale.

But before we speak of Boone's agency in the actual clearing and peopling of Kentucky, we ought to refer to an individual who explored the central portion of the State during the summer in which the North Carolina pioneer was engaged in rescuing the surveyors, and who built the first house in the West. This was James Harrod, the founder of Harrodsburg, where he erected his log-cabin in 1774, although Dunmore's war obliged him to abandon it for a season the same year. Harrod was not a man of education, that is, of book-learning; he knew the woods, and, partially, the world; his rifle he knew exactly and perfectly; and the heart of man had been read by him with care, though not with selfish care. He was a bold, dashing, active man; fond, like Boone, of forest life, but far less solitary and silent in his moods than that white Indian. He was a kindly man, too; a natural, born gentleman, a practical philanthropist, one who would spend hours of hard labor, and risk his life, to reclaim a poor neighbour's horse or cow. He was too much a hunter and a lover of frontier life to play a great part in the politics of the West; but over his comrades his influence was very great, and his name deserves to be held in respect by all who feel respect for those manly qualities which a border life so much calls for. He was forced to return, as we have said, from the valley of the Kentucky to that of the Kanawha, during the summer or early fall of 1774, to take his part in the war with the Shawanese. That war, however, was soon over; the battle of Point Pleasant and the treaty of Camp Charlotte having closed it by November, 1774. Then began the real settlement of Kentucky, which, till that time, lay in all its forest beauty. The rude shed which Finley and Boone had built in 1769 had crumbled away, and the hut of Harrod was empty. Here and there trees had been felled, perhaps corn planted; but, save in the brains of speculators, the land was still, in reality, the same virgin wilderness which the first explorers had found it. And this leads us back to Boone again.

In North Carolina, at that period, there prevailed the same fever which filled Virginia, a fever for Western lands. Among those who were infected was one Richard Henderson, a man of note in his own neighbourhood. He had grown to manhood without learning even to read or write; then he taught himself. He saw the world lying about him ready for use, and, filled as he was with energy, intellect, warm blood, and unguided ambition, he determined to use it for his own advancement. So he ran for constable, and won; then for under-sheriff; next began to creep up the slimy hill of legal renown and profit, until, while still young, he became associate chief judge of the colony. Meanwhile, he was no pedant, no dusty, dry recluse, but a gay, dashing, joking, popular man of the world. He lived freely, spent freely, speculated freely, and so lost all he had. What next? Thinking how to extricate himself, the rumors of the fine lands beyond the mountains came to his mind again. Some of his near friends had long known Boone, and had heard from his own lips the tales he delighted in of the paradise toward the setting sun. Would it be possible to get those far-off lands? If so, how? From the king or the Indians? Henderson saw the signs of the times; he felt King George's hand slipping off the unruly colonies; so he determined to get his fee from the savages. He soon learned the claim of the Southern Indians, and quietly sought the leaders of the Cherokees, and with them blocked out a treaty for the purchase of the lands lying between the Kentucky and Cumberland Rivers. Having associated with himself a number of rich and influential gentlemen for the prosecution of his scheme, a final deed was given by the Cherokees, on the 17th of March, 1775, at a meeting held on the Wataga, a branch of the Tennessee.

At this meeting Boone was present, on behalf of Henderson and his associates; and at once set forward upon its conclusion, and probably before its signature, to open a road to the region first purchased. It was a difficult and dangerous task. The Northern Indians were still smarting under the injuries which had caused the war of the year previous, and though the pipe of peace had been smoked with the Long Knives, it was no reason why their hunting-grounds should be invaded. As for the purchase from the Cherokees, what was it worth? The Cherokees never owned the land. Boone understood all this, and went upon his way with armed men, and muffled footsteps. Over the mountains, across the valleys, through the tangled thickets, round the rough knobs, silently and safely the road-makers, blazing the trees as they went, passed along; and at length the levels they were seeking came in sight. Though the Indians had not, up to that time, shown themselves, yet no sooner were the invaders within the plain than they were attacked. But the savages found their skill met by equal skill, and although they succeeded in killing four of the whites, they were unable seriously to impede their progress; and on the 1st of April, 1775, the little band, having reached the Kentucky

River and selected a site for their first station, began the construction of Boonesborough.

It was a fort, consisting of block-houses and cabins, which at first was the sole representative of the borough that bore Boone's name ; a fort some two hundred and fifty feet long by a hundred and fifty in breadth, placed sixty yards south or west of the river, near a salt-lick. Two months and a half of labor were devoted to it, — labor not without danger ; the pioneer worked with his axe in one hand and rifle in the other. Immediately upon its completion, Boone prepared to return to Carolina, and bring his family to the new home he had made ready for them. But before he went, he had borne his part in the organization of the new government which was to oversee the affairs of Henderson's colony, the colony or province of Transylvania.

Upon the very day on which Boone and his assistants commenced their station, Henderson, with forty armed men, reached Powell's valley, on his way westward, and, following the road marked out by Boone, on or before the 20th of May, came to where his pioneers watched and labored. It was his purpose at once to organize his followers, agree upon articles of union, and commence the process of legislation. Accordingly, word was instantly sent to the four stations which by that time had been begun ; for in the interval between Boone's arrival, late in March, and Henderson's, late in May, James Harrod had returned with a company, and commenced a settlement at a spot called Boiling Spring ; while Benjamin Logan, who had crossed the mountains in company with Henderson, had established himself at St. Asaph's. To these two germs of towns, and also to Harrodsburg and Boonesborough, Henderson sent solemn greeting, inviting each town to send delegates to the place we have last named, there to hold counsel and pass such laws as might seem fitting. On the 23d of May, according to summons, seventeen men took their places, as representatives of the youthful republic, under a vast elm-tree which grew about fifty yards from the Kentucky River, and around which the white clover spread as a carpet for their hall of legislation. A chairman and a clerk were chosen; God's blessing was asked by the Rev. Mr. Lythe, a delegate from Harrodsburg, and then the proprietors were informed that the meeting was ready to hear from them; whereupon Colonel Henderson made them a speech of some length on behalf of himself and associates. He laid down some of the great principles of legislation, and then drew the attention of his hearers to the peculiar laws required for them in their position. Among other subjects, he spoke of the need of laws providing for the recovery of debts, and referred with extreme severity to a proclamation which Lord Dunmore had issued when he heard of the purchase from the Cherokees, and wherein he put the world upon their guard against the baseless assertion of the Carolinians, that they were the true owners of the lands they claimed. Those lands the governor asserted to be within Virginia, and he treated the whole proceedings of the Transylvanians as illegal, and originating in a design to afford an asylum for debtors and desperadoes. The Carolina judge and his friends, many of whom were among the first men in America, treated with indignation, and rightly, this impudent assertion, that they wished to be the founders of an American Alsatia, — a prophetic picture of Texas. But while this ascription of base motives to them was needless and scandalous, Dunmore was perfectly right in the main point of Virginia's claim over the land in question; and his proclamation prevented that sale of lands by Henderson which might otherwise have taken place, besides serving as notice of the intention of Virginia, afterwards carried into effect, to exterminate the colony of Transylvania as an interloper.

Meantime, the members of the convention responded to the assertion of the proprietors, that they were entitled to frame rules for their own government, and proceeded forthwith, with praiseworthy speed, to the business of legislation. They were in session three working-days, and in that time passed nine laws, and framed a compact between the proprietors and people of the province. The laws they passed were as follows: — for establishing courts; for punishing crimes; for regulating the militia; for punishing swearing and Sabbath-breaking; providing for writs of attachment; fixing fees; for preserving the range; for improving the breed of horses; for preserving game. It is pleasant to notice that the last three bills were brought in by the Boones, both of whom were members of the convention. Such were the labors of the first Western legislature; they were, as we have intimated, all in vain, in consequence of the superior claim of Virginia; but they show that there was a free and self-sustaining spirit in the colony, and prove the presence of right principle among its founders. The first settlers of Kentucky have had no little injustice done them, in consequence of the existence at a later period of a class of "river men," who became, in the view of many, the representatives of the whole race of pioneers. But nothing could be more unlike the boasting, swearing, fighting, drinking, gouging Mike Finks, than Boone, Logan, Harrod, and their comrades, the founders of the commonwealth.

No sooner was the fort of Boonesborough completed than its founder prepared to do that which his heart had long been set upon, and which he had once before undertaken; we mean, the transfer of his family to the West. He therefore left, about the middle of June, 1775, for the borders of the Clinch River, where his wife and children were still staying; and, having packed up his few household matters for the second time, in September he returned to Kentucky with his own and three other families, the party numbering twenty-seven fighting-men, and four women, — the first four that had ever entered the wilderness, the "mothers of the

West." These bold females were Mrs. Boone, Mrs. McGary, Mrs. Denton, and Mrs. Hogan. And well may they be called bold. The contest with England was just commencing; Washington was besieging Gage; and all through the colonies the feelings of men were growing more and more embittered. Amid this gathering storm, it was clear that the British might be expected to use the Indians of the West and North as auxiliaries in the war which seemed to be inevitable, and those who made the frontier their home could look for nothing but the terrors of a border contest of unknown duration. Notwithstanding the dangers which beset them, emigrants flocked to the Eden of Kentucky. Some went thither, moved only by an insane love of gain, by a hope of making fortunes without labor in land speculation; others saw in the new settlements the germ of a great community, which was to be guided and governed, and trusted to obtain that power which so many souls covet as life-food; others, again, hoped for a society free from the evils and diseases of older communities; while the fewest were moved, as Boone and Harrod were, by a love of nature, of perfect freedom, and of the adventurous life in the woods. Some have held the opinion, that the great pioneer, Daniel himself, was a mere land-jobber, and have even thought him a very selfish and dishonest one; but that idea is passing away, we believe, from the few minds which ever held it. That he entered a good deal of land is perfectly true; and that his entries were singularly incorrect, and subjected him and all holding from him to utter loss, and that they led him to claim what was not his, is not to be questioned; but no reader of his life, we think, can long hesitate to believe, that, if he had made a fortune by his lands, he would have been unable to use it beyond those supplies which his forest-life called for. He would have pined and died as a nabob in the midst of civilization. He wanted a frontier, and the perils and pleasures of a frontier life, not wealth; and he was happier in his log-cabin, with a loin of venison and his ramrod for a spit, than he would have been amid the greatest profusion of modern luxuries.

Among those men who came to Kentucky in 1775 was George Rogers Clark, of whom mention more than once has already been made in this work. He was a leader and a master spirit; full of genius, full of energy and enterprise, his heart was as large and as fearless as his mind was penetrating and capacious. His biography yet remains to be written; the necessary papers were once placed in the hands of Mr. Bliss, of Louisville; but his sudden and violent death left the contemplated work undone, and we understand that the persons having possession of the materials for a full account of the "Western Washington" are unable to agree upon any individual at once able and willing to undertake the task. But we trust, that, before it is too late to elucidate many subjects which the manuscripts alluded to must treat of, by oral communications from surviving pioneers, the biography of Clark may be completed. He first entered the West in 1775, as we have said; and, returning in 1776, at once assumed that prominent place in the affairs of his adopted land which he ever afterward retained. He saw the political importance of the new settlements, and perceived how great a benefit it would be to meet the British beyond the mountains, instead of suffering them to unite and concentrate the whole power of the Indians, north and south, upon the scattered positions along the mountain range, and thus create a powerful diversion in favor of the English armies, by assailing the colonies behind, while the regular troops were hunting the bleeding Continentals from Long Island to Germantown.

We have referred to the fact, that Virginia, even under her royal governor, denied the right of the Transylvanians to the lands they had purchased of the Cherokees. In addition to the trouble arising from this claim of the Old Dominion, the settlers under Henderson were not satisfied with the situation of mere tenants, nor yet to be under a set of proprietors; and this dissatisfaction was made more pressing by an unwise increase in the price of their lands on the part of the North Carolina purchasers. Clark easily saw just how the matter stood, and determined in his own mind that Kentucky should either be a part of the State of Virginia, and her citizens have the rights of Virginians, or that she should be independent of all the world. Acquainted as by instinct with mankind, and possessing that power, common to all leaders of mankind, the power of binding by enthusiastic sympathy other men to himself, he had not been long in the West before he had set such agencies at work as he trusted would accomplish his purposes. And he did not fail; in June, 1776, while the Declaration of Independence was ripening in the Philadelphia Congress, a little congress at Harrodsburg met, and appointed Clark himself and Gabriel Jones as members to represent Kentucky in the Assembly of Virginia. At this meeting, Clark was not present; had he been, instead of sending members to the legislature of the mother State, Kentucky would have sent persons with power to treat for admission into the rights of Virginia, or proclaim the independence of the Western colonies. And such, in substance, did he make his mission; and, after no little vexation and labor, he procured the erection of the frontier settlements into the separate county of Kentucky.

Those settlements, meanwhile, were with open eyes watching the movements of their Indian neighbours. All along the border the impression grew daily more and more definite, that the savages, instigated and backed by the British, would suddenly swoop down, as in the time of Pontiac, and lay all waste. The hated race of "cabiners," those speculators who came out to obtain a preëmption right by building a cabin and planting a crop; the wretched traders who were always wandering about the frontier; the hunters who were revelling among the countless herds of game now for the first time seen, — all began, during the winter and spring of 1776, to draw closer to the stations, and shrink from the shadows. And, within the stations, men sat round the fire with loaded rifles, and told their tales of adventure and peril with new interest, as every sound reminded them how near their deadly enemies might be. And from hour to hour scouts came in with rumors of natives seen here or seen there, and parties of the bold rangers drew their belts, and left the protection of their forts to learn the truth of these floating tales. But there was one who sat at such times silent and seemingly unheeding, darning his hunting-shirt, or mending his leggins, or preparing his rifle-balls for use; and yet to him all eyes often turned. Two or three together, the other hunters started by daylight to reconnoitre; silently he sat working, until the day had drawn herself into the shadow of the earth, and the forest paths were wrapped in gloom. Then, noiselessly as the day had gone, he went; none saw him go, — he had been among them a moment before, and then was missing. "And now," said the loiterers by the smouldering logs, "we shall know something sure; for old Daniel 's on the track." And when, by and by, some one yet wakeful saw the shadow of Boone, as he reëntered the cabin, unheard as a shadow, he found, as usual, that the solitary scout had learned all that was to be known, and the watchful slept in peace. We know of nothing more characteristic of Boone than this habit of his, so quietly, alone and in the darkness, to undertake the searching of the forest infested by Indians.

The spring of 1776 passed rapidly by, and summer came, and the grand woodlands lay in all their majestic beauty, clothed in leaves and blossoms, and the dreaded flood from the North had not yet come. But with July, — that memorable July, — the scene changed, and bands of Shawanese from beyond the Ohio, and of Cherokees from beyond the

Cumberland, suddenly swarmed in the forests. Every day brought news of some one murdered; the speculators and traders turned their faces eastward, and fled; even farms, just commenced, were abandoned, and, by the 20th of July, more than three hundred emigrants had sought the shelter of the mountain posts. From station to station the news of the immense desertion spread like a pestilence, breeding new desertion. In some forts scarce enough remained to man them; terror and anxiety were the common feelings of all but the calmest and bravest.

It was in the midst of this panic, on the afternoon of July 14th, that a daughter of Daniel Boone, some thirteen or fourteen years old, with two of her friends, daughters of Colonel Calloway, one about her own age, the other older, ventured upon the Kentucky in a little skiff within sight of Boonesborough. The bushes on the bank opposite the fort were thick, and came down to the water's edge; and little by little, the playful, laughing girls, paddling and splashing, drew near unconsciously to the thicket. A white man or two, lazily lounging in the shade of the station, watched the canoe as it rolled and danced, and said there would be an upset yet if those girls were n't careful. And from the bushes ten other keener eyes watched the dancing bark, — the eyes of savage and wily enemies. Little by little, as the skiff drew nearer, one dark form, like the noiseless serpent, slid to the water's edge, slid, hidden by overhanging boughs, into the bosom of the river, and was lost to sight. Suddenly the girls looked at each other half amazed, half alarmed; their boat, which was floating leisurely with the leisurely current, had turned its bow toward the northern bank, and, by unseen agency, was skimming the water directly towards that shore. One of them sprang forward, and just then rose to sight the head of the cunning Shawanese who had seized the rope dangling from the bow, and who laughed aloud as the bitter shriek of the entrapped maidens rung through the drowsy air. One shriek, and they were beneath the branches, and stout arms seized them, and rough hands closed their mouths, and they were borne away. That shriek the loungers on the opposite shore heard; had the boat upset, then? No, there she was, just passing into the shadow of the boughs; and they saw the girls struggling, and the dark forms of the captors, and heard the half-suppressed yell of triumph that they uttered, and the whole truth flashed on them. Then came the alarm, the hurry, the rapid council, and the inquiry, "Who will swim over for the canoe?" There was no other; but to seek that one, was it not certain death? The Indians perhaps still lay there under those green curtains, waiting to pick off the garrison one by one, should they seek to pursue.

How this problem was solved, how the boat was regained or another procured, we have no means of knowing. We merely learn from Colonel Floyd, that the want of a canoe detained the whites for some time, so that the pursuers were able to go but five miles before nightfall. By daybreak, however, Boone had recovered the trail, and the avengers set forward; but soon the track entered a cane-brake, through which the Indians had gone in such a manner as to make it impossible to follow them without spending hours in disentangling the maze, and hours could not be wasted. Life and death, freedom or captivity, hung upon the right use of every moment. Boone was not long at a loss; turning southward with his companions, so as to leave the track upon his left, having carefully observed its general direction, and feeling sure that the captors would take their prisoners to the Indian towns upon either the Scioto or the Miami, he boldly struck forward, and travelled with all speed thirty miles or more; then, turning at right angles toward the north, he looked narrowly for marks of the passage of the marauders. It was a bold and keen device, and the event proved it a sagacious one; for, after going a few miles, they came upon the

Indian trail in one of the great buffalo-paths. Inspirited with new hope and strength, the whites pushed forward quickly but quietly, and on the alert, lest unexpectedly they might come upon the red men. And well was it that they used great caution; for when, after going ten miles, they at length caught sight of the natives as they were leisurely, and half-stripped, preparing their dinner, the quick-eyed sons of the forest saw them as soon as they were themselves discovered. Boone had feared, that, if their approach was known, the girls would be killed instantly, and he was prepared for instant action. So soon, therefore, as the savages were seen, he and three of his companions fired, and then the whole body rushed forward so suddenly as to cause their opponents to take to their heels, without waiting for scalps, guns, knives, moccasons, or blankets; and the three terrified girls were recovered unhurt.

The remainder of 1776, and the whole of the next year, were passed by the Western settlers in the midst of danger, and want, and ceaseless anxiety. At times, the stations were assailed by large bodies of savages; at times, single settlers were picked off by single, skulking foes. The horses and cattle were driven away; the corn-fields remained uncultivated; the numbers of the whites became fewer and fewer, and from the older settlements little or no aid came to the frontier stations, until Colonel Bowman, in August, 1777, came from Virginia with one hundred men. It was a time of suffering and distress through all the colonies, which was in most of them bravely borne; but none suffered more, or showed more courage and fortitude, than the settlers of the West. Their conduct has excited less admiration out of their own section than that of Marion, and men like him, because their struggles had less apparent connection with the great cause of American independence. But who shall say what would have become of the resistance of the Colonies, had England been able to pour from Canada her troops upon the rear of the rebels, assisted, as she would have been, by all the Indian nations? It may have been the contests before the stations of Kentucky, and Clark's bold incursions into Illinois and against Vincennes, which turned the oft tottering fortunes of the great struggle.

But, however we may think of this point, we cannot doubt the picturesque and touching character of many incidents of Western history during the years from '77 to '80. Time has not yet so mellowed their features as to give them an air of romance precisely; but the essence of romance is in them. In illustration, we will mention one or two of these incidents, familiar enough in the West, but less known to the greater part of the readers of this journal.

One of the eminent men of Kentucky in those and later times was General James Ray. While yet a boy he had proved himself able to outrun the best of the Indian warriors; and it was when but seventeen years of age, that he performed the service for a distressed garrison of which we are about to speak. It was in the winter of 1776–77, a winter of starvation. Ray lived at Harrodsburg, which, like the other stations, was destitute of corn. There was game enough in the woods around, but there were also Indians more than enough, and had the sound of a gun been heard in the neighbourhood of the station, it would have insured the death of the one who discharged it. Under these circumstances Ray resolved to hunt at a distance. There was one horse left from a drove of forty, which Major McGary had brought to the West; an old horse, faithful and strong, but not fitted to run the gantlet through the forest. Ray took this solitary nag, and before day-dawn, day by day, and week by week, rode noiselessly along the runs and rivers until he was far enough to hunt with safety; then he killed his game, and by night, or in the dusk of evening, retraced his steps. And thus the garrison lived by the daring labors of this stripling of seventeen. Older hunters tried his plan, and were discovered; but he, by his sagacity, boldness, care, and skill, safely pursued his disinterested and dangerous employment, and succeeded in constantly avoiding the perils that beset him. We do not think that Boone or any one ever showed more perfectly the qualities of a superior woodsman than did Ray through that winter.

If any one ever did, however, it was surely Benjamin Logan, in the spring of that same year. Logan, as we have seen, crossed the mountains with Henderson, in 1775, and was of course one of the oldest settlers. In May, 1777, the fort at which Logan lived was surrounded by Indians, more than a hundred in number; and so silently had they made their approach, that the first notice which the garrison had of their presence was a discharge of fire-arms upon some men who were guarding the women as they milked the cows outside the station. One was killed, a second mortally wounded, and a third, named Harrison, disabled. This poor man, unable to aid himself, lay in sight of the fort, where his wife, who saw his condition, was begging some one to go to his relief. But to attempt such a thing seemed madness; for whoever ventured from either side into the open ground, where Harrison lay writhing and groaning, would instantly become a target for all the sharpshooters of the opposite party. For some moments Logan stood it pretty well; he tried to persuade himself and the poor woman who was pleading to him, that his duty required him to remain within the walls and let the savages complete their bloody work. But such a heart as his was too warm to be long restrained by arguments and judicious expediency; and suddenly turning to his men, he cried, "Come, boys, who 's the man to help me in with Harrison?" There were brave men there, but to run into certain death in order to save a man whom, after all, they could not save, — it was asking too much; and all shook their heads, and shrunk back from the mad pròposal. "Not one! not one of you help a poor fellow to save his scalp?" "Why, what 's the good, Captain? to let the red rascals kill us wont help Harrison." At last, one, half inspired by Logan's impetuous courage, agreed to go; he could die but once, he said, and was about as ready then as he should ever be. The gate was slightly opened, and the two doomed men stepped out; instantly a tempest of rifle-balls opened upon them, and Logan's companion, rapidly reasoning himself into the belief that he was not so ready to die as he had believed, bolted back into the station. Not so his noble-hearted leader. Alone, through that tempest, he sprang forward to where the wounded man lay, and while his hat, hunting-shirt, and hair were cut and torn by the ceaseless shower, he lifted his comrade like a child in his arms, and regained the fort without a scratch.

But this rescue of a fellow-being, though worthy of record in immortal verse, was nothing, compared with what this same Benjamin Logan did soon after. The Indians continued their siege; still they made no impression, but the garrison were running short of powder and ball, and none could be procured except by crossing the mountains. To do this the neighbouring forest must be passed, thronging with Indians, and a journey of some hundred miles accomplished along a path, every portion of which might be waylaid, and at last the fort must be reëntered with the articles so much needed. Surely, if an enterprise ever seemed hopeless, it was this one, and yet the thing must be tried. Logan pondered the matter carefully; he calculated the distance, not less than four hundred miles, in and back; he estimated the chance of aid from other quarters; and in the silence of night asked wisdom and guidance from God. Nor did he ask in vain; wisdom was given him. At night, with two picked companions, he stole forth from the station, every breath hushed. The summer leaves were thick above them, and with the profoundest care and skill, Logan guided his followers from tree to tree, from run to run, unseen by the savages, who dreamed not, probably, of the possibility of so dangerous an undertaking. Quickly but most cautiously pushing eastward, walking forty or fifty miles a day, the three woodsmen passed onward till the Cumberland range was in sight; then, avoiding the Gap, which they supposed would be watched by Indians, over those rugged hills, where man had never climbed before, they forced their way with untiring energy and a rapidity to us, degenerate as we are, inconceivable. The mountains crossed and the valley of the Holston reached, Logan procured his ammunition, and then turned alone on his homeward track, leaving his two companions with full directions to follow him more slowly with the lead and powder. He returned before them, because he wished to revive the hopes of his little garrison in the wilderness, numbering as it did in his absence only ten men, and they without the means of defence. He feared they would yield, if he delayed an hour; so, back, like a chamois, he sped, over those broken and precipitous ranges, and actually reached and reëntered his fort in ten days from the time he left it, safe and full of hope. Such a spirit would have made even women dare and do every thing, and by his influence the siege was still resisted till the ammunition came safe to hand. From May till September, that little band was thus beset; then Colonel Bowman relieved them. In the midst of that summer, as George Rogers Clark's Journal has it, "Lieutenant Linn was married, — great merriment!" This was at Harrodsburg, near by Logan's station. Such was the frontier life!

It was a trying year, 1777, for those little forts in the wilderness. At the close of it, three settlements only existed in the interior, — Harrodsburg, Boonesborough, and Logan's; and of these three the whole military population was but one hundred and two in number! Then 1778 came in; and the frontier men felt full of confidence, for the savages had tried, and in vain, to annihilate them, and had been forced to retire beyond the Ohio again, and the prospect of a quiet winter seemed reasonably good. One thing the stations much needed, however, — salt. So Boone, with thirty men, started for the Blue Licks, to enter upon the interminable business of boiling, the water being by no means strongly impregnated. Boone was to be guide, hunter, and scout; the rest cut wood and attended to the manufacturing department. January passed quietly, and before the 7th of February, enough of the precious condiment had been accumulated to lead to the return of three of the party to the stations with the treasure. The rest still labored on, and Boone enjoyed the winter weather in the forest after his own fashion. But, alas for him, there was more than mere game about him in those woods along the rugged Licking. On the 7th of February, as he was hunting, he came upon a party of one hundred and four foes, two Canadians, the remainder Indians, Shawanese apparently. Boone fled; but he was a man of forty-six, and his limbs were less supple than those of the young savages who pursued him, and in spite of every effort he was a second time prisoner. Finding it impossible to give his companions at the Licks due notice so as to secure their escape, he proceeded to make terms on their behalf with his captors, and then persuaded his men by gestures, at a distance, to surrender without offering battle. Thus, without a blow, the invaders found themselves possessed of twenty-eight prisoners, and among them the greatest, in an Indian's eyes, of all the Long Knives. This band was on its way to Boonesborough to attack or to reconnoitre; but so good luck as they had met with changed their minds, and turning upon their track, they took up their march for Old Chillicothe, an Indian town on the Little Miami.

It was no part of the plan of the Shawanese, however, to retain these men in captivity, nor yet to scalp, slay, or eat them. Under the influence and rewards of Governor Hamilton, the British commander in the Northwest, the Indians had taken up the business of speculating in human beings, both dead and alive; and the Shawanese meant to take Boone and his comrades to the Detroit market. On the 10th of March, accordingly, eleven of the party, including Daniel himself, were despatched for the North, and, after twenty days of journeying, were presented to the English governor, who treated them, Boone says, with great humanity. To Boone himself Hamilton and several other gentlemen seem to have taken an especial fancy, and offered considerable sums for his release; but the Shawanese also had become enamoured of the veteran hunter, and would not part with him. He must go home with them, they said, and be one of them, and become a great chief. So the pioneer found his very virtues becoming the cause of a prolonged captivity. In April, the red men, with their one white captive, about to be converted into a genuine son of nature, returned from the flats of Michigan, covered with brush-choked forests, to the rolling valley of the Miamis, with its hill-sides clothed in their rich, open woods of maple and beech, then just bursting into bloom. And now the white blood was washed out of the Kentucky ranger, and he was made a son in some family, and was loved and caressed by father and mother, brothers and sisters, till he was thoroughly sick of them. But disgust he could not show; so he was kind, and affable, and familiar, as happy as a lark, and as far from thinking of leaving them as he had been of joining them. He took his part in their games and romps; shot as near to the centre of the target as a good hunter ought to, and yet left the savage marksman a chance to excel him, and smiled in his quiet eye when he witnessed their joy at having done better than the best of the Long Knives. He grew into favor with the chief, was trusted, treated with great respect, and listened to with attention. No man could have been better calculated than Boone to disarm the suspicions of the red men. We have called him a white Indian, and, except that he never showed the Indian's bloodthirstiness when excited, he was more akin in his loves, his ways, his instincts, his joys, and his sorrows to the aboriginal inhabitants of the West than to the Anglo-Saxon invaders. Scarce any other white ever possessed in an equal degree the true Indian gravity, which comes neither from thought, feeling, or vacuity, but from a bump peculiar to their own craniums. And so in hunting, shooting, swimming, and other Shawanese amusements, the newly made Indian-boy Boone spent the month of May, necessity making all the little inconveniences of his lot quite endurable.

On the 1st of June, his aid was required in the business of salt-making, and for that purpose he and a party of his brethren started for the valley of the Scioto, where he stayed ten days, hunting, boiling brine, and cooking; then the homeward path was taken again. But when Chillicothe was once more reached, a sad sight met our friend Daniel's eyes; four hundred and fifty of the choice warriors of the West, painted in the most exquisite war-style, and armed for the battle. He scarce needed to ask whither they were bound; his heart told him Boonesborough; and already in imagination he saw the blazing roofs of the little borough he had founded, and saw the bleeding forms of his friends. Could he do nothing? He would see; meanwhile be a good Indian and look all ease and joy. He was a long way from his own white homestead; one hundred and fifty miles at least, and a rough and inhospitable country much of the way between him and it. But he *had* travelled fast and far, and might again. So, without a word to his fellow-prisoners, early in the morning of June the 16th, without his breakfast, in the most secret manner, unseen, unheard, he departed. He left his red relatives to mourn his loss, and over hill and valley sped, forty miles a day, for four successive days, and ate but one meal by the way. Such power there is in the human frame of withstanding all fatigue and hunger, when the soul is alive and strong within us.

He reached Boonesborough, — and where was his wife? Why did she not rush to see him? "Bless your soul," said his old companions, as they hailed him like one risen from the dead, and shook his hand till it tingled, "she put in to the settlements long ago; she thought you was dead, Daniel, and packed up and was off to Carolina, to the old man's." How Boone felt and looked we leave our readers to imagine; but he had little time to express his feelings, for he found the station wholly unprepared to resist so formidable a body as that which threatened it, and it was a matter of life and death that every muscle should be exerted to get all in readiness for the expected visitors. Rapidly the white men toiled in the summer sun, and through the summer night, to repair and complete the fortifications, and to have all as experience had shown it should be. But still the foe came not, and in a few days another escaped captive brought information of the delay of the expedition in consequence of Boone's flight. The savages had relied on surprising the stations, and their plans being foiled by their adopted son Daniel, all their determinations were unsettled. Thus it proved the salvation of Boonesborough, and probably of all the frontier forts, that the founder of Kentucky was taken captive and remained a captive as long as he did. So often do seeming misfortunes prove, in God's hand, our truest good.

Boone, finding his late relatives so backward in their proposed call, determined to anticipate them by a visit to the Scioto valley, where he had been at salt-making; and about the 1st of August, with nineteen men, started for the town on Paint Creek. He knew, of course, that he was trying a somewhat hazardous experiment, as Boonesborough might be attacked in his absence; but he had his wits about him, and his scouts examined the country far and wide. Without interruption, he crossed the Ohio, and had reached within a few miles of the place he meant to attack, when his advanced guard, consisting of one man, Simon Kenton, discovered two natives riding one horse, and enjoying some joke as they rode. Not considering that these two might be, like himself, the van of a small army, Simon, one of the most impetuous of men, shot, and rushed forward to scalp them, — but found himself at once in the midst of a dozen or more of his red enemies, from whom he escaped only by the coming up of Boone and the remainder. The commander, upon considering the circumstances, and learning from spies whom he sent forward that the town he intended to attack was deserted, came to the opinion that the band just met was on its way to join a larger body for the invasion of Kentucky, and advised an immediate return.

His advice was taken, and the result proved its wisdom; for, in order to reach Boonesborough, they were actually obliged to coast along, go round, and outstrip a body of nearly five hundred savages, led by Canadians, who were marching against his doomed borough, and, after all, got there only the day before them.

On the 8th of August, with British and French flags flying, the dusky army gathered around the little fortress of logs, defended by its inconsiderable garrison. Captain Duquesne, on behalf of his mighty Majesty, King George the Third, summoned Captain Boone to surrender. It was, as Daniel says, a critical period for him and his friends. Should they yield, what mercy could they look for? and he, especially, after his unkind flight from his Shawanese parents? They had almost stifled him with their caresses before; they would literally hug him to death, if again within their grasp. Should they refuse to yield, what hope of successful resistance? And they had so much need of all their cattle to aid them in sustaining a siege, and yet their cows were abroad in the woods. Daniel pondered the matter, and concluded it would be safe, at any rate, to ask two days for consideration. It was granted, and he drove in his cows! The evening of the 9th soon arrived, however, and he must say one thing or another; so he politely thanked the representative of his gracious Majesty for giving the garrison time to prepare for their defence, and announced their determination to fight. Captain Duquesne was much grieved at this; Governor Hamilton was anxious to save bloodshed, and wished the Kentuckians taken alive; and rather than proceed to extremities, the worthy Canadian offered to withdraw his troops, if the garrison would make a treaty, though to what point the treaty was to aim is unknown. Boone was determined not to yield; but then he had no wish to starve in his fort, or have it taken by storm, and be scalped; and he thought, remembering Hamilton's kindness to him when in Detroit, that there might be something in what the Captain said; and at any rate, to enter upon a treaty was to gain time, and something might turn up. So he agreed to treat; but where? Could nine of the garrison, as desired, safely venture into the open field? It might be all a trick to get possession of some of the leading whites. Upon the whole, however, as the leading Indians and their Canadian allies must come under the rifles of the garrison, who might with certainty and safety pick them off if treachery were attempted, it was thought best to run the risk; and Boone, with eight others, went out to meet the leaders of the enemy, sixty yards from the fort, within which the sharpest shooters stood with levelled rifles, ready to protect their comrades. The treaty was made and signed, and then the Indians, saying it was their custom for two of them to shake hands with every white man when a treaty was made, expressed a wish to press the palms of their new allies. Boone and his friends must have looked rather queer at this proposal; but it was safer to accede than to refuse and be shot instantly; so they presented each his hand. As anticipated, the warriors seized them with rough and fierce eagerness, the whites drew back struggling, the treachery was apparent, the rifle-balls from the garrison struck down the foremost assailants of the little band, and, amid a fire from friends and foes, Boone and his fellow-deputies bounded back into the station, with the exception of one, unhurt.

The treaty trick having thus failed, Captain Duquesne had to look to more ordinary modes of warfare, and opened a fire which lasted during ten days, though to no purpose, for the woodsmen were determined not to yield. On the 20th of August, the Indians were forced unwillingly to retire, having lost thirty-seven of their number, and wasted a vast amount of powder and lead. The garrison picked up from the ground, after their departure, one hundred and twenty-five pounds of their bullets.

With this invasion from the North terminated the first period of the history of Kentucky; and here we shall close our article. Had a Clark, instead of a Duquesne, led the band which besieged Boonesborough, the West would probably have been wrested from the Americans, notwithstanding the conquest of Kaskaskia, — the stations were so few, and the garrisons so feeble. But in 1779 and 1780, emigrants poured in in crowds, and, after the siege of Boonesborough, there never was a time when the force in the interior and at the Falls was not such as to put all serious injury to the settlements out of the question. In 1779, the public lands were disposed of; Lexington, Bryant's station, and several others, were commenced; Clark took Governor Hamilton prisoner at Vincennes; and the progress of events thenceforward became more that of a society, and less purely individual.

Of the progress of that society we may at some future time speak. In this paper we have wished chiefly to hint at the characters and acts of the few men who led the little band which, from 1769 to 1779, was the ceaseless object of the hostility of the Indians, and to whom, as we have said, so much injustice has been done by confounding them with the vicious braggarts and cutthroats of a later period.

VIII.

BORDER WAR OF THE REVOLUTION.*

The border wars of the American Revolution were full of deep interest. The Indian tribes, having long fought to no purpose against the power of Britain, which seemed ever ready to support the "Long Knives" in their encroachments upon Indian lands, suddenly found the state of things reversed. The red-coats were with *them.* White had turned against white, brother against brother; and the English everywhere cheered on the savage against the very settlers who were, the year before, English themselves. The red men were, and well might be, puzzled at this sudden division of their old foes into British and "*Bostonais*"; but in it they saw cause for hope. The spirit of Pontiac bade them be of good cheer, and strike once more for their homes and hunting-grounds. From Lake Superior, along the North to Maine, and southward to the Gulf of Mexico, the oppressed and broken tribes took courage again; and, had Tecumthé then been but a full-grown man, God alone knows what might have been the result of our own Revolution. For, had

---

* *Life of Joseph Brant* [*Thayendanegea*]; *including the Border Wars of the American Revolution, and Sketches of the Indian Campaigns of Generals Harmar, St. Clair, and Wayne,* &c., &c. By William L. Stone. In Two Volumes. New York: George Dearborn & Co. 1838. 8vo. pp. 513 and 601.

From the North American Review, for October, 1839.

the Western tribes been guided by one spirit, and that acting in concert with the power of England, the "stations" of Kentucky would soon have been tenantless; and, with the West in possession of Britain and her red allies, man cannot say how our armies might have withstood the enemy.

But it was not so ordered. Pontiac was dead; Tecumthé a little child; and Brant, able as he was, had neither the temper nor position of those great chieftains. If he was not a half-breed,* neither was he in training and tone a full Indian.

The border wars of the Revolution, we say, were full of interest. They were the wars of a falling race, struggling for all that was dear to them; and, though we must shudder over the bloodshed and the burnings, we cannot compare the acts of the savage man with those of the civilized and Christian man of those days, without feeling pity and sympathy for the former. What was the scalp-taker of the wilderness, in point of atrocity, when measured with the scalp-buyer, Hamilton? What were the worst acts of the red men, when placed side by side with the massacre on the Muskingum? †

To understand the border wars of the Revolution, we must first understand the position of the Indians when those wars began.

In the remote Northeast were the Penobscots and their kindred tribes; while amid those wild regions, through which Arnold passed on his way to Quebec, dwelt "Natanis, the last of the Norridgewocks," with the poor remnants of those nations, among whom Father Ralle, the Catholic,‡ long labored, but who were too poor, even in 1775, to stop or

---

* Some suppose Brant to have been the son of Sir William Johnson. See Stone, *Life of Brant*, Vol. I. pp. 1, 2.

† For an account of Hamilton and of the Moravian massacre, see below.

‡ See *Lettres Edifiantes.*

annoy the troops which were toiling along the Kennebec and Dead River, on their way to the capital of Lower Canada.*

In New Hampshire were a few lingering bands of the Penacooks, and other warrior tribes of that Granite land. In Massachusetts there remained the portion of the Mohegans called the Stockbridge Indians, together with a few Pequots and Narragansets. In New York still stood that famous and much-feared alliance, known as the Iroquois, or Six Nations; an alliance from of old bound to England by strong ties, and, at the opening of the Revolution, under the direct control of the Johnson family, a set of stanch Tories. To the south of the Six Nations were the Delawares, a race of the most noble character, and whose councils were divided between those who wished to throw off the yoke of the white man, and those who saw that the white man must rule, and wished to live in peace and good faith with him. West of the Six Nations and the Delawares, that is to say, west of the Muskingum River, in what is now the State of Ohio, came the Shawanese, fierce, bold, cruel, and wholly adverse to the Europeans; the Wyandots, of whom it was said, in after days, that one could not be taken alive; the Miamis, once the head of a confederacy mightier even than that of the Iroquois, and still strong and determined; the Ottawas, Chippeways, and all the painted nations of the Northwest. South of this great band, and on the other side of those Kentucky stations, which had sprung up between the rival nations of the North and South, lay the Creeks, Chickasaws, Cherokees, and Catawbas; while in the extreme Southern country, though not within the limits of the British colonies, were the Seminoles, and other yet unconquered races of the *hammocks* and swamps.

Thus was the little band of Provinces fairly hemmed in by the tribes of red men; most of them certain foes.

---

* Sparks's *Washington*, Vol. III. p. 112.

The influence which these tribes might have upon the Revolutionary contest was evident to both parties. Lord Dunmore, in the autumn of 1774, made peace with the Shawanese upon the Scioto, and stopped the progress of the Virginians, who had just gained a victory at Point Pleasant, under the undoubted influence of calculations respecting the policy of having a strong force to hang upon the rear of the rebellious colonists.* He also, by his course, pacified the Six Nations, who had taken some part in that war. It arose, indeed, out of the wrongs done to Logan and a few others, and was immortalized by the speech of Logan, and he was a Cayuga.† In truth, the influence of the Indians could not be lost sight of; for, notwithstanding the peace of Fort Charlotte, made by Dunmore, the Shawanese of the Miami valleys never ceased from annoying the settlers within striking distance; in March, 1775, Boone and his party of surveyors, then engaged in laying out the first road in Kentucky, lost several men by the Indians; and from that time forward a partisan warfare was kept up.‡

In the North, meanwhile, the Americans had seen the dangers to be feared from the action of the Indians, and early in April the Provincial Congress of Massachusetts wrote to the Reverend Samuel Kirkland, then a missionary among the Oneidas, informing him, that, having heard that the British were trying to attach the Six Nations to their interest, it had been thought proper to ask the several tribes, through him, to stand neutral. Steps were also taken to secure the coöperation, if possible, of the Penobscot and Stockbridge Indians; the latter of whom replied, that, though they never could understand what the quarrel between the Provinces and Old England was about, yet

---

* See Doddridge's *Notes*, p. 236.

† For proofs of the feelings of the Iroquois with regard to Dunmore's war, see Stone, Vol. I. pp. 65 and 68.

‡ Butler's *Kentucky*, 2d ed., p. 27.

they would stand by the Americans. They also offered to "feel the mind" of the Iroquois, and try to bring them over.*

But the Iroquois were not to be easily won over by any means. Sir William Johnson, so long the king's agent among them, and to whom they looked with the confidence of children in a father, had died suddenly, in June, 1774, and the wild men had been left under the influence of Colonel Guy Johnson, Sir William's son-in-law, who succeeded him as superintendent, and of John Johnson, Sir William's son, who succeeded to his estates and honors. Both these men were Tories; and their influence in favor of England was increased by that of Mr. Stone's hero, Brant, now nearly thirty-three years old. This trio, acting in conjunction with some of the rich old Royalists along the Mohawk, opposed the whole movement of the Bostonians, the whole spirit of the Philadelphia Congress, and every attempt, open or secret, in favor of the rebels. Believing Mr. Kirkland to be little better than a Whig in disguise, and fearing that he might alienate the tribe in which he was from their old faith, and, through them, influence the others, the Johnsons, while the war was still bloodless, made strong efforts to remove him from his position. Of these efforts Mr. Stone speaks at some length, though with a confusion of dates, as we read his account. The first attempt was made, he says, in February, 1775 (Vol. I. p. 60). The cause of this attempt, he suggests, was a correspondence which took place the following April (p. 55). It failed, however, but was renewed and succeeded in the spring, as appears by a letter, dated January 9th (p. 61).†

---

* Stone, Vol. I. pp. 55-58. — Sparks's *Washington*, Vol. III. pp. 495, 496.

† The date, "January," may be a misprint for "June"; but we think not, as no reference is made in the letter to the communication from Massachusetts, as a cause of suspicion.

Nor were the fears of the Johnsons groundless, as is shown by another of the original papers presented us by Mr. Stone, the address of the Oneida Indians to the New England Governors, in which they state their intention of remaining neutral during so unnatural a quarrel as that just then commencing. But this intention the leading tribe of the great Indian confederacy meant to disturb, if possible. The idea was suggested, that Guy Johnson was in danger of being seized by the Bostonians, and an attempt was made to rally about him the savages as a body-guard; while he, on his part, wrote to the neighbouring magistrates, holding out to them, as a terror, the excitement of the Indians, and the dangers to be feared from their rising, if he were seized, or their rights interfered with.

So stood matters in the Mohawk valley, during the month of May, 1775. The Johnsons were gathering a little army, which soon amounted to five hundred men; and the Revolutionary committees, resolute never to yield one hair's breadth, " never to submit to any arbitrary acts of any power under heaven," were denouncing Colonel Guy's conduct as "arbitrary, illegal, oppressive, and unwarrantable." In truth, the Colonel was fast getting obnoxious. " Watch him," wrote Washington to General Schuyler in June; and, even before that order was given, what with the Tryon county men above him on the river, and the whole Provincial force below him, he was likely to be well watched. Finding himself thus fettered, and feeling it to be time to take some decided step, the Superintendent, early in June, began to move westward, accompanied by his dependents and the great body of the Mohawk Indians, who remained firm in the British interests.* He moved first to Fort Stanwix (afterwards Fort Schuyler, near the present town of Rome), and then went on to Ontario, where he arrived

* Stone, Vol. I. p. 77.

early in July, and held a Congress with thirteen hundred and forty warriors, whose old attachment to England was then and there renewed. Joseph Brant, be it noted, during all this time, was acting as the Superintendent's secretary.

All of the Six Nations, except the Oneidas and Tuscaroras, might now be deemed in alliance with the British. Those tribes, chiefly through the exertions of Mr. Kirkland, were prevented from going with the others, and upon the 28th of June, at German Flats, gave to the Americans a pledge of neutrality.*

While the members of the Northern Confederacy were thus divided in their attachments, the Delawares of the Upper Ohio were by no means unanimous in their opinions as to this puzzling family quarrel which was coming on; and Congress, having been informed on the first day of June, that the Western Virginians stood in fear of the Indians, with whom Lord Dunmore, in his small way, was, as they thought, tampering,† it was determined to have a Congress called at Pittsburg, to explain to the poor red men the causes of the sudden division of their old enemies, and try to persuade them to keep peace. This Congress did not meet, however, until October.‡

Nor was it from the Northern and Western tribes only, that hostilities were feared. The Cherokees and their neighbours were much dreaded, and not without cause; as they were then less under the control of the whites than either the Iroquois or Delawares, and might, in the hope of securing their freedom, be led to unite, in a warfare of extermination, against the Carolinas. We find, accordingly, that early in July, Congress having determined to seek the alliance of the several Indian nations, three departments were formed; §

---

* Stone, Vol. I. p. 81. † *Old Journals*, Vol. I. p. 78.

‡ Heckewelder's *Narrative*, p. 136.

§ *Old Journals*, Vol. I. p. 113, &c.

a Northern one, including the Six Nations and all north and east of them, to the charge of which General Schuyler, Oliver Wolcott, and three others, were appointed; a Middle department, including the Western Indians, who were to be looked to by Messieurs Franklin, Henry, and Wilson; and a Southern department, including all the tribes south of Kentucky, over which commissioners were to preside under the appointment of the South Carolina Council of Safety. These commissioners were to keep a close watch upon the nations in their several departments, and upon the King's Superintendents among them. These officers they were to seize, if they had reason to think them engaged in stirring up the natives against the Colonies, and in all ways were to seek to keep those natives quiet and out of the contest. *Talks* were also prepared to send to the several tribes, in which an attempt was made to illustrate the relations between England and America, by comparing the last to a child ordered to carry a pack too heavy for its strength. The boy complains, and, for answer, the pack is made still heavier. Again and again the poor urchin remonstrates, but the bad servants misrepresent the matter to the father, and the boy gets ever a heavier burden, till at last, almost broken-backed, he throws off the load altogether, and says he will carry it no longer. This allegory was intended to make the matter clear to the pack-carrying red men, and, if we may judge from Heckewelder's account, it answered the purpose; for, he says, the Delawares reported the whole story very correctly. Indeed, he gives their report upon the 137th page of his "Narrative," which report agrees very well with the original speech, preserved to us in the Journals of the Old Congress.*

The first conference held by the commissioners was in the Northern department, a grand congress coming together at Albany in August. Of this congress a full account may

---

* Vol. I. p. 115.

be found in Colonel Stone's first volume.* It did not, however, fully represent the Six Nations, and some, even of those who were present, immediately afterwards deserted to the British; so that the result was slight.

The next conference was held at Pittsburg with the Western Indians. This was in October, and was attended by the Delawares, Senecas, and, perhaps, some of the Shawanese. The Delaware nation were, as we have already said, divided in their views touching the Americans. One of their chieftains, known to us as Captain White-Eyes, a man, as it would seem, of high character and clear mind, of courage such as became the leader of a race, whose most common virtues were those of the wild man, and of a forbearance and kindness as unusual, as fearlessness was frequent, among his people, — this true man was in favor of peace; and his influence carried with him a strong party. But there were others, again, who longed for war, and wished to carry the whole nation over to the British interest. These were led by a cunning and talented man, called Captain Pipe, who, without the energy, moral daring, and unclouded honesty of his opponent, had many qualities admirably suited to win and rule Indians. Between these two men there was a division from the beginning of the Revolution till the death of White-Eyes. At the Pittsburg conference, the Peace-Chief, as he was called, was present, and there asserted his freedom of the Six Nations, who, through their emissaries present, tried to bend the Delawares, as they had been used to do. His bold denial of the claim of the Iroquois to rule his people was seized upon, by some of the war-party, as a pretext for leaving the Muskingum, where White-Eyes lived, and withdrawing toward Lake Erie, into the more immediate vicinity of the English and their allies.

The Shawanese and their neighbours, meantime, had

* pp. 94 - 104. Appendix, iv.-xxxi.

taken counsel with Guy Johnson at Oswego,* and might be considered as in league with the king. Indeed, we can neither wonder at nor blame these bewildered savages for leaguing themselves with any power *against* those actual occupants of their hunting-grounds, who were, here and there in Kentucky, building block-houses and clearing corn-fields. Against those block-houses and their builders, little bands of red men continually kept sallying forth, supplied with ammunition from Detroit and the other Western posts, and incited to exertion by the well-known stimulants of whiskey and fine clothes.†

However, it is hardly correct to say, that this was done in 1775, though the arrangements were, beyond doubt, made in that year; Colonel Johnson having visited Montreal, immediately after the council with the Shawanese and others at Oswego, for the purpose of concluding with the British governor and general upon his future course.

During 1775, therefore, there was no border war, if we except the small predatory incursions into Kentucky. In the South all remained quiet; in the West there were doubt and uneasiness, without action; in the North, a distinct siding with the king by the great part of the Indians, though no warfare.

But the next year found the mass of the red men openly in arms against the colonies. Brant, who had gone to Canada in the pacific guise of Colonel Johnson's secretary, in 1776 appeared at the head of the most numerous tribes of the Iroquois, threatening, with all the horrors of Indian warfare, the valley of the Mohawk.‡ His preparation for this service was of a curious nature, being nothing less than a visit to London, where for a time he was the lion of the city, and particularly patronized by Boswell, for whom he had his

* Stone, Vol. I. p. 102.
† Ibid., Vol. I. p. 187.
‡ Ibid., Vol. I. p 149.

portrait taken. Returning thence in time to be present at, and share in, the battle of the Cedars in May, he, for unknown reasons, suffered the summer and autumn to pass without taking any decisive step; keeping the poor women and children of Cherry Valley and the neighbouring settlements in a state of continual anxiety to no purpose.

In the West, however, there was more of movement. Traders were stripped, men slain, and stations attacked. The Shawanese and the Wyandots were both at war for England; and great efforts were made to involve the Delawares.*

But it was in the South, that the border wars of our Revolution first broke out in all their strength and horror. Upon the 30th of July, Congress was informed that the Cherokees had commenced hostilities; and from that time, or rather from the 15th of that month, when the war began, until the middle of October, the forces of the Carolinas, Georgia, and Virginia were engaged in one of those protracted contests which have ever marked the struggles of the whites and Southern Indians. But at length Colonel Andrew Williamson, who commanded the South Carolina forces, carried his arms into the interior of the Cherokee country, destroyed their villages, and brought them to terms. Of the details of this war we know very little. The causes of it, the means by which the Indians were induced to rise, and all the after-steps, have been but very imperfectly exhibited, as yet, by any writer. We trust, however, that some one, with the industry and perseverance of Mr. Stone, may be led to turn his attention that way, and compile the Annals, if not the History, of that time in the South.†

* Heckewelder and Butler.

† Holmes's *Annals*, Vol. II. p. 258. — *Journals of the Old Congress.* — Ramsay, &c. — Washington (Sparks's ed., Vol. III. p. 210) refers to evidences of efforts on the part of Britain to engage the Southern savages in 1775.

The year 1776 might be said, then, to have passed without any serious injury to the colonists from the various tribes, although it was clear, that those tribes were to be looked on as engaged in the war, and that the majority of them were with the mother country. Through the West and Northwest, where the agents of England could act to the greatest advantage, dissatisfaction spread rapidly. The nations nearest the Americans found themselves pressed upon and harassed by the more distant bands, and, through the whole winter of 1776-77, rumors were flying along the frontiers of Virginia and Pennsylvania, of coming troubles. Nor were the good people of New York less disturbed in their minds, the settlers upon the Mohawk and Upper Susquehannah standing in continual dread of incursion.* No incursion, however, took place during the winter or spring of 1777; though why the blow was delayed is what we cannot well know, until Great Britain has magnanimity enough to unveil her past acts, and, acknowledging her follies and sins, to show the world the various steps to that union of the savages against her foes, which her noble Chatham denounced as a "disgrace," and "deep and deadly sin."

That blow was delayed, however; and, alas! was struck at length, after, and as if in retaliation for, one of those violent acts of wrong, which must ever be expected from a frontier people. We refer to the murder of Cornstalk, the leading chieftain of the Scioto Shawanese; a man, whose energy, courage, and good sense place him among the very foremost of the native heroes of this land.† This truly great man, who was himself for peace, but who found all his neighbours, and even those of his own tribe, stirred up to war by the agents of England, went over to the American fort at Point Pleasant, at the mouth of the Great Kenhawa,

---

* *Journals of the Old Congress.* — Stone, &c.

† See Stone, Vol. I. p. 191. — Doddridge's *Indian Wars*, &c.

in order to talk the matter over with Captain Arbuckle, who commanded there, and with whom he was acquainted. This was early in the summer of 1777. The Americans, knowing the Shawanese to be inclining to the enemy, thought it would be a good plan to retain Cornstalk and Redhawk, a younger chief of note, who was with him, and make them hostages for the good conduct of their people. The old warrior, accordingly, after he had finished his statement of the position he was in, and the necessity under which he and his friends would be of "going with the stream," unless the Long Knives could protect them, found that, in seeking counsel and safety, he had walked into a trap, and was fast there. However, he folded his arms, and, with Indian calmness, waited the issue. The day went by. The next morning came, and from the opposite shore was heard an Indian hail, known to be from Ellinipsico, the son of Cornstalk. The Americans brought him also into their toils as a hostage, and were thankful that they had thus secured to themselves peace; — as if iniquity and deception ever secured that first condition of all good! Another day rolled by, and the three captives sat waiting what time would bring. On the third day, two savages, unknown to the whites, shot one of the white hunters, toward evening. Instantly the dead man's comrades raised the cry, "Kill the red dogs in the fort." Arbuckle tried to stop them, but they were men of blood, and their wrath was up. The Captain's own life was threatened, if he offered any hindrance. They rushed to the house where the captives were confined; Cornstalk met them at the door, and fell, pierced with seven bullets; his son and Redhawk died also, less calmly than their veteran companion, and more painfully. From that hour peace was not to be hoped for.

But this treachery, closed by murder, on the part of the Americans, though perhaps the immediate cause of the outbreak in the West, was not, in any degree, the cause of the great border war. Two years had been spent by Britain in arranging and organizing that war. Cornstalk fell into the snare, because that war was organized. Before his death the whole Cherokee contest was begun and ended, and Brant, in person, had commanded an expedition against Cherry Valley, which was attended with slight results, but was still proof of the condition of matters and the temper of men. And, almost at the moment when Cornstalk was dying upon the banks of the Ohio, there was a congress gathering at Oswego, under the eye of Colonel Johnson, "to eat the flesh and drink the blood of a Bostonian"; in other words, to arrange finally the measures which should be taken against the devoted rebels by Christian brethren and their heathen allies.*

And here, before entering upon the actual bloodshed, it may be as well, perhaps, to say what we have to say upon the comparative merits, or demerits, of the parties to the Revolutionary contest, in respect to their measures for the employment of the Indians.

The first mention of the subject, which we meet with, is in the Address of the Massachusetts Congress to the Iroquois, in April, 1775. In that they say, that they hear the British are exciting the savages against the colonies; and they ask the Six Nations to aid them, or stand quiet.† It would seem, then, that, even before the battle of Lexington, both parties had applied to the Indians, and sought an alliance. Nor was this strange or reprehensible. Both parties had been used to the employment of the natives in contests between the whites, and both knew that a portion of the coming struggle, at least, must be inland, among the tribes of red men, and that those tribes could not be expected to stand wholly neutral. In the outset, therefore, both parties

---

* Stone, Vol. I. p. 186.

‡ Sparks's *Washington*, Vol. III. p. 495.

were of the same mind and pursued the same course. The Congress of the United Colonies, however, during 1775, and until the summer of 1776, advocated merely the attempt to keep the Indians out of the contest entirely, and instructed the commissioners, appointed in the several departments, to do so. But England was of another mind. Promises and threats were both used to induce the savages to act with her,* though, at first, it would seem, to little purpose, even the Canada tribe of Caghnawagas having offered their aid to the Americans. When Britain, however, became victorious in the North, and particularly after the battle of the Cedars, in May, 1776, the wild men began to think of holding to her side, their policy being, most justly, in all quarrels of the whites, to stick by the strongest. Then it was, in June, 1776, that Congress resolved to do what *Washington had advised in the previous April*, that is, to employ the savages in active warfare. Upon the 19th of April the Commander-in-Chief wrote to Congress, saying, that, as the Indians would soon be engaged, either for or against, he would suggest that they be employed for the colonies;† upon the 3d of May, the report on this was considered; upon the 25th of May, it was resolved to be highly expedient to engage the Indians for the American service; and, upon the 3d of June, the General was empowered to raise two thousand to be employed in Canada. Upon the 17th of June, Washington was authorized to employ them where he pleased, and to offer them rewards for prisoners; and, upon the 8th of July, he was empowered to call out as many of the Nova Scotia and neighbouring tribes as he saw fit.‡

Such was the course of proceeding, on the part of the colonies, with regard to the employment of the Indians.

* Sparks's *Washington*, Vol. III. p. 55.

† Ibid., p. 364.

‡ *Secret Journals*, Vol. I. pp. 43 – 47.

The steps, at the time, were secret, but now the whole story is before the world. Not so, however, with regard to the acts of England; as to them, we have the records of but few placed within our reach. One thing, however, is known, namely, that, while the colonies offered their allies of the woods rewards for *prisoners*, some of the British agents gave them money for *scalps*.* And this leads us to speak of a distinction, which we would have kept in mind by those who read our remarks, with regard to the employment of the savages. It is this; that whatever tends to produce animosity between the individuals of two warring nations is to be avoided, as leading inevitably to enmity during peace, and thence to renewed war. The great cause of the bitterness of frontier and civil wars is the individual hatred that mingles with, and envenoms, the public hostility. This same individual feeling had much to do with the perpetual warfare of those times, when men fought hand to hand, instead of destroying whole ranks by cannon and musket shot; and the production of this individual feeling is one of the great, *peculiar* objections to privateering. Now, so far as the employment of the Indians helped to produce this personal, rather than public hatred, we think it wholly objectionable. We do not see, that it would help to do this necessarily, and we do not learn, that it did in fact. But the British plan of paying the savages for scalps, and thus setting a bounty on murder, one may well conceive, would produce personal, angry feelings, because it was unusual; whereas the employment of the red men, as between those warring in America, was not so.

We regard the British, then, as more culpable than the colonists in three respects; first, for trying to involve the Indians, in the South, West, and North, *from the outset*,†

* Jefferson's *Writings*, Vol. I. p. 456.

† Not culpable because the natives were savages, but because they were not in war, and the British sought to involve them in war. The

whereas the Americans tried to keep them out of the contest for more than a year; secondly, for offering money for scalps, an unusual measure, and one calculated to irritate individual feeling; and thirdly, for keeping the whole matter in the dark to this day.

Having disposed, thus summarily, of a point that might be discoursed on through twenty pages or more, we return to our history.

It was some time in July, probably, that Guy Johnson, with his loyalist and Indian friends, ate their Bostonian at Oswego. He was there, soon after, joined by Colonel St. Leger, with about two hundred British regulars, who, in conjunction with the Tories and savages, were to move up the river, and across to Fort Schuyler, and thence down the Mohawk to join Burgoyne on the Hudson. It was a pleasantly arranged plan, and does credit to the British ministers. New England, containing the most rebellious of the rebel provinces, was to be cut off from her sisters, and the same blow which did this was to clear the Mohawk valley of its Whig population, and so leave all north of New York the king's own. A good plan it was; but it failed. Burgoyne, as we all know, found a lion in his path; and his coöperator, St. Leger, was not more happy.

This last-named officer, withseventeen hundred men, got under way toward the last of July. Of his march and proceedings, Mr. Stone gives a clear and full account from the original papers.* His vanguard, with which was Brant, came before Fort Schuyler on the 2d of August, just after a reinforcement of two hundred men, and several boat-loads of provisions, had been safely housed. The main British force reached the post on the 3d. St. Leger, as we have said, had seventeen hundred men; Colonel Gansevoort,

---

wrong would have been the same, had it been a civilized neighbour whom they sought to bring into the quarrel.

* Stone, Vol. I. pp. 209–264.

who commanded the Americans, had seven hundred and fifty, with food and powder, however, for six weeks. Thus supplied, the provincials were prepared to stand a strong siege, although their works were in a bad condition. One thing they needed, a flag ; but this they soon furnished from red and white shirts, and a blue camlet cloak which was at hand, and the stars and stripes were, in a little while, waving above them.

Meantime, news having gone down the Mohawk of the approach of the British army, the militia of that region were called in, and assembled at German Flats, to the number of near a thousand, under the command of General Herkimer. This brave old officer, while on his march to the relief of Fort Schuyler, was induced, by circumstances related by Mr. Stone, to doubt the propriety of advancing; but, being taunted by some of his subordinates with Toryism and cowardice, he suffered his judgment to be overruled, and gave the order to march on. His body of untrained soldiers marched on at the command, in such form and disposition as to expose themselves not a little. By and by they came to a ravine. In the same loose order, in which they had hitherto been advancing, they entered it. When nearly the whole body of troops were within its limits, those in advance and upon the flanks were shot down by an unseen enemy, and the forest rang with the true Indian yell. It was Brant and his warriors; and the battle that followed is known as the battle of Oriskany. The British force, under the direction of Brant, as Mr. Stone thinks, had disposed itself in a circular form, so that, no sooner had the provincials entered through a gap left at one point of the circle, than the whole of them were surrounded, with the exception of the rear-guard, which ran away. And then began one of those contests which are very like to the battles of Homer and Scott, had we but a Homer or Scott to describe them ; — a battle of man against man; of individual prowess; of individual glory; not a battle of *manœuvre* (which, despite its name, is not hand-work, but head-work), but of the true hand-work, and well worthy of being sung, if we could but get rid of the Dutch names of Herkimer, and Visscher, and Van Sluyck. It was a battle, too, we regret to say, of that individual hatred which the knights of old did not feel for one another. Here were the rebels who had denied their king; there the traitors who were fighting against their country. Bitter indeed was the feeling between them, brother even seeking the life of brother.

Two men, especially, distinguished themselves on that day, Captain Gardinier and Captain Dillinback. The former, seeing one of his men seized by a pretended friend, but real enemy, sprang upon the captor, and levelled him with his spear (for he fought with the arms as well as the spirit of Hector and *Cœur-de-lion*), and rescued the man. Others sprang upon him. The first that came, "with mortal thrust he slew," and the second, sent howling and limping back to the British ranks. But those ranks were yet full, and three of the enraged Tories (for he was contending with Americans and neighbours) sprang upon him. Not even three, however, could conquer him. He kept them at bay, until, in the struggle, one of his spurs caught in the clothes of an opponent, and he was tripped, and fell. Now his case seemed desperate indeed. Two of the three Tories instantly struck with their bayonets, and pinned both legs to the earth. The third aimed a more deadly blow at his heart, but Gardinier caught the bayonet, and, by main strength, drew his assailant down upon his own body, and held him there as a shield against the thrusts of the others. All this had passed like thought; but, the instant his men saw the condition of their leader, they sprang to his rescue. Relieved from the bayonets above, Gardinier released the Tory who was upon him, and, seizing his spear in his lacerated hand, half rose, and buried it in the body of his antagonist.

The other hero of this battle, Captain Dillinback, was one who had often said, that he would never be taken prisoner. In the midst of the uproar, three of Johnson's men, who knew well the Captain's saying, rushed together to seize him. One of them succeeded in seizing his gun, for they came upon him unexpectedly. But Dillinback, though surprised, was not captured; he wrested his weapon from his antagonist, levelled him with the but, shot the second, and bayonetted the third! So he fulfilled his saying, that he would never be a prisoner; but, even at the instant of fulfilment, a ball struck him, and he fell dead.

Herkimer had been badly wounded early in the action; but he remained upon the field, and, sitting in his saddle, supported by a tree, smoked his pipe, and ordered the battle. It lasted six hours, and was, in spite of odds, a drawn game at last. The British killed most men, and the Americans remained masters of the field.

Meanwhile, during the battle of Oriskany, a sortie had been made from the besieged fort, by Colonel Willett, against the nearly deserted camp of John Johnson. It was entirely successful; much plunder and some prisoners being taken, without the loss of a man on the part of the Americans. The British colors, that were found, were immediately hoisted under those of America (the old camlet cloak and red shirt), and the besiegers treated to a hearty cheer by the inspirited garrison. Of the various steps taken, after this time, to secure the fort for the King and for the Province, we cannot speak. The rebels, in the end, were successful. St. Leger abandoned the siege, and marched back to Lake Ontario. Of all these steps, Mr. Stone gives a full account from original sources. From him we have derived the facts just given, and to him all that may write of those events will be indebted for much that is interesting, and now first brought to light.

While in the North the Iroquois were acting with the

British against the colonists, in the South all remained quiet, and in the West all remained uncertain. The Shawanese, irritated by the death of Cornstalk, still pretended to wish for peace, while they continually annoyed the settlers in Kentucky, and all those who passed up and down the Ohio River. The Delawares were, as ever, divided, though great efforts were made by the Wyandots, and other tribes more nearly under British influence, to persuade or drive them into the war.* Those more distant nations themselves waited only for the opportunity to strike some decided blow, and, meanwhile, continued to harass the frontiers of Pennsylvania and Virginia, causing great distress and fear. Through their incursions during the autumn of 1777, the steps taken by Hamilton, then Lieutenant-Governor of Detroit, to enlist the savages, became known, some of his proclamations having been left by them during their visits; and Congress was led to feel the necessity of now becoming masters, if possible, of those Western posts, from which arms, ammunition, and spirits were supplied to the inimical red men. Upon the 20th of November a report was made to Congress, in which this necessity was urged, and also the need that existed of taking some measures to prevent the spirit of disaffection from spreading among the frontier inhabitants.† Three commissioners also were chosen to go to Fort Pitt, for the purpose of inquiring into the causes of the frontier difficulties, and of doing what could be done to secure all the whites to the American cause, to cultivate the friendship of the Shawanese and Delawares, and to concert with General Hand some measures for pushing the war westward, so as to obtain possession of Detroit and other posts. General Washington was also requested to send Colonel William Crawford, an old pioneer, to take the active

---

* Heckewelder's *Narrative*, pp. 150, *et seq.* — Butler's *Kentucky*.

† *Old Journals*, Vol. II. p. 340.

command in the West; and he accordingly left head-quarters upon the 25th.*

While Congress was resolving upon the necessity of capturing Detroit and Lieutenant-Governor Hamilton, there was one man west of the mountains, who was also resolving, not only that it must be done, but that he would do it. This was George Rogers Clark, a man whose biography is not yet written, but who may compare with any general of our Revolution, except the matchless one, for decision, intrepidity, energy, forethought, and good sense. He was the best soldier that has ever led our troops against the Indians, and knew better than any other man of his day how to control those uncontrollable beings. Clark was the true founder of Kentucky, and deserves to have his name enrolled among those of whom full and detailed biographies are written. We hope that some one of the innumerable penmen of the day will be wise enough, and patriotic enough, to collect the papers and anecdotes which are still accessible, and combine them into such a form as he can. We care not very much, indeed, what the form of such a work, published now, is, provided it does but collect and perpetuate the materials, from which a nobler and more perfect work may be prepared by and by.

Clark went to the West in 1775. In 1776 he was busy in organizing his adopted land, Kentucky, in order to prepare her for becoming an independent State. In 1777, perceiving that it was from Kaskaskia, Cahokia, Vincennes, and Detroit, that the Indians, who never ceased to annoy the pioneers, were supplied, he sent spies to examine the state of things at and about those posts; and, having received their report, upon the 1st of October he started for Virginia, to lay the matter before the Governor of the parent State. Patrick Henry was then in the executive chair of Virginia;

---

* Sparks's *Washington*, Vol. V. p. 169.

and to him Clark made known his plans early in December. The Governor liked the proposed campaign very much, but could scarce think it possible it should succeed, so distant were the posts to be attacked, so small the force that could be used for the purpose, and so mighty the power of Britain. However, Burgoyne had been defeated, and the colonists were gathering courage; Clark was well known as a most active and persevering man; and his purposes having been fully explained, and fully approved by competent and critical judges, he succeeded in getting the Governor and Council to enter heart and soul into his scheme, and upon the 2d of January received his orders and outfit. Of his various acts and his wonderful success, we shall say little, referring our readers to the account already given by us of him, when reviewing Mr. Butler's "History of Kentucky." *

We have now, in our rambling way, brought matters down to the opening of 1778. During the spring of that year, there continued the same uncertainty as to the intentions of the Western and Northern tribes, and the outposts still suffered from incursions and petty attacks. A fort was built, early in the summer of that year, upon the banks of the Ohio a little below Pittsburg, near the spot where Beaver now stands. It was built by General McIntosh, and was named with his name.† From this point it was intended to operate in reducing Detroit, where mischief was still brewing. Indeed, the natives were now more united than ever against the colonies. In June we find Congress in possession of information, that led them to think a universal frontier war close at hand.‡ The Senecas, Cayugas, Mingoes (by which, we presume, were meant the Ohio Iroquois, or possibly the Mohawks), Wyandots, Onondagas, Ottawas,

---

* *North American Review,* Vol. XLIII. pp. 1, *et seq.*

† Doddridge, p. 243. — Silliman's *Journal,* Vol. XXXI. Art. 1.

‡ *Journals of the Old Congress,* Vol. II. p. 585.

Chippeways, Shawanese, and Delawares, were all said to be more or less united in opposition to America. This union, Mr. Stone hints, was brought about by Brant; * but he gives us no evidence on that point. Indeed, he has not much to say about the subject of his biography in this portion of it, most of his pages being filled with accounts of those events in which Brant took part only now and then. Congress, learning the danger to be so immediate and great, determined to push on the Detroit expedition, and ordered another to be undertaken up the Mohawk valley against the Senecas, who might otherwise very much annoy and impede the march from Fort Pitt. For the capture of Detroit, three thousand Continental troops and two thousand five hundred militia were voted; an appropriation was made of nearly a million of dollars; and General McIntosh, who had been appointed late in May, † by Washington, to succeed General Hand as commander of Fort Pitt and the Western forces, was to carry forward the needful operations.

All the flourish which was made about taking Detroit, however, and conquering the Senecas, ended in the Resolves of Congress, it being finally thought too late in the season for advantageous action, and also too great an undertaking for the weak-handed colonies. ‡ Clark, however, held on his way, and did his work, reducing Kaskaskia, Cahokia, and Vincennes, and catching the "hair-buying General" Hamilton.

But, strange to say, on the very night on which Clark entered Kaskaskia, far away in the Western wilderness, and sent his men yelling, like Indians, round the town, in order to scare the inhabitants into non-resistance, on that same night *genuine* Indian yells,

---

* Stone, Vol. I. p. 304.

† Sparks's *Washington*, Vol. V. p. 382.

‡ *Journals of the Old Congress*, Vol. II. p. 633.

"And sounds that mingled laugh, and shout, and scream,"

were echoing through the vale of Wyoming.

Of all that was horrible in the transactions of that night, and of the many errors and exaggerations in the accounts of it, we shall say nothing, but refer the reader to Mr. Stone, who purges the Indians in part, and Brant entirely, of blame. Indeed, the Mohawk chieftain had been acquitted of any share in that night's doings by Campbell, who had damned him to everlasting fame as a monster, some years since.

Nor was Wyoming the only place which suffered during the summer of 1778. It was on the 4th of July, that the beautiful valley of the Susquehannah was sacked, and, on the 18th, Brant, with his fire and knife, was busy on the Mohawk. In the remote West there was trouble too. Boone, who had passed his winter and spring among the Shawanese, a prisoner, and yet a trusted friend (so genuine a woodsman was he), went from them upon the 16th of June "at sunrise," leaving no message, for he saw that near five hundred warriors were gathering to attack Kentucky. Four days he travelled, averaging forty miles a day, and ate one meal on the journey, and then reached Boonesborough. Here he prepared every thing for war, and sat recruiting until the 1st of August, when he started with nineteen men to attack a town on the Scioto, far in the enemy's country. He was gone a week, and got back just before his post was called to surrender by a large body of Indians, who came, with a dozen Frenchmen, to demand the country in the name of his British Majesty. Boone, having no acquaintance with his British Majesty, but being intimate with the Shawanese, and knowing their pleasant mode of treating prisoners, declined; and then came a siege of ten days, in which so many guns were fired, that the besieged afterwards picked up one hundred and twenty-five pounds of bullets on the ground about the fort. The British force of French and Indians, having used up their ammunition, and lost about forty men, at last determined to retire, and leave Kentucky in peace again.*

The siege of Boonesborough was raised upon the 20th of August, and within a few days after that time another movement was made by Brant and his bloody followers against the settlement of German Flats. This settlement was about the junction of West Canada Creek, the stream on which are Trenton Falls, with the Mohawk River, and was one of the richest frontier posts. This attack was followed, in November, by the destruction of the settlement at Cherry Valley, nearly south of the Flats. Here the scenes of Wyoming were reënacted, and, as most have written, under the eye of Brant again; but Mr. Stone is prompt to defend his hero against all charges of cruelty, and presents us with strong reasons for thinking this, too, a slander. He had not the command, he says, and, though present, did all in his power to prevent, not to forward slaughter.

We have only one other act to record of 1778; the movement of General McIntosh. When it was found to be beyond hope to take Detroit at once, it was resolved, that the forces in the West should move up, and attack the Wyandots and other Indians about the Sandusky; † and a body of troops was accordingly marched forward to prepare a half-way house or post, by which the necessary connection might be kept up. This was built upon the Tuscarawas, a few miles south of where Bolivar now is, and was called Fort Laurens; the Ohio Canal, in these peaceful days, passes directly through it.‡ Here Colonel John Gibson was left with one hundred and fifty men to get through the winter as he best could, while McIntosh himself returned to Pittsburg, disappointed and dispirited.§ Nor was Congress in a very good

---

* Butler's *Kentucky*, pp. 96, *et seq.*

† *Journals of the Old Congress*, Vol. II. p. 633.

‡ Doddridge, p. 244. — Silliman's *Journal*, Vol. XXXI. p. 57.

§ Sparks's *Washington*, Vol. VI. p. 156.

humor with him, for already had six months passed to no purpose. Washington was consulted, but could give no definite advice, knowing nothing of those details which must determine the course of things for the winter. McIntosh, at length, in February, asked leave to retire from his unsatisfactory command, and was allowed to do so. His garrison at Fort Laurens, meantime, had been suffering cruelly, both from the Indians and famine, and, though finally rescued from starvation, had done, and could do, nothing.

But, while McIntosh was groaning and doing nothing, his fellow General, Clark, was very differently employed. Governor Hamilton, having made his various arrangements, had left Detroit, and moved down to St. Vincent's (or Vincennes), on the Wabash, from which point he intended to operate in reducing Kaskaskia and Cahokia, and also in conquering Kentucky, and driving the rebels from the West. But in the very process of taking St. Vincent's, he met with treatment that might have caused a more modest man to doubt the possibility of conquering those rebels. Hamilton came upon that post, which had been surrendered to the Americans in the summer of 1778, in December of that year. He came with a large body of troops, and unexpectedly; so that there was no chance of defence on the part of the garrison, which consisted of only two men, Captain Helm, of Fauquier in Virginia, and one Henry. Helm, however, was not disposed to yield, absolutely, to any odds; so, loading his single cannon, he stood by it with a lighted match, and, as the British came nigh, bade them stand, and demanded to know what terms would be granted the garrison, as otherwise he should not surrender. The Governor, unwilling to lose time and men, offered the usual honors of war, and could scarce believe his eyes, when he saw the threatening garrison to be only one officer and one private. However, even this bold conduct did not make him feel the character of the people with whom he was contending; and so, thinking it too late to operate in such a country, he scattered his Indians, of whom he had some four hundred, and sat himself down for the winter.

Information of all these proceedings having reached Clark, he saw, at once, that either he must have Hamilton, or Hamilton would have him; so he cast about him, to see what means of conquest were within his reach. On the 29th of January, 1779, the news of the capture of St. Vincent's reached Kaskaskia, and, by the 4th of February, a "battoe," as Colonel Bowman writes it, had been repaired, provisioned, manned, and armed, and was on her way down the Mississippi, in order to ascend the Ohio and Wabash, and coöperate with the land forces which were assembling. These forces, on the 5th of February, numbered one hundred and seventy men, "including artillery, packhorsemen, &c.," and, with this little band, on that day Clark set forward to besiege the British Governor, who had under him about half as many men, as a garrison. It was "rain and drizzly weather," and, the "roads very bad with mud and water"; but through those prairie ways, and the waters which covered some of the plains, the little rebel band slipped and spattered along, crossing rivers on trees felled for the purpose, and killing a buffalo occasionally, but all the way marching through unceasing rain, till, upon the 13th, they reached the Wabash. This they crossed in a canoe, it being three miles from shore to shore, the whole country between the Great and Little Wabash, near the junction of which they were, being under water, in consequence of the extraordinary rains; and "still raining," writes Colonel Bowman, every day. It was what we call in New England "a spell of weather." And, in addition to all this water, there was lack of provisions; on the 19th, says Bowman's Journal, "No food of any sort for two days"; and, on the 20th, he writes, "Camp very quiet, but hungry." But the wet and hungry little army was now almost in sight of St. Vincent's, and heard the Governor's guns, morning and evening, so that provisions were less necessary. They at times killed a deer, also, and had a mouthful all round. On the 23d, however, matters seemed desperate. The weather had grown cooler, so that it froze, and the men were marching across a plain, four miles in diameter, with the water breast high. Notwithstanding all this, though, they made progress, and on that day saw the town; and that night, with "colors flying, and drums braced, and water up to their arm-pits," marched up to the post and besieged it. The next morning, the poor drenched army had a breakfast, "the only meal's victuals" for six days.

Through all the toil, the marching, the wading, and the starving, Clark had been, as we might suppose, foremost; and he now felt disposed to show no favor to those who had brought him so far, and through such roads. His demand upon the Governor to yield was not, therefore, written with that regard to formal diplomacy, which the Briton would have liked. Thus ran the missive.

"Sir, — In order to save yourself from the impending storm which now threatens you, I order you immediately to surrender yourself, with all your garrison, stores, &c.; for, if I am obliged to storm, you may depend on such treatment as is justly due to a murderer. Beware of destroying stores of any kind, or any papers or letters that are in your possession, or hurting any house in town; for, by Heaven! if you do, there shall be no mercy shown you. G. R. CLARK."

To this the Governor replied, that he could not think of being "awed into any action unworthy a British subject"; but his true feeling peeped out in his question to Helm, when the bullets rattled about the chimney of the room in which they were playing piquet together, and Helm swore that Clark would have them prisoners. "Is he a merciful man?" said the Governor.

Clark, finding the British unwilling to yield quietly, began "firing very hot." When this came on, Helm cautioned the English soldiers not to look out through the loopholes; for these Virginian riflemen, he said, would shoot their eyes out, if they did. And several being actually killed by balls which came through the portholes, Hamilton was led to propose a truce, and some conversation; which ended in a surrender of the fort to Clark.*

Detroit was now within the reach of the enterprising Virginian, had he but been able to raise one third as many soldiers as were starving and idling at Forts Laurens and McIntosh. He could not; and Governor Henry having promised him a reinforcement, he concluded to wait for that, as his force was too small to both conquer and garrison the British forts. But the results of what was done were not unimportant; indeed, we cannot estimate those results. Hamilton had made arrangements to enlist the Western and Southern Indians † for the next spring's campaign; and, if Mr. Stone be correct in his suppositions, Brant and his Iroquois were to act in concert with him.‡ Had Clark, therefore, failed to conquer the Governor, there is too much reason to fear, that the West would have been indeed swept, from the Mississippi to the mountains, and the great blow struck, which had been contemplated from the outset by Britain. But for his small army of dripping, but fearless Virginians, the union of all the tribes from Georgia to Maine, against the colonies, might have been effected, and the whole current of our history changed.

Before leaving Clark, we would notice one expression, used by Mr. Stone, which does that bold partisan injustice. He says, "An expedition was organized against Kaskaskia, and Clark intrusted with the command of it"; § whereas the truth was, as we have stated, that Clark *originated* and carried through the whole plan.

---

* Butler's *Kentucky* and Bowman's *Manuscript Journal.*

† Butler, p. 80. ‡ Stone, Vol. I. p. 400. § Ibid., p. 352.

Turning from the West to the North, we find a new cause of trouble arising there. Of the six tribes of the Iroquois, the Senecas, Mohawks, Cayugas, and Onondagas had been, from the outset, inclining to Britain, though all of these but the Mohawks had now and then tried to persuade the Americans to the contrary. During the winter of 1778–79, the Onondagas, who had been for a while nearly neutral, were suspected, by the Americans, of deception; and, this suspicion having become nearly knowledge, a band was sent, early in April, to destroy their towns, and take such of them, as could be taken, prisoners. The work appointed was done, and the villages and wealth of the poor savages were annihilated. This sudden act of severity startled all. The Oneidas, hitherto faithful to their neutrality, were alarmed, lest the next blow should fall on them, and it was only after a full explanation, that their fears were quieted. As for the Onondagas, it was not to be hoped that they would sit down under such treatment; and we find, accordingly, that some hundred of their warriors were at once in the field, and from that time forward, a portion of their nation remained, and, we think, justly, hostile to the United Colonies.*

Those colonies, meanwhile, had become convinced, from the massacres at Wyoming and Cherry Valley, that it was advisable to adopt some means of securing the northwestern and western frontiers against the recurrence of such catastrophes; and, the hostile tribes of the Six Nations being the most numerous and deadly foes, it was concluded to begin by strong action against them. Washington had always said, that the only proper mode of defence against the Indians was to attack them, and this mode he determined to adopt on this occasion. Some difference of opinion existed, however, as to the best path into the country of the inimical Iroquois; that most lovely country in the West of New York,

---

* Stone, Vol. I. p. 405.

which is now fast growing into a granary for millions of men. General Schuyler was in favor of a movement up the Mohawk River; the objection to which route was, that it carried the invaders too near to Lake Ontario, and within reach of the British. The other course proposed was up the Susquehannah, which heads, as all know, in the region that was to be reached. The latter route was the one determined upon by Washington for the main body of troops, which was to be joined by another body moving up the Mohawk, and also by detachments coming from the Western army, by the way of the Alleghany and French Creek; upon further thought, however, the movement from the West was countermanded.* All the arrangements for this grand blow were made in March and April, but it was the last of July before General Sullivan got his men under way from Wyoming, where they had gathered; and, of course, information of the proposed movements had been given to the Indians and Tories, so that Brant, the Johnsons, and their followers, stood ready to receive the invaders.

They were not, however, strong enough to withstand the Americans; and, having been defeated at the battle of Newtown, were driven from village to village, and their whole country was laid waste. Houses were burned, crops and orchards destroyed, and every thing done that could be thought of to render the country uninhabitable. Of all these steps Mr. Stone speaks fully. Forty towns, he tells us, were burnt, and more than one hundred and sixty thousand bushels of corn. Well did the Senecas name Washington, whose armies did all this, "the Town-Destroyer." Having performed this portion of his work, Sullivan turned homeward again from the beautiful valley of the Genesee; leaving Niagara, whither the Indians fled, as to the stronghold of British power in that neighbourhood, untouched. This conduct

* Sparks's *Washington*, Vol. VI. pp. 183, *et seq.*

Mr. Stone thinks "difficult of solution,"* as he supposes the conquest of that post to have been one of the main objects of the expedition. Such, however, was not the fact. Originally it had been part of the proposed plan to attack Niagara; † but, early in January, Washington was led to doubt, and then to abandon, that part of the plan, thinking it wiser to carry on merely "some operations on a smaller scale against the savages." ‡

One of these smaller operations was the march of Colonel Daniel Brodhead, who had succeeded McIntosh in command at Fort Pitt, against the tribes along the Alleghany and up French Creek. These tribes Washington speaks of as "the Mingo and Muncey tribes," to which Mr. Stone *adds* the Senecas,§ as though he were ignorant that the Senecas formed one of the Mingo tribes, the very one, doubtless, referred to by Washington under the general term. The towns of these Indians were also laid waste, and their crops destroyed.

The immediate result of these prompt and severe measures was to bring the Delawares, Shawanese, and even the Wyandots, to Fort Pitt, on a treaty of peace. There Brodhead met them, on his return in September, and a long conference was held, to the satisfaction of both parties. Farther west, in July, Colonel Bowman had made an unsuccessful attack upon the Shawanese village, known to us as Chillicothe, in the Miami country; and, in November, Rogers and Benham suffered terribly in a battle with the savages opposite the mouth of the Little Miami. Into the particulars of these battles we cannot enter. Indeed, much as has been written about them, we are yet in the dark touching many points that ought to be perfectly understood. For instance,

---

* Vol. II. p. 36.

† Sparks's *Washington*, Vol. VI. pp. 120, 146.

‡ Ibid., pp. 162-166. § Vol. II. p. 41.

there is still some doubt as to the position of the Indian towns, against which expeditions marched from Kentucky, in 1779, 1780, and afterwards. And with respect to those very savages, from whom Rogers and his comrades suffered so much, there is doubt. Butler says, they were going against Kentucky, "under Birde, a Canadian Frenchman," and quotes from a letter written to him by the son of Benham, who was with the sufferers, and one of the greatest of them. But did not Mr. Benham, the son, refer to that expedition, under Colonel Byrd, in June, 1780, spoken of by Butler a little farther on? *

The events of 1779, in the West, with the exception of Clark's grand blow, were far less favorable than among, and east of, the mountains. The next year, however, saw the scene reversed; for though Byrd, with forces such as had not been before seen on the Dark and Bloody Ground, marched into the very centre of it, and seemed in the way of utterly sweeping it of its settlers and stations, he in truth did but little. And that little was more than avenged by the excursion of Clark against the Miami Shawanese. With nearly a thousand men he marched from the spot where Cincinnati now stands, against the towns upon the Little Miami and Mad River, all of which he destroyed, together with the crops standing about them, and so effectually defeated

---

* See Butler, pp. 103, 110, 550. Upon this and many similar points of Western history, we hope to be enlightened by a work, which we hear that Dr. Drake, of Cincinnati, has in hand; a full history of that city, founded upon an Address, delivered by him at the celebration of the fiftieth anniversary of the settlement of that growing place. This writer, as a writer of fact, takes precedence, in our opinion, of all those that have thus far arisen in the West. His "Picture of Cincinnati," published twenty years since, is still sought after, and deservedly so. It is just what it claimed to be. And we do not doubt, that his forthcoming work will be equally creditable to him and his adopted land; for we believe that he is not a native of the West, though early there.

and stripped the savages, as to prevent any considerable annoyance, on their part, for more than a twelvemonth afterwards.* The Mohawk valley, during that same summer, saw other scenes enacted. The Johnsons and Brant came upon it three several times, burning, killing, wasting; so that, by autumn, the whole country, above Schenectady, was a wilderness. It was a fearful retaliation for the devastations of Sullivan. In the course of that sad summer many curious and interesting events and adventures occurred, of which Mr. Stone speaks fully. Indeed, this is among the most interesting and original portions of his volumes. Into most of his details we cannot, of course, follow him, but must ask our reader's patience, for a few moments, while we tell the story of the Sammons family, greatly abridged, however, from the narrative given by our author.†

Old Mr. Sammons, with three sons and one or more daughters, lived upon the old Johnson estate, which had been sequestrated. Sampson, the father, was a sturdy old Whig, and well known to Sir John, whom he had often had a talk with about the rebellion. His sons, Frederick, Jacob, and Thomas, the youngest eighteen at the time of which we write, were much of the same mind and body; young Sampsons, knotty and fearless. Sir John, knowing their characters, thought he would catch them alive, and take them to Canada; so he sent his Indians out of the way, and, by good management, captured the whole race early in the morning, without a blow. The old man and his boys were at once bound, and marched off in the direction of Canada, though but a little way. That night the youngest boy, by the aid of the wife of a British officer, managed to escape; and the next morning, the father, having procured an interview with the Tory chief, read him such a lecture upon the ingratitude of thus treating one who had formerly stood by him, and upon the iniquity of his conduct generally, that he

* Butler, pp. 110, 117.

† Stone, Vol. II. pp. 72–136.

too was set free, and a span of his horses returned to him. But Frederick and Jacob were less fortunate, and were taken to the fortress of Chamblee, just within Canada, between Lake Champlain and the St. Lawrence. At that post there were about seventy prisoners, and not a very strong garrison; so that the first thing, to which the young Sampsons made up their minds, was an escape. Finding, however, their fellow-captives indisposed to do any thing for themselves, Jacob and Frederick determined to act without the rest; and, accordingly, the first time they were taken out of the fort together, to assist in some common service, they sprang from the ranks, at a concerted signal, and "put," as the phrase is in the West. The guards, startled, and less fleet of foot, could not catch them, and, though Jacob fell and sprained his ancle, he managed, under cover of the smoke produced by the gun-shots made at them, to hide himself in a clump of bushes, which his pursuers did not think of searching. It had been agreed, previously, between the brothers, that, in case of separation, they were to meet at a known spot at ten o'clock at night. Jacob, the lame one, mistook the hour, and, having gone to the spot and not finding his brother there, he left it, with the intention of getting as far from the fort as possible before daylight, his accident making time especially important to him. He accordingly pushed up the western bank of the Sorel River toward Lake Champlain, intending to swim it just below the lake, and then find his way along the eastern shore. Various events, however, occurred to prevent his doing this; but, after running great risk, by putting himself within the power of a Tory, whose chief excellence seems to have been the possession of a most kind and fearless wife, he was so lucky as to find a canoe, of which he took charge, and in which he made good headway toward home, until, in one of the narrow passes of Champlain, the British fortifications, on both sides, forced him to leave his vessel and take to the woods again.

He was without shoes, food, or gun, and had to find his way to Albany, through an unknown wilderness, along the Vermont shore. For four days he lived on birch-bark. Then he caught a few fish, and managed also to secure a wild duck. The fish and duck he ate raw. Thus he labored on during ten days. His feet, meanwhile, had become so badly cut, and so intolerably sore, that he could scarce crawl, and swarms of mosquitos made every moment of rest a moment of misery. While thus wretched and worn out, he was bitten upon the calf of the leg by a rattlesnake. And what did this young Sampson do then? Yield and die? Not he. With one stroke of his jackknife he laid his leg open, producing a plenteous flow of blood; and, with another, slew the poisonous reptile. And then came a day or two of such experience as few meet with in this life. Sammons, worn to a skeleton, with feet ragged from wear and tear, — his leg wounded and not a soul within twenty miles to help, — lay there under the log where he had been bitten, a little fire burning by him, which he had kindled by the aid of a dry fungus, — living on the rattlesnake which he had slain! He ate the heart and fat first, says Mr. Stone, and felt strengthened by the repast. What a power there is in such a soul! Truly he might say with Sampson of old, "Out of the eater came forth meat, and out of the strong came forth sweetness." There he lay, under that log, for three days; patient and surgeon, sick man, hunter, cook, and nurse, all in one. On the third day his snake was nearly picked to the bones, and he was too weak to fetch wood to cook the remainder. Sammons made up his mind, that death could not be postponed; and, having already shown how little division of labor was needed in such cases, determined to essay one more office, and by his knife proceeded to carve his epitaph on the log by his side. But God was not afar off from that brave man. He fell asleep, and strength from unknown sources flowed into his limbs. On the fourth day he rose refreshed, and, having made sandals of his hat and waistcoat, proceeded to hobble on his way once more, taking with him, as stores, the unconsumed portion of his snake. That night, again, he was comforted, being assured, by some means unknown to him, that he was near fellow-men. Rising with this faith, he struggled on till afternoon, when he reached a house and was safe. It was the 28th of June, 1780. Such were the fortunes of Jacob Sammons.

His brother Frederick was less fortunate. He had made many efforts, to no purpose, to find Jacob, who, when he fell, would not permit Frederick to stop and help him ; and, in seeking him, had run many risks. At length he crossed the Sorel ; killed an ox ; made himself some jerked beef ; and for seven days travelled along the eastern shore of Champlain without ill-luck. But, on the morning of the 8th day, he awoke sick ; a pleurisy was upon him ; a fever in his veins ; pain in every limb. It began to rain also, and there he lay, this other young Sampson, close by his brother, who, at that very moment, in that very neighbourhood, was nursing his rattlesnake bite ; — there he lay, knowing not that any was near him, for three days, on the earth, in the summer rain, and his blood all on fire. For three days, we say, he lay thus helpless. On the fourth day he was better, and tried to eat a little of his beef, but it was spoiled. He managed, however, to crawl to a frog-pond near by, a green and slimy pond, where the last year's leaves were rotting, and the bubbles rose of a hot day. He crawled thither, and put aside the green coating of the pool, and drank. He caught frogs, too, and feasted, though not a Frenchman in any of his tastes probably. There he lay, for fourteen days and nights, living by the life that was in him. Having expected death, he put up his hat upon a pole, so that it might be seen from the lake. It was seen by an enemy ; and he was found senseless and speechless, and carried — shame on the human creature that bore him — back to his prison again. And not to his prison only, but to its darkest dungeon; and there, for fourteen months, in utter darkness, he lay in irons; in irons so heavy and so tight, that they ate into the flesh of his legs, so that the flesh came off to the bone. And for fifty-six years afterwards, — for this young Sampson was living in 1837, and may be living yet, — the wounds then made did not heal. The British officer, whose heart enabled him, knowingly, to do this thing, was named (how aptly!) Steele. He was a Captain in the thirty-second regiment. May God have mercy upon his soul.

But our Sampson's adventures are not yet ended; for neither was his captivity over, nor his spirit broken. In November, 1781, he, with others, was transferred to an island above Montreal, in the rapids of the St. Lawrence. There he, as a first step, organized another plot for escape, which failed, and, as a second step, jumped, with one other, from the island into the rapids of the great river. For four miles, through those rapids, our hero and his comrade swam, navigating among the sharp rocks and fearful shoals with what skill they had. Landing on the north side of the St. Lawrence, they fought a club-battle with a village full of Canadian Frenchmen; conquered; killed a calf; and, seizing a canoe, tried to cross to the south side of the river. They were above the rapids of the Cedars, where no canoe can live long unguided, when their paddle broke in the mid-stream; and once more destruction seemed certain. A fallen tree, in the branches of which they caught, saved them, however; and, crossing the next day below the falls, they struck into the forest to seek the Hudson. For twelve more days they toiled on, living on roots, without shoes, without clothes, without hats, and reached Schenectady at last, in a plight that made Christian men give them a wide berth.

To close this strange, eventful history, — strange, and yet nowise improbable, — we have a statement which is of a kind to make men doubt, — perhaps to doubt the whole. We will give it. When Frederick reached Schenectady, — so runs the tale, — he wrote to his father. This letter went to a Mr. De Witt's, who lived some five miles from old Sampson, and there got misplaced. Jacob, who had long since settled into his usual ways once more, when he came down to breakfast one morning, said, that he had dreamed that Frederick was well and safe, and that a letter from him lay at neighbour De Witt's. The old father laughed at the fancy of the boy, and the sisters smiled, and shook their heads, and wished it were so ; but Jacob persisted it was so, and saddled his horse and rode over. Neighbour De Witt heard his young friend, and chuckled over his notion, but said there was no such letter. "Look," said Jacob ; so the good man looked, but said there was no letter there. "Look harder," said Jacob, "move the things, and see if it has not fallen down somewhere." The worthy farmer humored his adventurous neighbour, and moved this table, and that ironing-board, and the great settle, and by and by the flour-barrel. "Ha ! what 's that ? a letter, true enough. 'To Sampson Sammons, Marbletown.'" — "Well," said De Witt, "if this is not strange ! Why, it must have been left by that officer, that went along to Philadelphia last night." "Hark to me," said Jacob, "and see if dreams don't reveal things. Do you open the letter and read it, and see if I cannot tell you what 's in it." The amazed countryman opened and read, and Jacob repeated it word for word.

Such is Mr. Stone's account, based upon the statements of the Sammonses and De Witt. One question naturally occurs to the reader : — Did Mr. Stone write it after his studies in Animal Magnetism at Providence ?

But we must leave these details, and return to finish, in a few words, our process of skeletonizing. It is one of the great miseries of historical review writers, that they must often confine their labors to the most barren sketching, leaving it for others to supply those minute and personal matters to which history owes so much of its value and charm.

But, before returning to what little remains of our dry narrative, let us briefly look back over the six years which have passed since the campaign of Dunmore, in the autumn of 1774.

During 1775 offers were made, both by the Americans and English, to the Indians, and attempts to hold them neutral, or win them to one or the other side. The savages, longing generally to see the invaders driven from their hunting-grounds, and knowing, apart from all merits, that the Americans possessed those grounds, were inclined to side with England; and hesitated, in most instances, only till the result of the first campaign should show them the probable result of the contest. The Oneidas, and the branch of the Delawares led by White-Eyes, were exceptions to this general state of the red men. They were from the outset, and continued till the last, true friends of the Provinces. The year 1775, therefore, produced no results, so far as active operations were concerned. But the general tendency of the Iroquois in the North, the Delawares, Shawanese, Wyandots, Miamis, and Chippeways in the West, and the Cherokees, Creeks, and Chickasaws in the South, was in favor of England.

In 1776, the Iroquois went over openly to Britain ; the Shawanese and their more western neighbours, were also minded to war for the mother country ; and in the South the Cherokees rose, laid waste the Carolina frontiers, and were conquered.

The years 1777 – 1780 found the Iroquois first scourging the valleys of the Mohawk and Upper Susquehannah ; then houseless themselves ; and then once more in the ascendant, laying waste the country of their foes, till it was a desert from Ontario to the Hudson. Those same years found the Delawares still divided, but the American party faithful to their original undertaking. This fidelity at last, after the death of White-Eyes, who died in the winter of 1779-80, at Fort Laurens, of small-pox, obliged the chiefs to leave their country and go to Pittsburg; Pipe having, after the decease of his great rival and controller, obtained a strong influence in the nation. In the autumn of 1780, therefore, we may say that the Delawares were mainly in the British interest.

The Shawanese, from 1776 to 1780, were also in the main against the colonies, one tribe only being with them; but this nation had suffered so much from the Kentuckians, that in the autumn of 1780 they were very quiet.

Their Northwestern neighbours had suffered less, and were less overawed, but yet had been much cooled in their loyalty to England, by Clark's campaigns on the Mississippi and Wabash.

The Cherokees, during this time, had been quiet, but were fast rousing to action again. Had not Hamilton been captured, they would have been with him in his devastation of the Western country; and they stood ready to strike whenever the time came. That time came, as they thought, in the summer of 1781, and an attack was made by the Cherokees and Chickasaws upon the frontiers of South Carolina. It did, however, but little damage; and General Pickens, with about four hundred men on horseback, having ridden into the Indian country, and tried upon them a new mode of attack, — namely, a sudden charge with swords, — the warriors gave way. In fourteen days the General destroyed thirteen towns, and took many prisoners, and all without the loss of a man. In the autumn a new treaty of peace was made, and after that time no further trouble occurred with those two tribes. Their neighbours, the Creeks, tried their hand against General Wayne, near Savannah, in

June of the following year. They fought well, and for a time had the better of the battle; but in the end were defeated. Peace was preserved with them also from that time.*

During 1781 the Iroquois and their helpmates, the Tories, were wasting and slaughtering with renewed vigor, and but one happy event for the colonists occurred in the regions which they visited. That was the death of Walter N. Butler, the famous Tory leader, a man of great ability, great courage, and vile passions; a sort of reversed Marion. He was killed in one of the skirmishes of October, 1781, by an Oneida Indian.† After that autumn no hostile events of importance occurred in the Mohawk valley.

We have left us, then, for examination only the doings in the West, and they were too bad to speak of otherwise than briefly. We have, already, in the course of this sketch, presented, or rather hinted at, our views of British proceedings respecting the employment of the savages. The mere enlisting of those wild allies we cannot think, in the men of that day, reprehensible. The patriots of Massachusetts and Washington would never have advocated such an enlistment, had the measure possessed to their minds the objectionable features which some see in it now-a-days. For ourselves, we see no more objection to an alliance with red men than white men, unless it can be shown to perpetuate bad blood, and produce renewed quarrel. The secrecy of the British orders and acts, we think, should long since have been dropped. If England did right, why hide her doings? If wrong, let her own them and repent. The scalp-buying we object to, as leading to personal hostility. The conduct of the Tories and Indians at Wyoming, Cherry Valley, and during the invasion of the Mohawk, was full of evil, as war must be; but we have no charge against Britain for those acts.

---

* Holmes's *Annals,* 1781 and 1782. † Stone, Vol. II. p. 191.

Upon the whole, then, the very considerable outcry against British cruelty, during the border wars, we think unfounded. We do not know of an act equal in treachery to the capture and murder of Cornstalk; nor any that can compete, in point of cruelty, with those scenes in the West which it now becomes our painful duty to relate.

We have already said not a little respecting the Delawares upon the Muskingum; but, in order to make intelligible those events to which we are now coming, we must speak of them more particularly. Some years before the Revolutionary war began, those Delaware Indians, who had been converted to Christianity by the United Brethren, or Moravians, had been invited by the Delawares living upon the Muskingum, to come and settle in their country.* This they did, and built there several flourishing towns. There were, therefore, at the time of which we have been treating, three classes of Delawares upon that river; the heathen peace party, which was led by White-Eyes, the heathen war party under Pipe, and the Christian Delawares. The last-named people had nothing to do with the contests between the colonies and the mother country; but, as their towns were situated about the forks of the Muskingum, and near the great war-path from the Wyandot and Miami country to the frontiers of Pennsylvania and Virginia, they were at times visited by bands from each of the warring parties. This exposed them to suspicion; the Indians thought them renegades and spies; the whites called them secret foes, and accused them of aiding their heathen brethren.

So matters stood when, in the summer of 1781, Colonel Brodhead led a body of troops against some of the hostile Delawares. This, a portion of his followers thought, would be an excellent opportunity to destroy the Moravian towns, and it was with difficulty he could withhold them. He sent

* Heckewelder's *Narrative*, Doddridge, &c.

word to Heckewelder, and tried to prevent any attack upon the members of his flock. In this he appears to have succeeded; but he did not, perhaps could not, prevent the slaughter of the prisoners taken from the hostile Delawares. First, sixteen were coolly killed, and then nearly twenty. A chief, who came under assurances of safety to Brodhead's camp, was also murdered by a noted partisan, named Wetzel.

This took place in the spring or summer of 1781. About that same time, the British commanders in the Northwest made up their minds, that the settlements of the Moravians were a great evil in their way; as the Christian Delawares continually notified the frontier men of war-parties marching against them. It was therefore determined to destroy those settlements and remove the Indians, unless they would go, of their own accord, to some other point. This they would not do; and in the autumn, after long and frequent talks, which may be found in Heckewelder's "Narrative," the towns were abandoned, and the inhabitants removed to the Sandusky country, where they passed the winter in a most miserable condition. This removal the Americans appear to have looked on as a voluntary going over to the British.

In the spring of 1782, some of the Moravians, who had been literally starving through the winter, returned to their old places of abode, to gather what they could of the remainder of their property, and busied themselves in collecting the corn which had been left in the fields. About the time they returned for that purpose, parties of Wyandots came down upon the settlements, and slew many. This excited the frontier-men; and believing a connection to exist between the acts of the Wyandots, and the late movements of the Moravians, it was determined to attack and exterminate the latter, or, at least, to waste their lands and destroy their towns. Eighty or ninety men met for the purpose of effecting the objects just named, and marched in silence and swiftness upon the devoted villages. They reached them; by threats and lies got hold of the gleaners scattered among them, and bound their prisoners, while they deliberated on their fate. Williamson, the commander of the party, put the question, Shall these men, women, and children be taken to Pittsburg, or be killed? Of the eighty or ninety men present, sixteen or eighteen only were for granting their lives; and the prisoners were told to prepare for death. They prepared for death, and soon were dead; slaughtered, some say in one way, and some in another; but thus much is known, that eighty or ninety American men murdered, in cold blood, about forty men, twenty women, and thirty-four children, — all defenceless and innocent fellow-Christians.

It was in March of 1782, that this great murder was committed. And as the tiger, once having tasted blood, longs for blood, so it was with the frontier-men; and another expedition was at once organized, to make a dash at the towns of the Moravian Delawares and Wyandots upon the Sandusky. No Indian was to be spared; friend or foe, every red man was to die. The commander of this expedition was Colonel William Crawford, Washington's old agent in the West. He did not want to go, but found it could not be avoided. The troops, numbering nearly five hundred men, marched to the Sandusky uninterrupted. There they found the towns deserted, and the savages on the alert. A battle ensued, and the whites were forced to retreat. In their retreat many left the main body, and nearly all who did so perished. Crawford himself was taken and burnt to death, under the most horrible circumstances. We cannot detail them. In short, the whole expedition was a failure, as none ever better deserved to be.

Crawford's campaign was in June. In August a very large body of Indians appeared in Kentucky. They were met by the whites at the Blue Licks, on the Licking River, and a defeat was suffered by the Americans, which was long felt in that region, and is still familiar to all who live there. It was not too severe, however, to prevent Clark, with a thousand men, from marching into the Indian country, in September, and laying it waste so effectually as to awe the natives into comparative quiet. After that time Kentucky suffered little.

This march of Clark's in the autumn of 1782 was indeed the last decided movement in the border wars of our Revolution. After that, personal encounters alone took place. It is true, that the Western wars did not cease with the Revolution. The Miamis and their allies afterwards came more prominently forward, and the well-known campaigns of Harmar, St. Clair, and Wayne wound up, for the time, the long Indian contest. From 1774 to 1795 there was not peace, northwest of the Ohio, between the white and red man. But into these wars we cannot enter, having already gone beyond our proposed limits.

Before closing, let us ask, however, What may be learned from a rapid survey of those wars which we have been glancing at?

We may learn, that England was less blameworthy than we have been used to think her.

We may learn, that the Indians took less pleasure in slaughter than we have been in the habit of saying they did. Even at Wyoming and Cherry Valley, the Tories were more murderous than their red allies.

We may learn some national modesty, by finding, that Americans were guilty of the greatest treachery and the most cold-blooded murder done in those times.

We may learn, in fine, tolerance for all. The Tory felt that he was contending against traitors, disorganizers, locofocos of the worst tint; the Whig against the tools of a tyrant, who had sold themselves into bondage for vile lucre; the Indian against the usurpers of his ancient and deep-rooted right. In all, the lowest and most desperate part of man's nature was called into action, and the result was, that all did evil and wrong, times without number.

IX.

SETTLEMENT OF THE NORTHWESTERN TERRITORY.*

We know of nothing which illustrates more forcibly the rapid growth of the vast region northwest of the Ohio River, than the fact that the author of the volume before us, a man still active and vigorous, a bank director and politician, was a leader among the first true law-makers, the earliest legislators, of that immense realm. Ohio, Indiana, Illinois, Michigan, and Wisconsin, — with all their swarming millions, their gigantic granaries and clustering workshops, their canals and railroads, school-houses and churches, their libraries of statutes and reports, their piles of legislative documents, their monstrous debts, and yet more monstrous possessions, — have risen into existence under the eye of one who is still as much a citizen of the busy world as he was when his pen traced the first laws and sketched the dawning policy of that "mother of empires," the Northwestern Territory.

It was in 1796 that Jacob Burnet, then twenty-six years of age, left his home in New Jersey, and passed into the Western wilderness, the inhabitants of which, north of the

---

* *Notes on the Early Settlement of the Northwestern Territory.* By Jacob Burnet. Cincinnati: Derby, Bradley, & Co. 1847. 8vo. pp. 501.

From the North American Review, for October, 1847.

28 *

Ohio, were estimated at that time at about fifteen thousand souls. The young lawyer was bound for Cincinnati, a little aguish village of log cabins, where a brick had never been seen. On the eastern edge of this village stood Fort Washington, commanded at that time by a young lieutenant, named William Henry Harrison, who had served as aide-de-camp to Wayne, in 1794. The army and the bar — and within those two folds were contained most of the educated and refined men then in the Northwest — were chiefly remarkable for the exaggerated tone of dissipation which prevailed in them. Of nine lawyers who were at the bar when Mr. Burnet came to the Territory, eight died confirmed sots, and a large proportion of the officers under St. Clair, Wayne, and Wilkinson were hard drinkers.* The greatest man of the early West, George Rogers Clark, died a drunkard.† In this respect, a great change has been taking place within the last twenty years; the earlier pioneers not of the army or bar were by no means so abandoned in their habits as their more refined fellow-laborers; but among their children, born in comparative ease and wealth, and accustomed from childhood to the loose ways of the higher classes, there was a fearful amount of dissipation, and many, whose talents fitted them to rank with the foremost, sank into early graves or hopeless obscurity in consequence of their folly; but with a third generation have come greater inducements to labor, better examples, and a higher tone; so that throughout the West there is far less to regret and censure than there was even twelve or fifteen years since.

When Mr. Burnet entered the Territory, it was divided into four counties, to which a fifth was soon added; the county seats being Marietta, Cincinnati, Kaskaskia, Vincennes, and Detroit. At these points the courts were held at

---

* Burnet, pp. 36, 37. Harrison was one of the few exceptions.

† Ibid., p. 81.

which the members of the bar were in the habit of practising; but those from Cincinnati seldom went to Kaskaskia or Vincennes, though the writer of the work before us states, that, from the time he entered the practice until the State of Ohio was organized, he did not miss attending a single term at Detroit or Marietta. The journeys from one point to another were made on horseback, occupying from six to twelve days, the path lying for the most part through an uninhabited wilderness. The exposure and the risks were, of necessity, very great; but it was that very exposure, as we are informed, which made of our author, whose health was delicate, a robust man, who now, at seventy-seven, seeks amusement in a journey from the banks of the Ohio to the White Mountains of New Hampshire.

In 1798, the change of government took place which elevated the young attorney to the rank of a law-maker. This change grew out of the Ordinance of 1787, which provided that whenever the Northwestern Territory contained "five thousand *free* male inhabitants, of full age" (not, as Judge Burnet states, "five thousand *white* male inhabitants"), it should be entitled to choose representatives, and have a government of its own. In this government, besides the House chosen directly by the people, there was a Legislative Council, consisting of five persons, who were to be selected by the President of the United States from a list of ten sent him by the representatives of the Territory.

At the head of the Council first chosen stands the name of Jacob Burnet. Of his labors in the sphere to which he was called it will be enough to say, that during the first session he prepared and reported sixteen bills or laws (the whole number passed being thirty-seven), a system of rules for the Council, an answer to the Governor's address, a memorial to Congress, and an address to the President of the United States.

In connection with the last, the address to Mr. Adams, a

question arises which is worthy of our attention. In the paper referred to, Mr. Burnet "alluded very specially to the firmness with which he [Mr. Adams] resisted the efforts of the British commissioners, during the negotiations at Paris, to make the River Ohio the northern boundary of the United States"; * and in a note to the work before us, the writer affirms, that, Dr. Franklin having suggested a compliance with the proposition to make the Ohio the north line, Mr. Adams replied, "No," and said that he would sooner "withdraw from the negotiation, return home, and exhort his countrymen to continue the war as long as they could keep a soldier in the field. Mr. Jay was equally determined." † The claim thus advanced by Judge Burnet was also made by him in his address to John Quincy Adams at the founding of the Cincinnati Observatory, in November, 1843; and the fact, that the son of the statesman for whom the claim is made received it in silence, has been, though surely without reason, regarded as an indorsement by him of the correctness of Judge Burnet's statement. But is it correct? Does it do justice to Mr. Jay? We ask our readers to weigh the following facts.

Mr. Jay reached Paris, whither he was called by letters from Dr. Franklin, on the 23d of June, 1782.‡ From that time until September, little or no progress was made in negotiation, in consequence of the dilatory steps of the English government, which at first issued a commission wherein the United States were termed colonies,§ a term to which Mr. Jay resolutely objected, although Dr. Franklin and the Count de Vergennes thought it "signified little." Mr. Jay's opposition, and his arguments to Mr. Oswald, the British commissoner, carried the day, however, and on the 27th of September a new commission, drawn in accordance

* Burnet, p. 315.

† Burnet, p. 315, *note*.

‡ Sparks's *Dip. Corr.*, VIII. 113.

§ Ibid., X. 76.

with Mr. Jay's views, reached Paris.* Meantime, it had become evident that Spain, and probably France also, would oppose the claims of the United States to the West.† Mr. Jay was convinced that they would uphold the English claim to all the country north of the Ohio. Against the views thus entertained by her allies, the commissioner of the United States (Mr. Jay ‡) took a stand as decided as could be taken; and fearing that the court of England might be influenced by the Spanish and supposed French views, he sent a special messenger to converse with Lord Shelburne on the subject of boundaries, and to urge the full American claim.§ With Mr. Oswald at Paris, little or no difficulty appears to have occurred; and articles were drawn up by the 8th of October, which Mr. Oswald recommended to his court for adoption.|| By these articles, the northern boundary of the United States was to have been, as at present, from Maine to the point where the 45th parallel crosses the St. Lawrence, " thence straight to the south end of the Lake Nepissing, and thence straight to the source of the River Mississippi." ¶ These lines, it will be seen, would have given us, not only the chief part of the Northwestern Territory, but also the greater portion of Upper Canada, and the complete control of the Lakes. This boundary the British ministry, however, would not consent to, and Mr. Oswald was so informed on the 23d of October; three days after, for the first time since the negotiations began, Mr. Adams reached Paris.*

In Mr. Adams Mr. Jay found a bold and able coadjutor, and in the discussions which followed the two were together,

---

* Sparks's *Dip. Corr.*, VIII. 136, 143, 204.

† Ibid., VIII. 150 - 160, 202 - 205.

‡ Dr. Franklin was sick, and did little. (*Dip. Corr.*, VI. 451.)

§ Ibid., VIII. 164 - 169.

|| Ibid., VIII. 204.

¶ Ibid., X. 90.

** Ibid., VIII. 205, 206; VI. 436.

as far as we can discover, upon all leading points.* In respect to boundaries, however, there is nothing to show that the British wished at that time to force the United States south to the Ohio. Two lines were talked of, the one being the 45th parallel from the St. Lawrence to the Mississippi, the other the present line through the Lakes.† Mr. Oswald agreed to the former, which would still have given the United States the control of the Lakes, and a second set of articles, embodying that boundary, was prepared November 5th ; ‡ but these also the British ministry objected to, and twenty days after *offered* a third set,§ defining the boundary as it now exists.

We should not have dwelt upon this point so long, did we not deem it a duty to place in a just light every act of a man so true, pure, and patriotic, and yet so little estimated and basely maligned, as John Jay. That Judge Burnet may remember correctly the understanding of the time, and the tone of the papers of the day, we do not question ; Mr. Adams was preëminent for his services and his abilities ; but the evidence to which we have referred is the best to be had, and shows, we think, distinctly, that the main battle as to boundaries was fought by his colleague.

Among the most interesting portions of Judge Burnet's volume are the sketches of the men who were distinguished in the early annals of the Northwest. Among these, no one, both from rank and misfortune, is so prominent as Governor St. Clair. St. Clair was a man born never to succeed, and upon whom the consequences of ill-success were visited as crimes. He was born in Scotland, in 1734, of a wealthy and influential family. Having received a university education, he joined the army, and was with Wolfe in 1759 at the battle of Quebec. After the peace of Paris he left the

* *Dip Corr.*, VI. 436, 439, 448, &c.

† Ibid., VI. 442, 465.

‡ Ibid., X. 94.

§ Ibid., X. 101.

army, and bought a farm in the interior of Pennsylvania, in which Province he held various commissions. Among the duties which came upon him as a representative of the Penn family was that of arresting, in 1774, Dr. John Connolly, who, under a commission from Lord Dunmore of Virginia, had arrived upon the Monongahela with a view to seizing Pittsburg and the neighbouring lands, all of which were claimed by the Old Dominion; and it is from St. Clair's letters that we learn the connection between that seizure, which was ultimately effected, and the Indian war which followed; the fact having been, that Connolly, to reconcile the Virginia Burgesses to his extravagance in fortifying and providing against the Pennsylvanians, thought a little Indian skirmishing advisable, so that warlike expenditures might be charged to that account, and thence came the murder of Logan's family and its consequences.*

When the Revolution broke out, St. Clair was made a colonel in the American army; in 1776 he was created brigadier, and in 1777 major-general, and was placed in command of Ticonderoga. That important post, however, he was forced to yield in July of the same year, and did it, although he anticipated that it would bring upon him, as was the fact, a storm of popular censure, and perhaps his own ruin. "I know," he said to Wilkinson at the time, "I could save my character by sacrificing the army; but were I to do so, I should forfeit that which the world could not restore, and which it cannot take away, the approbation of my own conscience." † The self-sacrifice was made; and although his companions in arms, the court-martial which examined the affair, and Congress, all considered his conduct wise, right, and honorable, the poison of calumny had entered the public mind, and was never eradicated.

---

* See the original papers in *American Archives*, I. 252–288, 435, 459, 470, 484, 506, 774, &c.

† Wilkinson's *Memoirs*, I. 85.

At the close of the war he again retired to his farm, whence he was called to serve in Congress, over which body he presided for some time. When the Northwestern Territory was about to be organized, in 1787, St. Clair was desirous of being appointed its governor; and such was his influence in Congress, that Dr. Cutler, the agent of the New England associates, found it wise to withdraw the Massachusetts candidate, General Parsons, and to support the Pennsylvanian,* who was chosen in October.

As governor of the Northwest, St. Clair was unfortunate, both in his civil and military capacities. His love of official show and fondness of power displeased some, his strong Federal politics disgusted others, and with the Territorial legislature, when first organized, he came into conflict by the exercise of his "veto," having refused his assent to eleven acts. But his famous defeat was a more general ground of complaint than even his political course. Never, indeed, was a man more denounced than he for an affair in which little or no blame attached to him. As the exact circumstances of that second "Braddock's field" have not been generally presented correctly, we will, in justice to the commander's memory, state them.

On the 3d of November, 1791, St. Clair's army reached the banks of a small tributary of the Wabash, at the spot afterwards named by Wayne Fort Recovery. Here the regular troops rested in a position of considerable security, the militia being thrown across the stream a quarter of a mile beyond the main force. Colonel Oldham was in command of the militia, and was instructed to send out scouts in all directions, to ascertain if the Indians who had been hovering about the army for some days were present in force or not. In addition to this, a volunteer body of regulars, picked

---

* See Cutler's *Journal*, in *N. A. Review*, Vol. LIII. 334, &c. (Oct. 1841).

men, was sent under Captain Slough * to take a position in advance of the militia, and make a yet more careful examination of the woods. This done, the commanding general, who was miserably sick, sat down with Major Ferguson to plan a slight work as a place of deposit for his stores. Slough during the night advanced a mile and a quarter into the forest beyond the stream, and doubtless into the immediate vicinity of the great council of the natives, who occupied a camp three quarters of a mile in extent, when, finding the Indians very numerous, and being satisfied that the army would be attacked in the morning, he withdrew his troops to give warning to their comrades. On his way back to the main camp, he stopped among the militia, and reported his observations to Colonel Oldham, who, in reply, told him that his spies brought in similar information, and that he also expected an attack by daylight. Oldham's message Captain Slough agreed to carry to head-quarters, reporting it, together with his own discoveries, to General Butler, the second in command, and who had charge of the first line, — from which, if we remember rightly, Slough was detached. General Butler was an old Indian trader and fighter, and was regarded as the best man in the camp for the business on hand; but at the time he was not on good terms with St. Clair, and neither communicated the information he had received to the commander-in-chief, nor took any precautions himself.

The night passed on, and the troops mustered before daylight in the morning as was usual; but not a word reached St. Clair of the enemy which filled the woods around him. But when the soldiers, dismissed from their ranks again, were in confusion and unprepared for action, the yells that rose about the devoted band told too plainly the presence of the foe; and in a moment, before the troops could be fairly

† In *Am. State Papers*, V. 139, this name is misprinted "Hough."

reorganized, the militia, flying like deer before the hunters, rushed into the camp and produced a disorder that could not be remedied. In addition to this, the soldiers, trained to European warfare, were gathered in masses round the cannon, and thus became a target to the hidden riflemen of the woods. St. Clair did all that could be done; but, disabled by illness, his officers killed, and his troops at length panic-stricken, after three hours and a half of hard fighting, he was forced to turn his back, himself almost the last man on the field. Thus was his army destroyed through the gross negligence of General Butler, and the false, though usual, policy of placing his militia in advance, and fighting in close rather than open order.

General Butler died on the field of battle, and no explanation of his conduct can be given; but had he reported to his superior officer the facts made known to him by Slough, the army, St. Clair assures us, would have been moved at once upon the enemy, and the result might have been a victory.*

In relation to General Butler's death there are various accounts, which, to the skeptic in the details of history, must be full of comfort. Some say he was killed by a half-breed Shawnee chief, his own son; this is the account given by John Johnston, of Piqua, Ohio, a prominent Indian agent.† Stone, in his Life of Brant,‡ tells us that he was badly wounded, and left upon the field of battle, and that, seeing Simon Girty, he asked that worthy to kill him; this, Girty, being unused to acts of mercy, refused to do; but an Indian, learning the sufferer's rank, kindly buried his tomahawk in his brain. A third statement, given in Butler's Kentucky,§

---

* In reference to this battle, see *American State Papers*, V. 137, 198. Ibid., XII. 37, 44. Slough's deposition in St. Clair's *Narrative*, pp. 213 – 219. Marshall's *Kentucky*, I. 380. Dillon's *Indiana*, I. 308. St. Clair's *Narrative*, pp. 31 – 36, 135. *American Pioneer*, II. 150.

† Cist's *Cincinnati Miscellany*, II. 299.

‡ p. 204.

§ II. 310.

informs us that he was wounded and taken back of the lines to be attended to; but that while they were dressing his wounds, an Indian broke through the ranks in pursuit of the officer, whom he had seen borne away, and killed him in the arms of his attendants. Other variations might be added, but it is needless, as these are enough to show the worthlessness of minute historical statements, even in relation to what happened in our own country but a half-century ago.

To return to St. Clair. His unpopularity was brought to a climax by his opposition to the efforts of the people who inhabited the eastern portion of the Territory to obtain a State organization. This opposition he continued up to the meeting of the convention to form the State constitution, in November, 1802, and, having obtained permission to address that meeting, he did it in a manner which caused Mr. Jefferson instantly to remove him from office. He then returned to Pennsylvania, worn out, poor, and without hope. A claim which he had against the United States was refused payment, because barred by the statute of limitations, and a bill to grant him an annuity was lost in the House of Representatives. Pennsylvania acted more generously, and bestowed upon him a yearly income sufficient for his wants, which he enjoyed until his death, in the eighty-fourth year of his age, August, 1818.

Judge Burnet dwells at considerable length upon the Indian wars of the Northwest; and they deserve to be dwelt on, especially at this time, as they show how Washington treated a weak neighbour whose demands were unreasonable and whose conduct was unjust, fearing neither the charge of weakness, nor the accusation of a want of proper national pride. The Indian wars of the Northwest, which in their day were vastly more important to the Union than our present contest, grew up in the following manner. When England made the peace of 1783, she left her Indian allies along the frontier entirely unprovided for, at the mercy of the Americans. Congress naturally regarded the victory over England as a victory also over her helpers, and looked upon the lands of the Northwest as forfeited by Britain in consequence of her treaty, and lost by the natives through the right of conquest. The Indians, accordingly, were offered peace, and portions of their own lands were allotted them as residences and hunting-grounds, while what was needed by the States was taken for nothing, or at a merely nominal price. This is the language of the treaty of Fort McIntosh, made in January, 1785, with the Wyandots, Delawares, Chippeways, and Ottawas; and in that concluded at the mouth of the Great Miami, a year later, not only are their lands "allotted" to the Shawanese, but they are made expressly to acknowledge "the United States to be the sole and absolute sovereigns of all the territory ceded to them by a treaty of peace made between them and the king of Great Britain," January 14th, 1784.* With this understanding on the part of the whites, were made the treaties of Fort Stanwix in 1784, of Fort McIntosh in 1785, of the Great Miami in 1786, and of Fort Harmar in 1789.

But the great body of the Indians refused to acknowledge the validity of these treaties. The celebrated Brant had early seen that the red men, when left to themselves, would soon be stripped of all they had, unless they determined upon and persevered in union. It became with him, therefore, a leading object to secure such a union of the Northwestern and Northern tribes as would put it out of the power of any one nation to dispose of its lands without the consent of the others. And he succeeded in forming such a confed-

* See also Report to Congress of October 15, 1783 (*Old Journals*, IV. 294). Instructions to Indian Commissioners, same date (*Secret Journals*, I. 257). Knox's Report of June 15, 1789 (*American State Papers*, V. 13). Statement of Commissioners in 1793 (*American State Papers*, V. 353).

eracy, though at what period precisely we do not learn, either from Mr. Stone or any other source; its first appearance, so far as we know, was through a very able paper addressed to the United States, in November, 1786, by a meeting of the Indian congress, held at the mouth of the Detroit River.* But, although this union of the tribes does not appear till 1786, we find the earlier treaties objected to on the part of Brant and others, because they were made, in opposition to the known wishes of the natives, with single tribes. This point, indeed, seems to have arisen at a very early period; as we find that in October, 1783, it was ordered by Congress that the commissioners to make peace with the Indians should treat with them unitedly; but, in the following March, it was directed that they should meet the tribes at various places and different times,† which policy was adhered to. There was, therefore, on the red man's side, a determination to resist all transfers of land unless made by universal consent, while the whites were disposed to obtain what they could from the fears, the wants, or the weakness of separate tribes; and, inasmuch as the Indian confederacy had no recognized national existence, the whites were able to attain their ends despite the protests of the savages. Indeed, those protests do not make any appearance on record, until, as we have said, the autumn of 1786, although it is alleged that they were made as early as the treaty of Fort Stanwix.

We cannot, therefore, accuse our fellow-countrymen of unfair dealing with their copper-colored brethren, but neither can we be surprised that the children of the forest regarded the growing invasion of their homes with impatience and anger. Of old they had hoped to stop the career of European conquest at the Alleghanies, and had failed; then the

* It is in the *American State Papers*, V. 8.

† *Secret Journals*, I. 255, 261.

Ohio became their landmark; but now that, too, was passed, and they were to be driven they knew not whither. Impatient and angry, war-parties harassed the whole Ohio border, on both sides of the river, and Gamelin, a trader who was sent in April, 1790, up the Wabash, found evidences of a spirit of hostility which led to the useless and unfortunate campaign of Harmar, who was to strike a blow upon the Maumee that would terrify the restless savages into good behaviour. He struck his blow, but the red dogs struck back again; he burnt their towns and corn, but they killed and scalped his "regulars," while his foolish and cowardly militia took to their heels.*

This blow, therefore, served only still further to irritate and encourage the natives, who meanwhile were hoping for direct aid from England. Indirect aid they seem to have had, if not from the authorized upper agents of Britain, at least from her traders and under-functionaries; and soon they were swarming again with torch and tomahawk along the devoted frontier. When this state of facts became known to the President, it was determined to adopt a three-fold plan of action, calculated, as it was hoped, to meet all difficulties. By this plan there was to be sent to the confederacy on the Lakes a messenger of peace, under the protection of certain friendly Iroquois chiefs, Corn-Planter and others; in case he failed to satisfy the natives that the United States desired to do justice, expeditions were to go from Kentucky, composed of frontier men, who were to repeat Harmar's blows upon the villages of the Wabash, and avoid his defeats, which were ascribed to the presence of the regulars; while, in the third place, a great army was to be

* See accounts of Harmar's campaign in *American State Papers*, XII. 20, &c., and V. 104, &c. Some writers have placed Harmar's actions on the Scioto; this is because there was a "Chillicothe" on the Maumee; there was a third Indian town of the same name on the Little Miami.

gathered, which should march to the Maumee, take, fortify, and hold the point at the Miami village, now Fort Wayne, and by this means completely overawe and control the unruly red men.* The commander-in-chief was St. Clair, the pacific messenger, Colonel Proctor, and the leaders of the Kentuckians, Scott and Wilkinson. Proctor's mission entirely failed, in part because he was unable to reach the confederacy, and in part because the Indians mistrusted the three-headed negotiation, which was military at two points, and civil at but one.† Scott and Wilkinson, in due time, attacked the unhappy villages on the Wabash, destroying some food and killing a few warriors. Of St. Clair's most fatal conflict we have already said enough.

When the news of that campaign reached the President, he felt that he must act with decision, and at the same time he was, with most others, still unwilling to lose any opportunity of avoiding further bloodshed. While, therefore, steps were taken to renew the army, and place it under a leader of undoubted ability and energy, means were also adopted to bring the intentions of the United States home to the minds of the natives more completely than had been done before. To this end, the Iroquois friendly to the United States were to go westward; Brant was invited to Philadelphia; Colonel Trueman, with a friendly message, was sent from Fort Washington (Cincinnati) to the Maumee; Colonel Hardin, with a similar message, was despatched to Sandusky; Captain Hendricks, chief of the Stockbridge Indians, was urged to attend the convention of the natives in the Northwest; and General Rufus Putnam, of Marietta, was authorized to go into the Indian country and make a treaty with as many tribes as he could. But all was of no avail; the most that could be done was to procure the submission of existing

---

* *American State Papers*, V. 171. Sparks's *Washington*, IX. 109.

† Stone's *Life of Brant*, II. 300, &c.

difficulties to a great council to be held in the following year, 1793, and this was obtained through the emissaries of the Six Nations. Brant visited Philadelphia, but did not return to his Western confederates; Hendricks stayed away from the council; Trueman and Hardin were murdered before reaching their destination; and General Putnam's treaty, made at Vincennes, was of no avail, having never been ratified by the Senate.

And here we pause for a moment, to notice a slight error of Judge Burnet in relation to the mission of Trueman. He states* that Trueman and Hardin went on the same embassy, leaving Fort Washington some time in June. He also observes, that "the discrepancies which have appeared as to the time, manner, and circumstances of that unfortunate embassy are somewhat remarkable." Such is, indeed, the fact, and we will note them, although unimportant in themselves, as one of the curiosities of historical detail. Marshall and Butler, in their Kentucky Histories, speak of Trueman as sent by Wilkinson; Atwater, in his History of Ohio, says he was sent by Wayne; Judge Burnet, in a former publication, the Transactions of the Ohio Historical Society, alleged that he was sent by Harmar; this, in the work before us, he speaks of as an error, and states, what is the truth, that he was a messenger of the United States executive, under instructions from the Secretary of War.† The author of the Notes now says he left Cincinnati in June; but in the fifth volume of the American State Papers, p. 243, we have a statement by William May, who says that he (May) was sent, on or about the 13th of April, "to follow on the trail of Trueman, who, with a French baker and another man, was sent as a flag to the Indians." He afterwards mentions the discovery of Trueman's body and those of his companions, "scalped and stripped." Many circum-

* p. 129. † *American State Papers*, V. 230.

stances render this statement suspicious, such as the fact that Trueman's instructions are dated in Philadelphia, April 3d, and that his death was not heard of until June 28th, even at Vincennes; and yet there is no reason on the face of it to question May's account. But from a letter in Dillon's Indiana, Vol. I. p. 312, written by Wilkinson, we learn that one *Freeman* left Fort Washington for the Indians on the 7th of April, and in the same letter May is ordered to follow on his track. It was then Freeman, and not Trueman, beyond a doubt, whose body May found. That it was not that of the latter we know, because we have in Cist's Cincinnati Miscellany, Vol. I. p. 18, another letter from Wilkinson, which clears up all difficulties, and enables us to correct our author; it is dated May 24th, and states that "Hardin and Trueman left us day before yesterday, the former for Sandusky, the latter for the Maumee."

But although the pacific overtures of 1792 availed so little, Washington was determined to send messengers the next spring whose position and characters should command respect. He at first selected Charles Carroll and Charles Thompson; but as they declined the nomination, Benjamin Lincoln, Timothy Pickering, and Beverly Randolph were chosen instead, and about the last of April left Philadelphia for the West. Of their proceedings Judge Burnet gives a full account. They were of the most conciliatory and pacific character. Every thing that could be done with propriety was done to allay the passions of the Indians and the jealousy of the English, who did not like it that they had not been called in as mediators. But all was in vain; the savages had worsted Harmar and annihilated St. Clair; they also fully expected aid from England, having received beyond doubt intimations from the British agents that the war between the United States and the mother country would be renewed; intimations which Lord Dorchester, in his famous speech of February, 1794, before the final conflict, fully seconded. The genuineness of this speech, it is true, was denied by Judge Marshall in his Life of Washington, and the note in Mr. Sparks's great work (Vol. X. p. 394) might lead one to suppose that he agreed with the earlier biographer; but we have reason to know that Mr. Sparks is satisfied that the speech is genuine, and the discovery of a certified manuscript copy among Brant's papers, made by Mr. Stone, places the fact beyond question. The commissioners of Washington were, therefore, forced to retrace their steps, and then Wayne was instructed to make his entrance, which he did slowly, but with such skill that the Indians found themselves outdone in their own particular branch of warfare, skulking and surprising, and had lost all their moral strength and their confidence before the battle of August 20th 1794, — the battle which closed, not only the Indian war, properly so called, but also the border contests that had lasted since Connolly, in 1774, began his Indian skirmishes, in order to excuse his expenditure of the treasures of the Old Dominion.

If our reader will for a moment dwell upon the course of proceeding we have thus hastily sketched, he will see that Washington, when a war had been rashly entered upon, — as the war of 1790 to 1795 certainly had been, by the expedition of Harmar, — was not, therefore, unwilling to approach the other party in a spirit of concession and compromise, even after that other party had been successful. Had St. Clair's campaign proved fortunate, instead of ruinous, the reasons for concession and pacific measures would have been vastly stronger. And can it be doubted, that, if we had paused at the Rio del Norte, and proper commissioners, with the power of offering just and wise concessions, had been sent to Mexico, our own consciences and the judgment of the world would have acquitted us, where both will now convict us, — and this equally whether we had succeeded, or, like Washington, failed in the effort to secure peace without further bloodshed?

Before leaving this subject of the Indian wars, we wish to call the attention of our readers to the last message sent by the Indians to Messrs. Randolph, Lincoln, and Pickering; an abstract of it may be found in the work before us, page 149, or the whole in the fifth volume of American State Papers, page 356; it is, we think, among the best papers to be met with in the diplomacy of nations, savage or civilized.

Among the most remarkable men connected with the period of which we are writing was General Wilkinson, and we cannot but hope that some one will attempt his biography before it is too late. His connection with Burr, and his failures during the war of 1812, have thrown a shade over his character and talents; but he possessed abilities of a very rare kind, and if unworthy of confidence, he was surely one of the profoundest and most successful concealers of roguery that ever lived; for three protracted trials, before a court of inquiry, the House of Representatives, and a court-martial, failed to lead to his conviction on any of the charges brought against him. His popular power was unbounded; he absolutely ruled Kentucky at one time, though a mere private man, and one lately from beyond the mountains. In his dealings with Burr, he was either innocent, or too deep for one who was not easily duped. As a business man, he opened the trade of the Mississippi. As a writer and speaker, he was perfectly adapted to his sphere. In social life, he exercised a fascination even over his enemies, and none, however prejudiced, could resist the charm of his eloquence, his manner, and his most subtle flattery.

But it is time that we ceased these rambling, and we fear uninteresting, remarks on the past of the West, to suggest some more connected thoughts on its history and its probable future.

Upon the surface of the earth there is no land which ought to be more interesting to us than the vast and wealthy realm which lies upon the Mississippi and its tributaries. The dead or dying hero is no more worthy of our regard than the new-born infant. Beyond the Alleghanies is to be tried the great question of our age and race, — that of self-government, as we call it, or, more properly, the question whether we can and will submit ourselves to the government of God. There is a Pagan Democracy, which looks to real self-control, or, in other words, no control at all, which demands its own rights, and aims at nothing higher than happiness; but there is also a Christian Democracy, which bows to the Controller of all, looks to the rights of others and its own duties, and aims at justice, truth, and God's kingdom among men. Upon those Western prairies, among those Western "knobs," along those winding rivers, and by the side of the countless little water-courses and "dry runs" of that vast valley, are the rival spirits of Heathen and Christian Democracy to contend for supremacy; already the battle is begun.

And what a battle-field! From the Alleghanies to the Rocky Mountains, from the frozen lakes of the North to the tepid waters of the Gulf of Mexico! Every soil, every climate, every variety of surface. Of all the great products of the world, coffee is the only one which does not, or may not, grow there. Take the people of Britain, Ireland, France, Holland, Germany, Italy, and Spain, and place the whole in the valley beyond the Appalachians, and it would continue to ask for "more." Ohio alone, without sinking a pit below the level of her valleys, could supply coal equal to the amount dug from the mines of England and Wales for twenty-five hundred years; and Ohio is but a pigmy, in the way of bitumen, compared with Western Pennsylvania and Virginia. Iron abounds from Tennessee to Lake Erie, and forms the very mountains of Missouri and Arkansas. Salt wells up from secret storehouses in every Northwestern State. Lead enough to shoot the human race extinct with is raised from the great metallic dikes of Illinois and Wisconsin. Copper and silver beckon all trusting capitalists to the shores of Lake Superior. And mark the water-courses, the chain of lakes, the immense plains graded for railroads by Nature's own hand, the reservoirs of water waiting for canals to use them. Already the farmer far in the interior woods of Ohio or Indiana may ship his produce at his own door to reach Boston, New York, Philadelphia, Baltimore, or New Orleans, and every mile of its transit shall be by canal, steamboat, or rail-car.

What a land is this for Democracy to try her hand in! How different from the hard, rough Attica, where the olive-tree, the peasant's cow and pig combined in one, clung to the fissured rock century after century, yielding its butter and lard; where the humming swarms of Hymettus were instead of the sugar-cane, and pastures and fields, and ease and plenty were not tempting men to sloth and neglect. Is not the very wealth of the West to be its ruin? Can virtue and self-control exist without hard labor and struggles? And can labor be the characteristic of a land so reeking with abundance?

Let us enter that land, and choose its most typical State, Kentucky; let us look at its towns, its people, its inner history, and see what light we can gather to aid us in a Yankee guess at the time to come. We leave the Ohio valley; we ascend the hills, if those deserve the name which are only "elevations of depression," the ridges left where the water has gullied the plain; * — how rounded, how feminine the landscape! Over the gentle undulations, symmetrical as the bust of Venus, the ripening wheat, the rising corn-fields, spread to the shadow of the emerald maple-boughs, or the feathery beeches. The blue sky softens in the distance into a hazy, sleepy white; the tulip-tree, left alone in the pasture, lifts its branchless trunk seventy or

* Such is the case, although the hills are from two to three hundred feet high; their tops are the true level of the country.

eighty feet heavenward, and the broad, glossy leaves twinkle and wink in the sunbeams; the cattle lie dozing, only their molar teeth wakeful; the pigs are deep in the mire by the brook-side; a gaunt horse, dragging after him at the plough-tail an unwilling negro, walks between the corn-rows, trampling, not eradicating, the weeds; through the open door of the farm-house, as you pass, you may see the mistress *lazing* in her easy-chair; when you reach the town before us, you may find her helpmate talking politics at the tavern door.

And now we come upon the town, the county seat. How old it looks! Nature so young and vigorous, and this poor place so decrepit and halt! The stone house at the corner has not a whole windowin it, and the chimneys look more ancient than the Pyramids; the hewn-log dwelling to the left totters and reels as if the steaming bar-room next door kept it perpetually half drunk; the hotel itself, red, and brick, and brazen, is the symbol of impudence and brutality, — of that Heathen Democracy whose life-blood is whiskey, and whose breath is oaths.

Let us join the group round the old gentleman, who, with his chair in the street, his feet on the window-sill, his left hand in his ruffled shirt-bosom, and his cud in his cheek, is laying down the law, pointed off with spirts of tobacco-juice. These men, common as they look, are not common men; lazy as they appear, leaning against the shoulder-polished door-posts, they are full of energy and ability. Such men as these won the battle of Buena Vista, and will rule the world if they choose to. Here is one, hard-featured and stern, with full veins, and a complexion like half-tanned ox-hide, who would, like Harry Daniel, of Mount Sterling,* murder the brother of his wife and see her go crazy, and

* Henry, commonly called Harry, Daniel, of Mount Sterling, Montgomery county, Kentucky, shot his brother-in-law in open court,

yet walk his way with an easy conscience, or, at any rate, the pretence of one. Next to him sits a man who could wage war with the human race for a lifetime, and enjoy it; a man of the Middle Ages, with all the vices of feudalism and all those of our money-seeking age combined. He has made his fortune by hunting up invalid titles, purchasing and prosecuting the legal claim, and turning the innocent holder to the dogs. And yet at home no one is kinder, more thoughtful, almost self-sacrificing. Send him to Mexico, and humanity is capable of no crime from which he would turn, or at which he would shudder. Take him to Boston, and his manner will be as pleasing as his conversation will be original. Search his pockets and you will find a plan for defrauding a neighbour of his farm, a most affectionate letter to an absent daughter, a bowie-knife, and Paradise Lost.

Beyond him, notice that face. How clear the eye, how confident the mouth, how strong and firm the chin! If he speaks, you will hear a voice like the Eolian harp, pouring forth words of such sweetness that the bees might cling upon his lips. If he moves, it is the Indian's motion, quiet and strong as sunlight. In his mind the Higher Democracy is forming itself a home; and amid the low contests of politics, he will be, unconsciously, acting as the messenger of the great Friend of man. Another comes by with a quick, springy step, as if with ankle-joints of India-rubber; he stops, joins in the discussion; words pour from his tongue more rapidly than the ear can drink them; he looks round, his eye all seriousness, and his mouth all smiles; men catch his idea, though they cannot his syllables, and their nods show that he has hit some nail on the head. That man, slight as

---

March 5th, 1845. Both were, in wealth and standing, among the first men of the neighbourhood. Daniel was acquitted, and is now again a leader in his district.

a girl, might be safely trusted to lead any corps in any battle; and yet in his life he never struck a blow. Go for ten miles round, inquire in any household, and you will hear of him as the kind adviser, the steadfast friend, the unostentatious helper; many a son has he saved from the gambling-table, the race-course, or the deadly duel, begun with rifles and finished with knives; — and he, too, is a child of the soil.

Now consider, that, while the murderer and the victim of assassination become known to you through the press, the virtues of the patriotic politician or the village philanthropist make no noise in the world. Believe us, also, that, while the towns and taverns of these Western States, reeking with tobacco and whiskey, are symbols of the evil Democracy of our land, and the bullies and cutthroats, the knaves and robbers, are its true children; and though you might, on first looking at such a society as you may see in almost any Western town, think anarchy was close at hand, yet are the villages ever improving, the taverns themselves growing more decent, and anarchy is going farther and farther away. Remember that this Kentucky was settled by men perfectly their own masters; no government, no religion, no police, no restraining power of any kind save the voice of God in their own breasts. Remember that among them were the most reckless, unprincipled, and bloodthirsty of human beings. Remember that for twenty years this population, thus gathered in anarchy, was demoralized by a border warfare, full of atrocities on both sides. Call to mind, that, without attachment to the Union, the people of Kentucky were courted by Spain, France, and England, and were more than once nigh severing themselves from the Atlantic States. And when you have recalled these things, observe how out of anarchy* has come a regular and untroubled govern-

* This is not too strong a term; in 1776, George Rogers Clark called the people together to take measures to procure a recognition of their

ment; out of indifference or antagonism to the Union, a true devotion to it; and out of a population scarce cognizant of law, a society which, even in its excesses and violations of statute, aims, however blindly, to obey the law of justice and public good. To understand the West, you must remember that it is socially a youth, in a state of transition, to be compared rather with England under the Plantagenets than with England now. You find, consequently, strange mixtures of statute law and Lynch law, of heathen brutality and the most Christian excellence, of disregard for human life and self-forgetting philanthropy. But amid all the confusion, you may find evidence, we believe, that the Higher Democracy, the rule of God, is advancing.

And here we may relate a curious scene, calculated to illustrate our meaning, which took place in a part of the State where some of us from "Down East" were visiting a few years since. It was a county town that we were staying at, and the Circuit Court was in session. The presiding judge was a large, kindly, easy gentleman, respected and beloved by most that knew him. But still, like all public men in Kentucky, he had his enemies, persons that he had charged against as suitors, or rebuked as witnesses, or reprimanded as jurymen; and among them was a sort of half-outlaw who dwelt upon the outskirts of the town we were in. This man, silent, unsocial, and determined, had vowed his revenge, and the judge was always on the alert to meet his insult or his knife, as the case might be, and never saw him but he kindled from his kindly quietude like a chafed mastiff. On the second day of our visit, as it chanced, the worthy magistrate, as he walked court-ward after dinner, spied his old foe on one of the wooden benches which are placed

---

existence by Virginia, or to set up for themselves; there was then absolutely no government. — See Butler, Marshall, Morehead, or Clark's own Journal, in Dillon's *Indiana*, I. 128, &c.

under the trees around Western court-houses, and took it into his head that the semi-barbarian looked at him in a very peculiar, and of course insulting manner. Instantly he kindled, fixing his eye upon the enemy, who of course did not lower his; the judge strode toward the supposed delinquent, and without a word uttered, lifting his stout hickory sapling, dealt the offender blow upon blow across the face. Not many blows fell, however, ere the semi-savage plucked from his pocket a pistol, which, clapping it against the assailant's waistcoat, he fired; the judge staggered and fell. Instantly the death-dealer fled, but close upon his heels were two scions of the fallen magistrate, armed and equipped with pistol and bowie-blade. Two shots fired *in transitu* missed, and the knife thrown, as the Indian casts his tomahawk, passed the intended victim and stood quivering in the earth; the murderer reached his home unhurt. Then rose the cry of popular vengeance, for all loved the judge, and thirsted to avenge him. But vengeance must be legal; so, while the people watched round the outlaw's house, which he and a brother were barricading, the proper writs were issued for their arrest, and messengers sent to the four winds to summon a bench of justices to try the sudden crime. Meanwhile the fallen victim was stripped, and probes, knives, and lint were made ready; but, thank Heaven, to no purpose; for the ball, while it had bruised and thrown down the worthy man, had not — strange to say — even broken the skin, and was found somewhere among his vestments, the explosion having burnt a hole in his silk waistcoat. Then came the siege of the outlaw's den; protruded rifles, solemn oaths on the one side not to injure, violent ones on the other not to yield; nor was there much prospect of peace until news came that the accused had committed no murder. When he learned this, the astounded life-taker, surprised out of his boldness, gave himself up, and under due warrant and the guidance of a vast self-called *posse*, walked toward the court-house, where the justices were meanwhile gathering. Thither also came the judge, with a hole in his vest merely, his vitals untouched; and the court opened. Evidence was heard, and very brief argument. This done, the magistrates laid their wise heads together, and, having pondered all things,—*fined each party one cent and dismissed the case!* Then, leaving their high seats, the judge from the bar rose to the bench, and the ordinary business of the court went on.

But strange judicial scenes are not to be met with in the wilds of Kentucky alone. In Cincinnati, not many years since, the Court of Common Pleas appointed a clerk under circumstances which were of a character to excite suspicions as to the motives of the judges. The bar was not disposed to acquiesce, although the members had, in truth, nothing to say or do in the premises. And not only did the lawyers object, but the people also, in their majesty, objected. Two meetings, one of the bar, and one of the public, were therefore called at the court-house, to be held just before court hours, to take the matter into consideration. At the meeting of the profession, proper resolutions were passed and ordered to be presented to the court; and that being adjourned, the masters in large numbers organized themselves. After the choice of a committee, it was suggested that it would be as well to examine the judges as to some alleged attempts at bribery on the pårt of relatives of the successful candidate for the clerkship, which was a lucrative office. A second committee was accordingly appointed to wait upon the magistrates and desire their presence. Three of them, and one just off the bench, answered the popular summons; and then was to be seen the singular Democratic phenomenon of a judge standing upon the bar-table in his own court-room, in the midst of an assembly of merchants, mechanics, and laborers, turning from side to side, and undergoing an examination in reference to his official acts, and the efforts made to influence those acts improperly. The popular meeting, having heard the judges through, decided against the appointment that had been made, and then adjourned, giving place to the court, whose hour of meeting had long since passed. When the court was opened, the proceedings of the bar were read, but the president judge, who had refused the subpœna of the public meeting, treated the whole matter with contempt, and insisted upon consummating the appointment by entry on the record; this his fellow-magistrates, who had become alarmed, objected to, and one of the three, one who had opposed the appointment all along, spoke with much warmth, and was applauded by the people. The president judge ordered the clerk *pro tem.* to hand him the record, but the clerk declined; he commanded the sheriff to adjourn the court *sine die*, but the sheriff refused; he commenced an address to the bar and people, and was then fairly hissed from the bench! * The decision of the public and bar, thus announced, was not to be resisted, and the appointment was annulled.

The execution of Smith Maythe in Kentucky, in July, 1841, affords another illustration of that curious mixture of law and lawlessness, wholly free from passion, to which we have referred. Maythe was a Cincinnati boy of the most desperate character. He shrunk from no crime, and yet escaped, by one means and another, the consequences proper to his outrageous conduct. At length, in company with one Couch, he robbed a drover in Grant county, and cut his throat; but the wound not proving mortal at once made it probable that the law could do no more than imprison the criminals, and prisons, it was known, could not hold Maythe. The farmers and others who lived near by the spot where the crime was committed, being convinced that one who

---

* *Cincinnati Gazette*, April 13th, 1834. *Cincinnati Republican.* Pamphlet published by the Bar, &c.

attempted a murder was in truth a murderer, though the law would not adjudge him to be so, and fearing that Maythe would be turned loose to commit further crimes, determined to execute him themselves, in obedience to what they deemed the true law of the case. To the number of several hundred, they met and organized for the purpose of carrying their plans into effect. There was no concealment, no passion; but calm determination. Thirty-six hours' notice was given the criminals of their fate; the jailer was not asked to open the jail, as that would have ruined him, and its doors were forced. A clergyman was provided, and five hours were allowed the culprits to spend in his company; three speeches, praying them to desist, were listened to by the executioners, respectfully, but without causing any change of purpose. When the hour came, the whole body formed a procession and bore the murderers to the spot where their crime had been committed, and there, upon the tree under which their victim was found lying, hanged them.

This was all anarchy, but it was the anarchy of law-abiding men. It was no riot or mob; the proceedings were those of a people whose parents had settled a wilderness, had defended their hearths against the savage, and had begun a system of obedience to a self-imposed rule of right; these men regarded their doings as an extension of that system. And is it not true, that, under Democratic influences, many changes and advances in law will necessarily be made through the breach of law? Will judges and legislators, on many points, ever feel that they can carry God's law into effect, until popular feeling, overstepping statutes, leads the way? We may illustrate our meaning, which is not to excuse disloyalty to law, but to state what we believe to be a fact, by a single instance. Would seduction ever have been punished as it deserves, if there had not been on the part of individuals, juries, and "the masses," most distinct and emphatic protests — with pistols, verdicts of insanity, and shouts of congratulation — against the old heathen English common law which gave a man days' wages for the ruin of his daughter, because by her ruin he lost her labor? We may regret that Democracy should entail such evils on us, but, like the mischiefs of an election, these evils are the necessary friction of our machinery. Where the people rule, they must be heard; and on many subjects, not connected with politics, they never will be heard, we fear, unless through movements and acts in themselves revolutionary.

Now, the younger a Democratic community is, the more of this irregular action there will be; and in such a community the true question is, not whether laws are broken by popular will, but whether a regard for law, and a perception of its benefits, is growing or decreasing. In the West we believe such a regard and perception to be on the advance.

We have already adverted to the change of sentiment toward the general government, but it deserves to be more dwelt upon, as an evidence of what we say. When the Federal Constitution was discussed in the Virginia convention, Kentucky (then a part of the Old Dominion) sent fourteen delegates, eleven of whom voted against its adoption. And this vote was given after mature deliberation, and a full knowledge of the instrument. In the July previous to that convention (1787), Harry Innis, attorney-general of Kentucky, wrote to the governor of Virginia as follows: — "I am decidedly of opinion that this Western country will in a few years act for itself, and erect an independent government."* This spirit continued with little abatement at least till the time of the famous resolutions of 1798, when John Breckenridge announced in the legislature of Kentucky the doctrine, that if Congress attempted to enforce any laws which the States objected to, "it is then the right and duty

* Marshall's *Kentucky*, I. 270, 287.

of the several States to nullify those acts, and protect their citizens from their operation." And this doctrine received the unanimous support of the Senate, the approval of the governor, and met with but three opponents in the House, one of whom, William Murray of Franklin county, advanced the arguments since expanded and urged by Daniel Webster.*

Nor was Kentucky alone in her nullification; Ohio, in 1820-21, having taxed the United States Branch Banks fifty thousand dollars each, and having collected the tax by main force, passed resolutions recognizing and approving the doctrines asserted by Kentucky in 1798.† But has nullification remained the theory of the West? By no means. In February, 1833, Kentucky took back, in most express words, her former theory, and affirmed the powers of the central government and the federal courts; ‡ and although Ohio has not, we believe, so directly proved her change of views, it is perfectly well known that she is anti-nullification through every fibre.

Now all this change has been, we think, not owing to any change in political parties, or to a mere selfish conviction that the Union is for the interests of the West; it is a growing regard for, and loyalty to, law, as embodied in the national rule, that has caused the change of feeling, and that will preserve allegiance to the Union henceforward unimpaired.

There is another episode in Western history, which, in relation to this subject, is worthy of notice; we refer to the Whiskey Insurrection. It grew out of Alexander Hamilton's taxation of spirits, in 1790-91. The farmers of Western Pennsylvania and Virginia could not send their grain down the Mississippi, for it was closed by Spain; and neither railroad, canal, nor turnpike offered any easy conveyance over

* Butler's *Kentucky*, 282-289.

† *American State Papers*, XXI. 653, 654.

‡ Butler, 289.

the mountains. The rye was therefore condensed into whiskey, as a horse could carry but four bushels of the grain, while it could bear the whiskey distilled from twenty-four bushels. It was natural enough, therefore, in those days, when alcohol was regarded as a necessary of life, that the frontier men should deem themselves aggrieved, and the tax unequally inflicted. The consequence was a threefold rebellion; in the first place, the leading men of the suffering region, Albert Gallatin among them, protested, and in no measured terms, against the system of the Secretary; in the second place, the more thoughtless and reckless proceeded to tar and feather the collectors of the tax, and to commit other acts of violence; while, in the third place, a systematic opposition to the general government was organized, and measures were taken to produce a universal rising of the people. Mr. Gallatin and his friends, seeing how matters tended, soon desisted from their violent words; and although they had gone the length of proclaiming that they would withhold from the tax-officers all assistance, and "all the comforts of life which depend upon those duties that as men and fellow-citizens we owe to each other,"* they joined the peace party. The individual rioters, though troublesome, were not dangerous. It was the third body of opponents which threatened serious mischief, and spread a spirit akin to that of the Jacobins of France. At the head of this party was David Bradford, an attorney and politician of some note. He apparently thought that by means of the Democratic societies, and other similar associations, he could manage the Western people as he pleased; and, taking advantage of a very unwise step on the part of the government, namely, the sending of offenders against the excise law east of the mountains to be tried, he proceeded to kindle the spirit of resistance.

It was not hard to do this, as it was easy to compare the

* *American State Papers*, XX. 108.

course adopted by the Federal government to that of England before the Revolution, which had required criminals to be sent to Britain, and by means of a society similar to, but independent of, the regular Democratic clubs, he was able to effect an organization which was in reality formidable. The fact, that it was not an affiliated society that Bradford used, deserves especial notice, as Washington and others ascribed the Western difficulties to those associations. In the neighbourhood of Pittsburg were three clubs, two of them independent of the Eastern bodies, the third a regular, affiliated scion of the orthodox stock; — in this last nothing was done to encourage outbreaks; in the two former every thing was done; and moreover, when the crisis came, the Eastern clubs united in condemning the measures of Bradford and his friends.* Those measures were such, that the United States Marshal and General Neville, the inspector of the district, were fired upon by a party, while serving a warrant, and the next morning, July 16th, 1794, General Neville's house was surrounded by a number of men who wished to destroy his papers. These men belonged to the Mingo Creek association, one of the two already referred to, and do not appear to have contemplated any criminal proceedings beyond the destruction of the inspector's official documents. He, however, was alarmed, and, without waiting for an attack, fired upon the crowd, wounding five and killing one of them.

This of course brought matters to a crisis. The militia of the Mingo Creek settlement, who were all embodied in the

* For Washington's views, see Sparks, X. 429, 437, &c. For proof of our statement, see Brackenridge's *Incidents of the Insurrection*, III. 25, 148, and Findley's History of it, p. 166. These were both on the spot, and men of character. The proceedings of the Eastern societies may be found in the *United States Gazette* of August 26th, September 1st and 6th, 1794, and the *Boston Independent Chronicle* of August 18th and October 6th, 1794; or other papers of the day.

club, were instantly notified, and the next morning found Neville's house surrounded by five hundred men. To meet this force, Neville had but his own negroes and family, and a body of eleven soldiers from the garrison of Fort Pitt. Regarding the case as desperate, the inspector managed to escape and conceal himself; the besiegers, learning this, demanded his papers, and also required that the soldiers should come out and give up their arms. The United States officer was willing to have the house searched, and whatever the rioters pleased taken away, but absolutely refused to capitulate. Firing then commenced; the buildings were ignited; the regulars forced to surrender; the property of Neville destroyed; and one of the leading insurgents killed. This killing took place after a call from the house to stop firing, and was in consequence of the exposure consequent upon that call; a fact which made the rioters regard it as murder. We speak of those without the house as rioters; but they were perfectly organized, and the attack was deliberately made, under the direction of a committee, who sat upon a hillock and ordered the various movements.

The rebellion being now fairly opened, meetings were held, characterized by a fury which alarmed all concerned. The United States mail was stopped and robbed by Bradford and others, to learn who were their leading enemies in Pittsburg; these, when known, the people of that town were forced to expel; and it was proposed to attack the arsenal and seize the United States arms, and to sack and burn the city at the Fork. Terror pervaded all classes, and it was with great difficulty that Pittsburg was saved from a conflagration. And when commissioners went West to strive to adjust matters, the Western people refused the overtures of the government, who put the matter to vote in the primary assemblies. Then followed the march of troops, the flight of Bradford and others, and the general submission.

Such is a brief outline of this movement, as given by Findley, Brackenridge, Hamilton, in his report of August,* and the papers of the time. Now, is it possible that such an opposition to law and government could be organized at this time anywhere in the West? A repetition of Shays's rebellion in Massachusetts and New Hampshire is just as possible, —just as probable.

We believe the experiment of Democracy at the West, then, to have tended thus far from, not toward, anarchy; we believe the higher view, of submission to God's will, to have gained upon the lower one, of self-government. There is far too much of Pagan Democracy still, beyond all question; far too much of laziness, idleness, drunkenness, brutality, bloodthirstiness; the leading power is still selfishness, and vanity is still the most popular teacher; but, despite all this, we feel assured that a spirit of true self-submission is growing; and, in the midst of populations that seem lost in sensuality and idle gratification, are coming up men of the highest and most practical Christian wisdom. And this we ascribe, not, as some do, entirely to the influence of New England Puritan principles transplanted to the West, but equally at least to the springing up of the right principles there among the native-born. Such men are found where Puritan principles have never reached. And though the wealth of the land will embarrass the growth of good habits, as it does the growth of corn, by an immense production of weeds, we have confidence that a power is at work that will root the tares out, and leave the grain unhurt.

When we say that we do not ascribe the progress of the West in wisdom to the transplanting of New England principles, we do not mean, of course, to undervalue those principles; our danger is, of necessity, a likelihood to overestimate them. And we rejoice to believe that every year

* *American State Papers*, XX.

carries more of the better portion of the "universal Yankee nation" into the recesses of the West. Miss Beecher's plan of sending teachers from New England thither is full of sound sense, and promises great good; as single women, or married ones, her emigrants will be "teachers" equally. But we would suggest, that, independent of our corner of the Union, there is an abundance of good and wise souls always pressing forward. If Democracy is not a form of Antichrist, every community standing as the West did, without rule, must of necessity grow self-submissive, obedient to God's law. If the West has not done so, then indeed do we fear that our idea of society is all wrong and evil; but the truth is, we believe, that whatever is truly anti-Christian in the land beyond the mountains, and peculiar to that land, may be traced to slavery, that is, to the foe of Democracy, rather than to a spirit of the largest liberty. Of all the real riots, for example, which have occurred in the West, most — those at Cincinnati in 1836 and 1841, that at Alton, Illinois, that at Lexington, Kentucky, and others elsewhere — have been outbreaks of the spirit of slavery; a spirit which is by no means confined south of the Ohio. From 1796 to 1807, various efforts were made by the people of Indiana Territory to procure the repeal or suspension of the article of the Ordinance of 1787 forbidding slavery therein; * and to this hour Ohio retains her Black Laws, which close the public schools to the negro, forbid his appearance as a witness in court where a white is interested, and discourage his entrance into the State. But even this spirit is yielding; and if that yields, what may not be hoped for?

In fine, let none conclude, from reports of assassinations and strifes in the great valley, that anarchy is on the increase; even the "street-fights" and murders of Tennessee

* *American State Papers*, XVI. 68, 160; XX. 387, 450, 467, 477, 485.

grow out of her stringent law against duelling.* Consider that you may travel ten thousand miles in those Western States, where a peace-officer would be as great a curiosity as an elephant, and meet with no harm; remember that Cincinnati, with a population bordering on eighty thousand, has no police worth mentioning, and yet is as quiet and safe as any place of the size on the earth, we presume; and recall to mind what we have already noticed, that Kentucky began in anarchy, and has risen to law, — that she was once the Alsatia of the United States, and is now in comparison quiet and peaceable, — that she once hung to the Union by but a thread, and is now bound to it with clamps of iron; and you cannot but have some faith in the workings of Democracy.

* The brother of our present chief-magistrate, now one of our representatives abroad, was tried for killing a man in a street-fight, and acquitted on the ground of self-defence. These fights are growing less common and less reputable.

X.

FIFTY YEARS OF OHIO.*

"A LITTLE after eleven o'clock, on the night following our elections in this place," says a letter from Cincinnati, written in October, 1837, "I was called to the door by a very vigorous rapping. It was some one in great haste to know the result of the day's work, and who had mistaken our house for the one in which the votes were to be counted. After directing him aright, I threw the door open a little wider, that I might see what young patriot this was, that so keenly desired to know the state of parties. The light of the hall lamp fell full on his face. It was Hezekiah Flint, one of the first band of white men that ever came to reside in the wilds of Ohio."

Such facts are startling. In the stranger to Ohio history, it requires an effort of imagination to conceive of one of the

---

* 1. *The Statutes of Ohio and of the Northwestern Territory, adopted or enacted from* 1788 *to* 1833, *inclusive; together with the Ordinance of* 1787. Edited by SALMON P. CHASE. Cincinnati. 1833-1835. Three volumes, large octavo.

2. *The Ohio Gazetteer and Traveller's Guide; containing a Description of the several Towns, Townships, and Counties, with their Water-courses, Roads, Improvements, Mineral Productions,* &c., &c. First Revised Edition. By WARREN JENKINS. Columbus. 1837. 12mo. pp. 546.

From the North American Review, for July, 1838.

founders of that great and populous State as still an active and strong man, out at midnight to learn the result of an election. But a few facts and a little thought do away the wonder; for it was but fifty years, last April, since the first band of white residents entered what now forms the State of Ohio; and every one of the many men of seventy, yet vigorous and stirring, was entering into busy life, when the plain upon which Cincinnati is built was sold for less than fifty silver dollars!

Nor is this growth surprising, except that it is without precedent. The causes fully explain the result. Land so cheap, and labor so high, that a day's work would buy an acre; titles direct from government; a climate temperate and healthful; and, above all, a national compact, forbidding slavery, securing civil and religious freedom, and all those privileges that others had struggled for through ages of blood and turmoil, — these were mighty inducements to the worn soldiers and impoverished yeomen of Massachusetts and New Jersey. Never, since the golden age of the poets, did that song, of which Mr. Butler makes mention in his History of Kentucky, "the siren song of peace and of farming," reach so many ears, and gladden so many hearts, as after Wayne's treaty at Greenville in 1795. "The Ohio" seemed to be, literally, a land flowing with milk and honey. The farmer wrote home, of a soil "richer to appearance than can possibly be made by art"; of "plains and meadows, without the labor of hands, sufficient to support millions of cattle summer and winter"; of wheat lands, that "will, I think, vie with the island of Sicily";* and of bogs, from which might be gathered cranberries enough to make tarts for all New England; while the lawyer said, that, as he rode the circuit, his horse's legs were dyed to the knee with the juice of the wild strawberry. At that time the dreadful

* Written in 1786. *Secret Journals of Congress*, Vol. IV. p. 322.

fevers of 1807 and 1822 were not dreamed of; the administration of Washington had healed the divisions among the States; the victory of Wayne had brought to terms the dreaded savages; and, as the dweller upon the barren shore of the Atlantic remembered these things, and the wonderful fact, in addition, that the inland garden to which he was invited was crossed in every direction by streams, even then counted on as affording means for free commercial intercourse, and that it possessed, beside, nearly seven hundred miles of river and lake coast, the inducements for emigration became too strong to be resisted; the wagon was tinkered up at once, the harness patched anew, and a few weeks found the fortune-seeker looking down from the Chestnut Ridge, or Laurel Hill, upon the far-reaching forests of the West.

But, should the inquirer turn from the bare fact of Ohio's growth, and a view of the great causes which have produced it, and ask a detail of the operation of those causes, we are forced to tell him that even the *annals* of that State are still to be compiled. A philosophical history cannot be yet looked for. The great movement which has begun at the West, the men of this day cannot see the scope or end of. They can but note down what passes before them from hour to hour, as the astronomers of old noted the motions of the sun and stars; in the hope that, by and by, a political Copernicus and Newton may come, who will reduce their seeming discords to harmony, and, amid apparent chaos, show order and beauty.

Even the labor of collecting historical materials has but now begun. The first effort of importance was made by the Historical Society of the State last December, and that will avail nothing unless followed up by strong and persevering action. Of individual effort nothing is worth notice except Mr. Chase's three volumes, containing the whole body of statute law, beginning in 1788 and extending to 1833, prefaced by a sketch of the State history. This work may rank first among the materials for the future historian, as the legislation of a democratic community is the best permanent exponent of its character; and, but for the compiler of these volumes, portions of even the legislation of this young land would, probably, soon have been lost. "It was absolutely impossible," says Mr. Chase, "to procure a complete set of the territorial laws. Of the laws of 1792 but a single copy is known to have existed in the State. The State library contained none, and none remained among the rolls in the office of the Secretary;* and those that have written mere local and partial sketches have done it too often carelessly, and have produced a strange confusion respecting many recent facts, some of which we shall have occasion to mention further, by and by.

From what we have said, it must be evident, that, although the completion of the first half-century, since the settlement of Ohio, makes a notice of its progress natural and proper at this time, any thing like a complete view of that progress must be out of the question. Had we the materials, they could not properly be presented in a general sketch; and a critical examination could embrace, at any one time, in a work of this kind, but a small portion of the century and a half, elapsed since the first Europeans visited the Ohio valley. We shall, therefore, speak principally of the results, giving such details only as are least accessible and most interesting.

There were a few events, connected with Ohio, previous to the Revolution, which had a bearing upon her present condition. One was the rejection by France, in 1755, of the offer, made by England, to give up all her claim to the territory west of a line drawn from the mouth of French Creek,† twenty leagues up that stream toward Lake Erie,

---

* Chase, *Statutes*, Vol. I. p. 5.

† The spot where Franklin, Venango County, Pennsylvania, now

and from the same point direct to the last mountains of Virginia which descend toward the ocean.* The Indians between this line and the Mississippi were to be considered independent; but France was to retain Canada, and her settlements on the Illinois and Wabash. Had this offer been accepted, there is little doubt, from the ability always shown by the French in the management of the Indians, that their colonies would have been planted upon the Scioto, the Miami, and the Maumee; so that, even though the country had finally come under the control of the British colonists, it would have borne the marks of French manners, prejudices, and habits. Another event worthy of notice (we omit the war of 1756, as too well known to need comment) was the proclamation of the king in 1763, after the treaty of Paris, forbidding his governors in America to grant any warrants of survey or patents "for any lands beyond the heads or sources of any of the rivers which fall into the Atlantic Ocean from the west or northwest"; or upon any lands not ceded by the Indians.† The effect of this proclamation was to prevent all attempts to settle any part of what now forms the State of Ohio; which, had it been done by Virginia (within whose charter the Northwest Territory was thought to lie), would have been accompanied, probably, by the introduction of slavery; and at any rate by a tinge of monarchical feelings and ways of thought, that, in the twelve years which elapsed before the Revolution, might have obtained some foothold in that territory.

In this manner, the soil of Ohio remained wholly un-

---

stands. — French Creek was in those times called by the French *Rivière aux Bœufs;* and by the English, *Beef River* and *Buffalo River.* — The Alleghany was called sometimes by that name, sometimes *Ohio;* Washington, in his Journal of 1753, uses both. French Creek was used by the French as their great thoroughfare to the Ohio.

* *Secret Journals of Congress,* Vol. IV. p. 74.

† *Land Laws,* p. 84.

touched by Europeans until the Revolution. And, during that struggle, it was preserved from settlement by the contest which arose among the States with reference to the ownership of the vacant lands; slavery being thus again prevented from entering its bounds, and the less worthy and moral kept back, until the settlers of Marietta and Cincinnati had given somewhat of a character to the population. Nor was this all; for, when Jefferson's proposal to exclude slavery from the Northwest Territory after 1800 was defeated, it was so by the favorers of slavery, all the Free States voting for it; and yet it was to that defeat, that its *total* exclusion was owing, three years later.* — Thus was the State, of which we write, reserved, apparently, until all was ripe, to try within her limits the experiment of democratic institutions, originating under the most favorable circumstances. The first men that trod her soil as citizens were soldiers of the Revolution; the companions and friends of Washington; and they went to a land which could, when they entered it, bear up, as it has been said, no other than freemen.

The first step that was taken towards settling the Northwest Territory was by the presentation of a memorial to Congress, from the officers and soldiers of the Revolutionary army, entitled to land-bounties under the Resolves of September 16th, 1776, and August 12th, 1780.† This memorial was forwarded to General Washington by Rufus Putnam, upon the 16th of June, 1783; and by him was transmitted to the President of Congress, together with General Putnam's letter, which gave at length his views respecting the settlement of the Western country, and the location of military posts there.‡ But at that time the final

* See *Old Journals*, Vol. IV. p. 373. — Dane's *Abridgment* (Supplement), Vol. IV. Appendix, Note A.

† *Land Laws*, p. 337.

‡ The letters relating to this petition were sent by Mr. Sparks to

grants of Virginia, Connecticut, and Massachusetts had not been made; and the Federal legislature, upon the 29th of October, 1783, having under consideration a memorial from General Armand, resolved, that, much as they desired to fulfil their engagements to the officers of the army, they could not, at that time, assign to them any particular district.*

We cannot enter into an examination of the protests, remonstrances, and petitions, which resulted in the cession, by all the States, of their vacant lands to the Union; † but

---

the Committee for the Celebration of the Settlement of Ohio, at Cincinnati, 1835, and were by them published, with the Oration of the day, &c.

* *Land Laws*, p. 339. — *Old Journals*, Vol. IV. p. 304.

† The only account of the steps which led to the cessions of Virginia, &c., that is at all complete, is in Blunt's *Historical Sketch*. — The best statement of the grounds upon which Virginia and the other States claimed the West, is to be found in *Secret Journals of Congress*, Vol. III. p. 175. We may here notice an error in Blunt's *Sketch* (p. 71), which Mr. Chase has copied (p. 13). After mentioning the Resolution passed by Congress upon the 30th of October, 1779, recommending Virginia to forbear from issuing warrants for unappropriated lands, Mr. Blunt says, "Congress did not confine itself merely to remonstrances, but ordered Colonel Broadhead to be stationed in the Western country, with a competent force to prevent intrusions upon that territory. In the execution of these orders, that officer, in the month of October, 1779, being informed that certain inhabitants of Virginia had crossed the Ohio, he ordered them to be apprehended," &c. The date of the letter from Colonel Broadhead, informing Congress that he had expelled these Virginians from beyond the Ohio, is given in the Journals of Congress, and proves it to have been written four days before the passage of the Resolution, in consequence of which, Mr. Blunt's account would lead us to think he was sent to the West; — in which sense Mr. Chase understood it; as he says, "To enforce this recommendation (of October 30th) Colonel Broadhead was stationed in the Western country," &c. — The facts were these; the General Assembly of Pennsylvania sent to Congress, early in 1779, a representation of the exposed state of their frontiers, then threatened by the Indians, acting under British incite-

must content ourselves with the bare statement, that New York conveyed her claims to Congress on the 1st of March, 1781; that Virginia released hers upon the first of that month, three years later; while Massachusetts delayed till the 19th of April, 1785, and Connecticut till the 14th of September, 1786.

Meanwhile, upon the 22d of October, 1784, the Five Nations had relinquished to the United States all their claims to the grounds west of Pennsylvania;* and, upon the 21st of the following January, the Wyandots and Delawares, by the treaty of Fort McIntosh (which post stood near the ground now occupied by Beaver, Pennsylvania), gave to the whites the whole south of what is now Ohio.† The Indian title being thus done away, and all the State claims but that of Connecticut given up, Congress, upon the 20th of May, 1785, passed their ordinance for the disposal

---

ment. This, upon the 25th of February, was sent to Washington; who, early in March, sent Colonel Broadhead to Pittsburg, as director of Indian affairs there. At that time the Delawares, who lived along the Ohio from the Muskingum towards Pittsburg, were divided; some, under White-Eyes, being for peace, and others, under Pipe, for war. (See Thatcher's *Indian Biography*, Vol. II. p. 122.) — Broadhead, called by them the Great Sun, more than once prevented a union of the whole nation against the Americans, by defending their property from the ravages of the frontier-men; and for this purpose acted as stated in his letter of October 26th; which says, expressly, that he turned the Virginians from the Indian lands, not the disputed territory. While acting to prevent the savages from being wronged by the whites, Broadhead offended many of the latter; but Congress agreed to support him (*Old Journals*, Vol. III. p. 449), and, when suits were brought against him, indemnified him (*Old Journals*, Vol. IV. p. 183). — For Washington's letter, sending Broadhead to the West, see Sparks's *Washington*, Vol. VI. p. 205. — In the Appendix to Vol. VIII. of that work are some remarks, by Madison, on the opposition in Congress to the Western claims of Virginia, &c.

* *Land Laws*, p. 122.

† Ibid., p. 148.

of lands in the West.* Under this ordinance, Thomas Hutchins, Geographer of the United States, assisted by a surveyor from each State, proceeded to examine and divide the newly acquired territory.

Among those who at that time visited the region in question was Colonel Benjamin Tupper. During the summer and fall of 1785, this gentleman, acting as temporary surveyor for Massachusetts, made himself acquainted with the country about the Muskingum; and, being fairly carried away by its beauty and seeming fertility, was strongly instrumental, it is believed, in causing its selection as the resting-place for the colony that went out nearly two years afterwards, under the patronage of the Ohio Company. Indeed, there is reason to think that Tupper's visit to the West was the immediate cause of the formation of that company; which resulted from a meeting of those entitled to land bounties, called through the newspapers by General Putnam and Colonel Tupper, in January, 1786. The meeting took place upon the 1st of March; the "Ohio Company of Associates" was organized; and the resolution taken, to collect a million dollars' worth of certificates, and to employ some one at the West, who should select a spot, for which they might definitely contract with Congress. Congress, on their part, showed a disposition to do all in their power to forward the settlement of the Northwestern lands; and with that view, upon the 21st of April, 1787, passed a resolution, authorizing the sale of those surveyed townships which might remain after the portion assigned the army had been

* Ibid., p. 349. It is worthy of remark, that the first ordinance reported to Congress, May 28th, 1784, proposed to divide the public lands into townships or "hundreds" of ten miles square, each divided again into a hundred parts; the plan next reported, April 26th, 1785, proposed townships seven miles square; and this, during the debate, was altered to six miles square, which was the size suggested by Putnam, in 1783.

drawn for, for public securities; the sale to commence upon the 21st of the following September, and the price not to be less than one dollar per acre.*

Before this public disposition of the lands commenced, however, it was the purpose of the Associates to make a separate contract for that part of the territory which their agent in the West might select as most suitable. This agent was General Samuel Holden Parsons, who, as Indian commissioner, had, in the year 1786, visited the Ohio country as far down, at least, as the mouth of the Great Miami, where a treaty was concluded, on the 31st of January, with "the Shawanoe nation." † This gentleman, in the spring of 1787, selected, after due examination, the same spot which had pleased Colonel Tupper, — the valley of the Muskingum. At the mouth of this river he proposed to have the chief city, while the purchase was to stretch along the Ohio to the mouth of the Scioto,‡ so as to include the half of the rich valley that borders that stream. Many things acted as inducements to this selection; the beautiful scenery and rich soil upon the banks of the clear "Elk-eye"; § the protection that would be afforded to the settlers by Fort Harmar, built in 1786, and then the frontier post; the near neighbourhood of Western Virginia, from which men and food might be had in time of need; the knowledge, that within the selected territory were coal, salt, and iron,|| and (as strong an inducement as any) the expectation, then

* *Old Journals*, Vol. IV. p. 739.

† Ibid., p. 627. — *Land Laws*, p. 258.

‡ The Scioto was early famous for its rich bottoms; "for forty miles on each side of it," says Dr. Franklin in his *Albany Plan of Union*, 1754, "and quite up to its heads, is a body of all rich land; the finest spot of its bigness in all North America."

§ The meaning of the Indian word "Muskingum."

|| In the passage, part of which we have given, from Franklin, in 1754, he refers to "the particular advantage of sea-coal in plenty, (even above ground,) in two places," which recommended the Scioto valley.

entertained, that through the Cuyahoga and Muskingum would be the communication between the Ohio and Lake Erie, while the bulk of the Atlantic trade, it was thought, would pass the mountains from James River and the Potomac, and flow down the Kenhawa.*

One other thing is said to have influenced General Parsons; this was the advice of some persons, that were supposed to be good judges, that he should *not* select the spot he did. The story is this, and, as our informant had it from General Rufus Putnam, we presume it to be correct. After General Parsons had examined the country immediately about the junction of the Muskingum with the Ohio, he proceeded up the valley of the former, that he might have a view of the interior. Having gone many miles, he met with one of the Zanes, four of which family were among the most noted of the frontier rangers.† Zane was probably engaged in salt-making at Salt Creek, which runs into the Muskingum, about ten miles below the present town of Zanesville.‡ Parsons, well knowing that the man he had chanced upon knew, from an acquaintance of fifteen years or more, the whole of what now forms the State of Ohio, asked his advice touching the location of the purchase which the Ohio Company proposed to make. Zane, having pondered the matter, and consulted with some of the old Delaware Indians that lived thereabout, recommended the General to choose either the Miami country, or the valley of

---

* See Washington's *Correspondence*, during 1785–86; particularly a letter to Knox (Sparks's *Washington*, Vol. IX. p. 110), in which he says, that the confluence of the Kenhawa and Ohio may in time "be a more eligible place than Pittsburg." Under the impression that it might be, the Ohio Company laid out, opposite to the Kenhawa, the town of Fairhaven; which is still but a small village, and will, probably, never be more.

† They founded Wheeling in 1770. See Silliman's *Journal*, Vol. XXXI. p. 3.

‡ Silliman's *Journal*, Vol. XXXI. p. 84.

the Scioto, in preference to that which he was then examining. What it was that made Parsons doubt the good faith of the pioneer, we know not; but he came to the conclusion that Zane really preferred the Muskingum to any other point, and wished to purchase it himself when the sales should begin during the following September.* This impression did away what little doubt still remained in his mind; and, returning to the East, he laid his proposal to contract with Congress for all the land along the Ohio, between the seventh range of townships and the Scioto, and running back as might be afterwards agreed upon, before the directors of the Company of Associates.

His choice being approved by them, he addressed a memorial to the legislature of the Confederation, asking them to empower the Board of Treasury to make the proposed contract. This memorial was reported upon on the 14th of July, the day after the passage of the well-known Ordinance of 1787; † and the report was passed, and the Board authorized to make the contract, upon the 23d of that month.‡ Information of this act of Congress having reached New York, Rufus Putnam and Manasseh Cutler, for themselves and their associates, wrote upon the 26th to the Board of Treasury, offering to accept the proposition of the report with some few variations, but providing that the company should receive no more land than they paid for. Three months passed before the contract was finally concluded,§ the in-

* This anecdote has been told, somewhat differently, in the *American Quarterly Review*, for March, 1833, p. 100. Had the writer of that article looked at the contract made by the Ohio Company, he would not have said their choice was made when the first settlers were on their way to the West; nor, had he thought a moment, would he have supposed Yankees so shiftless as to take any man's opinion *pro* or *con* as conclusive in a matter of such importance.

† *Old Journals*, Vol. IV. p. 755.

‡ Ibid., *Appendix*, p. 17. — *Land Laws*, p. 362.

§ These matters may be found at length in the *Land Laws*. The

denture bearing date October 27th; and when the patents issued, in 1792, the million and a half of acres named in this contract were diminished to something over eleven hundred thousand, the rise in Continental certificates having prevented the Company from securing the sum they had expected. In consequence of this non-performance, by the Associates, of their original plan, they lost the rich lands upon the Scioto, their western range of townships being the fifteenth.

All being now ready for actual emigration, a plan of the city, which was to be built at the mouth of the Muskingum, was prepared in Boston; and, by a vote of the Company in November, one hundred settlers were to be sent forward at once; being furnished with provisions while on the way to the new country, and taken into pay at four dollars per month, from their arrival at Pittsburg till the following May. Each man was to provide himself with "a good musket, bayonet, and cartridge-box"; and if he had besides an axe and hoe, and the mechanic his needful tools, he was to be transported free of cost.* Accordingly, in December, one party assembled at Danvers, Massachusetts, and upon the 1st of January a second detachment left Hartford. Their route was the old road, nearly that followed by Braddock; and it was April before the united parties left the Youghiogany, and began to float down toward their destined home; so that any who might have counted upon the wages which they were to receive after passing Pittsburg, and which were to be paid in land, must have found their farms but small, compared to their expectations.

Upon the 7th of April, 1788, this little band of forty-seven

---

price of the land was to be one dollar per acre, subject to a deduction for bad lands, not to exceed 33 cents per acre throughout. One seventh of the purchase might be paid for by warrants for military bounties.

* Carey's *Museum*, 1787, Vol. II., *Chronicle*, page 14.

persons landed, and encamped upon the spot where Marietta now stands; and from that day Ohio dates her existence.* The river, at whose mouth this first colony of the new settlers placed itself, was noted, even then, as the scene of many interesting historical events. At the forks of the Muskingum, upon the 9th of November, 1764, Bouquet had received from the Indians two hundred and six persons who had been made captive during the short but bloody war of Pontiac.† Near that spot the first Protestant Christians that lived in Ohio, the Moravians, built their house of worship, in 1772.‡ There dwelt the noble-spirited Logan, § and the well-known peace chief of the Delawares.|| Heckewelder labored upon its banks; there, upon the 16th of April, 1781, was born his daughter Maria, the first of the "Buckeyes"; ¶ and, in one year from that time, was enacted there the most disgraceful of all frontier acts, the murder of the Moravian Indians.**

---

* Many of the facts which we state are derived from oral testimony, in the general accuracy of which we have full confidence; many others might be brought to light by examining the newspapers of the day. The measures taken by the *Ohio Historical Society*, at its last session, will make permanent the testimony of most of the early pioneers still living. See also some papers on the history of Ohio in the *Western Monthly Magazine*, for 1833.

† An account of Bouquet's Western expeditions of 1763 and 1764 was published in Philadelphia. The Indians gave up two hundred and six prisoners, and the Shawanese gave hostages for the delivery, in the spring, of a hundred more still in their hands. Holmes (*Annals*, Vol. II. p. 131) says Bouquet made peace with the savages; but he only agreed to the selection of emissaries to go and make peace with Sir William Johnson; he had no authority to make peace himself.

‡ Doddridge's *Indian Wars*, p. 257.

§ McClung's *Sketches of Western Adventure*, p. 279.

|| Thatcher's *Indian Biography*, Vol. II. p. 122.

¶ Silliman's *Journal*, Vol. XXXI. p. 66.

** Ibid., p. 64. Doddridge, p. 248. The writer in Silliman's *Journal* says Crawford was in this expedition; but, from Doddridge's account, we think this a mistake.

Upon these matters we cannot dwell; nor can we, indeed, refer to more than a few events relative to the settlement made by Putnam and his companions. As this settlement was undertaken at a time when Indian hostilities were much to be apprehended, the more remote savages having, the preceding fall, avowed their intention to oppose all attempts to civilize the Northwestern wilderness, upon the ground that those who had made the treaties of 1785 and 1786 were not authorized to do so,* one of the most prominent objects of the settlers was the renewal of these treaties; and the Indians were invited to meet the whites for that purpose in May, at a spot seventy or eighty miles up the Muskingum. Meanwhile, the Governor, Arthur St. Clair, who had been appointed upon the 5th of the preceding October, not having reached the West, it became necessary to erect a temporary government for their internal security; for which purpose a set of laws was passed, and published by being nailed to a tree in the village, and Return Jonathan Meigs was appointed to administer them. It is a strong evidence of the good habits of the people of the colony, that, during three months, but one difference occurred, and that was compromised.† Indeed, a better set of men, altogether, could scarce have been selected for the purpose, than Putnam's little band. Washington might well say, "No colony in America was ever settled under such favorable auspices as that which has just commenced at the Muskingum. Information, property, and strength will be its characteristics. I know many of the settlers personally, and there never were men better calculated to promote the welfare of such a community." ‡

With the information which belonged to them was mingled a little of that pedantic love of ancient learning which

* Carey's *Museum*, Vol. II., *Chron.*, p. 2.

† *Western Monthly Magazine*, 1833, Vol. I. p. 395.

‡ Sparks's *Washington*, Vol. IX. p. 385.

tinged the better educated of those days. This showed itself in a meeting of the directors and agents held, July 2d, upon the banks of the Muskingum, for the purpose of naming the city which had just been laid out, and also the public squares. As yet the settlement had been called merely "The Muskingum," but the name Marietta was now formally given it, in honor of Marie Antoinette; the square upon which the block-houses stood was christened "*Campus Martius;* the square No. 19, *Capitolium;* the square No. 61, *Cecilia;* and the great road through the covert way, *Sacra Via.*"* Nor was the taste in English composition much more in accordance with that of our days, than the conceits just mentioned. Of this we have evidence in an Oration, now before us, delivered upon the 4th of July, 1788, by James M. Varnum, who, together with S. H. Parsons and John Armstrong, had been appointed to the bench on the 16th of the previous October.

The Governor, as we have said, had not yet arrived, which fact gives occasion for the following passage.

"May he soon arrive! Thou gently-flowing Ohio, whose surface, as conscious of thy unequalled majesty, reflecteth no images but the grandeur of the impending heaven, — bear him, O, bear him safely to this anxious spot! And thou, beautifully-transparent Muskingum, swell at the moment of his approach, and reflect no objects but of pleasure and delight."

But at the close of this first-fruit of Ohio literature, the Judge looked forward, with prophetic eye, to the fortunes of the just-entered wilderness; and, in these dim and seer-like terms, foretells the future.

---

* Carey's *Museum*, Vol. IV. p. 390. In the fifth volume of that periodical, page 284, is an account of the city of Athens, which the Spaniards at this time proposed to build at the mouth of the Missouri. "On the very point" where the rivers joined was to be Fort Solon; not for defence, however, "but for the retirement of the governor from the busy scenes of public employment"!

"Religion and government commenced in those parts of the globe, where yonder glorious luminary first arose in his effulgent majesty. They have followed after him in his brilliant course; nor will they cease till they shall have accomplished, in this Western world, the consummation of all things.

"Religion inspires us with certain hope of eternal beatitude, and that it shall begin upon the earth, by an unreserved restitution to the common centre of existence. With what rapture and ecstasy, therefore, may we look forward to that all-important period when the universal desires of mankind shall be satisfied! When this new Jerusalem shall form one august temple, unfolding its celestial gates to every corner of the globe! When millions shall fly to it, 'as doves to their windows,' elevating their hopes upon the broad-spreading wings of millennial happiness! Then shall the dark shades of evil be erased from the moral picture, and the universal system appear in all its splendor! Time itself, the era and the grave of imperfection, shall be ingulfed in the bosom of Eternity, and one blaze of Glory pervade the Universe!"

It would appear that the Ohio listened to the prayer of the orator, for, upon the 9th, St. Clair arrived. The Ordinance of 1787* provided two distinct grades of government for the Northwest Territory, under the first of which the whole power was in the hands of the Governor and the three judges, and this form was at once organized upon the Governor's arrival. The first law, which was "for regulating and establishing the militia," was published upon the 25th of July;† and the next day appeared the Governor's proclamation, erecting all the country that had been ceded by the Indians east of the Scioto River into the County of Washington.‡

We have spoken of a proposal made to the Indians early in 1788, to hold a treaty with the whites in May, at a spot seventy or more miles up the Muskingum. The proposed meeting was delayed from time to time; but stores, presents,

* This instrument is so well known, and so easy of access, that we have not thought it worth while to detail its provisions.

† Chase, Vol. I. p. 92.

‡ Carey's *Museum*, Vol. IV. p. 433.

and other valuables were collected at the designated spot, to wait there until both nations were ready. Upon the 12th of July, however, a party of Chippeways attacked this post; and though they were repulsed, and six of them made prisoners by the Delaware Indians, who were friendly to the settlers, it was thought best to withdraw the stores to Fort Harmar, and there hold the treaty.* This was done, though the Indians could not be brought to conclusive action until the 9th of the following January,† when the business was "ended to the entire satisfaction of all concerned."

"The progress of the settlement," says a letter from the Muskingum, "is sufficiently rapid for the first year. We are continually erecting houses, but arrivals are faster than we can possibly provide convenient covering. Our first ball was opened about the middle of December, at which were fifteen ladies, as well accomplished in the manners of polite circles as any I have ever seen in the old States. I mention this to show the progress of society in this new world; where I believe we shall vie with, if not excel, the old States, in every accomplishment necessary to render life agreeable and happy."

The emigration westward even at this time was very great; the commandant at Fort Harmar reporting four thousand five hundred persons as having passed that post between February and June, 1788; many of whom would have stopped on the purchase of the Associates, had they been ready to receive them.

During the following year, and indeed until the Indians, who, in spite of treaties, had been committing small depredations all the time, stealing horses and sinking boats, went fairly and openly to war, the settlement on the Muskingum grew slowly, but steadily, and to good purpose. During the years from 1790 to 1795, it suffered severely, sometimes coming to the brink of destruction from famine and

* Carey's *Museum*, Vol. IV. p. 203.

† *Land Laws*, p. 149.

savage foes. But when that war was ended, though its comparative sterility had become known, and thousands passed its barren hills scoffing, as they guided their keels to the richer regions about the Miami, its progress was of the most encouraging kind. The men that stopped there were those that were willing to work hard, and gain no more than independence after all; and the general character of the settlers about Marietta, from that time forward, afforded the best guarantee that the population of the Purchase would be industrious, persevering, and economical. On the rough "knobs" of Meigs, and Athens, and Washington, were laid the foundations of quite as much true wealth, as upon the fertile plains of the lower country; for true wealth is as much in the habits of the tiller, as in the soil that is tilled.

In later years, the Muskingum valley suffered very severely from sickness; and, when the financial troubles of 1817–18 brought the richest citizens of Ohio to the verge of utter poverty, the poorer emigrants from New England had cause enough to groan, and to lament that they had been persuaded to leave their homes.

"Marietta," says an epistle written about that time, "I find a poor, muddy hole; — the mud here is more disagreeable than snow in Massachusetts. My advice to all my friends is, not to come to this country. There is not one in a hundred but what is discontented; but they cannot get back, having spent all their property in getting here. It is the most broken country that I ever saw. Poor, lean pork at twelve cents; salt, four cents; poor, dry fish, twenty cents. The corn is miserable, and we cannot get it ground; we have to pound it. Those that have lanterns grate it. Rum twenty-five cents a gill; sugar thirty-seven cents a pound; and no molasses! This country has been the ruin of a great many poor people; it has undone a great many poor souls for ever."

The melancholy picture presented by this letter-writer

was, even then, one half imagination. The idea of the corn being "miserable," for instance, was, we presume, drawn from the shrivelled appearance of the Southern and Western corn, which, to a raw Massachusetts man, seems an evidence of worthlessness; though we admit the lantern grating* to have been an evil, as also the absence of molasses; — and the mud of which our writer complains is a good objection to the whole Ohio valley to this day.

At present the Ohio Company's purchase is but thinly settled, compared to other parts of the State; but its population is, generally, of an excellent character. The expected communication through the Muskingum did not take place. That river is, at this time, undergoing improvements, that will make it as valuable for navigable purposes as it is now for its water-power; and along the Hockhocking valley also the State is constructing a canal.

But the worldly well-being of that portion of Ohio, of which we have been speaking, is more in prospect than possession; and, much as has been said about the unlucky choice of the Associates, for their posterity and the world we believe that choice to have been an admirable one. We believe the day will come, when as perfect a union of knowledge and good habits with wealth, and the means of attaining wealth, will be found in the purchase of the Company, as in any part of the State. The uplands of that region afford most excellent wheat lands;† and the hill-sides, the best sheep pastures. Iron abounds in the immediate vicinity, and salt and coal extend through the whole district.

* Doddridge tells us, that this was in common use among the frontier settlers.

† For many sections, that were a few years since called barrens, and for which at tax-sales but from two to five cents an acre could be had, the purchasers are now paying to the original owners Congress price, as the land will bring from fifteen to twenty-five bushels of wheat to the acre.

Some of the salt-springs yield from two to four hundred bushels a day, and it is generally of excellent quality. The coal exists in unknown abundance, in veins from five to twelve feet in thickness; some above and some below the bottoms of the valleys.* We have here, therefore, all that can be wished of the means for acquiring comfort and wealth, and these means so placed as to demand toil and economy for their development. This fact, united to the very admirable character of the original settlers, and the slow growth hitherto, leads us to think that General Parsons's selection will, in the end, prove a very fortunate one.

Having, in this brief manner, given an outline of the planting of the first colony in Ohio, we next turn to the settlement of the Miami country, the most important, in immediate results, of all the early settlements.†

The region between the two Miamies of the Ohio ‡ was early known to the whites as one of great fertility. In 1751, Christopher Gist, the agent of the old English Ohio Company, went a hundred and fifty miles up the larger of those two streams; § and in 1752 the English had made a fort,

---

* For a full account of the mineral wealth of the Purchase, see Dr. Hildreth's excellent article in Silliman's *Journal*, Vol. XXIX. The State Geologists (1838) state, that probably 12,000 square miles of Ohio are underlaid with coal, and 5,000 with workable beds, averaging six feet in thickness; each square mile of this thickness contains six millions of tons; and in England the annual consumption is but fifteen millions.

† In 1800 the population of the Miami country was 15,000, one third of that in the whole State; in 1790 it was two thirds of all in the State, viz. 2,000; in 1810, more than one quarter, viz. 70,000.

‡ Beside the Great and Little Miami emptying into the Ohio, there were two rivers of that name which emptied into the lakes; one was the Maumee; the other, running into Lake Michigan, was, according to some, the Chicago, according to others, Fox River, and, as a few think, the St. Joseph's. We may take occasion, in some future paper, to examine this question and others connected with it.

§ Sparks's *Washington*, Vol. II. pp. 37, 480.

or trading station, among the Piankeshaws, a tribe of the Twigtwees, or Miamies, on what is now called Loramie's Creek, forty-seven miles above Dayton; which post was attacked and taken by the French during that year.* The Miami valleys were afterwards examined by Boone, during his captivity among the Shawanese in 1778;† and by the war parties, which Bowman and Clark led against the Indian villages on the Little Miami and Mad River. But as the Shawanese were among the most inveterate enemies of the whites, and the unceasing plagues of the Kentucky settlers, no attempt was made to effect a lodgment near their towns until after the treaty made with them in January, 1786. During the spring of that year, Benjamin Stiles, of Redstone (now Brownsville), on the Monongahela, visited the newly ceded district, and, being much pleased with it, went to Philadelphia for the purpose of interesting some of the leading men in its purchase and settlement.‡ He was introduced to John Cleves Symmes, a representative in Congress from New Jersey. Mr. Symmes was so much interested by the accounts given him of the beauty and fertility of the Miami region, that he determined to visit it himself, which he did; though at what period precisely we do not know. Finding the representations of his informant to fall short of, rather than exceed, the truth, he applied himself, upon his return, to the task of interesting others in the proposed purchase; and, on the 29th of August, 1787, wrote to the President of Congress, requesting that the Board of Treasury might be empowered to contract with him and his associates for all the lands between the Miami rivers, and running as far north as the north line of the Ohio Company's

---

* *Land Laws*, p. 148. — Sparks's *Works of Franklin*, Vol. IV. p. 71.

† Carey's *Museum*, Vol. II. p. 324.

‡ *Cincinnati Directory*, for 1819, p. 16. The historical sketch in this volume was compiled from the evidence of the first settlers then alive.

purchase; the terms of the contract to be substantially the same as those to be made with "Messrs. Sargent, Cutter, and Co." His petition was referred to the Board, with authority to contract, upon the 2d of the following October.*

Upon the 26th of the next month Symmes issued a pamphlet, addressed "to the respectable public," stating the terms of this contract, and the scheme of sale which he proposed to adopt.† This was, to issue his warrants for not less than a quarter-section (a hundred and sixty acres), which might be located anywhere, except, of course, upon reservations, and spots previously chosen. No section was to be divided, if the warrant held by the locator would cover the whole. The price was to be sixty-six cents and two thirds till May, 1788; then one dollar till November; and, after that time, was to be regulated by the demand for land. Every locator was bound to begin improvements within two years, or forfeit one sixth of his purchase to whosoever would settle thereon and remain seven years. Military bounties might be taken in this as in the purchase of the Associates. For himself Symmes retained one township at the mouth of the Great Miami, at the junction of which stream with the Ohio he proposed to build his great city; to help the growth of which he offered each alternate lot to any one that would build a house and live therein three years.

As Continental certificates were rising, in consequence of the great land purchases then making with them, and as difficulty was apprehended in procuring enough to make his first payment, Symmes was anxious to send forward settlers early, that the true value of his purchase might become known at the East. He had, however, some difficulty in

---

* *Land Laws*, p. 372.

† See *Land Laws* for the terms and final settlement of Symmes's contract.

arranging with the Board of Treasury the boundaries of the first portion which he was to occupy.*

In January, 1788, Matthias Denman, of New Jersey, took an interest in Symmes's purchase, and located, among other tracts, the section and fractional section upon which Cincinnati has been built.† Retaining one third of this particular locality, he sold another third to Robert Patterson, and the remainder to John Filson; and the three, about August, 1788, agreed to lay out a town on the spot, which was designated as being opposite Licking River, to the mouth of which they proposed to have a road cut from Lexington, Kentucky, to be connected with the northern shore by a ferry. Mr. Filson, who had been a schoolmaster, was appointed to name the town; and, in respect to its situation, and as if with a prophetic perception of the mixed race that were in after days to inhabit there, he named it Losantiville, which, being interpreted, means *ville*, the town, *anti*, opposite to, *os*, the mouth, *L*, of the Licking.‡ This may well put to the blush the *Campus Martius* of the Marietta scholars, and the Fort Solon of the Spaniards. What the connection may have been, it is out of our power to say; but Mr. Filson was killed in about a month from this time by a single Indian, near the Great Miami.§

Meanwhile, in July, Symmes got thirty people and eight four-horse wagons under way for the West. These reached Limestone (now Maysville) in September, where they found Mr. Stiles with several persons, from Redstone. But the mind of the chief purchaser was full of trouble. He had

* *Manuscript Letters* of Symmes.

† Many facts relative to the settlement of Cincinnati we take from the depositions of Denman, Patterson, Ludlow, and others, contained in the report of the chancery trial of *City of Cincinnati* v. *Joel Williams*, in 1807.

‡ *Cincinnati Directory*, for 1819, p. 18.

§ Symmes's *Letters.* — Patterson's *Deposition.*

not only been obliged to relinquish his first contract, which was expected to embrace two millions of acres, but had failed to conclude one for the single million which he now proposed taking. This arose from a difference between him and the government, he wishing to have the whole Ohio front between the Miamies, while the Board of Treasury wished to confine him to twenty miles upon the Ohio. This proposition, however, he would not for a long time agree to, as he had made sales along nearly the whole Ohio shore.* Leav-

* It may be as well to give here a sketch of the changes made in Symmes's contract. His first application was for all the country between the Miamies, running up to the north line of the Ohio Company's purchase, extended due west. On the 23d of October, 1787, Congress resolved, that the Board of Treasury be authorized to contract with any one for tracts of not less than a million acres of Western lands, the front of which, on the Ohio, Wabash, and other rivers, should not exceed one third the depth. On the 15th of May, 1788, Dayton and Marsh, as Symmes's agents, concluded a contract with the Commissioners of the Treasury for two millions of acres in two equal tracts. In July, Symmes concluded to take only one tract, but differed with the Commissioners on the grounds stated in the text. After much negotiation, upon the 15th of October, 1788, Dayton and Marsh concluded a contract with government, bearing date May 15th, for one million of acres, beginning twenty miles up the Ohio from the mouth of the Great Miami, and to run back for quantity between the Miami and a line drawn from the Ohio parallel to the general course of that river. In 1791, Symmes found this would throw his purchase too far back from the Ohio, and applied to Congress to let him have all between the Miamies, running back so as to include a million acres, which that body, on the 12th of April, 1792, agreed to do. When the lands between the Miamies were surveyed, however, it was found that the tract south of a line drawn from the head of the Little, due west to the Great Miami, would include less than 600,000 acres; but even this Symmes could not pay for, and, when his patent issued upon the 30th of September, 1794, it gave him and his associates but 248,540 acres, exclusive of reservations, which amounted to 63,142 acres. This tract was bounded by the Ohio, the two Miamies, and a due east and west line, run so as to comprehend the desired quantity. As Symmes made no further payments after this time, the rest

ing the bargain in this unsettled state, Congress considered itself released from its obligation to sell; and, but for the representations of some of his friends, our adventurer would have lost his bargain, his labor, and his money. Nor was this all. In February, 1788, he had been appointed one of the judges of the Northwest Territory, in the place of Mr. Armstrong, who declined serving. This appointment gave offence to some; and others were envious of the great fortune which it was thought he would make. Some of his associates complained of him, also, probably because of his endangering the contract to which they had become parties. With these murmurs and reproaches behind him, he saw before him danger, delay, suffering, and perhaps ultimate failure and ruin; and, although hopeful by nature, apparently he felt discouraged and sad. However, a visit to his purchase, where he landed upon the 22d of September, revived his spirits; and, upon his return to Maysville, he wrote to Jonathan Dayton of New Jersey, who had become interested with him, that he thought some of the land near the Great Miami "positively worth a silver dollar the acre, in its present state."

But, though this view of the riches now almost within his grasp somewhat reassured Symmes's mind, he had still enough to trouble him. The Indians were threatening; in Kentucky, he says, "they are perpetually doing mischief; a man a week, I believe, falls by their hands"; but still government gave him little help toward defending himself; for, while three hundred men were stationed at Muskingum, he had "but one ensign and seventeen men for the protection and defence of 'the Slaughter-house,'" as the Miami valley was called by the dwellers upon the "dark

---

of his purchase reverted to the United States, who gave those that had bought under Symmes ample preëmption rights. See *Land Laws*, pp. 372-382, *et seq.*

and bloody ground" of "Kentucke." And, when Captain Kearny and forty-five soldiers came to Maysville in December, they came without provisions, and but made bad worse. Nor did their coming answer any purpose; for, when a little band of settlers were ready to go, under their protection, to the mouth of the Miami, the grand city of Symmes that was to be, the ice stove their boats, their cattle were drowned, and their provisions lost, and so the settlement was prevented. But the fertile mind of a man like our adventurer could, even under these circumstances, find comfort in the anticipation of what was to come. In the words of Return Jonathan Meigs, the first Ohio poet with whom we have any acquaintance,

> "To him glad Fancy brightest prospects shows,
> Rejoicing Nature all around him glows;
> Where late the savage, hid in ambush, lay,
> Or roamed the uncultured valleys for his prey,
> Her hardy gifts rough Industry extends,
> The groves bow down, the lofty forest bends;
> And see the spires of towns and cities rise,
> And domes and temples swell into the skies." *

But alas! so far as his pet city was concerned, "glad Fancy" proved but a gay deceiver; for there came "an amazing high freshet," and "the Point," as it was and still is called, was fifteen feet under water.

But before Symmes left Maysville, which was upon the 29th of January, 1789, two settlements had been made within his purchase. The first was by Mr. Stiles, the original projector of the whole plan; who, with other Redstone people, had located themselves at the mouth of the Little Miami, where the Indians had been led by the great fertility of the soil to make a partial clearing. To this point, on the 18th of November, came twenty-six persons, who built a block-house, named their town Columbia, and prepared for

* A Poem delivered at Marietta, July 4th, 1789, slightly altered.

a winter of want and hard fighting.* But they were agreeably disappointed; the Indians came to them, and, though the whites answered, as Symmes says, "in a blackguarding manner," the savages sued for peace. One, at whom a rifle was presented, took off his cap, trailed his gun, and held out his right hand, by which pacific gestures he induced the Americans to consent to their entrance into the block-houses. In a few days this good understanding ripened into intimacy, the "hunters frequently taking shelter for the night in the Indian camps"; and the red men and squaws "spending whole days and nights" at Columbia, "regaling themselves with whiskey." This friendly demeanour on the part of the Indians was owing to the kind and just conduct of Symmes himself; who, during the preceding September, when examining the country about the Great Miami, had prevented some Kentuckians, who were in his company, from injuring a band of the savages that came within their power; which proceeding, he says, "the Kentuckians thought unpardonable."

The Columbia settlement was, however, like that proposed at the Point, upon land that was under water during the high rise in January, 1789. "But one house escaped the deluge." The soldiers were driven from the ground-floor of their block-house into the loft, and from the loft into the solitary boat which the ice had spared them.

This flood deserves to be commemorated in an epic; for, while it demonstrated the dangers to which the three chosen spots of all Ohio, Marietta, Columbia, and the Point, must be ever exposed, it also proved the safety, and led to the rapid settlement, of Losantiville. The great recommendation of the spot upon which Denman and his comrades proposed to build their "Mosaic" town, as it has been called,

* *Cincinnati Directory*, for 1819, and Symmes's *Letters*. The land at this point was so fertile, that from nine acres were raised 963 bushels of Indian corn.

appears to have been the fact that it lay opposite the Licking; the terms of Denman's purchase having been, that his warrants were to be located, as nearly as possible, over against the mouth of that river; though the advantage of the noble and high plain at that point could not have escaped any eye. But the freshet of 1789 placed its superiority over other points more strongly in view than any thing else could have done.

We have said that Filson was killed in September, or early in October, 1788. As nothing had been paid upon his third of the plat at Losantiville, his heirs made no claim upon it, and it was transferred to Israel Ludlow, who had been Symmes's surveyor. This gentleman, with Colonel Patterson, one of the other proprietors, and well known in the Indian wars, with about fourteen others, left Maysville upon the 24th of December, 1788, "to form a station and lay off a town opposite Licking." The river was filled with ice "from shore to shore"; but, says Symmes, in May, 1789, "perseverance triumphing over difficulty, they landed safe on a most delightful high bank of the Ohio, where they founded the town of Losantiville, which *populates* considerably."

It is a curious fact, and one of many in Western history that may well tend to shake our faith in the learned discussions as to dates and localities with which scholars now and then amuse the world, that the date of the settlement of Cincinnati is unknown, even though we have the testimony of the very men that made the settlement. Judge Symmes says, in one of his letters, "On the 24th of December, 1788, Colonel Patterson of Lexington, who is concerned with Mr. Denman in the section at the mouth of Licking River, sailed from Limestone," &c. Some, supposing it would take about two days to make the voyage, have dated the being of the Queen City of the West from December 26th. This is but guess-work, however; for, as the river was full of ice, it might have taken ten days to have gone the sixty-five miles from Maysville to the Licking. But, in the case in chancery to which we have referred, we have the evidence of Patterson and Ludlow, that they landed opposite the Licking "in the month of January, 1789"; while William McMillan testifies, that he "was one of those who formed the settlement of Cincinnati on the twenty-eighth day of December, 1788." As we know of nothing more conclusive on the subject than these statements, we must leave this question in the same darkness that we find it, and proceed to more certain events.

The settlers of Losantiville built a few log huts and block-houses, and proceeded to lay out the town; though they placed their dwellings in the most exposed situation, yet, says Symmes, they "suffered nothing from the freshet." The Judge spent a little time with them, and then fell down to North Bend,* accompanied by the small army which had been allowed him for his protection. Here they built "a camp," "by setting two forks of saplings in the ground, a ridgepole across, and leaning boat-boards, which had been brought from Maysville, one end on the ground and the other against the ridge-pole; inclosing one end, and leaving the other open for a door, where the fire was built to keep out the cold, which was very intense."

Finding his point to be so low, that a city could not be safely built there, unless, as he says, "you raise her like Venice out of the waters," he surveyed the grounds between the north bend of the Ohio and the Miami; thinking a plan might be arranged so as to have the advantage of both rivers still, it being but a mile across the isthmus. He found the land, however, to be too hilly and broken, and was forced to content himself with a small town-plat reaching a mile and

* So called, from its being the most northerly bend of the Ohio below the mouth of the Kenhawa.

a half along the Ohio, of which he offered the alternate lots to settlers, of whom forty came within two months, and built themselves "comfortable log cabins."

But his longing for a city still continued; and, after much consideration, he determined in favor of a spot twelve miles up the Miami, and within half an hour's ride from North Bend; he preferred this to the Ohio shore, because he thought it better to concentrate the trade of the Miami valley, than to be one of many cities along the larger stream. The Miami was then considered navigable, and was for many years afterwards navigated by keel and flat boats; and, in Symmes's estimation, the country about the river was "superior in point of soil, water, and timber, to any tract of equal dimensions to be found in the United States." The hope that a great city was to arise at this point long continued to comfort the harassed mind of the projector; and when St. Clair informed him that he was about to visit and organize the Miami purchase, Symmes doubted much whether a new town which he had laid out at South Bend, or Losantiville, would be best fitted for the county seat; but, as the former was more central, thought, that, if it were made the county town, "it would probably take the lead of the present village (Losantiville) *until the city can be made somewhat considerable.*"

But the mind of this persevering and just man, which had never been at ease since he first embarked in the enterprise of reclaiming the wilderness, was to be still further tried. The Kentuckians, seeing that he, by his clemency, his moderation, and his firmness, still remained on good terms with the Indians, and that settlers were flocking to his lands, represented the boasted fertility of the soil as a lie, and the safety of the settlers as a delusion. Some even threatened to make it so, by destroying every Indian they could find in the Miami purchase. The soldiers that were with him were idle, disobliging, and burdensome. His surveyors and settlers were at times " put to great shifts from want of bread." Continental certificates were rising, and his purchase was endangered by the difficulty of obtaining them. Many, that had bought of him on speculation, threw up their contracts. Then came information that the British were urging the Indians to war; and his expected recruits did not come. Next was actual warfare, and his settlers left him, fifty at one time. And, to complete his disquiet, his friends beyond the mountains wrote to him, that great attempts would be made to turn him from the bench; that he was universally disliked, almost hated, by the settlers, and that his Eastern co-proprietors were displeased by his management.

The perils of warfare Symmes was prepared to meet. At the beginning he had said, " Disasters I expect; if I can prevent a defeat, it is as much as I hope for the first year." " We may talk of treaties as we please; I am certain we must fight or leave the ground." And now that the day of trial was near by, he shrunk not. " What will be the issue," he says, " God only knows. I shall maintain the ground as long as I possibly can, ill prepared as we are. I can but perish, as many a better man has done before me."

But dislike and opposition, which his heart assured him he had not merited, he did not meet without suffering. While yet on his way to the West in the summer of 1788, he said of his accusers, that " the only revenge he wished to have against them was, that they might have equal success in their views, attended with equal calumny and censure "; for which he thought he had " pretty good security, if they undertook to do business for many "; and the bitterness which he then tasted was increased every year that he lived.

It was not destined, however, that this frontier post of the West should perish. In June, a force of a hundred and forty men was sent to Cincinnati; and Fort Washington was commenced upon the spot since made classic by the Bazaar of Mistress Trollope. In December, this band was increased to four hundred and forty, by the arrival of General Harmar, who was about to march against the Indians of the Maumee and Wabash. At this time Losantiville contained eleven families and twenty-four bachelors, beside the garrison.

In January, 1790, the governor and judges arrived at that village, for the purpose of organizing the county; which Symmes, whom "the Governor complimented with the honor of naming" it, called Hamilton, after the well-known Alexander, then Secretary of the Treasury. At this time, also, the name of Losantiville was abandoned, and Symmes and St. Clair adopted that of Cincinnati, or, as the former wrote it, Cincinnata, "in honor of the order of the Cincinnati, and to denote the chief place of their residence." The name is a good one, but the place ill suited for the residence of those honorable "knights," whose constitution could not even withstand the semi-aristocratic air of the seacoast.

In the spring of 1790, various stations were formed and garrisoned in the neighbourhood of Cincinnati; and General Harmar began to prepare for his campaign against the old Miami village at the junction of the St. Joseph's and St. Mary's, though he was not able to leave till the following September. Of his march, his ill success, amounting to a virtual defeat, and the outburst of savage warfare that followed, we shall not speak, as they may be found in any history of those times. The return of the troops, mournful as it was, had its ray of comfort, however, for our adventurer. "It is impossible," he says, "to describe the lands over which the army passed; I am told that they are inviting, to a charm."

But in 1791 came new troubles. It was found that it would be very hard, if not impossible, for Symmes and his comrades to pay for the million of acres, extending twenty miles only on the Ohio, as so much of it lay back from that stream that he could not find purchasers. And this brought him into conflict, in some way, with St. Clair, a self-willed and arbitrary man, who had also, about this time, seen fit to proclaim military law in a "part of the town of Cincinnati"; an act which the Judge thought "bordered hard on tyranny." And when Symmes offered to accompany the Governor in the expedition for which he was then preparing, his Excellency gave him an answer that led him to think his presence would be rather disagreeable than otherwise. Next came the fear that Congress might open a land-office, and, by competing with, ruin him; and then the panic that resulted from St. Clair's defeat on the 4th of November, 1791. When the news of that event reached the settlers, they left their farms with scarce an exception; dismay went through the whole West; and a savage warfare commenced, that for two years and eight months nearly equalled that of 1763. These things were all sources of great discomfort and loss to Symmes, who had amid them all but one cause for joy, and that a poor and unchristian one, — the general dislike that was brought upon his old foe, St. Clair, whose pride, no doubt, he was very glad to see humbled.

We say nothing of the particulars of that general's defeat, because they are well known. The effect was, as we have said, dreadful. It almost stopped emigration; nor was confidence felt again until the decisive victory of Wayne, in August, 1794, which led to the treaty of Greenville in the same month of the year following.

When the knowledge that peace had been made with the Indians became general, however, "all Kentucky," as Symmes says, "and the back parts of Virginia and Pennsylvania ran mad with expectations of the land-office opening" in the West; "they laugh me full in the face, when I ask them one dollar per acre for first-rate land, and tell me, they will soon have as good for thirty cents." Even his North Bend settlers left him, to push their fortunes in those interior valleys, of which the soldiers of St. Clair and Wayne gave such descriptions. The mere prospect of a treaty diminished the population of his young town one half, and its completion gave his hopes almost a death-blow. So uniformly unfortunate was this founder of the most thriving colony of the Ohio, that warfare and peace, prosperity and adversity, seemed equally to injure his interests; and, to complete the picture, he was now at variance with his friend and adviser, Dayton.

But we cannot follow any farther his individual fortunes. No man ever seemed in a surer path to wealth, influence, and honor, than Judge Symmes when he first began his Western operations. He was a man of good sense and very general information; just, kind, courageous, and persevering; but he had still some faults, which, coöperating with that fatherly but inscrutable Providence which governs all our external fortunes, thwarted his projects, destroyed his most promising plans, and involved him in quarrels and lawsuits, so that at last he died poor and neglected. But the cloud that is still upon his memory will one day rise. It is clear that, in despite of his failings, he was a true and high-minded man; and the future historian of Ohio will feel, as he examines his character, that it is one upon which he may dwell with pride.

From the conclusion of the treaty of Greenville, the rapid growth of the Miami valleys may be dated; for, after that time, but one great event occurred to embarrass the settlers of that region. This was the failure on the part of Symmes to pay for much of the land which he had sold. But even this difficulty was almost entirely removed by the preëmption laws to which we have referred. The country lying about the junction of Mad River and the Miami was one of the most valuable portions which were in this situation. Seventeen days after Wayne's treaty, that is, upon the 20th of August, 1795, this tract was purchased of Symmes by St. Clair, James Wilkinson, Jonathan Dayton, and Israel Ludlow, who, during the next month, sent surveyors to lay out their purchase; and, in November, Mr. Ludlow named and surveyed the town of "Dayton," now one of the most flourishing in the State. The settlement of the new town began in the following April.

When it was found, however, that this purchase would not be included in Symmes's patents, the proprietors refused to accept the benefit of the preëmption law, and abandoned their contract; which was taken by Daniel C. Cooper, who realized a fortune from it.

From Cincinnati and Dayton, settlers spread in every direction. And it was not till the country was pretty well filled, that the towns began to grow; the population of Cincinnati increasing but two hundred persons from 1800 to 1805, while the whole region back received about twenty-five thousand emigrants during that time.

The great causes of the rapid advance of the Miami country were, its fertility, ease of access, healthful character, and uncommon amount of water-power. The Muskingum and Scioto valleys are not so broad as those of the Miamies; and the uplands between these last-named streams being upon limestone, while those about the former are based on sandstone, are richer, as well as more level. But the superiority of the Miami country, in respect to water-power, was still more striking. Though as yet but poorly improved in proportion to its capabilities, it at this time moves a very great amount of machinery; as may be seen by the following statement, which we take from a letter written to us by an inhabitant of Dayton, the population of which in 1833 was but three thousand four hundred.

"We have within our corporation three cotton factories; a carpet factory, four stories high, one hundred by forty feet, and now turning out one thousand yards of Ingrain and Venetian carpeting weekly; a gun-barrel manufactory, four stories high, which sends its work through the whole Mississippi valley from Illinois to Louisiana; three large establishments for the making of machinery ; a large merchant flour-mill ; a fulling-mill ; a saw-mill, with a lath factory, and machine for jointing, planing, and grooving boards ; and an establishment for sawing stone. All these works are driven by the water of Mad River ; and we hope soon to see three times as much more in operation. A company has been formed and chartered to bring the water of this river from a point three miles from town, and throw it into the canal (Miami), above all the works now in use. They will be able to use all the water of the river at one point, with a fall of seventeen feet. Mad River, above the town, affords mill-sites for many miles, at an average distance of about a mile apart."

This writer also says, that, nine miles above Dayton on the Miami, the whole of that river may be applied, with a fall of from thirteen to sixteen feet. And, in addition to these streams, are four large creeks with falls ; twelve locks upon the canal ; and several springs affording water enough for mills ; "in one case a single spring acts upon three successive wheels of twenty-five feet each."

With such advantages of situation and soil, the valleys of the Miami rivers must become thickly settled and highly cultivated. A canal already connects the interior with Cincinnati, and in a few years, beyond a doubt, the whole region from that city to Lake Erie will be traversed by a canal and a railroad ; while from Cincinnati, as a centre, will radiate, in addition to these, a most admirable Macadamized turnpike-road (now in a great measure finished) ; a canal and a railroad to Indiana ; three other McAdam turnpikes, already constructed in part, two to meet the National Road in Ohio, and the third to reach the centre of Kentucky ; and that giant railroad, which, crossing Kentucky, Tennessee, and South Carolina, with branches to North Carolina and Georgia, is to rival the Mississippi, and make the West and the South one, as the West and Southwest are already one.*

The population of the region in question, though, like that

---

* The Licking is also to be made navigable by slack-water improvements, now in progress. This river runs into the heart of Kentucky.

of all very fertile countries, less generally hard-working than that of the more hilly tract purchased by the Ohio Company, is, to a very uncommon degree, industrious and sober. In the neighbourhood of Dayton great numbers of Germans are settled; and their steady, straightforward, plodding habits exert a good influence over our more fickle and enterprising countrymen.

Some idea of the nature and amount of the productions of the country lying back of Cincinnati may be had from the following return of articles received at that point by the Miami Canal, during the year ending December 1st, 1837.

89,000 bushels of corn.
75,000 barrels of flour.
22,000 " " pork, beside nearly three million pounds of bulk pork, and 1900 hogsheads of hams and shoulders.
54,000 barrels of whiskey.
249,000 pounds of butter (printed in the canal report " kegs ").

The exports of Cincinnati in 1826 amounted to but one million of dollars; in 1835 they were computed by an accurate observer at more than six millions. This includes, besides receipts by the canal and wagons, the produce in pork, lard, &c., of 162,000 hogs, driven to Cincinnati and there killed; and also one hundred steam-engines, two hundred and forty cotton-gins, twenty sugar-mills, and a great variety of other manufactured articles of all kinds; — the results of more than fifty steam-factories at work in and about the city.

This same writer gives the following calculation of the exports of 1836: —

Of Pork,	$ 3,000,000
" Flour,	600,000
" Whiskey,	750,000
" Iron manufactures,	2,000,000
" Hats, books, &c.,	1,350,000
" Sundries,	400,000
	$ 8,100,000

During that year, also, there were built in Cincinnati thirty-five steamboats, costing $ 850,000.

In illustration of the rapidity of the increase in the Miami valley, as compared with that of the Ohio Company's purchase, the following facts are worthy of attention. In 1834, the average value of lands * in Washington county was, by tax appraisement, $ 1.23 per acre; in Meigs county, .92; in Athens county, .63; in Gallia county, 1.05. These are in the tract bought by the Associates. Let us now look at Symmes's purchase. Hamilton county, $ 10.00; Montgomery county, 4.53; Butler county, 6.04; Warren county, 5.11.

Turning from the fortunes of the two main settlements made in Ohio before the final peace with the Indians, we come to the history of Galliopolis.† And here we must confess our extreme deficiency of materials, although many of the original settlers are still residing in their "city of the French." And to this deficiency is added confusion, which we have in vain tried to do entirely away.

In May or June, 1788, Joel Barlow left this country for Europe, "authorized to dispose of a very large body of land" in the West.‡ In 1790, this gentleman distributed proposals in Paris, for the sale of lands, at five shillings per acre, which promised, says Volney, "a climate healthy and delightful; scarcely such a thing as frost in winter; a river called, by way of eminence, 'The Beautiful,' abounding in fish of an enormous size; magnificent forests of a tree from which sugar flows, and a shrub which yields candles; venison in abundance; without foxes, wolves, lions, or tigers; no taxes to pay; no military enrolments; no quarters to find for soldiers. Purchasers became numerous, individuals and

* This does not show the real value of the land, the appraised value being but about forty per cent. on the true value; but, for comparison, it answers as well as if it were nearer the truth.

† Commonly written *Gallipolis*.

‡ Sparks's *Washington*, Vol. IX. p. 386.

whole families disposed of their property; and, in the course of 1791, some embarked at Havre, others at Bourdeaux, Nantes, or Rochelle," each with his title-deed in his pocket.* Five hundred settlers, among whom were not a few carvers and gilders to his Majesty, coachmakers, friseurs and peruke-makers,† and other artisans and *artistes* equally well fitted for a backwoods life, arrived in the United States in 1791–92; and, acting without concert, travelling without knowledge of the language, customs, or roads, they at last managed to reach the spot designated for their residence, after expending nearly, or quite, the whole proceeds of their sales in France.

They reached the spot designated; but it was only to learn, that the persons whose title-deeds they held did not own one foot of land, and that they had parted with all their worldly goods merely to reach a wilderness, which they knew not how to cultivate, in the midst of a people of whose speech and ways they knew nothing, and at the very moment when the Indians were carrying destruction to every white man's hearth. Without food, without land, with little money, no experience, and with want and danger closing around them, they were in a position that none but Frenchmen could be in without despair.

Who brought them to this pass? Volney says, the Scioto Company, which had bought of the Ohio Company; Mr. Hall says, in his *Letters from the West* (p. 137), a company who had obtained a grant from the United States; and, in his *Statistics of the West* (p. 164), the Scioto Company, which was formed from or by the Ohio Company, as a subordinate. Barlow, he says, was sent to Europe by the Ohio Company; and by them the lands in question were

---

* *View of the Climate and Soil of the United States, &c.* — The sugar-tree was the maple, and the wax-bearing myrtle the shrub that yielded candles.

† Brackenridge's *Recollections*, p. 42.

conveyed to the Scioto Company. Kilbourn says, "The Scioto Land Company, which intended to buy of Congress all the tract between the western boundary of the Ohio Company's purchase and the Scioto, directed the French settlers to Gallipolis, supposing it to be west of the Ohio Company's purchase, though it proved not to be." The Company, he tells us, failed to make their payments, and the whole proposed purchase remained with government.*

The last we believe to be the true account. No other connection existed, so far as we can learn, between the Ohio and Scioto Companies than this, that some persons were stockholders in both; so that the want of good faith, charged by most writers on those of whom the French bought, cannot apply in any degree to the Ohio Company. Nor do we know that there was a want of faith at all; the lands were believed to be what Barlow represented them. A contract with government was to have been regularly made, and funds (as we learn) were collected toward the payment. But the treasurer of the Company became bankrupt, and the funds were lost, how we know not. The spot to which the French were directed was supposed to be within the limits of the intended purchase; and, once there, the Company, which had failed, could do nothing for them. As we hold it to be good philosophy, as well as true charity, to choose of two sufficient causes that which involves the least moral guilt, we should ascribe that mingling of private and company concerns, which seems to have ruined the latter, to want of care, and not want of honesty.

But, whatever doubt there may be as to the causes of the suffering, there can be none as to the sufferers. The poor gilders, and carvers, and peruke-makers, who had followed a jack-a-lantern into the literally howling wilderness, found that their lives depended upon their labor. They must clear

---

* Kilbourn's *Gazetteer*, 1831.

the ground, build their houses, and till their fields. Now the spot upon which they had been located by the Scioto Company was covered in part with those immense button-wood or sycamore trees, which are so frequent along the rivers of the West, and to remove which is no small undertaking even for the American woodman. The coachmakers were wholly at a loss; but at last, hoping to conquer by a *coup-de-main*, they tied ropes to the branches, and while one dozen pulled at them with might and main, another dozen went at the trunk with axes, hatchets, and every variety of edged tool, and by dint of perseverance and cheerfulness at length overcame the monster, though not without some hair-breadth escapes; for when a mighty tree, that had been hacked on all sides, fell, it required a Frenchman's heels to avoid the sweep of the wide-spread branches. But when they had felled the vast vegetable, they were little better off than before; for they could not move or burn it. At last a good idea came to their aid; and, while some chopped off the limbs, others dug, by the side of the trunk, a great grave, into which, with many a heave, they rolled their fallen enemy.

Their houses they did not build in the usual straggling American style, but made two rows or blocks of log cabins, each cabin being about sixteen feet square; while at one end was a larger room, which was used as council-chamber and ball-room.

In the way of cultivation they did little. The land was not theirs, and they had no motive to improve it; and, moreover, their coming was in the midst of the Indian war. Here and there a little vegetable garden was formed; but their main supply of food they were forced to buy from boats on the river, by which means their remaining funds were sadly broken in upon. Five of their number were taken by the Indians; food became scarce; in the fall, a marsh behind the town sent up miasmata that produced fevers; then winter came, and, despite Mr. Barlow's promise, brought frost in plenty; and, by and by, they heard from beyond seas of the carnage that was desolating the firesides they had left. Never were men in a more mournful situation; but still, twice in the week, the whole colony came together, and to the sound of the violin danced off hunger and care. The savage scout that had been lurking all day in the thicket, listened to the strange music, and, hastening to his fellows, told them that the whites would be upon them, for he had seen them at their war-dance; and the careful Connecticut man, as he guided his broad-horn in the shadow of the Virginia shore, wondered what mischief "the red varmint" were at next; or, if he knew the sound of the fiddle, shook his head, as he thought of the whiskey that must have been used to produce all that merriment.

But French vivacity, though it could work wonders, could not pay for land. Some of the Gallipolis settlers went to Detroit, others to Kaskaskia; a few bought their lands of the Ohio Company, who treated them with great liberality; and, in 1795, Congress, being informed of the circumstances, granted to the sufferers twenty-four thousand acres of land opposite Little Sandy River, to which, in 1798, twelve hundred acres more were added; which tract has been since known as *French Grant.*

The influence of this settlement upon the State was unimportant; but it forms a curious little episode in Ohio history, and affords a strange example of national character.

Marietta and Cincinnati with their outposts, and Gallipolis, were the only settlements made in Ohio before Wayne's treaty. After that event, the Scioto valley and the Western Reserve were rapidly peopled; but we are unable to give any facts of value relating to their settlement. The tract between the Little Miami and Scioto Rivers had been originally reserved by Virginia for her soldiers; but, as she allowed locations to be made without having the ground previously surveyed into regular portions, a great deal of overlapping, or shingling of titles (as it is called in the West), has taken place; and the uncertainty and litigation, therefrom resulting, have diminished the value of a very excellent body of land; the higher portions being among the best wheat lands in the West.

The fertility of the Scioto valley is proverbial. For the cultivation of maize it is unsurpassed, and the stock-farms which border upon it are among the largest and best in the State. The valley itself is subject to that miasma which produces intermittent fevers; but this is yearly diminishing. East of the Scioto lies a broken country, through which, from the southwest to the northeast, passes the great iron deposit. There are several beds, and different kinds of ore, all of which dip toward the east. With the iron is associated bituminous coal; which, though of an ordinary quality in general, and in thin layers, answers for the steam-engines which are used at the furnaces. The amount of available ore in the counties of Jackson, Lawrence, and Scioto, it is estimated by the State geologist, will supply four hundred thousand tons a year for two thousand seven hundred years; and these contain but a third or fourth of the whole deposit, though, from their proximity to the Ohio River, it has been little wrought but in them; there being in the two last-named counties fourteen or fifteen furnaces, producing an average of one thousand tons of pig metal a year. Nor can we omit the Buhrstone deposit, which, adjoining the iron, passes through the very midst of a country that will, in time, be yellow with wheat-fields; and which, for milling purposes, there is reason to think, will afford stone nearly or quite equal to the French, when the same skill is used in selecting the blocks.

But that portion of Ohio, which at this time is most flourishing, all things considered, is the Western Reserve, or Connecticut Reserve. This district was retained by Connecticut when she made her transfer to the United States, in 1786, though against the judgment of many of our wisest statesmen.* In 1800, however, the right of jurisdiction was relinquished by the State to the Union, and patents were issued by the United States to the Governor of Connecticut, for the use of those persons who had previously bought from her; † by which means all difficulties were quieted. The Reserve included all the land north of the forty-first degree of north latitude, and extended west from Pennsylvania one hundred and twenty miles.‡ It is a level and fertile country; and, though much of it was so wet, when covered with forests, that it was thought by many to be of little value, it has become dry as it has been opened to the sun, and presents at this time as fine an extent of arable and meadow land as can be seen anywhere; diversified, in the southern counties, by little lakes of crystal clearness; and, in point of cultivation, fences, and buildings, no district in the West surpasses, if there be any that equals, the Reserve. This is in part owing to the habits of the original settlers, who were principally from Connecticut and Massachusetts; and in part to the fact, that the ground has to be well cleared, ditched, and cultivated, in order that it may be productive. A soil that demands labor that it may be made to yield, and yields a large return when that is given, is the soil that will make its owners most independent; and that boasted fertility of the prairies, which requires little or no pains on the part of the farmer, however much it may suit man's love of ease, is a misfortune, not a blessing.

The Reserve is peculiarly fitted for grazing, and is fast

---

* *Old Journals*, Vol. IV. pp. 645-648. — Sparks's *Washington*, Vol. IX. p. 178.

† *Land Laws*, p. 104.

‡ The writer in Silliman's *Journal*, for October, 1836, p. 34, says, the Reserve is bounded south by the Ohio. As it is not marked on our maps, this might mislead some.

becoming a great cheese and butter making region; some of the cheese made there is not unlike the Stilton cheese of England. Vast numbers of cattle are also raised there for the market. In point of mineral wealth, this district is not wanting, as the great iron deposit crosses it, and the coal-beds reach its southern borders. And, in respect to water-power, it is, at one point, unsurpassed; the Cuyahoga falling, at the new town called Cuyahoga Falls, two hundred and forty feet in two miles and a half; and affording from four to twenty thousand cubic feet of water per minute.* This point is destined, beyond doubt, to be one of immense importance. The Ohio Canal is within two miles; and the Pennsylvania and Ohio Canal will pass directly through the town, connecting this point, by complete water communication, with New York and New Orleans, and by canal and railroad with Philadelphia. Every acre in its neighbourhood is capable of cultivation; and coal, lime, and freestone are found in the immediate vicinity.

Of the people of the Reserve we have spoken. They are hard-working and sober. Not more than half the townships, it is said, assess any poor tax. The temperance reform has been more general here than in any other part of Ohio. Thousands have abandoned distilling, notwithstanding its profits; and many farmers will not sell their corn for distillation. The young, also, are taught that industry and economy, which their fathers learned in New England. We have known three Western Reserve boys leave home for Connecticut "to get their education," with fifteen dollars among them, and reach New Haven with twelve still in their pockets.† But such journeys are no longer necessary,

---

* *Ohio Gazetteer*, article *Cuyahoga*. — Silliman's *Journal*, for October, 1836, p. 45.

† The Reserve boys cannot compete with the native Yankees, however; one of whom, a year or two since, being in the South of Ohio and wishing to go home, bought him a cow, and, trudging at her

as the people of the Reserve are building colleges for themselves.

The section of Ohio which was last settled was the northwest corner; that portion having been retained by the Indians until 1819.* Since it came into the market, it has been rapidly filling up, the land being of an excellent quality, and well watered; and, when the Miami Canal shall be completed to the Maumee, as it will be in a year or two, this will be a very thriving section. Here, also, is a great water-power, the Maumee falling from sixty to seventy feet in the eighteen miles above Perrysburg.

Having thus glanced at the different portions of the State whose fiftieth birthday was commemorated last April, we will but ask our readers to bear with us a little longer, while we touch upon some points in which the State at large is concerned.

The first form of Territorial government was organized in July, 1788; the Governor, and most of the leading men of that day, being Federalists. In September, 1799, the legislature, which the people were at that time, under the Ordinance, entitled to elect, assembled at Cincinnati. This body very naturally possessed some of the democratic temper, then prevalent; and the free use which the Governor made of his veto power caused some clashing between the representatives and himself. In November, 1802, Congress having passed an act authorizing the formation of a State government, a convention met at Chillicothe to form a constitution. This convention was very thoroughly Jeffersonian; and the result of its meeting was a thorough democratic constitution. Of the excellences and defects of this instrument, we have not time to speak; but they are those of a truly

heels with his book, lived on her milk and what he got in exchange for it, and sold her at an advance, when he reached his point of destination.

* *Land Laws*, p. 187, *et seq.*

popular form of government. Neither can we say any thing, in detail, of the laws that have been passed by the State legislature. They have, in the main, evidenced the good sense and correct principles of the people. The great faults have been, haste in their preparation, continual change, and too much local legislation; all which have resulted from too great a love of making laws.*

But there are three things which have had, and will hereafter have, so great an influence upon the fortunes of Ohio, that we cannot close without a reference to their history; we mean steamboats, canals, and common schools.

The idea of using steam in the navigation of the Ohio and Mississippi occurred to Mr. James Rumsey, of Virginia, as early as the year 1782.† In 1784, his invention had been made known to Washington, who mentions it at the close of his letter to Governor Harrison, respecting internal improvements, dated October 10th of that year; and speaks of it more fully in a letter to Dr. Williamson, written upon the 15th of the following March.‡ Mr. Rumsey also obtained, in 1784, patents from two States; but his plan, which was essentially to pump up water at the head of the boat, and force it out again at the stern (which pumping and forcing were to be done by an old-fashioned atmospheric steam-engine), did not ever come into use, though the model of it worked well.

From that time, until Fulton determined to try his steamboats on the Western waters, people contented themselves with arks, keels, and flats. In 1811 and 1812, Mr. Fulton caused to be built at Pittsburg the *Orleans*, of four hundred tons. She left that place in December, 1812, and, passing

---

* Ohio has now thirty-six volumes of general laws. In 1837 were printed one hundred and forty-four pages of general, and six hundred and seventy-eight of local laws.

† *Cincinnati Directory*, for 1819, p. 64.

‡ Sparks's *Washington*, Vol. IX. pp. 68, 104.

down the river, presented for the first time to the dwellers upon its banks the spectacle of a self-moving boat.* But, though this did very well for a voyage down the stream, it was found to be even less available than the keel-boat for the passage against the stream; and, from 1812 to 1816, it was thought hopeless to make a steamboat that should stem the current and ascend the rapids of the Mississippi and Ohio. In 1816, however, Captain Henry M. Shreve (since famous as the inventor of the snag-boats, or "Uncle Sam's tooth-pullers," as the river-men call them) built at Wheeling the *Washington*, having one large boiler on her upper deck; and though she was so unlucky as to burst this boiler while at Marietta on her way down,† she reached New Orleans in safety; and, returning to the Falls, first convinced the merchants and mariners of the West that such boats might supersede the keels. But even after this many doubted; and, when the first boat, the *Vesta*, was built at Cincinnati, in 1817, those best fitted to judge scoffed at the idea, that she could bring freight up stream cheaper than the keel-boats. "Gentlemen," said the builder, a sanguine, and, as they thought, mad man, "you now pay five and six dollars a hundred from New Orleans; but we shall some of us live to see steam doing the work for one half that." — He and they have lived to see it reduced to one eighth.

We need say nothing as to the immense influence which has been exerted upon the whole West by the use of steamboats; their value is self-evident. At present, between six and seven hundred are plying upon the waters that discharge themselves through the Mississippi.

But, vast as must have been the effect of rapid and cheap carriage upon the great rivers and lakes, it would have done

* *Cincinnati Directory*, for 1819, p. 55.

† Silliman's *Journal*, for October, 1836, p. 1. The writer erroneously states the *Washington* to have been the first Western steamboat.

but little toward developing the resources of Ohio without those roads and canals which connect the interior with the coast. Long after steamboats were in full operation, a wet fall and heavy roads made it so difficult to get produce to a market, that wheat-stacks rotted where they stood, or were given over to the swine, as not being worth the threshing. Now, the farmer in the interior may put his cheese or pork into the canal-boat, and, without touching land again, it passes to either extremity of the Union.

The great New York canal was suggested by Gouverneur Morris, in 1777;* but, as early as 1774, Washington tells us, that he had thought of a system of improvements by which to connect the Atlantic with the Ohio;† which system, ten years later, he tried most perseveringly to induce Virginia to act upon with energy. In the letter to Governor Harrison, to which we referred a page or two back, he also suggests, that an examination be made as to the facilities for opening a communication, through the Cuyahoga and Muskingum or Scioto, between Lake Erie and the Ohio. Such a communication had been previously mentioned by Jefferson, in March, 1784; he even proposed a canal to connect the Cuyahoga and Big Beaver.‡ Three years later, Washington attempted to interest the Federal government in his views, and exerted himself, by all the means in his power, to learn the exact state of the country about the sources of the Muskingum and Cuyahoga.§ After he was called to the presidency, his mind was employed on other subjects, but the whites, that had meantime begun to people the West, used the course which he had suggested (as the Indians had done before them), to carry goods from the Lake to the settlements on the Ohio; so that it was soon

* Sparks's *Life of Morris*, Vol. I. p. 497.

† Sparks's *Washington*, Vol. IX. p. 31.

‡ Jefferson's *Correspondence*, Vol. II. p. 222.

§ See Sparks's *Washington*, Vol. IX. pp. 214, 291, 303, *et seq.*

known definitely, that upon the summit level were ponds, through which, in a wet season, a complete water connection was formed between the Cuyahoga and Muskingum.

From this time till 1817, the public mind underwent various changes; more and more persons becoming convinced that a canal between the heads of two rivers was far less desirable, in every point of view, than a complete canal communication from place to place, following the valleys of the rivers, and drawing water from them. In 1815, Dr. Drake, of Cincinnati, proposed a canal from some point on the Great Miami to the city in which he resided;* and in January, 1818, Mr., afterwards Governor Brown, writes thus: — "Experience, the best guide, has tested the infinite superiority of this mode of commercial intercourse over the best roads, or any navigation of the beds of small rivers. In comparing it with the latter, I believe you will find the concurrent testimony of the most skilful and experienced engineers of France and England against the river, and in favor of the canal, for very numerous reasons." †

In accordance with these views, Mr. Brown made every inquiry respecting the feasibility of canals from the mouth of the Cuyahoga to the Ohio, and from Dayton to Cincinnati; and in 1820, being then executive of the State, laid his views before the legislature.‡ Four years were devoted to making surveys and estimates, and arousing people to the utility of the proposed measure; and, in 1824, two lines were definitely determined on, the one beginning at the mouth of the Scioto River, crossing by the valley of the Licking to the Upper Muskingum, and thence to the Lake; the second connecting Cincinnati with the Lake, by the valleys of the Great Miami, Loramie's Creek, the Auglaize,

---

* Drake's *Picture of Cincinnati*, p. 224.

† *Cincinnati Directory*, for 1819, p. 73.

‡ Chase, *Statutes*, Vol. I. p. 44.

and the Maumee. The subject was now ready for legislative action, and in February, 1825, an act was passed, authorizing the construction of the route from the mouth of the Scioto, through to the Lake; and of the other, to Dayton. The only opposition to this act was by some of the land-owners in the eastern part of the State, and most of them were finally led to change their views.

The first cost of the Miami Canal, which connects Cincinnati with the fertile country lying back, was about 900,000, it being a little more than sixty-seven miles long. During the year ending October 31st, 1837, this canal received in tolls, &c., deducting contingent expenses, about $ 57,000.

The Ohio Canal cost $ 4,244,539; its length being three hundred and thirty-three miles. During the year ending October 31st, 1837, the net income was something over $ 280,000.*

The Miami Canal has been since extended thirty miles beyond Dayton; and, at this time, the whole line, with the exception of fifty-three miles, is under contract, to its junction with the Wabash and Erie Canal, near Defiance.

The Wabash and Erie Canal begins at the head of steamboat navigation upon the great river of Indiana; and, after passing into Ohio, extends about eighty-seven miles, and then enters the Maumee. The whole line is under contract.

The other State works now in progress are the Walhonding Canal, which passes from the Ohio Canal up the Walhonding or Whitewoman's River, and which will ultimately be extended up the various branches of that river into the counties of Richland, Knox, Holmes, and Wayne; the Hocking Canal, by which the Ohio Canal and Ohio River will be connected; the Muskingum River improvements, by which the Ohio Canal and Muskingum will be connected,

---

* This is the net income paid into the treasury, without deducting repairs, &c.

and the latter be made navigable for steamboats; the National Road; and a side cut from the Miami Canal, of twenty miles. In addition to these public works are two company canals connecting the Ohio Canal and Ohio River at different points; the one entering Pennsylvania and passing down the Big Beaver River, the other entering the Ohio just at the State line; and also the Whitewater Canal, connecting Cincinnati with the great Indiana Canal, and so with the whole interior of that State. There are also in progress two railroads from Sandusky, one to connect with the Miami Canal at Dayton, the other running into the centre of Huron county.

But perhaps the best idea that we can give of the commercial facilities, natural and acquired, of Ohio, will be by the following statement, showing the number of counties bordering on the Ohio and Lake Erie, and also how many are crossed by a canal, railroad, or Macadamized road, now *actually made or in progress.*

There are in Ohio seventy-five counties.*

Upon the Ohio River lie 14

and, of these, seven have through their interior either a canal, railroad, or Macadamized road.

Upon the Lake lie 7

and, of these, three have through their interior a railroad or canal.

Canals, now made or making, pass through .	32
Railroads, now in progress, pass through . .	6
Macadamized roads, made or in progress, pass through	5
Of the seventy-five, remain unimproved by canal, railroad, or McAdam road, though most have turnpike-roads, ...	11
	75

And nowhere, among those yet mentioned, have we included ten canal, and forty-one railroad companies, which have

* Not including a new county erected last winter, called Erie.

as yet done nothing; though in some of the largest, sufficient stock is taken to enable them to begin operations as soon as the money market is easier.

Nor should we omit to mention, that by a law of 1836–37, when one half of the stock of a turnpike-road, or two thirds of that of a canal, or railroad, is taken by individuals, and the object is approved of by those who have charge of the public works of the State, the Governor is authorized to subscribe in the name of the State for the balance. Under this law, in January last, nine turnpike-roads, three railroads, and two canals had been approved of by the Board of Public Works; and, in February, the State had become interested with individuals and companies to the amount of $1,054,311.10.

The third of these improvements, which have produced, and will produce, the most permanent influence on Ohio, is the system of common schools.

The Ordinance of 1787 provided, that, "religion, morality, and knowledge being necessary to good government and the happiness of mankind, schools and the means of education shall be for ever encouraged." In the previous Ordinance of 1785, regulating the sale of lands in the West, Section No. 16 of every township was reserved "for the maintenance of public schools within the said township." And the Constitution of Ohio, using the words of the Ordinance of 1787, says, that "schools and the means of instruction shall for ever be encouraged by legislative provision." In accordance with the feelings shown in these several clauses, the governors of Ohio always mentioned the subject of education with great respect in their messages, but nothing was done to make it general. It was supposed, that people would not willingly be taxed to educate the children of their poor neighbours; not so much because they failed to perceive the necessity that exists for all to be educated, in order that the commonwealth may be safe and prosperous; but because a vast number, that lived in Ohio, still doubted whether Ohio would be their ultimate abiding-place. They came to the West to make money rather than to find a home, and did not care to help educate those whose want of education they might never feel.

Such was the state of things until about the year 1816, at which time several persons in Cincinnati, who knew the benefits of a free-school system, united and commenced a correspondence with different portions of the State. Their ideas being warmly responded to, by the dwellers in the Ohio Company's purchase, and the Western Reserve more particularly, committees of correspondence were appointed in the different sections, and various means were resorted to, to call the attention of the public to the subject; among the most efficient of which was the publication of an *Education Almanac* at Cincinnati. This work was edited by Nathan Guilford, a lawyer of that place, who had from the first taken a deep interest in the matter. For seven or eight years this gentleman and his associates labored silently and ceaselessly to diffuse their sentiments, before any attempt was made to bring the subject into the legislature. At length, in 1824, it having been ascertained, that a strong feeling existed in favor of a common-school system through the eastern and northeastern parts of the State, and it being also known that the western men, who were then bringing forward their canal schemes, wished to secure the assistance of their less immediately benefited fellow-citizens, it was thought to be a favorable time to bring the free-school proposition forward; the understanding being, that, as neither the friends of canals, nor those of schools, were strong enough by themselves to carry their project, each should assist the other. This understanding, which was rather implied than expressed, has led some to say, that the free-school system was attained by "log-rolling"; which saying, though true in one sense, is not to be understood in the sense that refers to individual solicitation and promise. On this occasion Cincinnati sent to the Senate Mr. Guilford, whose avowed and main object in thus entering public life was to help on the accomplishment of his favorite project, and to that he devoted himself during the session. Many thought his toil useless; some of the leading men said, the measure was unconstitutional, unwise, and against popular feeling entirely; but they proved false prophets, as it was carried by a very large vote, and became a popular measure.

The Reverend Manasseh Cutler, one of the leading directors of the Ohio Company, stood by the side of the chief projector of the school law at the bar of the House of Representatives when the final vote was taken upon it; and, as the Speaker announced the result, the old man raised his hands and uttered the words of Simeon, "Lord, now lettest thou thy servant depart in peace, according to thy word; for mine eyes have seen thy salvation!" It was a touching and true tribute.

Mr. Guilford, having brought about the particular good which he had in view, became a private citizen again, setting to the common political aspirants of the country an example well worthy their consideration. He still lives, and praise would here be misplaced; but no one can doubt, looking only to the object he effected, that his name will ever be remembered with those of the great benefactors of Ohio and the West.

During the thirteen years that have passed since free schools were first established, some changes have been made in the laws respecting them, one of the most important of which was the appointment, eighteen months since, of a Superintendent, whose business it is to collect all the information possible respecting the state of the public schools, of the school funds, and of the effects of the system, which he is to make public annually, in the form of a Report to the legislature ; and, to assist in the diffusion of his knowledge, he is, by the school law of the past winter, to publish a journal every second month, devoted to education. The Superintendent made his first Report last January, which Report was very favorable, inasmuch as it represents the people throughout the State to be very anxious to have such measures taken as shall render the means of general education more accessible than they have yet been made. The Report contains sixty-five pages, and exhibits at length the evils of the present arrangement, with suggestions for the future ; which suggestions, having been embodied in an act, were, in the main, adopted with great unanimity by the legislature, much of whose time and attention last winter was given to the subject of education. The great evils have been a want of funds, and an injudicious division of those that the State possessed. The idea now brought forward is, to have, yearly, two hundred thousand dollars, at least, distributed through the State, according to the number of youth in each township, on such principles as will secure to each township an equal additional sum, to be raised by the townships respectively ; by which plan every child in the State would have about eighty cents yearly.

Another legislative step, which showed the feeling that exists on the subject of education, was the commission given to Professor Stowe, two years since, to examine the public schools of Europe, whither he was going to purchase a library for Lane Seminary. His Report was made to the legislature during the last winter, and is a very interesting one ; clear, condensed, and practical. This feeling has shown itself also by education conventions, and in the yearly meeting of teachers, which takes place at Cincinnati.

Nor have High Schools and Colleges been disregarded by Ohio, though it is the general feeling that they, as the Superintendent says, " will, as a natural consequence, grow out of good common schools." In the Ohio Company's purchase two townships were given by Congress for a university, and its place of location was called Athens. The present income from the lands owned by this institution is four thousand dollars. There are four professorships, and, during 1835–36 this college had from ninety-five to one hundred students; during the present year there are but fifty-three.

There is another college at Marietta, established in 1832, which is doing very well.

In the Miami neighbourhood are, — the Miami University, at Oxford, Butler county, chartered in 1809, endowed with one township of excellent land, and now containing about one hundred and sixty students; — the Cincinnati College, at Cincinnati, incorporated in 1819, but, for many years previous to 1835, entirely quiescent; now, however, in full operation again, having, in March last, an Academical Department with one hundred and eighty-two scholars, most of them youths in the primary and preparatory classes; a law class of eighteen; and a medical class of one hundred and twenty-five; with eighteen teachers; — the Woodward College and High School, at Cincinnati, well endowed, and having about one hundred and fifty students; — and the Lane Seminary, about two miles from Cincinnati, which is now a purely theological seminary, of the Presbyterian sect. This institution, in March last, contained forty-two students, and five teachers; it also possesses a library of ten thousand volumes, which is, for its size, one of the most complete in the United States.

In the Western Reserve, we have the Western Reserve College, at Hudson, Portage county, with one hundred and seven scholars two years since; the Willoughby University, in Cuyahoga county, incorporated in 1834, and but partially organized; and the Oberlin Institute, in Lorraine county, incorporated in 1834, and containing, in 1836, three hundred and ten students, ninety-two of whom were girls.

Besides these, are Kenyon College, at Gambia, Knox county, an Episcopal Seminary, with one hundred thousand dollars' worth of property, and educating more than two hundred students; Franklin College, in Harrison county, chartered in 1825, from which, in 1837, graduated nine young men; and two Medical Colleges, one at Worthington, Franklin county, and the other at Cincinnati, the latter being a State institution.*

We may also mention, in this connection, the State Institution for the Deaf and Dumb; the ninth Annual Report of which, in 1837, shows that one hundred and twenty-seven persons have received instruction therein; — that for the Blind, opened a year since, and containing eleven pupils, under the temporary arrangement which exists until the building, now erecting, is finished; — and the Lunatic Asylum, which, it is thought, will be in operation during the coming autumn; the building (of two hundred and ninety-five feet front, and capable of containing one hundred and twenty patients, each having a room, beside officers, and those patients that require strict confinement) being nearly completed.

We have thus, in a hasty and incomplete, but we trust not wholly useless manner, presented an outline of the agricultural, manufacturing, and commercial advantages of the State of Ohio; together with the prospect she has for affording to all her children an ample intellectual education. We will now only point to some of the more prominent influences, that will bear upon the individual spiritual well-being of her citizens; — that object for which government, civiliza-

---

* For most of these facts we are indebted to the *Ohio Gazetteer*, of 1837.

tion, and knowledge all exist; and leave our readers to prophesy, each for himself, her future destiny.

The necessity for industry on the part of the people of Ohio, to which we have already referred, we regard as an important element toward determining the spiritual character of that people. To this we now add, — the climate, that permits labor, and, during most of the year, makes it grateful; the absence of slavery, which prevents the unnatural prejudice against bodily labor, which that institution produces; the division of the soil among its tillers; their freehold tenure; the mixed character of the people, in respect to religious faith, social views, political and sectional prejudices, — which mixture tends to make men less bigoted, and more catholic in their spirit; the ease with which every community is approached by those from other portions, which forbids local habits and prejudices; political freedom; a continual striving for social equality, which is, in substance, an antagonism to a reverence for mere wealth and professional knowledge, unsupported by ability and worth; and a general disposition not to reject religion, but to refuse to receive any form of religious faith on the mere word of a teacher. These, with almost universal comfort in physical matters, and very general wealth; and, also, universal information; and every form of Christianity; are, we believe, the influences that Ohio contains within herself for the future development of her children. Whether they may be expected, considered with reference to the external influences that will also bear upon her, to produce something like a Christian State, socially, politically, and religiously, all may judge as well as we. But if they do not, — if, on the contrary, they lead to worldliness, and anarchy, and irreligion, — are we therefore to despair? Because this people is not fitted for freedom, is freedom, therefore, not fitted for man? We reject all such views. Through freedom alone can man become what he should be; and, though America may but prove, what other lands have proved, each in its time, that he is still unfitted to escape wholly from pupilage, we look forward with not only hope, but faith, to the day when society shall be, not a mass of warring parties, but a Christian brotherhood; and we do this because, in the past, we see man ever advancing to this point.

XI.

THE FRENCH REVOLUTION.*

WE have heard the question asked more than once, within a twelvemonth, "How can any man at this day think of writing another History of the French Revolution?" The answer is obvious to all who have studied that great social and political phenomenon, for to them it is known that we have not yet a truly complete history of it; and, until the publication of the three whose titles we give below, we had scarce an approximation to one. Madame de Staël, Mignet, Scott, and a host of inferior writers, had done something toward presenting in one view the thousand events of that strange movement; but until Thiers and Alison published their first volumes, there had not been an approach made to a thorough and complete view. Nor is the want yet supplied. Alison and Thiers are clear, minute, sensible, and worthy of deep study; Carlyle is bold, sagacious, profound,

* 1. *History of Europe, from the Commencement of the French Revolution, in* 1785, *to the Restoration of the Bourbons, in* 1815. By ARCHIBALD ALISON, F. R. S. Edinburgh and London. 1836–1839. Vols. I.–VII. 8vo.

2. *Histoire de la Révolution Française.* Par M. A. THIERS. Paris. 1836. 10 vols. 8vo.

3. *The French Revolution: a History.* By THOMAS CARLYLE. London. 1837. 3 vols. 8vo.

From the New York Review, for July, 1839.

comprehensive, and demands deep study ; — but neither of the three gives us what we want. Thiers is superficial, Alison commonplace, and neither presents to us with power a picture of the causes of the revolution ; and Carlyle, whose insight is far greater, and whose imagination is a thousand-fold more mighty, still lacks simplicity, distinctness, and an earnest unconsciousness. Thiers tells his story with the flow, and glitter, and shallowness that mark the French mind so very generally ; Alison talks like a good, sound advocate, very sensibly, and to the point, but not as one whose eye can see far into a millstone ; while Carlyle, with the power of a true poet, and the grasp of a true philosopher, lays before us the wonderful story with such grimaces, and so sneeringly, that wonder, admiration, disgust, and regret divide our bosom, and baffle our judgment.

In truth, to comprehend the French Revolution, we must have written for us a work yet unattempted ; a full and living picture of the seventy years which preceded the meeting of the States General. Of this time, there are extant records innumerable, in the shape of memoirs, journals, letters, and writings, — but there is as yet no connected view of it. Carlyle, in his pictorial way, gives us the results of his reading upon that time, and in doing so does more to make the revolution intelligible, than all other writers with whose works we are acquainted ; but we want more than this ; we want a true and complete history of the changes of mind, the developments of first principles, the disappearance of old landmarks, the rise of new ones, — in short, a history of France, commercially, socially, intellectually, and morally considered, from 1715, or thereabouts, to 1789. We know not a field upon which a man of industry, impartiality, and imagination could better employ twenty years of his life, than in the preparation of such a work. Of the conquests and amours of Louis the Fourteenth, we have records enough ; but of the far more important conquests of the thinkers, writers, and scoffers that followed him, we have only piecemeal sketches, or biographies, that by their extent set the reader at defiance. And yet it was from the conquests last named, as the world is coming to see, that the great social tornado, known to us as the French Revolution, received its bent and character.

It is true, that not many years have passed since reviewers seriously contended, that it was not *merely* the financial troubles of France, that rent her whole frame asunder; and it is also true, that most writers are still busily demonstrating, when the question arises, that it was not La Fayette and Mirabeau that produced the general overturn, but Louis the Fifteenth and his followers, with all their sins of commission and omission; — but it is none the less true, that there are yet others who see that the sins of Louis were only those of the most noted man in the kingdom, — that the cause of the revolution lay deeper than the character or acts of king or court, — that it came from a source of universal extent, and tore in pieces the whole society of France, because the whole social system, from court to hovel, was wrong, and out of joint.

In this paper it is our purpose, not to criticize the works before us, but to inquire into the causes and extent of that social disease which led to the great convulsion, and to apply the lessons drawn from that time and land to our day and our country. Some may doubt the possibility of showing that we are in any danger from those causes which were operating in France; but, to us, it appears that very much is to be feared from those causes. In what we may say on this point, we cannot expect a general agreement; indeed, we must look to offend those of the most opposite views. We would only say, in reference to this, that surely truth-seekers in this country ought to be willing to hear the opinions of all, and calmly to accept or reject them; if dangerous, then branded as such; if only weak and worthless, then in pitying silence.

Every one that is acquainted with the working of a steam-engine knows how necessary it is to have every joint perfect, and all the gearing which it moves complete. Let but a bolt slip, let but a timber be wrongly inclined, let the least disproportion between the moving power and the apparatus moved exist, — and all is shake, and racket, and danger. There must be, in mechanical contrivances, a very thorough adaptation of the parts that are put in play to one another, and also to that which produces the central action. Now, society is so far mechanical in its operation, that this rule of mechanics applies to it; and the spirit of a society, its central moving power, if unadapted to its forms, habits, classifications, and other gearing, will produce a jar and wear that must sooner or later wreck the whole machine; and if a bolt, shaft, or even little pinion-wheel, get so far out of place as to produce a strong cross-strain, there will be an instant crash and general disorganization. For instance, if the spirit of the people be republican, and the forms of society be aristocratic, things cannot work well; the strain will grow more and more unequal, the movement more and more awry, until something gives way. So, also, if the spirit be aristocratic, and the form republican. It matters not what the social and political gearing of a country be; so long as it is unsuited to the central force, mischief must come. It is not in our republican form that our safety lies; nor is England insecure because of her aristocratic institutions: our safety lies in the perfect adaptation of our spirit to its forms; and her danger, in the ever-increasing want of adaptation that is visible in her arrangements.

And why are we so fortunate as to have forms that match our national character? If we mistake not, it is because they, in some measure, grew out of that character, and were not made and fitted to it. The old constitutions of France were like so many broadcloth coats, cut and sewed by Sieyes and other tailors, and put upon a drunken giant; but ours is, measurably, the skin that grows as we grow, fitting itself to every part, and stretching to every need. Nature is a better workwoman than Madame Sieyes, and what she does may be relied on as well done. If the social and political organization of a country be the growth, the natural, vital growth, from the spirit of that country, all will be well; but if it be the result of art, the work of man, the poor product of mechanism, it will wear and tear, and need patching and alteration; and if the alteration be not made, but, while the spirit changes, the forms remain, then comes the want of adaptation, the jar, and wrench, and ruin.

It may be doubted, however, if the forms of society, man being the fallen creature that he is, can ever be wholly a natural and vital growth. Certain it is, that hitherto there has been very little of nature's handiwork seen in political and social systems. The English system was, like ours, measurably natural; and it has, accordingly, accommodated itself most wonderfully to the growing and changing kingdom; seams have opened now and then, but have soon healed. One great error, to be sure, England has made, and is still making; she never wants to have her children born, but tries, in the face of nature, to rear them within her own bosom; nor did the birth-pangs of these United Provinces teach her wisdom.

It may be doubted, we say, whether forms are ever wholly natural, and consequently, after a lapse of years or ages, the want of adaptation of which we spoke must come, and revolution, more or less violent. This thought need not trouble us, however, for, though it leads of course to disbelief in the permanency of the institutions of our country, yet, be it noted, the change need not be violent. For, though man cannot, like nature, alter by a never ceasing and never seen process, but must use patching in the stead of growth; yet there need be no disruption, and no other evil than a momentary stoppage of movement.

Of natural social systems, there are, perhaps, only two, which we may call the paternal and the fraternal. The ancient systems were all of the former kind, even among republicans. The great prophet of the paternal form was Moses; it belonged to an early time. In our day, the tendency is toward the fraternal; but, alas! none have, as yet, reached it, but all of Christendom is in the valley between the heights; the great prophet of fraternity was Jesus; it will be exemplified in some day yet to come.

And now, turning to France, we find her, in old times, under the dominion of the warrior and the priest. Men, in those days, followed leaders, the strong and the wise; the mass was weak and was ignorant, and the preëminence of some few was natural and just. The feudal system was, to no small extent, a vital system; the growth of the wants of the time. Then all was of the paternal type; there was no free inquiry, no free following of individual wishes; but the pope and the bishop, the king and the count, naturally and properly were looked up to.

Ages rolled on. The system essentially remained the same that it had ever been, but the spirit and the wants of those under it had vastly altered. The men of the southern mountains, Wickliffe, Huss, and, at length, Luther, spoke and acted free inquiry, truth-seeking, — scarce knowing what they did; and as ignorant of the results of their deeds, as the Marquis of Worcester was of steamships and locomotives. The instinct of dependence was weakening; science was extending; gunpowder, printing, travels, commerce, were changing the whole tissue of life. No man stood in the same relation to his neighbour that his father had stood in to his fellows. Why, in the time of the peasant's father, the count, whose castle crowned the hill near by, was a brave man, and a strong man, and a good leader, — and he was followed and looked up to; he was labored for cheerfully, because he fought well, and was a great man; but now gunpowder has stripped the count's burly son of the might that should lay in his prowess and his courage, and has bestowed that might on some stripling engineer, or some quick-witted commander; and the present lord of the castle can neither defend his vassals, nor command the reverence of the world; and yet he must be labored for, even as his father was. Will such labor, think you, be cheerful?

So, through the whole tissue of society, we say, was creeping another spirit. The idlers who had once fought, now hunted, drank, displayed themselves at court; the mailed suit was changed for the gilded suit, the gauntlet for the silk glove; expenses increased, money must be had, and the sullen peasant was worked harder to feed the worthless lord, than his fathers ever were to uphold their true leader. Meanwhile, in the villages, instead of trial by combat, and trials by fire, have come trials by thought and evidence; men, too, were born, here and there, who, leaving the old spiritual guidance, thought of religion for themselves; but still the old guides stood there, near by, not now with shepherd staves, but with torch and sword.

So changes the spirit of the French nation, and the needs of the French nation; but the forms change not. While in England the voice of the mass, whose wants there too are altering, is heard more and more fully, and the old religious faith, as it weakens, is supplanted by a new and living faith; in France, the mass is yet dumb, and the old reverence is wearing to a shell, and no successor appears. In England, the commons kick and cry, and continually shiver off something of the old feudal rind; and, as they are resisted, there come to aid them men whose minds have run far toward vagueness, but who still have deep faith, and recognize the existence of mystery, and worship a living God. In France, there is no knowledge yet of what is wanted, though a vague feeling of want grows stronger yearly. Louis the Great sweeps along, and for a time all seems well on the surface;

for glory, like a torch at the mouth of a tomb, dazzles the eye, and hides the uncleanness within. Nay, there has been, perhaps, a momentary flicker of true loyalty again, but it soon dies away; and debt, and doubt, and despair, come instead.

Thus, gradually, has it come to pass, that the feudal system is utterly unsuited to the spirit of those that are moving in it. The lords should be at work; the peasants should be enjoying the fruit of their own labor; every man should be allowed some scope of thought, and a true, living, religious faith, such as filled many of the Huguenots, should be let in to take the place of the dying. But no; the forms, iron and immovable, must remain. Wasteful expenditure by king, and priest, and noble, must be met by harder work on the part of the peasant. Idleness, unchecked by reverence, breeds immorality in the highest; all respect for woman ceases, chastity is no longer a virtue, and the unchaste no longer to be shunned. Parents send their sons to learn manners and politeness at the palace of Ninon de l'Enclos, a prostitute upon principle.

At length, the whole machinery of politics, society, and religion, being unadapted to the spirit that was moving men, which was a spirit of acquisition, — first of wealth, and then of knowledge, — a new process began, a process of inquiry into the worth of all this machinery; the need of it; the best substitute; the true ideal of society. While Louis the Fifteenth was yet a mere child, Montesquieu had gathered the materials for his great work upon government; and within two years after that most miserable of monarchs ascended the throne, was published the Telemachus of Fénelon, a work which Louis the Great had prohibited the printing of, thinking its pure and high views a satire upon his court and reign.

It would have been well had all those who now come forward as inquirers, been like Fénelon and Montesquieu; as devoted in soul, and as free and bold in intellect. But a new phasis in the action of European mind was just then beginning, which brought forward into the field many whose natures had little resemblance to those of the theologian of Cambray, and the philosopher of Bourdeaux.

The wild credulity, keen inquiry, and worthless empiricism of the Middle Ages had been succeeded by the discriminating method of the Baconians, and the deep, fearless exercise of logic and faith, by the great minds of the time of Milton, Barrow, and Cudworth. But the tendency toward a thorough comprehension of all earthly things stopped not there; in 1687 appeared Newton's Principia, and in 1690, Locke's Essay, — works that evidence the great progress which had been made in analysis. In truth, there seemed now to be no limits to the power of the mind of man; it could ascend to heaven, and unravel the mystery of the planetary system; it could lay bare the sources of knowledge, and bring every faculty of the human understanding to the touchstone. Nor was it only to the abstract sciences that the dissecting knife was applied. Forty years before Locke's Essay was published, Thomas Hobbes had, almost with a prophet's voice, borne his testimony against the whole range of thoughts, sentiments, and acts, which spring from man's spiritual nature; and in 1681, Peter Bayle had dared to write in France, that atheism was less to be feared than superstition. The whole intellectual world was looking toward experiment and logic, waiting thence a new revelation. Earnestness and spiritual power seem to have died out; and the opponents of freethinking spoke the same icy dialect, and from the same shallow pool, as the minute philosophers themselves. Berkeley, in 1713, calls the infidels of the day "a set of poor, ignorant creatures, that have not sense to discover the excellency of religion"; and again, "unthinking wretches, of short views, and narrow capacities, who are not able to penetrate into the causes or consequences of things." And this strong abuse was bestowed upon them because they held virtue to be lovely in itself, while he looked on it as a thing which should be followed, in order to gain some great future good! They would have men love it as they would have them love pictures and statues, because it was lovely; he would have them pursue it as a trade, whereby to gain heaven; neither seemed to recognize that idea in man which looks beyond the known Beautiful and Useful, and sees the Right; sees it in the faith, too, that it is one with the Beautiful and the Useful, though our facetted eyes yet dissever them. Surely, in those days did the words of Milton come true; and "to all the duties of evangelical grace, instead of the adoptive and cheerful goodness which our new alliançe with God requires, came servile and thrall-like fear. . . . . . Which fear of his, [the superstitious man, or professing believer,] as also his hope, fixed only upon the flesh, rendered, likewise, the whole faculty of his apprehension carnal."

It was indeed a sad time, the opening of the eighteenth century. The face of Europe was covered thick with the carcasses of feudal institutions, and with the yet moving bodies of diseased monarchies and faiths, — full of putrid sores. And, to remove these, arose a great army of scavengers, who would also fain have removed every green thing, and have killed every living creature, lest they should die too. It was a time of destruction and denial; the wrong was there before them, and must be put away, and the right might grow if it would, they cared not. Indeed, they denied all right; they had dissected plants and animals, and had found no such thing as Life in them, — it was merely an accident of their formation; and so, too, they had examined with microscopic eyes the heart of man, and the head of man, and there was no idea of Right there, but only a love of the Pleasant, here or hereafter.

It was a time when faith had ceased to act, for the recognition of mystery had been abandoned by all. The wonders of the stars had been explained, and the composition of all earthly bodies was to be made known, and the intellect had been weighed, and measured, and gauged, — and where could mystery remain? Here stood man, his mind a blank, and there the world; and that world wrote upon this mind, as the late-invented Daguerreotype upon the paper, all its secrets. Faith was, therefore, full belief in some asserted fact; religion was the keeping up such an intercourse with God as would insure his favor; and morality was obedience to his laws for fear of punishment. Such these things were to the believer; but to the infidel, religion was a scarecrow, with which priests kept others from the rich fields of tithes and preferments; — and morality was the pursuit of pleasure.

We have called the opening of that century a time of Doubt and Denial; old errors were daily discovered, and attacked, and all men gave their minds to the pursuit. "If," said Shaftesbury, in 1708, "the knowing well how to expose any infirmity or vice were but a sufficient security for the virtue which is contrary, how excellent an age might we be presumed to live in." It was in truth an age of exposure; not of cure, but of exposure. During the time of Louis the Thirteenth, the process was going on; through the whole reign of the great Louis, it worked secretly, and spread widely. The religious contests carried skepticism into the hearts of every family in France; Bayle, in that respect, was an exponent of the men of his day, — first a Calvinist, then a Catholic, then a Calvinist again, — and, in the end, a doubter; not a denier, — denial had not yet come, — but one balancing, believing nothing. Into every corner of France, this spirit spread; the lawyers — corrupt because the courts were corrupt, half-educated, half-developed, readers, debaters, flaw-finders — were admirably adapted to nourish and preach the new faith of faithlessness. The court, a great heart, every throb of which sent poison to the ends of the land,—the court was all infidel, not in form, but in fact. Rotten to the core, it called forth no deep pity, or manly condemnation;—epigrams, satires, sneers, were all that the professedly virtuous had for the vice that was about them. The only unpardonable sins were those of opinion, and the nobler the opinion, the deeper the sin; before 1700, the pure Fénelon had been condemned and exiled for believing that a man might love God without being led to do so from fear of punishment or hope of reward. And no wonder that they exiled him for such heresy, for it was heresy to the whole course of their lives, and every principle of their conduct. Fénelon and his faith stood without them as visible conscience-prickers, and they wished him away.

Into this evil time—a time of practical wickedness in high places, and of misery in low ones; a time of general inquiry, and uncertainty, and doubt; of denial, forming, but as yet unspoken; of the pursuit of pleasure, and no faith to curb it—were born successively Voltaire (in 1694), Buffon (in 1707), Rousseau (in 1712), Diderot (in 1713), Condillac and Helvetius (in 1715), and the Baron d'Holbach (in 1723).

And now Denial began to find her mouth-pieces. The keen, quick Voltaire—leaving the course which his father had chalked out for him, preferring rather to keep fine company and write fine verses—was not slow to see how admirably the time was suited to his nature. With the mighty instinct of vanity, he knew that the world was waiting to hear, not vice merely, nor weakness merely, but all those forms and institutions which men had come unconsciously to think weak and wicked ridiculed, sneered at, and annihilated. He smelt the carcass afar off, and hastened to the banquet. His was, indeed, a nature strangely suited to the day in which he lived; mystery was to him synonymous with absurdity, and faith with folly; he would have men kind, was kind himself; would have them moral, though immoral in his own conduct; he had a certain belief, too, and as late as 1762 talked of the "religion of our Saviour, Jesus Christ, and the extension of his kingdom"; — but in spirit he was the impersonation of irreverence and doubt. He embodied one leading idea of his time, that of serving truth by merely laying bare and sneering at untruths.

He saw in the visible Church of France evils and absurdities beyond number, and, wholly unable to look farther, opened his quiver of keen shafts to smite Religion. It was somewhere about 1732 that he began the warfare openly and seriously, while the public mind was all astir with the quarrels of the Jesuits, or Papal Catholics, and the Jansenists, or anti-Papal members of that Church: at that moment, when half the French world were laughing at religion, and half were angry with it, appeared his Philosophical Letters. They were read, for the author was well known, but the parliament of Paris ordered the volume to be publicly burnt, and the author to be seized. He escaped, but his book was burnt, and, as is usual in such cases, was thereby burnt into the memories of men. This, be it noted, was done by the parliament, a body which at that very time took one of the boldest steps ever taken in those days; for, having declined to register some anti-Jansenist and highly Papal acts, the king forced them to do it, in a bed-of-justice; — but on the morrow the parliament, with a spirit prophetic of 1788, protested against that act, and followed the king to Marly to make him listen to their complaints. He would not listen, and St. Antoine was not yet conscious, so that no result followed; but had previous events prepared the people of the capital for action, the Revolution might have begun then.

Voltaire began the attack upon religion in 1732 or 1733; from that time, nothing of a strong and serious character was published until 1746, when Diderot put forth his Philosophical Thoughts, his first-fruits of long-established practical atheism. The life and character of this man, Denis Diderot, are sufficiently familiar to all our readers. He was a marked and peculiar product of that time, and could have been what he was in no other age or country. He, too, embodied a great idea of that day, the idea of conforming conduct, not to our sense of duty, nor even to our instincts and affections, but to our bare logical understanding. He was the typical moralist of the day; could maltreat his wife, and write letters on virtue to his mistress, calling upon her to support him in the path of excellence, and love him, so that he might ever dread vice. He was a man of strong understanding; was fearless, kind in his own eyes, probably honest; but the world was to him a lifeless clod, and its on-dwellers the creatures of circumstance and chance. To him a good man was good luck, a bad man misfortune. He would not have any one angry with the evil-doer, any more than with a wind which fills our eyes with dust. He bade his disciples to neither rejoice nor regret that they were what they were; for they were the mere results of physical causes. Never to reproach others or repent ourselves was, in his eyes, the beginning of wisdom.

To such a man the pursuit of pleasure was the only conceivable end of life, and, lead whither it might, was the true end. The deep mystery of purity, the deep mystery of disinterestedness, were to him unknown depths. Why should there be decency, modesty, chastity? Try these virtues by the understanding, and what are they? Shadows. And as such Diderot regarded them, and lived in constant contempt of them.

At the age of thirty-three, this man wrote his first noted philosophical treatise; and though it was at once burnt by the hangman, and the author imprisoned, it was read extensively, and with so much favor, as to lead him to write three works of somewhat similar character, which came out from time to time until 1751, when the great Encyclopædia was commenced.

Meanwhile, before the publication of that work, which gave a name to the circle of infidels who were the mouthpieces of the French people, Condillac, the metaphysician of atheism, Buffon, its naturalist, and Rousseau, its sentimentalist, had appeared in public. Condillac's first work, that on the origin of human knowledge, had appeared in the same year with Diderot's executed pamphlet. It was a work of great acuteness, and pushed forward many steps the principles promulgated by Locke, and now known to France through the writings of Voltaire and others of the same school. Buffon's History began to appear in 1749, and in 1750 Rousseau maintained his paradox, that the sciences had injured moral growth, and bore away the prize from all commonplace competitors. The ground taken on this occasion, and so well defended by Jean Jacques, was, we are told, pointed out to him by Diderot. If such was the case, it was either a most curious coincidence, or Rousseau's whole course of life was strongly colored by that one act; for that ground was essentially the same that he occupied during his whole after life.

And now we have come to that point whence the movement was comparatively direct and certain. Let us look with some care at its phenomena.

The great mass of the French people was suffering from actual want; they were hungry, and had not food to eat; and as to intellectual or moral supplies, there was an utter famine. Above this mass were those whose minds had been somewhat opened, — whose power had been somewhat developed, — whose ambition had been somewhat kindled; but they were kept down, were forced to work, were constrained in every act and thought; they longed for a change, an opening, — for a chance to gain power and glory. To these men, the infidelity which had sprung up among the higher thinkers had come down, and, silently or openly, they too had no faith but in pleasure; their whole philosophy chimed in with their natural depravity, and lowered their aims and narrowed their views. Above these, again, came a class of better educated and wider looking men, who saw the immense absurdity of such a king as Louis the Fifteenth, and the immense evils of all the relations of society. They longed for remedies, they dreamed impossible perfections, and societies without a want or an evil. Impregnated with the prevailing ideas first impressed upon the world by Locke, they hoped to know all things by analysis and experiment; they saw no reason why men should not be made devoid of evil passions, and all be virtuous affection and reciprocal kindness. From this class came St. Pierre; to this class Rousseau spoke; it furnished, in after days, the Girondists. And above them again came, in strange commixture, an ignorant, formal, and weak noblesse, a thoroughly corrupt court, a worthless clergy, and a band of regenerators who denied every ground of religious faith, every idea of duty, and every feeling that revolted from indecency and licentiousness.

The lowest spoke not; indeed, they scarce recognized their misery, and knew far too little to know the causes of it, or their own power. They were slaves, and as such lived without hope, and died in sullen despair.

The next class, consisting of small lawyers, doctors, and poor priests; of merchants whose business carried them now and then from home; of the more quick and sensitive shopkeepers, and all those whose instincts sought power, and whose souls were not above selfishness; — this class, whence came the Jacobins by and by, spoke but softly, and within their narrow village limits. There they caught, as they could, Voltaire's wit, and Diderot's daring impiety, and Condillac's acute materialism, and dealt them out to their neighbours. Religion, through those villages, was, substantially, a mere crust, which it needed but a single move to shiver into atoms. Self was the only god truly worshipped; and that was bowed to in its lowest forms, for the worship of its higher ones was forbidden. Reverence for supernatural things, for moral excellence, for king, country, every thing, was rapidly passing. Try reverence by the understanding, and you will learn to revere your own pleasure only.

The third class, of better educated and purer hearted men and women, the dreamers of the day, talked much and freely among themselves, seeking a cure for the devastating disease which was blackening their country. Montesquieu's *Esprit des Lois*, which had appeared in 1748, was read, and pondered over, and debated with very deep interest. The affairs of government, the conduct of matters in France, the debt, expenditure, the whole economy of the kingdom, became the prevalent topics of conversation.

But the chief speaking, though perhaps the least thinking, was among the yet higher class, which was composed, as we have said, of most curious materials, — first the court, next the parliament, third the clergy, and last the philosophers. Upon the character, purposes, and proceedings of each of these bodies, a volume might be written with all ease; and to such an understanding of the causes of the Revolution as we could wish all historical students might have, a volume on each would be necessary. We can, however, give but hints and references. The court was, as is proverbially known, a sink of impurity. The ruler during the minority of Louis the Fifteenth, the Duke of Orleans, was an open scoffer at all religion and morality; and so bad were his wife and daughters, that over the former was placed this epitaph: — "Here lies Idleness, the mother of all the vices." And Orleans was but the type of the court in his time; nor did it improve in after times; — Richelieu was the incarnation of licentiousness; and if you would know something of Louis himself, a slight but all-sufficient view may be found in Madame Campan's memoirs.

The parliament was of a temper and habit wholly different from the court, but, so far as the public was concerned, did often as much harm as the worthless nobles. The parliaments of France, we scarce need say, were in no respect like the body of the same name in England. They were, in their origin, courts of justice; but, in the course of time, had become a kind of popular body, restraining the kings in their attempts to plunder the public. It is true that the members represented no persons but themselves, and those with whom direct interest and sympathy connected them. They bought their places in the parliament, and generally used them for their own purposes, and often to the great injury of the public. However, it was inevitable that a body composed of such materials should catch something of the liberalizing spirit of the day, both as to government and religion. That spirit had been long growing, and by the middle of the eighteenth century, the time of which we write, the parliament of Paris was ready to take strong steps in favor of comparative freedom.

The clergy, meanwhile, had become divided into two great masses, — the Jesuits, which practically included all of the old-school Catholics, the favorers of Papal authority; and the Jansenists, which body embraced those who, still claiming to be Catholics, were for throwing off to some extent the power of Rome and the power of the priesthood. In short, the Jesuit body represented the despotic and spiritual leaders of the day, and the Jansenists the liberalists, who yet dared not become Protestant. The former waged of course a deadly war against the latter, with very various success. Parliament favored the Jansenists, the court upheld the Jesuits, — not because they had any sympathy with them, for the Pompadour, who was then true king of France, was a liberalist, — but in order to gain certain political ends.

In the course of the movement which took place in consequence of the division between court and parliament, the latter denounced the *lettres de cachet* by which government secured its victims, in return for which the leaders in the denouncing body were seized, imprisoned, and an attempt made to organize other courts to take the place of the parliaments; but the plan did not succeed, the court was too weak to carry through its measures, the parliament triumphed, and the Jesuits were thrown into the shade for a while. This was in 1754.

Behind these jarring and quarrelling bodies stood the firm little band of atheistical philosophers, ready and willing to do battle with them all. Republics were not talked of as applicable to France, it is true, but in the abstract, as the phrase is, they were applauded to the skies. Louis the Fourteenth was looked back upon with contempt and dislike, because of his selfish and unprincipled profusion of blood and treasure; the reigning king was heartily and rightfully held in execration. Indeed, the proofs were many, that the French monarchy was approaching a crisis; Louis the Fifteenth himself said, that it was very old, but would last his time, he thought. But our *philosophers*, while they despised the court, were too wise to think the parliaments worthy of support; they saw them to be what they were, monopolies of the worst kind, and only possible in a kingdom which was so wretchedly governed as France. Nothing, in truth, strikes a man of this day of written constitutions more than the perfect chaos which prevailed in France. Most truly did the Great Louis say, "I am the state"; and with scarce less truth might the harlots of his successor have repeated the saying.

But it was against religion, Jesuit and Jansenist, close and liberal, high and low, old and new, against all the *prejudices* which religion had brought in, against priestcraft in every shape, and intolerance in all but themselves, that the philosophers chiefly waged war. Their instincts assured them, that, if they could but succeed in doing away with the sense of duty, the sentiment of reverence, and the recognition of mystery, loyalty to king, and parliaments, and all but self, would soon follow; and their steps were taken accordingly.

It was in 1751 that the *Encyclopædia* began to appear. It was the result of a wish on the part of certain Parisian booksellers to make all they could out of the rapidly increasing taste for various knowledge; and of a desire on the part of a poor and persecuted author to get money, distinction, and that learning which must be acquired in its preparation. Diderot and his publishers accordingly began to pour forth upon the world their new lights, assisted by the whole fraternity of analyzers and atheists, to a greater or less extent. Voltaire had rejoiced when he heard in Prussia of the proposed work, for he had great reliance upon it as a means by which truth and virtue might be established upon a surer ground than religious faith, and the idea of right. Nor was the sage of Ferney mistaken; the Encyclopædia soon proved to be a most complete collection of the new critical opinions held by its editor and his friends. The clergy began to fear; the public was all a-tiptoe; Diderot became, day by day, more noted, and all was going on swimmingly, when a chance hit of the mistress of one of the ministers stopped his labors, and consigned him to prison. This, however, was but for a little while, and the worthy destroyer soon came back to freedom and his labors. The publisher, Le Breton, was alarmed, however; the government showed symptoms of uneasiness, and after the atheist had written, the more careful bookseller blotted, — saving himself some trouble, and the world much vile and worthless matter.

Now, too, was forming that delightful circle of which the Baron d'Holbach was centre. Of the doings of that little world of practical infidelity, Diderot's letters, published by his daughter, have given a broad and terrible picture. We need say nothing of it. There the friends of virtue, based on a love of pleasure, met, and rioted, and read, and flattered each the other. There might be seen Helvetius, the shallowest of them all, taking some guest aside, to talk over with him his book, "De l'Esprit," published in 1758. There might, at times, be heard under discussion Rousseau, whose strange views of man and society were dividing the thoughts of men, and rivalling the fame of the Encyclopædia itself, but whose admiration of the whole spirit of the life of Christ was not to be tolerated by the liberalists of Grandval.

Of the admiration of those liberalists for one another, we can have but a faint idea. Voltaire they looked upon as the highest specimen of nature's handiwork; he was called by them the apostle of goodness. Diderot was compared with Plato and Cicero; he has not, said his friends, less light of intellect, warmth of imagination, or goodness and purity of heart, than those great men. To talk of Diderot's purity is bitter mockery; but let us look for one instant at the code of moral action proposed by an abbé, the Abbé Raynal, author of the History of the Indies. "I will do good," thus his catechism began, "because it is agreeable"; which, being translated, brings us to the rule that we should do whatever is agreeable; a rule rigidly followed by Louis the Fifteenth, by Philip of Orleans, by Mirabeau, Robespierre, Napoleon; in truth, it was the great rule of the Revolution, and may explain some of its strangest scenes; for what is it but this,—Follow the dictates of thy passions? This rule, and most of the notions of the purer minds of that time, were based upon a total disbelief in man's sick and depraved nature. Raynal thought virtue would be as pleasant as honey to all men.

So stood matters in France during the last twenty years of the miserable Louis. Defeated by England, in the war of 1756; thwarted at home by his provincial parliaments, which were reducing to practice the democratic tendencies of the age; hated by the Jesuits, whom he had once undertaken to support, but had at last been obliged to abandon, in obedience to the Pompadour and the nation; suspected by all the clergy, who, already possessors of one third of the kingdom, groaned because a decree prevented their gaining the remainder; despised by the philosophers, feared and disliked by the middling classes, and made a mere tool of by his courtiers; it was only the force of habit that prevented the nation from rising, and casting him from the throne. His new mistress, Dubarry, was not far from right when she hung the portrait of Charles the First before him, and bade him beware the fate of that monarch. The Duke of Choiseul, who headed the liberal party against the Jesuits and their friends, for a time warded off the great pressure upon the old institutions; but Choiseul fell before the influence of Dubarry, and in his place was put D'Aiguillon, a well known and thoroughly hated upholder of the old forms and influences, religious and political. In Brittany, where he had been governor, and where the liberal ideas, as to property, government, and faith, were as strong as in any part of France, he was utterly hated, and had been engaged in an open quarrel with the parliament. This quarrel was brought, for settlement before the parliament of Paris, and there decided against the Duke. Notwithstanding this decision, the king made him minister, and then reprimanded the parliament, tearing from their registers the record of their sentence. At once, the parliament, whose influence was felt throughout the whole kingdom, ceased to act as a court of justice. Its members were then seized by the military, and, still refusing to act, were degraded from office, and exiled to various points. These were strong steps, for, though neither the *philosophers* nor people had much confidence in the parliaments, yet, at that moment, they stood the representatives of freedom. The government, seeing the danger that existed, and fearing popular commotion, determined to take one strong, popular step, and promised to the nation new courts, new laws, and new proceedings, all to be in accordance with the prevailing ideas of the time, which favored freedom, and looked toward equality.

From that day, perhaps, the Revolution might properly be dated; for from that day the vague wishes and unspoken plans of the oppressed people began to find voice and form. The proposition of a change of gearing (to go back to our original illustration), to suit the new spirit, came from government, and when the question was asked, What machinist shall make this change? the answer was inevitably, "The whole nation, the States General." So do the events of this world come about. For the most selfish ends, D'Aiguillon and his fellows climbed into the chair of state, in opposition to the liberal will of the country; and to secure themselves there, and make peace with that will, proposed a measure which no liberalist had, as yet, dared to propose openly and seriously.

The measure proposed by the new ministry was a reform of the prevailing evils; but among their leading acts were an increase of taxes upon the poor, and a diminution of the interest on the public debt one half. It was clear that such acts would lead to reform in a way not to be desired; for the people were starving, and the moneyed classes, to whom much of the debt belonged, were as little disposed to be plucked, as moneyed men in general.

In 1770 Choiseul left the ministry; in 1774 Louis the Wretched died. Of his deathbed, with all its horrible, disgusting, ridiculous, and noble accompaniments, — for the devotion of his neglected daughters was noble, — Carlyle gives a picture so vivid, so minute, so true, that our flesh creeps as we read it. His History opens with the death of that monarch, when the French kingship, as he says, was dying too; and from that time on he gives a most wonderful sketch of the progress of events. We cannot extract from him, —

38 *

we do not care to make the useless attempt of epitomizing him. We say to the reader, go and study the first books of Carlyle's History, forgetting the peculiar style, or analyzing it, and acknowledging its beauties; and then study any of the other writers upon the Revolution, and you will see how true it is that imagination is the power which an historian needs to use, and will own the eminence of the Scotchman in that particular. No writer has approached him in the explanation of the first movements towards the bloody catastrophe of 1792.

Leaving him, therefore, we will briefly close our view of the incipient stages of the Revolution, by a glance at the events of Louis the Sixteenth's reign, which preceded the summoning of the States General in 1788.

When the old king died, there was general rejoicing; for in the young one the people hoped to find a friend and help. And had Louis the Martyr possessed the moral power of some of his ancestors, he might have saved France. When his reign began, there was immense physical suffering in France; great poverty among the working classes, and very heavy taxes, which fell wholly on them and the other commoners. These taxes resulted from the profusion of Louis the Great in war, and of Louis the Wretched upon his prostitutes, a hundred million livres having been spent in that cause. Louis the Sixteenth wished to relieve this misery, for he and his queen were young and tender-hearted; but he had been brought up with high religious notions, and though he instantly turned out the infamous ministry then in place, it was only to install the feeblest of ministers, Maurepas, in whom his father had had some confidence. Maurepas, however, was less of an absolutist than when known to the Dauphin; since that time he had had some connection with the philosophers, and had caught some of the spirit then prevalent. Accordingly, when appointed prime minister, he chose as governor of the finance department Turgot, a thorough liberalist and economist of the new school. This was a great step for the thinkers of the day, — they had now their representative in the administration. But, alas! it was only for a little season; for the whole mass of privileged people, nobles, clergy, and parliaments, took up arms against the radical reforms proposed by Turgot, and after a vain effort on the part of the king to support him, he was dismissed. Here, then, we have another step in the revolutionary process, — the union of the privileged classes against the popular party, and a refusal by them to share in the burdens of the state; for that was the point in dispute.

To Turgot soon succeeded Necker, his opponent upon points of theoretic economy, but his fellow-laborer in the great cause of liberalism. He, too, had soon to march, having first, however, effected one great step, namely, a representation of the commons equal to the united representation of the nobles and clergy, in certain provincial assemblies which he instituted. Before that time, the idea never prevailed that the commons could be more than a third of the interests to be represented in any assembly, and of course the privileged orders could easily control them. The example which Necker's new arrangement gave was remembered and improved upon by the bolder spirits that came after him.

While Necker was in the ministry for the first time, another event also took place, which excited indirectly a very great influence upon France; this was the American Revolution. In the result of that struggle, and in the form and character of the government which grew from it, and which, in spite of its faults, had that popular character which charmed the suffering subjects of a despotic prince, the more sanguine patriots of France saw much to admire and struggle for.

Before the close of the American contest, another change had taken place in France, which hastened the rapidly approaching dissolution of the monarchy; — this was the acquisition by the queen of a strong influence over her royal husband, who had hitherto had little reliance upon her. The consequence of this change was an identification of both king and queen with the anti-popular party. And as a great deal had been hoped from the accession to the throne of a young and pure prince, just so much additional disappointment and bitterness came from the failure of that prince to relieve those deep-rooted evils which nothing but a total social change could have removed. Nay, the very failures of the seasons were charged upon poor Louis and his ministry; and famishing men cried aloud against the government, because God had cut short the harvest. When, therefore, it was supposed that the privileged classes, through the queen, had gained the king's confidence, and that the people were to have no help, there was general lamenting. To lower the queen in the eyes of the people, stories were put in circulation as to her conduct, which added to the growing dislike of her. She was an Austrian, haughty and unwise, and every day increased the dissatisfaction.

Meanwhile Calonne had become financier, and tried by a system of beggary and expense to make all the wrong right; but daily the deficiency of means in the national treasury increased. Finding the nation rapidly verging to bankruptcy, and that some new taxes must be laid, Calonne in desperation determined to try Necker's plan, and tax the privileged classes; but he proposed to do this by their own consent, which he hoped to gain we know not how. Accordingly, early in 1787, the leaders of the privileged classes, or notables, were called together, and the measures laid before them. To be made to pay their share of the public burdens was, however, no part of the calculation of the nobles, and still less of the clergy. To avoid the need of doing any thing for the public, those who favored the old state of things turned against Calonne, because of his wasteful expenditure, and those who, with La Fayette, favored a new *régime*, cried out upon the ministers for utter inadequacy and worthlessness. He fell, and was succeeded by Lomenie de Brienne. Lomenie was very ambitious, very wicked, and very weak ; he wished to avoid the general land tax proposed by his predecessors, and yet he found it impossible to do so. He hesitated, and stammered, and doubted awhile, and then laid an edict, imposing such a tax, before parliament. The parliament was fully of the mind to reject it, upon two grounds, — the one, that it took money from them ; the other, that, by taxing the privileged orders, the balance against the power of the crown would be destroyed, and the monarch become an absolute despot. Of the first reason little was said, and of the last what was said was said in whispers. But, though thus minded, the parliament was unwilling to take the whole opprobrium of rejecting a measure desired by the country, and flatly declared themselves unable to lay taxes, thus abandoning the claim which they had upheld for ages, in order to save themselves. They even went farther, and said that the States General, representing the nation, could alone tax the nation.

The minister, vexed at this unlooked for declaration, was weak enough to force the parliament to register the proposed tax ; a step against which they at once protested, and, assuming the popular side against the court, declared the forced registry void. The minister exiled them. But in exile no business was done, and clients cried aloud. Brienne then bargained with the parliament for a new loan to meet immediate necessity, and they came back to Paris. But they came only to be threatened with a worse fate, for means were secretly taken to annihilate this refractory body and its fellows in the provinces, and substitute others. The parliaments got wind of the plan, however, and refused to be annihilated. They were then forcibly dismissed, though throughout the whole of France with trouble, discord, and opposition.

And now the demand was general for the assemblage of the representatives of the nation; for all were sick of the perpetual contest around the throne. Even the court thought it best to have the estates convened. Brienne, meanwhile, becoming penniless, and a mob being feared in consequence of the excitement, he was dismissed, and Necker reinstated. By him it was decided, that the commons should have half the representatives in the States General, which met, as all know, on the 5th of May, 1789. From that day the Revolution is usually dated.

We have now hastily, but we trust intelligibly, given the outline of those events which we wish to recall to the minds of our readers, dwelling longest upon those positions to which we more particularly would call their attention.

The efficient cause of the French Revolution was the entire want of adaptation in the political and social relations of the country to the spirit of the time. It is wonderful how a society so constituted could hold together at all. Priesthood against parliament, parliament against court, court against people; — the balance was preserved by means of ceaseless internal discord, — threatening every few years to end in a revolution. The *efficient cause* of the Revolution was, we say, the injustice and iniquity of the political and social systems of France; systems which all true men were, and should have been, rejoiced to see in the way to change.

The *immediate or exciting cause* was the derangement of the finances. This was the bolt in the machine which fell from its place, and produced the crash; but this fell from its place only because of the deep and long-continued derangement of the whole of society.

The *character* of the Revolution was owing to an entirely different set of causes, in a great measure, from those which produced the movement itself; and to these we wish to call our readers' thoughts, for it was in the character of the Revolution that its chief evils lay, and from that we think our country may learn many lessons. What the character referred to was, we need not say; it is a proverb over the whole earth; we shall but attempt to show whence that character mainly came.

We believe that it came from a want of reverence; that it was the result of a total absence of that sentiment of veneration, which is the only groundwork of a deep sense of right, an efficient feeling of duty, and an upright life.

What is man without that sentiment of veneration? What being can be more miserable than the human being who looks up and sees no God; who looks around him, and in the movements of nature and the events of life sees no mysterious and venerable agency; to whom the world is a lifeless clod, and its master shallow chance? No orphan is as destitute as he. He has lost his father indeed. He is without help, guide, or adviser. The earth, and all that is on it, he has comprehended; he has solved all mystery, and laid bare to his intellect all secret things. Virtue is to him enlightened self-interest, and vice mere folly. Right he defines to be the way of comfort, convenience, and pleasure; and duty the instinctive desire of happiness. He walks under the stars and sun, and with his instruments ascertains their movements, and measures their heavenly paths; but the mystery of their whole being is hid from him, and he looks up at them, not reverently, but scientifically, not in humility, but in pride. He walks among his fellow-men, and reads their history, and witnesses their actions, and in all he sees the influence of circumstances; he looks at the relation of man and woman, and, it may be, thinks it well for the state that marriage is customary, but the existence of any principle bearing upon that relation, but convenience and brute pleasure, he denies; chastity is to him desirable, provided the state wants peopling, but in a land already full he would have every woman a prostitute. And man, the living man, is what? A strange growth of a strange world.

An animal whose organization allows him to know, speak, think, and act more perfectly than brutes. The life of man has no sacredness to him, for sacred implies reverential feeling. If murder is blameworthy, it is because the state needs its members, or because insecurity of life is unpleasant; not because the taking of life is awful in itself. The man without veneration has no rule to walk by, save that of the Abbé Raynal, — to do what is agreeable; and if he be brought to a bloodthirsty mood, why, he will drink blood.

Now the French people had been long drifting toward utter faithlessness, utter irreverence. The veneration called loyalty had died out, from the absence in those, toward whom it should have been felt, of all the qualities that could command it. The reverence for the ceremonies and ministers of the Church had passed by, too, as those ministers became worthless or wicked, and those ceremonies forms instead of symbols. The respect for woman had ceased with the cessation of self-respect among the leading women of the land. The respect for property had passed, for the right to property was disputed and denied, and the unholy distribution and use of it undeniable. The reverence for life had disappeared with the coming in of a philosophy among the thinking, and a second-hand belief among the unthinking, which made man a happy accident, a fortunate formation, with a mind of excellent white paper, and capital *Daguerreotype* senses to write upon it. Virtue was no longer venerable, for a good man was, in Diderot's phrase, good luck. Lastly, all reverence for God was gone, because there was no God. One reverence only remained, a reverence for actual, living, acting men; — for Voltaire and his fellow-thinkers; for Mirabeau and his fellow-workers; for Robespierre and his fellow-pretenders; for Napoleon, the thinker, worker, and pretender in one. This reverence could not die out as the rest did, for it rested, not on faith, but on sight.

With the views now presented, the character of the French Revolution may be partially, at least, understood; though, at last, one of the greatest mysteries itself that man has looked on.

We wonder, sometimes, at the September massacres and the Reign of Terror; that women should come with their work, and witness the executions with the composure of those that look on the mock-murders of the stage; but with their views of the life of man, what was death by the guillotine? No more than death by the sword is to the soldier. The September slayers embraced and wept over the true men whom they were not bound to slay; but when an aristocrat, or, in other words, a foe, criminal, and oppressor, was thrown out to them, their axes crushed his skull with the same good-will which winged the rifle-balls of our brothers of the frontier, when an Indian crossed their path. Most truly does Carlyle say, when speaking of Montgaillard's statement that four thousand persons were slain in the Reign of Terror, — "It is a horrible sum of human lives, M. l'Abbé; some ten times as many shot rightly on a field of battle, and one might have had his glorious victory, with *Te Deum*."

And now we must seek, most briefly, to apply whatever we have learned from the French Revolution to our own time and our own country: for safe as we may feel from revolution, it is very evident that we are not safe from those causes which we suppose to have given its dreadful character to the struggle in France, — and which may in some way affect our welfare and overthrow our hopes.

The cause which we have supposed gave color to the French Revolution was the want of reverence. In feudal times, reverence was universal, except, perhaps, among a few of the best informed. As the world has grown older, the veneration for things formerly venerated has disappeared, because, too often, acquaintance has proved them to be undeserving; and, while the old objects have ceased to be venerated, new objects, deserving reverence, have not been brought before us. In addition to this, the success which attended analysis and logic as applied to matter, and many old prejudices and habits, has given us an undue faith in those processes, and men incline to trust and rely upon no truths save those reached through logic and analysis. In the United States, all favors the growth of confidence in the intelligible only; of reliance upon the tangible, the useful, the comprehensible. Efforts have been made from time to time to introduce among us more faith and reverence, and, if we are not mistaken, there is reason to think a philosophy now in progress that will help to sustain those efforts; but, as yet, the favorers of reverence are few and scattered, separated by religious, or political, or social differences, — and the want of respect and veneration presents daily greater and greater dangers. Children do not reverence their parents, chiefly because those parents reverence nothing themselves. How can a father hope to be respected, who never expresses, by word or act, respect for his fellow-men or his Maker. Independence is, in our land, mistaken for freedom.

There was another circumstance, also, which has had a great influence upon us. Our country owed much to Mr. Jefferson, and was disposed to receive much from him; for, of our prominent men, he most thoroughly embodied the popular spirit of the time: thence came his power. But that spirit, in Jefferson, was from the outset of a French turn, and, after his residence in France, was most peculiarly and strikingly French. The contest between Jefferson and his opponents was not, essentially, about measures or forms; it was the unceasing struggle of change and conservatism, and, on his part, was tinctured with the true French feeling of denial, analysis, and irreverence. His Declaration of Independence, — let none think we speak of it, or its signers, irreverently; they saw it not from the point of view which we are taking, — his famous Declaration, unconsciously to himself, recorded his spiritual faith; it declares man's rights to be "life, liberty, and the pursuit of happiness." How much truer and nobler those original articles of confederation between the New England colonies, in which, not the pursuit of happiness, but the advancement of "the kingdom of our Lord Jesus Christ," and the enjoyment of "the liberties of the Gospel, in purity and peace," are said to have brought the Pilgrims across the ocean. Not that these *terms* could have been used by Mr. Jefferson; but the difference between him and the Puritans was much deeper than a difference of terms or of subjects; it was that which marked the French as distinguished from the English Revolution; which divides the pursuit of happiness from the pursuit of right.

We do think our country, then, in danger of becoming irreverent, irreligious, and sensual, rather than spiritual. We see among all, of every political creed, and every religious faith, a disposition to bring the universe of thought, sentiment, and feeling to the touchstone of the understanding. We are sadly afraid of mysteries. We want to comprehend every thing; to walk by sight, and not by faith. But we see, also, — thanks be to God! — among those of every political creed, and every religious faith, some who stand out from, and opposed to, the prevalent idea; men whose first philosophical principle is the recognition of mystery everywhere; whose ground of religious faith is full reliance, deep devotion, unquestioning self-sacrifice. Let them battle, undismayed by ridicule, abuse, contempt! Let them seek, untiringly, to present to men better grounds of hope and life, than are given by the philosophy of Locke, the ethics of Paley, the theology of Priestley.

It is a very common saying, that our freedom rests upon our national character; and men rush in crowds to the great cause of popular education. The saying is a true one, and education is sadly wanted; but mere education is not enough; it must be a religious education, or the influence of it, in preserving our liberties, will be slight. Liberty cannot live with irreverence. Liberty is one of the great conditions of spiritual growth; except on that account, it is worthless; unless that is going on, liberty will cease, from simple uselessness. A nation spiritually degraded cannot be free, let the government be what it may, for it has no use for freedom. But without reverence, there cannot be spiritual growth. The higher powers shrink and wither in the shallow soil of man's wisdom, and the philosophy of the understanding. Without reverence, then, there can be no abiding freedom, for it would be unmeaning. You may call a republic of unbelievers free, but that republican form confers no liberty; it may give scope to licentiousness, but it can confer no liberty. The land in which the mass rules is not the free land; that is the home of freedom where the truth rules. That is no true democracy in which all are on a level merely; the true democracy is that in which all are brothers, — some elder, some younger, but all helping one another. A democracy is impossible on any other than Christian principles.

"We boast our light," says Milton, "but if we look not wisely on the sun itself, it smites us into darkness." Let us, in this favored land, beware how we look upon the sun of freedom, for if we look not wisely, it will indeed smite us into darkness; and "the fear of the Lord is the *beginning* of wisdom."

We learn, then, from the French Revolution, the infinite dangers of national irreverence. For, be it noted as our faith at least, it was not the ignorance of the mass that caused that convulsion to be black with gore, but it was their irreverence. Had the mass been ignorant and reverent, and the few wise and reverent, the French Revolution had never been what it was. Look, how it paused, and crept to the abyss unwillingly, as if nature recoiled from the plunge into Jacobinism, and longed to turn at every step. She would have stayed the movement with constitutional reform; but alas! that reform was based on denial, and the *right* to be happy; it was the reform of sentimental abbés, and sneering *philosophers*, who proclaimed man's right to rule himself, and to be virtuous, — if it was agreeable; and so constitutional reform, and monarchy, passed into an unconstitutional republicanism. But a republic, a commonwealth, resting on individual selfishness, and the love of pleasure or power, was too absurd a thing even to assume shape; and it sunk, like frost in the sunbeams, into that Jacobinism which was the natural, true, genuine, and only fabric that selfishness and the love of pleasure would and could support. There is one supreme ruler in every man's breast, and one only; the sense of duty requiring the realization of right. Let that rule a man, and outward bonds fall from him like cords of tow from red-hot iron. Law, outward restraint, applies only to the partially or wholly irreverent and undutiful. But to the man who lacks the sense of duty, outward law must and will be applied. We say "will be," for let him live where he may, under despot or demagogue, he cannot fly that outward restraint which God has ordained that every one shall bear, who is not free through the truth. And the French Revolution wrote upon our earth, in letters of blood and fire, that as it is with the individual, so it is with the nation; that to trust in the wisdom of man, to rely upon the understanding of man, to leave the mysterious and cling to the intelligible only, to give up faith and confide in sight only, to substitute the love of happiness for the sense of duty, and the equality of the whole for the Christian brotherhood of the whole, is to take the sure way to crime, and disappointment, and slavery, and self-reproach.

XII.

A GLIMPSE OF AUSTRALIA.*

Since Pisistratus Caxton, his wild cousin, and speculative uncle, thought it worth their while to seek their fortunes in Australia, perhaps some review-readers may not be unwilling to take a trip there too, especially if they can do it in their arm-chairs, and without being exposed to winds strong enough to spoil a cigar, or disturb a quiet nap. In England, Australia is rather a pet topic, and books innumerable are published in respect to it; but few or none of them are reprinted on this side of the Atlantic, and not many among us, unless from some special cause, turn their studies toward the south-

---

* 1. *Two Expeditions into the Interior of Southern Australia.* By Captain Charles Sturt. Second Edition. London. 1834. 2 vols.

2. *An Historical and Statistical Account of New South Wales, &c.* By John Dunmore Lang, D. D. Second Edition. London. 1837. 2 vols.

3. *Physical Description of New South Wales.* By P. E. Strzelecki. London. 1845.

4. *Discoveries in Australia in* 1837 - 43. By J. Lott Stokes. London. 1846.

5. *Journal of an Overland Expedition in Australia from Moreton Bay to Port Essington.* By Dr. Ludwig Leichhardt. London. 1847.

6. *Journal of an Expedition into the Interior of Tropical Australia.* By Lieut.-Col. Sir P. Mitchell. London. 1848.

From the North American Review, for January, 1850.

ern land of wonders. Her egg-laying quadrupeds, black swans, and marvels of all sorts, which, as Sydney Smith says, rendered the latter half of Dr. Shaw's life miserable by their oddities, and filled Sir Joseph Banks "with mingled emotions of distress and delight," are now old stories, familiar to every child; while the more serious problems of her agricultural and commercial capabilities, her future political condition and moral influence, have hardly attracted the eye of any one who is not concerned in the immediate, pressing, practical problems of emigration. Indeed, we suspect many of those on this side of the water who have followed the fortunes of our "Anachronism," were forced to go to an atlas to know where the famous city of "Adelaide" was situated, and have puzzled their brains not a little, endeavouring to form, by the help of Mr. Pisistratus Caxton's note, a clear conception of what is meant by "the Wakefield."

As we have heretofore said little as to this second New World, which, looked at from the right point of view, is "farther west" even than Oregon or California, we embrace the present moment, and Mr. Caxton's introduction, to enter, examine, and imperfectly describe it.

And first, let us get a clear idea, if we can, of its size. Maps deceive us sadly. The wisest, even, scarce escape the optical delusion of thinking that that country is large which looks large on the map. As England, therefore, has commonly one sheet at least to herself, and England's youngest child, New Holland, only the corner of a sheet, we very naturally think of our antarctic sister as but a little affair. When we look closely, however, the proportions of this young land of the Anglo-Saxon change wonderfully. Should we place her northern point, for example, on the northern point of Maine, her southern would fall somewhere south of Cuba, or in the latitude of the city of Mexico; while longitudinally, her eastern extremity being as far "down" as Cape Cod itself, her western would not fall short of the new Mormon settlement by the great Salt Lake, beyond the Rocky Mountains. Or if we compare her rounded, compact area with our more scattered and outstretched domain, we shall find that she numbers about as many million square miles as we do, Texas, New Mexico, California, and all.* This, then, is the land we propose to visit; not a little, out-of-the-way island, but truly a New World. Thinly peopled, poorly cultivated, scarce known beyond the coast, it is true; but when as many years had elapsed after the settlement of Jamestown as have passed since the founding of Sydney,† namely, sixty-one, the colony of South Carolina was not in existence. New York had been but four years under the flag of England. "Jamestown was but a place of a State-house, one church, and eighteen houses, occupied by about a dozen families"; New England did not number fifty-five thousand souls; "Berkshire (in Massachusetts) was a wilderness"; "Lancaster and Brookfield, solitary settlements of Christians in the desert,"‡ and not a white man, save the half-apocryphal De Soto, had seen the prairies, or struggled through the forests of the West. Let the slow, early colonial growth of our own rapidly growing land teach us not to despise the comparative feebleness of Australia; it is impossible, by their size merely, to distinguish the new-born oak from the most trivial weed of the meadow.

And now, having a somewhat tangible notion of the extent of this island-continent, let us briefly recall the story of its discovery, its exploration, the facts brought to light by

---

* Say three million square miles. Murray's *Encyclopædia of Geography*, (American edition,) Vol. III. pp. 323, 371. — McCullock's *Gazetteer*, article "Australia."

† Sometimes incorrectly written Sidney. It was named after Lord Sydney, Secretary of State for the Home Department, in 1787. See Collins, quoted by Lang, Vol. I. p. 25.

‡ Bancroft, Vol. II. pp. 212, 92.

those who have explored it, its colonial ups and downs,—look into its present condition,—and thus try to realize this, to so many of us, mere nominal thing, "New Holland."

In the king's library at the British Museum is a chart by a French draftsman, dated 1542, and probably the same referred to by Rear Admiral Burney as drawn by Rotz, in which a coast is laid down that would appear to be the shores of Australia; but we know nothing of the voyages upon which this map was based. Sixty-four years later, in 1606, Pedro Fernandez de Quiros and Luis Vaes de Torres, sailing from Callao, in Peru, made a more or less complete examination of the northern part of the great "Terra Australis Incognita"; and the latter, who was second in command, even discovered the straits which bear his name. Nothing, however, came from this Spanish discovery, except countless memorials from the commanders to the king, praying him to colonize the new continent of the South; to all which suggestions and entreaties the court turned a deaf ear, for Spain was then just falling asleep, and, in the very year after the discoveries of Quiros, at the very time he was penning his memorials, probably, lost the Moluccas,* with their cloves and nutmegs, to the insatiable Dutch, and was nearly cut off by those busybodies from all her colonies, east and west. Then came the persevering Hollanders themselves upon the stage. The Duyfhen, a Dutch yacht, seems indeed to have touched near Cape York in 1605, but it was by mere accident; and those who were in her knew not what they had seen. But the labors of Dirk Hartog, in the good ship Endragt, extending from 1616 to 1622, were not labors wholly in the dark, though still it was the "great unknown south land" along whose western shores Dirk Hartog sailed, and upon the borders of whose bays he left memo-

* The Moluccas belonged to Portugal, but Spain and Portugal were then united.

rials of his visits.* The hero of Dutch discovery in regard to Australia, however, inasmuch as he sailed round it, was Tasman, Abel Janez Tasman, who — sailing from Batavia in 1642, during the rule of the excellent Anthony Van Diemen — passed west and south of New Holland; discovered the land which bears the name of the worthy governor; and continuing beyond Australia, he brought up against, and made known to the world, New Zealand. Finding but a murderous reception there, he pursued his course northward, and, after many perils, and visiting many new and strange places, at last reached Java again in safety. It would be no more than justice to the first circumnavigator of the southern continent, should the name "Tasmania" at last drive out the title of Van Diemen's Land," as at the present time it bids fair to do.

But the swarms from the Low Countries found nothing along the dry and barren coasts of Australia to tempt a settlement. No spices, nor jewels, nor precious metals; not even water enough to make a canal possible. So the shores which were visited by Hartog, and De Witt, and Nuyt, and Tasman, remained silent and desert as ever.

At length, in 1688, England began to bear her part in Australian research, her representative being the well-born, but, as we think in these times, not well-behaved, buccaneer, William Dampier. This celebrated and successful navigator made two visits to New Holland; first, in the capacity of a pirate or "privateer" (for so the fraternity called themselves), and next as the commander of his Majesty's ship Roebuck. His examinations were confined for the most part to the west and northwest coasts, which he found by no means inviting, neither soil nor inhabitants being such as to win any one's affections. Of the people he says, they "are the miserablest people in the world. The Hodmadods of

---

* King, Vol. II. p. 180.

Monomatapa,* though a nasty people, yet for wealth are gentlemen to these, who have no houses and skin-garments, sheep, poultry, and fruits of the earth, ostrich eggs, &c. . . . . . . They have great bottle-noses, pretty full lips, and wide mouths. They are long-visaged, and of a very unpleasant aspect, having no one graceful feature in their faces." In most respects, the accounts given by Dampier prove to be perfectly correct; he was a close observer, and had he fallen upon the eastern instead of the western coast, the colonization of Australia might have commenced more than half a century earlier than it did. As it was, the voyages of the British buccaneer effected no more than those of his Dutch predecessors had done.

From that time until Cook began to unravel the mazes of the Pacific and Australian seas, New Holland was left to her bottle-nosed savages, — her Indians, as they were termed, down almost to our own days. In April, 1770, however, the great circumnavigator, approaching, not from the north or west, as other discoverers had done, but from the east, came upon a shore which was green, fertile, well watered, and pleasant of aspect. Anchoring in a harbour, the shores of which furnished such treasures to the collections of Mr. Joseph Banks, afterwards the world-renowned Sir Joseph, that the bay was named Botany Bay, Cook began to make acquaintance with the advantages of the neighbouring country; and, coasting thence northward, examined and named in succession inlet after inlet, point after point. Of the north, west, and south coasts he saw nothing, and of the eastern, south of Botany Bay, learned no details. Nor was much added to his information during his after voyages, no other part of Australia being examined, and only so much of Tasmania as left it still, on the map, the southern extremity of its continental neighbour.

---

* East coast of Africa, back of Mozambique.

So stood geography sixty-two years since, Alexander Humboldt being at the time eighteen years of age, when the first body of convicts left England for Botany Bay. Let us see how much it amounted to. New Holland, which in those days of darkness included Van Diemen's Land, had been sailed round, and its dimensions and shape pretty well ascertained. Its western shore had been examined for a few miles inward, and found thirsty and inhospitable; its eastern had been skirted, and its comparative fertility and pleasantness placed beyond doubt. The natives were known to be extremely uncivilized, but neither very warlike nor very cruel, and appeared to be by no means numerous. No fruits or vegetables of value had been discovered by the industry of Banks and his companions; and no animal worthy of notice except the kangaroo. The shores were clothed for the most part with a sombre forest of evergreens, the mass of them unknown elsewhere; coral reefs skirted the coast in many parts; water was by no means abundant upon the whole, and in the west was sadly wanting; the power of the sun was such as the torrid zone and its vicinity might reasonably be expected to feel; and though hills and mountains rose in the distance, they did not seem to possess great height, or to promise valleys or table-lands of fertility among or beyond them.

Meanwhile, England needed a new outlet for her criminal population. America would receive them no more; the labors of Howard and of the Quakers had opened the eyes of men to the horrors of European prisons; the punishment of death for trivial crimes was becoming every day more and more offensive to the hearts and consciences of the masses. In this state of things, of growing crime and a growing indisposition to use the old home remedies, how natural to go back freely to the ancient constitutional depletive of transportation;* and what land of exile so fitting as that lately

* Dating from 39th Eliz., Chap. IV., A. D. 1597.

visited by Cook? So, in the early spring of 1787, a fleet of eleven sail mustered at Portsmouth to form the new colony of criminals at the south: six transports, three store-ships, a frigate, and a tender; the whole conveying six hundred male and two hundred and fifty female convicts, together with some two hundred and fifty soldiers, or rather marines, and forty of their wives. Over the whole presided Captain Arthur Philip, of the navy, who was to be first governor of New South Wales. The fleet sailed May 13th, and reached Botany Bay from the 18th to the 20th of the following January.

It was not an uneventful time. During the passage of that fleet, "The Ohio Company," which first settled our great Northwest, bought their lands of Congress; the ordinance that makes slavery impossible in that young empire was framed by the dying Confederation; Washington and his associates fashioned the constitution under which we live; while in Europe the political caldron began to simmer,— the parliament of Paris was "transported" for refusing to register the new taxes asked for by the court, and Philippe Egalité took open part against the king.

Into the details of Australian history we cannot, of course, enter. But we may notice three leading sources of trouble to the early inhabitants. The first was the proportion of the criminal population; proportion we say, for it was not intended or attempted to make the colony a mere prison, a larger jail. Free emigrants, men of means, and enterprise, and character, were encouraged from the outset to seek in the new settlement a field for investment and profitable labor.* But no high tone of character, no proper spirit of industry, no decency or moral purity even, could prevail in a colony the vast mass of which consisted of the most idle

* See letters of Governor Phillip and Secretary Dundas on this subject. Lang, Vol. I. pp. 39–43.

and abandoned of mankind. For years, the settlers of Sydney, unmolested by the natives, were dependent upon England for the bread they eat, and more than once nearly starved to death;* while the pioneers in Ohio, who reached their camping-ground not quite three months after the Australians moored in Port Jackson, raised their corn, their flax, their cotton even, spun their thread and wove their cloth, — and all in the face of the most formidable savages that the Anglo-Saxon has yet had to deal with.† Nor has England learned, until within the last few years, that her system of transporting the refuse of her population will never answer, unless, even after all the reformation which can be effected before they go, they are made so small a portion of the colony to which they migrate as to receive its character, not give their character to it.

The second cause from which the young New Holland nation suffered, ay, and yet suffers, was and is *the want of women*. It is a subject we cannot and need not dwell on; but whoever knows any thing of human nature, and especially of convict nature, knows that where masses of hardened men are collected together, and women are rare, there is not a vice which can, — we will not say brutalize, for the brutes are pure and true to their natures, — but which can *Yahoo* mankind, that is not soon forthcoming.

The third cause of idleness, low tastes, low morals, and slow progress in the realm of Botany Bay, was the unprecedented use of rum, which became at last the colonial currency, being the only thing universally desired.‡ During Governor King's administration, "from 1800 to 1806," says Dr. Lang,§ "the population of New South Wales consisted

---

* For three years, said an old settler to Mr. Lang, I lived in the constant belief that I should some day perish with hunger. Lang, Vol. I. p. 56.

† Hildreth's *Pioneer History*, p. 302, &c.

‡ Lang, Vol. I. p. 96. § Ibid., p. 81.

chiefly of those who sold rum, and those who drank it. Even the chief constable of Sydney, whose business it was to repress irregularity, had a license to promote it, under the Governor's hand, by the sale of rum and other ardent liquors; and although the chief jailer was not exactly permitted to convert his Majesty's jail into a grog-shop, he had a licensed house in which he sold rum publicly on his own behalf, right opposite the jail door."* We must not, however, leave it to be inferred that Governor King was so munificent in his licenses from mere love of mischief; the fact being that he was trying a sort of homœopathic experiment. He found upon his accession the leaders of society, and especially the officers of the military corps, the "New South Wales Corps," which had been raised for the colony, engaged in a monopoly of spirits that was immensely profitable, though immensely pernicious; and he was trying to dry up the streams of alcohol by diminishing the profits of those who dealt therein. He had also in view the lessening of the influence of his Pretorians, who were rapidly becoming too strong for the civil power, and whom he hoped to counterbalance by the emancipists† and free settlers to whom he gave the *entrée* of the rum traffic. He failed, however, in all points. The "New South Wales Corps" lost none of the influence which it had possessed, and rum remained, in spite of governors and clergy, strong measures and weak, prohibitions and licenses, even more influential than the "Corps" itself. Up to 1810, said Captain Kemp of the Pretorians, at a trial in England, "the Governor, clergy, officers civil and military, all ranks and descriptions of people, bartered spirits." "Every description of inhabitants," said, at the same trial, John Macarthur, a leading merchant and paymaster of the "Corps," "were under the necessity of paying for the necessaries of life, for every article of

* Lang, Vol. I. p. 83.

† Freed convicts.

consumption, in that sort of commodity which the people who had to sell were inclined to take," namely, — rum. As to the military, this very John Macarthur, and his friends of the body to which he was paymaster, deposed the successor of Governor King, Governor Bligh, who was a strong opponent of the spirit trade. They placed him in confinement, usurped the supreme power, turned out the old officers and put in new, and for a time were masters of the colony. For this decided step, however, the commander, Major Johnston, was cashiered, and the corps ordered elsewhere.

We have said the colony suffered from three great evils, the abundance of criminals and rum, and the scarcity of women. In a less degree it suffered then, and has, together with other colonies, suffered since, from the infamous system of *nepotism*, — if that word may be stretched so as to take in favoritism toward relatives and connections when practised by profane hands. The results of this system were well displayed in the events which led to the "whiskey rebellion" that overthrew Governor Bligh. That rebellion grew out of the opposition of Macarthur & Co. to the Governor; but sought an excuse in the character of the chief law officer of the colony, Richard Atkins, Judge Advocate, and, under the statutes of Parliament, President Judge. This man, the relative of some one in power at home, and therefore thus raised to authority and influence, was so utterly ignorant of law, that he had to employ the only regularly bred attorney in the colony, one who had been transported for perjury, to do his professional work; he was moreover a drunkard; had pronounced sentence of death, says Governor Bligh, when intoxicated; was irresolute, "his opinion floating and infirm," and wholly unable to keep a secret, however weighty.* Under such circumstances,

* Lang, Vol. I. pp. 113, 134, 150, 441.

certainly not favorable, were laid the foundations of the great antarctic Anglo-Saxon empire.

Two decades of Australian history closed with the deposition of Governor Bligh; a third opened and ended with a ruler who has left his name to rivers and harbours, capes and mountains, hospitals, jails, and roads, — Lachlan Macquarie. Upon his reign, which extended from 1809 to 1821, we must dwell with more detail, as it was marked by the clear presentation of problems, geographical and social, which are not yet wholly solved.

We will first state what these problems were, and how they came to be presented; and afterwards attempt to show in how far, and in what manner, they have as yet been answered.

And, first, as to the geographical. The general outlines of Australia, as we have said, had been ascertained before the time of Cook. That great sailor added to what had been known before a running survey of the eastern shore north of Botany Bay. But when the convict-colony was founded, in 1788, no one knew that Tasmania was a separate island, and the southern shores of Australia had never been examined with any degree of thoroughness. In 1797, however, there came into the sphere of southern research one who explored with such perseverance, and wrote so ably, that his name ought to be scientifically sanctified in the annals of the Australian Academy, — Lieutenant Flinders. As midshipman, he, together with Surgeon Bass, in 1789, explored in small and leaky boats the straits which bear the name of the adventurous doctor; and toward the close of the same year, while Washington was consolidating our Union, and the ruler of Britain's empire was unable to rule his own mind even, and the court of France had gone crazy with royal banquets and its people with king-conquering mobs, — just then, when the women of Paris led Louis prisoner, Flinders and Bass made themselves ready for the trip which, in a few weeks, demonstrated the geographical independence of Tasmania.

But the career of Flinders did not end, it only commenced, with the discovery of Tasmania's isolation; this merit was recognized by the powers at home, and in 1801, with John Franklin, whose name, like a vast *aurora borealis*, now fills the world's horizon, as his subordinate, — he began the survey of Australia's southern coast. During that survey, he discovered the whole of what is now known as the South Australian shore, Spencer Gulf, the Gulf of St. Vincent, and Encounter Bay. And yet those discoveries were almost unwelcome; for the word had gone abroad, no one knew whence, that a vast strait of the ocean passed from the great Australian bight, the Gulf of Carpentaria; and each voyager hoped along that strait to find the Mexico or Peru of New Holland. This strait vanished before our discoverer, and the interior of the southern continent yet remained a mystery.

It was not, however, without a struggle that Flinders abandoned the discovery of the reputed passage. In 1802, renewed and strong, he sailed northward, and strove to find, in the vast bay of Carpenter, some opening which would make accessible the treasures of the interior; but he found, we regret to say, only mud, — infinite flats, and shallows, and bars, and swamps, of mud. Many years passed, and that strange interior was still unknown. The colony of New South Wales had been, meanwhile, drunken with rum and convicts; staggering along from 1788 till 1813, and yet no one had been able to penetrate the rugged and precipitous range of the Blue Mountains, the highest peaks of which are less than one hundred miles from Sydney. But at length, in 1813, came a season of unusual drought. The pastures which lay along the Hawkesbury, the Nepean, and their tributaries, close to the original settlements, were dried up; and as grazing had become the chief occupation of many of the leading agriculturists, it became a most important point to learn what chance for cattle and sheep there was beyond the precipitous defiles which had thus far been the western limits of the colony. Three gentlemen, one of them a barrister, undertook to explore the passes of the hills. These passes (if such impassable ravines deserve the name) are of the most romantic and broken character. The streams flow through valleys bounded by walls of rock, a thousand or fifteen hundred feet in height; Strzelecki * says, he was unable to extricate himself and his men from them "until after days of incessant fatigue, danger, and starvation." Mr. Dixon, the surveyor, in attempting to reach Mount Hay, immediately west of Sydney, was for four days bewildered in the labyrinth of gullies through which flow the River Grose and its branches, and was at length thankful to escape from them alive, leaving the mountain for some more fortunate explorer to climb. Into this wilderness of basalt and sandstone the discoverers of the interior of Australia, urged by the thought of starving herds and scant larders, trusted themselves. Before that time, the most successful attempt to pass the range had been made by Mr. Caley, a botanist, who, having at length reached a point where all around him rose naked masses of weather-stained rock, while deep chasms yawned at intervals, turned back to the abodes of civilized men in despair. But to fill an herbarium is one thing, and to save one's life and property a very different matter. The three travellers, accordingly, urged by necessity, overcame the difficulties which had daunted the botanist, and, after great dangers and sufferings, reached the streams flowing westward, which pointed or led them to a country that seemed to their worn cattle and to themselves a paradise.† A road was instantly commenced;

---

* Page 57.

† The usual uncertainty of history in small matters attaches to these first explorers; Dr. Lang makes one of them, Lawson, a respectable

the whole convict-labor of the colony was devoted to its completion; settlers with their flocks and herds crowded across the before impassable barrier; Bathurst was founded in the valley of a fine stream, named, in honor of the Governor, "Macquarie"; and a new era seemed opening upon the Anglo-Saxon in the great island of the south.

The country beyond the Blue Mountains having been once made known, an examination of it followed as a matter of course. Mr. Evans, who, as deputy of the colonial surveyor, had constructed the road over the hills, was the first to carry on the investigation, and discovered another westward-flowing river, in size and appearance resembling the Macquarie, to which was given the Governor's first name, Lachlan. But where did these streams empty? Through what regions did they run? Were there not, somewhere on their banks, natives more civilized than those which as yet had been seen? Perhaps towns, wealth, the Australian Mexico, for which all adventurers had been looking? To determine these various matters, Mr. Oxley, the surveyor-general, prepared, in 1817, to trace the Lachlan to its mouth. But, strange to say, as he proceeded down its banks, it lessened and lessened, and dwindled away, till all its waters were lost in flooded marshes without end. The next year he tried the Macquarie, and with no better success. It did not, like the African rivers, dry up in deserts of sand, but was swallowed by what appeared to be a vast, shallow lake, covered with reeds, which made it impossible to examine its shores or learn its extent. Disappointed and astonished, the examiner turned back with the conviction, that the centre of Australia was a basin into which its interior rivers flowed, and from which they found no exit; so that the dreams of

---

old settler; Sturt says he was Lieutenant in the 104th regiment. Lang carries them, and some cattle with them, over the mountains; Sturt says they turned back when in sight of the western plains.

wealth, of cities, even of fine farms and countless herds, along the banks of the Macquarie and Lachlan, were forced to disappear as mere castles in the air. Nor was the experience of Mr. Oxley the sole ground of faith in respect to these central waters. The natives, in their hand-and-foot, mumbo-jumbo kind of talk, seemed to describe them; told how they were navigated by canoes, and imitated the spouting of the whales that played in them. So strong was the faith in this mediterranean sea, that, for ten years, no further effort was made to solve the problem as to the nature of the interior.

The western slope of the mountains, which rise not far from the eastern coast, was explored by Oxley, Mechan, Hume, and Allan Cunningham, the king's botanist. The Argyle country was discovered, the heads of the Murray were crossed, the region now known as Australia Felix was traversed and its excellences in part comprehended, while, to the north, partial surveys were made as far as Moreton Bay. Captain King, also, during the period between Oxley's attempt to trace the interior streams in 1817, and Sturt's in 1828, began and completed his survey of the Australian shores, and especially of the northern and western coasts. To these voyages of King we shall have occasion to refer hereafter; but for the present, we wish to keep our attention and that of our readers to the problem of the interior.

At length, in 1828, forty years after Sydney was founded, a second expedition was sent to inquire into the condition of that immense region in the centre of Australia, which had baffled Oxley ten years before, but into which colonists were perpetually pressing. The immediate motive for sending explorers at that time was the existence of a drought which, commencing in 1826, had made new fields and streams the one necessity of life; and which also, it was supposed with reason, must have changed the condition of the marshes that had stopped the previous inquirers, even if it had not wholly dried them up. To the command of this band of investigators was appointed Captain Sturt, the most successful, upon the whole, of Australian explorers. In 1828, Sturt and his comrades followed the Macquarie to where it was lost, — not in an interior sea, as Oxley had supposed, but in a vast plain covered with reeds and impassable by man, a plain alternately submerged and sun-burnt. He also discovered beyond this plain a river, which he named, after the Governor who then presided in New South Wales, the Darling. The course of this river was southwest, but the little water it at that time * contained was so impregnated with salt and alum, that it was impossible for the party to use it, and they were forced reluctantly to turn back. The Castlereagh, a stream north of the Macquarie, and flowing in nearly the same direction, northwest, was next examined and traced to the Darling. Thus much having, with great trouble and suffering, been learned, Sturt the next year turned his steps more to the southwest, in which direction ran the river through whose channel the Macquarie, Castlereagh, and all other streams thereabouts, as the traveller was convinced, discharged their waters. Striking the head of the Murrumbidgee, he traced that river to its junction with the Murray, followed their united waters to the union of a stream from the northeast, by him supposed to be, and which proves to be, the Darling, and thence pursued his way to Lake Alexandrina (named after her present Majesty, Victoria Alexandrina), and across that shallow basin to the ocean.

These two expeditions served to demonstrate that no great interior sea, such as had been imagined, existed in the southeastern corner of Australia; for after all his travels, Sturt had only been able to determine, half by sight and half by shrewd guesswork, the true outline of one corner of the continent. It was proved, pretty clearly, that the waters

* Mitchell afterwards found it sweet at the same point.

which fell upon the western slope of the mountains, that extend from Cape Howe to Moreton Bay, found their way through vast plains, in a southwest direction, toward Encounter Bay, or were lost by evaporation and absorption before they could penetrate to the shore. It was also proved, that those plains were by no means fertile, were ill-suited to tillage, were wanting in water, and during any season of drought, — and it was terribly apparent that droughts lasting through years might be looked for, — would be uninhabitable. The rivers were mountain streams, rising in a moment, inundating every thing, laying vast tracts under water; then passing away, and giving place to sand, and dust, and desolation. Our Western rivers are changeable enough; the Ohio rises in its flood from sixty-five to seventy feet; at one season, it is a torrent often a mile in width, and fit to bear navies; at another, it creeps along, a little "creek" that a man may ford on horseback, and travellers upon the bank (we speak literal truth) are annoyed and blinded by the sharp dust which drives from the bed of the river. But the Ohio is unchangeable compared with the streams of Australia. The Hawkesworth, back of Sydney, rises ninety feet above low water. The Macquarie is alternately deep enough to bear a line-of-battle ship upon its bosom, and so shallow that the fishes and frogs cannot live in it. One month, it is the Hudson in its strength and volume, and the next, a "dry-run." To-day, you may faint upon its banks from thirst, because between them all is waterless, and to-night be wakened by a distant roar of crashing logs and breaking tree-tops, and hurrying out may find a moving cataract, tossing the spoil of the forest before it, and filling the bed of the river in a moment with a torrent that you cannot pass.

Among such streams and with such a soil, in which, during dry weather, a horse will sink above his fetlock at every step,* tillage cannot flourish.† It is a land for flocks and herds, which can journey to and fro with the change of seasons; much of it is almost valueless. In 1843, Sir Thomas Mitchell stated before the legislative council, that in his belief, of about eighteen million of acres as yet not granted within the colony of New South Wales, five sevenths were not worth sixpence an acre. So scant is the vegetation, that from ten to twenty acres are allowed as grazing ground to a bullock, and from three to seven for a sheep. ‡

The investigations by Sturt, therefore, while they served to clear away the cloud which hung over the geography of Australia's southeastern corner, and gave an intelligible character to the rivers of that region, added nothing to the hopes of the colonists, gave no stimulus to speculation, and caused no mass of emigrants to divert their course from America to New Holland. And yet the Captain spoke hopefully and strongly § of the lands which lie upon the lower banks of the Murray, and between that stream and St. Vincent's Gulf, and recommended there the formation of an emigrant colony. ||

But although the Captain's discoveries immediately, and at once, caused no emigration to the regions he had passed through and near, indirectly they were connected with one of the four chief colonies of New Holland, — that of South Australia; and as the principles upon which that colony was based were promulgated in the same year in which Sturt

---

* See Sturt, Vol. II. pp. 64, 65, &c.

† Much may be done for Australia by systematic irrigation. See some suggestions by Strzelecki, p. 443, &c.

‡ See statements in Douglas Jerrold's newspaper of September 30th, 1848, p. 1268. Strzelecki, pp. 459, 370.

§ Too strongly; he makes a space of fifty-five miles by seventy-five contain seven million acres! See Vol. II. p. 247. It should have been 2,640,000.

|| Sturt, Vol. II. pp. 229, 246.

discovered the Murray, and as, besides, the steps for settling Swan River in the west were commenced in that same eventful twelvemonth, 1829, we think it but fair to leave our geographical problem here for a while, and turn to the social inquiries, which, as we have intimated, were more or less clearly presenting themselves to the English world during the rule of Lachlan Macquarie.

Those problems were, —

1. Ought any future settlements in Australia to be composed, in whole or part, of criminals?

2. How ought the criminals sent to New South Wales, or elsewhere, to be employed?

3. Should lands be granted or sold? If sold, in what manner, and at what price?

4. Is it desirable to concentrate the settlements, and if so, how can it be done?

These topics, mixed up with a vast amount of what was merely personal and political, were brought prominently before the people of England by the accusations which the Hon. H. Grey Bennet brought against Governor Macquarie; by the appointment of a Commissioner to visit New South Wales, and by the report of that functionary, Mr. Bigge, made in 1822.

In regard to the problem of future colonies, the effect of Australian experience upon the best minds at home was decidedly adverse to mingling convicts with free settlers. Immorality, social aristocracy, bad culture, and unequal profits, were but a few of the evils which were believed to flow from the system that had been pursued at Sydney. All future colonies, it was thought, ought to be merely penal settlements, larger prisons, or should be free from the taint of the dungeon and the gallows. The settlers of New South Wales, it is true, and those of Tasmania at a later period, found convict labor cheap and profitable; but even at that early day, the mischiefs which have since, for years at a time, put a stop to transportation were discerned by the keen-sighted.*

The second problem, how to employ the convicts sent to Botany Bay and its dependencies, was less easily answered. If government employed them, as Macquarie had done, on public works, a vast expense followed. If they were "assigned" to individuals, that is, made over as a sort of white slaves, after the old fashion † which had been pursued in America in early days, though the master made money, and though the convict, if well behaved, gained great privileges, yet the popular mind of England was likely to become displeased with this sort of servitude in those Wilberforcean times. And if the convict were set free, was it not saying to the honest man in Great Britain, "You must pay for a passage to our Australian empire," and to the rogue, "You shall go there for nothing"? Where was a fourth course to be discovered?

Up to the close of Macquarie's rule, the government had been the chief employer; free settlers were scarce, and the emancipists were poor and clung to the towns. After his time, the "assignment" system gained in favor for a while, both at home and abroad, and New South Wales grew rich and wicked; then it was denounced in Great Britain; in 1838 a committee of Parliament advised its discontinuance; and in 1840 it was abandoned. Sir Robert Peel and Lord Stanley, having come into power, next commenced (in 1843) an experiment in Van Diemen's Land, which collected the convicts, who were no longer sent to Sydney, into gangs under the superintendence of public officers; this was the "probation" system.‡ It was found, however,

---

* E. g. Sydney Smith, Dr. Whately, Bentham, and Bennet named above.

† See Bancroft, Vol. I. pp. 187, 188. — Macaulay's *England*, Vol. I. pp. 602, 603 (Harper's large edition).

‡ A full account of this system is in the *Edinburgh Review*, for July, 1847, p. 132, American edition.

worse, more demoralizing, and far more depopulating in its results, than even its enemies had foretold. One twentieth of the free population of Tasmania left it in six months; thefts and robberies by the Bushrangers, the escaped convicts, and those whose time was out, prevailed to an extent that made all men fear for life and property each hour of the day and night; * vices which Sodom would have blushed at were as common as the gangs were numerous; and from 5,500 to 12,000 men were stationed, in bodies of 200 and 300, from Southport all up through the interior, to the waters of the Mersey in the north. This system, therefore, had in its turn to be modified, and further transportation to Tasmania abandoned; and again the problem came back, What shall we do with our transported convicts? At present, if we are rightly informed,† they all go through a course of punishment and discipline in England to begin with, and then, as "exiles," with "tickets of leave," which make them in substance freemen within specified limits, and during good behaviour, go to the colony appointed. They can choose their own masters, make their own bargains, and while they keep within bounds, and conduct properly, are like any other good citizen; if they stray or misbehave, a summary proceeding by any magistrate may bring them to their marrow-bones. Such is the present half-solution, for it is no more, of the second problem we have stated.‡

The third, as to the sale of lands, has proved even yet harder to deal with; in that early day, however, it attracted comparatively little attention. When land was plenty and free emigrants scarce, the royal representatives found it convenient for all parties to make liberal gifts of his Maj-

* Crimes were from six to eight times as numerous as in England.

† Our latest information is through the article in the *Edinburgh Review*, of July last.

‡ The whole subject of transportation is just now in a state of transition; what will be done no one knows.

esty's Australian territory, and accordingly, tracts varying in size from ten thousand acres to fifty thousand were granted to various individuals, upon condition that they would employ a certain number of convicts. But in 1829 commenced a movement which was destined to change all this system of gratuities, and substitute in its place one phase or other of "the Wakefield."

Mr. Wakefield's theory of colonization, if we comprehend it aright, was substantially as follows: — The welfare of any community depends very much upon such a division of labor as shall fill every trade, profession, and employment with good men, and not overload any of them. If land in any country is so cheap that all are able to become freeholders, there will be no laborers, no farm-hands, or mechanics; a semi-barbarism will follow; no growth in wealth or civilization will take place, and the country will be stationary or retrograde. If, therefore, you would have a colony progressive and civilized, you must put your lands so high as to keep a proper proportion of the inhabitants in the labor-market, seeking employment, and yet not so high as to prevent as many from buying real estate as can use it to advantage with the help of such laborers. But still further, your colony cannot be supplied with laborers, especially if far from home, unless they are carried there free of expense, or with but little expense, to themselves. If, then, England wishes Australia to grow in riches and goodness, let her, instead of giving lands to all who will employ a few convicts, sell them at a fixed price, never taking less, and in fixed quantities, never selling less; and let her apply the revenue arising from these sales to the transportation of free, honest laborers to the points where they are needed. In this way, the labor-market of New Holland will be supplied; the expense of supplying working-hands will be paid by the lands of the colony; no more land will be taken up than can be worked to advantage; population will be concentrated; wealth accumulate; knowledge and virtue advance; and the millennium begin to dawn for this unhappy world of the antipodes, to say nothing of the relief England will feel when her paupers are thus economically provided for.

These views Mr. Wakefield gave to the world in his "Letters from Sydney," in 1829. They contained too much common sense, and Great Britain too many paupers, to fall dead upon the public ear, even during the political tumults of 1830; and in that year a society was formed to promote the scheme he had suggested. In 1831 the government adopted the leading principles which were advocated by the Wakefield school, and Lord Ripon, Secretary for the Colonies, forbade all further grants by the royal governors, East and West, instructing them to sell the royal lands at auction, at a minimum price of five shillings (one dollar and a quarter) an acre. Commissioners were also appointed to attend to the subject of emigration, and every effort was made to induce the starving laborers of England, Ireland, and Scotland to betake themselves to the plains of New South Wales, and the banks of the St. Lawrence. These measures and these efforts were not in vain; the number of emigrants to Sydney increased, in eight years, from 800 yearly to 5,000; the sales of land from 20,000 acres in 1832, to 271,000 in 1835.

But the greatest achievement of the Wakefield system was the founding of the colony of South Australia, near the mouth of the Murray. No sooner was it understood that the ministry were disposed to adopt the new theory of colonization, than efforts were made to secure a grant of those lands lately visited by Sturt,* as a field where that theory could be tried with some degree of confidence; as the

* The projectors of South Australia seem to have adopted Sturt's error of "seven million acres" without question. See a letter from Mr. Morphett in the second annual report of the Colonization Commissioners.

country was uninhabited by whites, and was sufficiently distant from New South Wales and Tasmania to prevent much trouble from stragglers. In 1831, accordingly, Lord Ripon was approached on the subject; after much trouble, a charter was obtained in 1834; and on the 28th of December, 1836, Governor Hindmarsh anchored in St. Vincent's Bay. But before we proceed to speak of South Australia, which commenced thus at the close of 1836, we have several arrearages to bring up, namely, the fourth problem stated above, as to the concentration of settlers; some items in the history of New South Wales; the progress of inland discovery; and the foundation of Western Australia on the banks of Swan River.

When the passage of the Blue Mountains opened the interior of the continent to settlers and squatters, and above all, when the experience of a few dry seasons demonstrated the need of vast pastures for their flocks and herds, it was a matter of course that the colonists began to scatter themselves to far distant stations, wherever grass and water beckoned them. This dispersion was felt to be injurious to the welfare of the community, and concentration became a recognized desideratum soon after the time of Macquarie; but how to prevent the dispersion was a question which none could answer. Wakefield's scheme, it was hoped, would do something, but could have no effect upon those who occupied lands without authority. Police officers and prosecutions were out of the question; and many were almost forced, by the increasing price of real estate, — which was raised by the rulers from one and a quarter to three, and then to five and seven dollars an acre as the minimum,* — to seek the wilderness, and become squatters on the royal domain. Some who bear this by no means honor-

* In 1838 to 12 shillings; to 20 shillings in 1843; and in some localities to 30 shillings.

able or euphonious name are wealthy; some own herds of 25,000 cattle, and flocks that number 60,000 head. Thus, "the Wakefield," misapplied and caricatured, led to a result the opposite of what was hoped for, — dispersion instead of concentration, barbarism in place of civilized society. Nor have some other governmental measures been more wise. For example, land is sold to the settler at five dollars the acre, and not less; but if he refuses to buy, he may, if he dislikes squatting, take out a license to pasture his sheep on the vast public commons, and for this he pays a mere trifle, lessthan four cents an acre.*

The fourth problem, accordingly, as to the concentration of society in Australia, is, we may say, still unanswered.

Turning next to the second of our arrearages, the state of things in New South Wales from 1821 to 1836, during the rule of Brisbane, Darling, and Bourke, we have, — in addition to the greater ingress of free emigrants, the popularity, growth, and death of the "assignment" system, and the introduction of Wakefield's plan, — to notice, first, the speculative spirit which, in 1825–26, played the same game with sheep and cattle in Australia, that it was playing in England with joint-stock companies of all sorts, and has since played with railroads and locomotives. Next, we would refer to the constant growth of that social aristocracy, which was inevitable in a community part convict and part free. Many of the emancipists became wealthy as years rolled by, but they remained as much a marked class as the free blacks of Philadelphia or Boston. Efforts were made to break down the wall of partition; governors and philanthropists tried it, but in vain. The shoemaker who had never seen the inside of a prison would no more ride in the carriage of the emancipist millionnaire, than a Virginia planter would marry his slave.

---

* See Howitt, pp. 99, 213.

A third point in the annals of Sydney and its dependencies is the continued power of rum. In the capital, there has been a bar-room or liquor-store of some kind to about every sixty inhabitants, from 1821 till nearly the present time. To these stores the laborers from the country — unable, as they say, to buy land at the high rates asked, and in the large tracts (640 acres) prescribed under "the Wakefield," and so having no motive to save — bring their earnings, two and three hundred dollars at a time, place them in the landlord's hands, and with a request to be helped till the money is gone, and then to be kicked out of doors, they gather their friends and commence an Australian spree.

And now, having hinted at the social problems which arose in the time of Macquarie, and at the partial solutions that have been given them, we return to the geographical investigations which have taken place since Sturt discovered the Murray, in 1829. During his sail down that river, the Captain found, as we have stated, a stream entering from the north which he thought was the Darling; to determine how this was, and what might be the character of the country along the latter stream, Major Mitchell, Surveyor-General of the Colony, was sent, in 1835, to examine the region from which the great drought of 1828 had driven the former explorers. During that year and the one succeeding, this gentleman traced the river in question from where Sturt had left it to its junction with the Murray; he also ascertained that its valley, though by no means as fertile as that of the Nile, was yet available for pasturage in ordinary seasons; and discovered several new native grasses. But the facts revealed by Mitchell respecting the Darling were unimportant compared with his examinations of the country about the heads of the Murray, and southward to Port Phillip, a region so fertile to eyes that had dwelt on the half-desert lands farther north, that he named it Australia Felix. It is a country, he says in his report of October 24, 1836, "more extensive than Great Britain, equally rich in point of soil, and which now lies ready for the plough in many parts, as if specially prepared by the Creator for the industrious hands of Englishmen." Since that expedition, Mitchell, now Sir Thomas and Lieutenant-Colonel, has attempted to find a stream which, flowing into the Gulf of Carpentaria, would open a route from Sydney to the northern coast, and avoid the difficult Straits of Torres. He started upon his enterprise in November, 1845, and succeeded in finding, as he thought, the very stream he was in search of, which he named the Victoria. He did not, however, prosecute the inquiry, but returned to Sydney in January, 1847, and left his second in command, Mr. Kennedy, to follow the Victoria through its lower course. This he undertook to do, but soon found that the river, instead of continuing to run northward, changed its course and ran, growing shallower and smaller as it went southwest, toward the as yet unknown centre of the continent.* From that point Kennedy turned back, and no one thus far, we believe, has learned the fate of Mitchell's Victoria, unless Dr. Leichhardt — who, a year ago last April, had just left the neighbourhood of Moreton Bay with the intention of pursuing the course of the Victoria, and then penetrating entirely across to Swan River — has been fortunate enough to do so.

After Mitchell, no late investigator deserves more praise than Dr. Leichhardt himself, and should he succeed in his present enterprise, he will place himself foremost among the Austral travellers. In his expedition of 1844 – 45, he succeeded in going from Moreton Bay to a point on the eastern shore of Carpenter's Bay, and thence, round the head of those waters, to Port Essington. In this journey, he saw large tracts of fine land, and discovered a considerable stream, which he named after the Surveyor-General, Mitch-

* Kennedy's report is in the Athenæum, for June 10th, 1848, p. 580.

ell. Captain Stokes, also, of late years, between 1837 and 1843, has examined in detail the shores of the Gulf of Carpentaria, and also some portion of the northern shores that King passed by; — the result of which researches has been the finding of four river-mouths, that seem to promise a fine inland country upon the banks; these are the Albert and Flinders, emptying into Carpenter's Gulf; the Adelaide, opening into Clarence Strait; and another, Victoria, which pours out its waters at the eastern extremity of the inlet, the western end of which King named Cambridge Gulf.

Less important, but not less interesting, than the researches of Mitchell, Leichhardt, or Stokes, have been those of Eyre, and our friend Captain Sturt, both of whom, starting from Adelaide, have tried to penetrate the realms north of that capital. Of their travels we have not seen any full accounts, and can only say that Eyre learned the existence of a vast horse-shoe lake, which seems formerly to have communicated with Spencer Gulf, and would seem to be the very mediterranean sea to which the natives have referred from time to time. All about it, as we gather, was salt and barren. Sturt went farther northward, to about the 25th parallel of latitude, and there found also salt lagoons and dry runs.

Thus stands the geographical problem to-day; as yet, no one knows any thing worth speaking of in Eastern Australia away from the sea-coast, and beyond the valley of the Murray and its tributaries, which reach, however, through some ten degrees of longitude, and thirteen degrees of latitude, from the tropic of Capricorn to the neighbourhood of Cape Howe; an extent of country equal to that which lies between Pittsburg and the Mississippi, Lake Michigan and New Orleans. On the north, west, and south, the shores alone have been visited by Europeans, if we except the neighbourhood of Swan River, and thence to King George's Sound on the south. To that colony we must now, for a few moments, turn our attention.

The southwestern corner of Australia was, in all probability, explored to some extent by the early Dutch navigators; they at any rate sailed along its shores, and left their mellifluous names as an inheritance; Vlaming-land, Leeuwin-land, and Nuyt's-land attest their presence to this day. But the first examination of the Swan River region, of which we have any account, was made by the officers under Captain Baudin, who, in the "Geographe," was engaged in surveying that portion of New Holland about the same time that Flinders was at work at his survey; indeed, the two discoverers met in Encounter Bay during April, 1802, and although France and England were at war, exchanged visits, acted like men, and left the name of the gulf to commemorate so sensible a *rencontre.* The French are stated to have gone up the river and along its banks for eighty miles, but no attempt, that we know of, was ever made by the Emperor to take possession of the realms which his officers had thus brought to light. Nor was any thing done by Britain, until Captain Stirling, who followed the footsteps of the French in 1826, reported that the lands bordering upon this western stream were fertile and worthy of cultivation, and, being so much more accessible from Europe, would be found far more desirable than those of the Hawkesworth and Macquarie. The British government, acting upon his suggestions, in 1829, offered the territory to such settlers as would pay their own expenses out, and take care of themselves when there, on these terms: — whoever would invest three pounds was to receive forty acres, and as soon as he could prove that that amount, about thirty-seven cents an acre, had been actually expended on the land, he was to have a title in fee-simple; and so for every three pounds invested; — provided, that if one fourth of any land thus allotted was not brought into cultivation in three years, there was to be an additional charge of sixpence on every uncultivated acre; and whatever remained wild at the end of seven years was to revert to the crown. Whoever took out laboring hands, male or female, above ten years of age, was to receive for each one two hundred acres of land in fee-simple.

This was the second colony on the southern continent, it will be remembered, and convicts were not to pollute it with their presence. Stirling, who had opened the way, was appointed the Governor of "Western Australia," and settlers flocked to the new Canaan; between June and December, 1829, twenty-five ships arrived at the mouth of the river. But the up-and-down kind of progress, which seems to be inseparable from the colonial condition, soon changed matters. Off from the river-banks the soil was poor; rains came in torrents, and then droughts turned all to dust; the thermometer stood at 105 in the shade;* the harbour was objectionable; the river navigable by boats only about forty miles; and, in short, men had hoped too much and had been disappointed. Then all went down; lands were abandoned after money had been spent on them; houses were given up half built, in despair of tenants; cultivation was neglected; the pendulum swung back, and Swan River was as much underrated as it had been overrated. But pendulums swing both ways, as we know; so, in 1833, we find all flourishing again; grants of land, which the year before sold for twenty-five pounds, worth a hundred, and rents netting ten per cent., from the rage for sheep farming.† And so, from that day to this, has West Australia risen and fallen; at one time, men have rushed from it as from a sinking ship, and then have clustered to it again, like the wreckers round that same ship, when high and dry on the beach. Of late years, since the wild grants of land which were made in early days

* Breton's Excursions, pp. 30, 31. Breton went to Swan River in the autumn of 1829.

† Letter of January 27th, 1833, appended to Sir James Stirling's Journals.

have ceased, and the Wakefield selling system has ruled, matters have been regularly and healthily progressive, in spite of the introduction of convicts, who now, under the modified system that is in operation, as we have stated above, are sent as laborers to the Swan with their "tickets of leave." About six thousand acres of land are now cultivated; the vine and olive have been introduced, and the exportation of sandal-wood, which is found some sixty miles inland, promises to open a profitable trade with China. Coal has been discovered; specimens of mercurial ores have been met with; and the mineral world may come to the aid of Western Australia, as it has to that of her southern and eastern sisters. The shore, however, of the west of New Holland is sadly unproductive and dry. The expedition of Captain George Gray, in 1840, from Shark Bay to Perth, disclosed a region which none but an Australian, who can live on "fragrant grubs" and raw roots, could inhabit. In the interior, the lands are better; well fitted in many parts for pasturage, and swarming already with half-wild bullocks and unconquerable cows.*

The third colony of Australia in point of seniority, and the second certainly, if not the first, in respect to wealth and progress, is that of which we have already said a few words in connection with "the Wakefield." "South Australia" was suggested in 1831, established by Parliament in 1834, and settled at the close of 1836. But to follow its varying fates from that time to the present would require not so much an article as a volume; and we must refer all curious readers to the works of Wilkinson, Stephens, Torrens, &c., and the various reports made from time to time to Parliament. We must notice, however, the main source of the adversity which tried the founders of South Australia,

* See Landor's account of a cow-hunt, in his "Bushman, or Life in a New Country."

and that of the prosperity which has since raised her to preëminence again. The plan of the colony was this; it was from the outset to support itself; not, however, by the sale of lands, for all the proceeds of the territorial sales were to be applied to emigration, in accordance with Wakefield's principles, — but by borrowing money to be repaid out of the future revenue; this was one peculiarity; a second was, that the Governor, instead of being sent out by the powers in England, in the usual way, was to be appointed by a board of commissioners, residing in London,* and named principally by the association which had brought about the formation of the colony. The result of these two peculiarities was a series of misunderstandings, mismanagements, and reckless expenditures, which plunged the colony in debt, perplexed and discouraged the settlers, and held out such visions of high taxes in future as effectually scared away all emigrants.† The expenses of the colonial government, in 1839, rose to £140,000, with a revenue of £20,000; an income one seventh of the outlay.

Such was the source of the troubles which, for a while, beset South Australia. But her fertile soil, her excellent climate, one of the most healthy in the world, and above all, the discovery of immense mineral treasures, copper, lead, iron, silver, gold even, have again made her popular and prosperous. The copper mines are among the richest in the world; ‡ and the iron is said to be remarkably pure. Agriculture is also flourishing, in spite of the high minimum price of public lands, which so long prevailed, five dollars an acre. § Sixty thousand acres are actually cultivated, and

* One commissioner resided in the colony, and overlooked matters.

† The land sales fell from 17,000 acres to 600 in one year. In 1842, the emigrants were not more than 150 in number.

‡ The value of ore exported in 1845-46 was £140,000, or $700,000; in 1847, it was £180,000.

§ The folly of such a price is well put by Strzelecki, page 459; it

three years ago 620,000 sheep and 38,000 cattle rejoiced in the luxuriant pastures which stretch from Adelaide inward.

Upon the higher branches of the same river, which discharges the waters of Southeastern Australia near Adelaide, lie the pleasant and fertile lands of that happy region which we have mentioned as having been partially explored by Messrs. Hovel and Hume in 1824, and as having been more fully surveyed by Mitchell in 1836. The "Port Phillip" country, the southern portion, politically, of New South Wales, is, next to South Australia, the most popular portion of the southern continent; and for agricultural purposes, whether tillage or grazing, is the most popular and promising of all. There has been, thus far, but one serious drawback, apparently, to its prosperity; although it is to be apprehended that the existing system of transportation will prove injurious in the end to Australia Felix, which is receiving largely of the "exiles," young and old; — the drawback to which we refer is the system of land-selling and renting. Under this system, such high prices were asked for land, and permits for grazing granted so low,* that dispersion was inevitable, settlers were discouraged, squatters became more numerous than ever,† and civilization was needlessly delayed. Nor was this all; the course pursued by the government led to speculations of the most

---

requires seven acres, worth thirty-four dollars, to feed a sheep worth fifty or seventy-five cents, and producing two and a half pounds of wool! The interest alone would make the wool cost eighty cents a pound.

* A section, or square mile, 640 acres, was sold by government for 3,200 dollars (£640), but rented for 25 dollars a year! See Howitt's Impressions of Australia Felix, pp. 99-213. Mr. Howitt was a sufferer, and his impressions are very unfavorable; too much so, we judge.

† In October, 1843, there were in New South Wales 879 squatters' stations, with a population of 800 souls, and containing 11,796 horses, 491,000 horned cattle, and 1,000,800 sheep.

extravagant character, and these were followed by almost universal bankruptcy. But this portion of New Holland, like our own Western country, which but a few years since went through a similar series of revulsions, contains the essential elements of prosperity, and must, at some future time, become the most densely peopled part of the island that has yet been entered. In 1847, indeed, the effects of the earlier convulsions had in a great degree passed away.*

One other point alone remains to be mentioned, — Northern Australia, or the north province of New South Wales; the site of Port Essington and Victoria.

In 1813, Captain King explored the strait which divides the two islands, named by him Melville and Bathurst. As the reports which he made proved the neighbourhood to be well suited for a settlement, and as the British ministry desired to take formal possession of the coast which King had examined, an expedition was sent out in 1824, under Captain Bremer, which founded a fort upon the western side of Melville Island, and there commenced a colony. The fort was named Dundas, and the harbour Port Cockburn; and one hundred and twenty-six persons, of whom forty-five were convicts, were left as the germ of the new province. This position, however, was abandoned in 1828 for Raffles Bay, on Coborg peninsula, near to Port Essington. The object of this change was to secure the trade with the Malays, who come in large numbers yearly to this coast to take the Trepang or *Bêche de mer*. This point was soon left uninhabited, however, in consequence of the incompetence of the commanding officer, and from that time till 1839 the northern coast was left to the natives and the Malays. In the year last named, Captain Bremer, who had meantime become "Sir Gordon Bremer," was again commissioned to colonize the desert "Arnheimland," and in due season

* See a letter in Douglas Jerrold's paper, October 14, 1848.

founded at Port Essington the third infant settlement of the north; a settlement which, in so far as we are informed, yet remains in an infantile state. Leichhardt found it, in 1845–46, a mere military station.

And now we have briefly, dryly, most imperfectly, sketched the history of discovery and colonization in the great unknown Southern land. We have seen it visited by the Spanish, Dutch, and French, without an effort on the part of either at colonization. We have pointed to the voyages of Dampier, Cook, Flinders, King, and Stokes, under the authority of Great Britain, by whose efforts the coast has been gradually brought to light with great distinctness, although not a year passes without some further additions to the perfectness of the surveys thus made, and even to the discoveries of river-mouths of importance; — as, for instance, the discovery lately made, or certainly about to be made, of the mouth of the River Boyne, which discharges its waters on the eastern coast not far from the tropic of Capricorn, probably into Harvey Bay. We have briefly reported the passage of the Blue Mountains, the expeditions of Oxley, Sturt, Hume, Mitchell, Eyre, Sturt again, and Leichhardt, which have made known to us the great valley of the Murray, the Victoria of Central Australia, the coast of the northeast, the region of the Austral Alps and Pyrenees, the slope towards Bass's Straits, Lake Torrens, and the deserts which lie between the gulfs of Spencer and Carpentaria. We have mentioned, for we could do no more, the problems as to convict labor, emigration, the price of land, and the dispersion of the settlers, which have arisen from time to time into prominence in the progress of New South Wales more especially, but which in some degree have been sources of disquiet in Western and Southern Australia as well. We have attempted to convey to our readers an idea of the fitness of this New Holland world more particularly for grazing; of the advantages for tillage that distinguish the southern district of New South Wales, "Australia the Blessed"; of the metallic wealth of the "Wakefield" colony; of the comparative barrenness, as far as we yet know, of the western and northwestern shores; and of the regular progress that is taking place in the region that reaches from Swan River to King George's Sound, and which is nearly equal in size to the State of Georgia, and about as far from the equator.

Two subjects alone remain for us to speak of, the geological and meteorological views which have been proposed to account for the peculiar soil and condition of Central Australia, and the character and situation of the natives. Of both we must speak very briefly.

A favorite theory for explaining the flatness, the barrenness, and the salt pools of the vast regions which stretch from the western slope of the Blue Mountains and Australian Alps to the eastern declivities of the Stanley range of hills beyond the River Darling, has been its recent rise from the ocean. According to this view, the fertile lands along the eastern coast were not long since (in a geological estimate of long and short) bounded on the west by a bay or gulf, which stretched from the neighbourhood of Adelaide, along the course of the Darling, to the region beyond the marshes of the Lachlan and Macquarie, where those rivers make a descend of 1,800 feet in from one to two hundred miles. As the whole continent rose above the ocean level, the bottom of this vast gulf became that plain which is now alternately flooded and scorched to dust. Hence its barren character, for as yet the influence of the ocean salt is felt, and only salsolaceous plants grow plentifully; and time has not yet brought from the uplands that vegetable mould which is essential to fertility; indeed, the uplands have not much to spare, for the evergreens that cover them afford but a short supply of leaves, and those fall so gradually as to lose most of their enriching virtues from the absence of a proper fermentation. When, in addition to this ocean origin of the interior, its flatness, the imperfect formation of its river channels, the absence of vegetable mould, and the frequent droughts, we consider the denuding effects of the floods which from time to time sweep portions of it, — its want of fertility is explained. But, according to this view, nature by these very floods is preparing these plains for the habitation of man; she is deepening the river channels, is manuring the soil, is changing the worthless ocean bed into a land fit for cultivation. Such, very briefly stated, is the view (as we understand it) of Sturt, of Mitchell, of M'Culloch, and others.*

Another theory, and one to our mind far better supported by facts, is ably stated, though in a somewhat scattered form, by Strzelecki, who has done more to make New South Wales and Tasmania scientifically intelligible than all other inquirers. He has done so much, indeed, that, before speaking of his views in relation to the subject before us, we must say a few words of the Count himself. He is a Pole, exiled, or self-exiled probably, because he would not renounce that nationality which he estimates so well.† For twelve years previous to 1845, he was engaged in wandering through North and South America, the West Indies, the South Sea Islands, New Zealand, New South Wales, Van Diemen's Land, the islands near Java, China, Hindostan, Egypt, and Europe. That he did not fail to use his eyes, his ears, and his mind, during these varied travels, is proved by the work before us, and by the extracts from his unpublished journals, which he here and there gives by way of illustration. If these are fair specimens of his manuscripts, no traveller since Humboldt (if "since" is applicable to that

---

* See M'Culloch's Gazetteer, art. "Australia," and references there given.

† See the note from his Manuscript Journal, p. 380.

wonderful man) so well deserves to have his writings published and illustrated at large.*

Strzelecki's view of New South Wales — for of New Holland as a whole no sane man would say any thing in our present state of ignorance — is this: the geology, or rather the mineral character, of the rocks which prevail determines the vegetation, the temperature, the moisture, and the fertility of that strange land, whose lightnings even are so often thunderless.†

The rocks of New South Wales are excessively silicious; the proportion of those containing more than sixty per cent. of silex to those containing less being as four to one; and so far as the country west of the Blue Mountains is known, this flinty formation almost universally prevails. Now the soil formed by the disintegration of such rocks is very unfavorable to vegetation, and especially to that kind of vegetation which causes *the earth readily to imbibe moisture from the air, and slowly to part with it;* in other words, such a soil, independent of rains, will always be dry, and rains will always run through it, or be shed by its surface. In addition to this, it is found that the silicious soils absorb solar heat, but do not retain it after the sun has passed away, a circumstance uniformly connected with non-productiveness. The amount of rain which falls in Australia was, for the years 1838 to 1842, both included, more than double that which falls in London; while the evaporation was not one

---

* It was Strzelecki who discovered "Gipp's Land," back of Cape Howe, a very valuable region, — to him almost a rat trap (p. 460), as he had to work four weeks, going three miles a day, and leaving every thing, in order to get out!

† Strzelecki, p. 190. — M'Culloch's Gazetteer, p. 215 (Am. ed.). Lightning without thunder has been witnessed on the Atlantic; men have been killed on board ship, when no other sound accompanied the electricity than a hiss. This we have from the commander of the ship, a man of the highest character.

third more. It is not, therefore, a dry climate. Neither is it a hot one, upon the whole; an average of three years does not show a summer heat above 90°, or an annual mean above 68°. The peculiar character of New South Wales, in short, is not to be traced to its climate, or its rains, although they fall unequally and often in torrents, so much as to its peculiar soil, growing out of the minerals which compose the mass of its rocks. If this view be correct, nature must not be left to turn the Macquarie into a Nile, but wise irrigation and wise planting must cure what nature cannot; and, a ter all, the time may never come when the valley of the Darling and its tributaries can be other than a thinly peopled, pastoral land.*

In reference to the aborigines of Australia, who are decreasing with truly frightful rapidity, Strzelecki states, as a fact based upon very extensive and varied observation among the natives of America, the South Sea Islanders, and Australians, that, by a law of nature, the aboriginal female, after having once borne children to a European, is barren to men of her own race.† In addition to this cause of decrease, the prevalence among the New Hollanders of the most poisonous complaints, as attested by Sturt ‡ and others, may be mentioned. Nor is there in the Australian nearly as much as in the Iroquois, the Delaware, the Huron, and the Blackfoot, to make us regret this God-directed — for such it seems to be — wasting away. Civilization and Christianity seem even less adapted to him than to our own red man. The British government, and especially the colony of South Australia, have favored the natives as far as the white man in this century can be expected to favor the brown. But it is all in vain. The New Hollander is not wanting in intelligence or good feeling. He is kind, forbearing, not devoid

---

* Strzelecki, from one end to the other. † p. 346.

‡ Sturt, Vol. II. pp. 124, 126, 148.

of ingenuity, not unworthy of sympathy; but he can no more live where the Anglo-Saxon once plants his foot, than his aboriginal weeds can where the plough and harrow and hoe are at their mission. The negro has a permanence; he fits into the white, and, in one relation or another, the two can and do live together. But the North American Indian and the Australian fill no crevice in the absorbing nature of the Caucasian; they cannot be slaves, they cannot be equals, of course they cannot be masters; and so, while might practically makes right, they die, or their race is lost by admixture with the race of their conquerors. It is not now, indeed, a question of right, but a question of fact; and before it can be made a question of right in practice, the sufferers will be gone from earth.

And here we must close. This topic of the natives, taken in connection with the aborigines of the Pacific islands and Africa, we may return to again. We might also fill another article as long, though perhaps not as tedious, as this, with sketches of Anglo-Australian life; but we prefer to turn the attention of such readers as may follow us thus far to some of the various English works which relate to this subject, — especially to those of Landor, Sidney, Howitt, Wilkinson, and Westgarth.*

---

* Landor on Western Australia; Sidney on Botany Bay and its Backgrounds; Howitt and Westgarth on Australia Felix; Wilkinson on Australia of the South.

END OF VOL. II.

www.ingramcontent.com/pod-product-compliance
Lightning Source LLC
LaVergne TN
LVHW020911110826
845150LV00004B/646

* 9 7 8 1 4 2 5 5 5 7 3 4 8 *